Mississippi: The Closed Society

James W. Silver

MISSISSIPPI: THE CLOSED SOCIETY

NEW ENLARGED EDITION

A Harvest Book

HARCOURT, BRACE & WORLD, INC., NEW YORK

For three native Mississippians
Bill, Betty, and Gail

B.4.66

Copyright © 1963, 1964, 1966 by James W. Silver

Library of Congress Catalog Card Number: 66-15957

Printed in the United States of America

Contents

v

A Note from the Author

From the White House at eight o'clock on the night of September 30, 1962, John F. Kennedy began to plead eloquently with Mississippi students to understand that they must not interfere with the court-ordered admission of Negro James Howard Meredith to their University. Unknown to the President, at almost exactly the moment his sober face appeared on television screens across the nation, tear gas was being fired by United States marshals into an unruly crowd in front of the Lyceum Building on the Ole Miss campus. Choking and gasping, the spectators fell back across the Circle toward the Confederate monument, pursued by the marshals as far as the flag pole.

Within ten minutes, five or six green army sedans, each carrying six white-helmeted marshals, came over the Illinois Central bridge, which spans Hilgard Cut between the campus and the town of Oxford, and moved toward the Lyceum. As they made the slow turn to the right at the Confederate monument, they were assaulted with a hail of bricks thrown at close range. Windshields and car windows were smashed. My wife and I could see the men inside huddling to protect themselves from the splintering glass. The pounding of the bricks on the cars and the screams—"The sons of bitches have killed a coed." "We'll kill the bastards." "We'll get the God-damned marshals!" —these, plus shrill cries of filth and obscenity, proved that eighteen- and nineteen-year-old students had suddenly been turned into wild animals.

My wife and I suspected then that we were in for a night of terror. Earlier in the afternoon, warned by our nine-year-old daughter Gail, who had heard the news over the radio, we had driven out to the airport to watch the arrival of the marshals and Justice Department officials, little dreaming of the agony in store for us. As our University-owned home is only a half mile from the administration building (Lyceum), which had been requisitioned for federal headquarters, we could not have avoided the excitement had we wished to do so. In front of that majestic ante-bellum structure, both of us did what little we could to help maintain the calm that prevailed until after six o'clock, partly by carrying to those assembled the Chancellor's message that the marshals and the Mississippi Highway Patrol were acting in concert to keep order. Governor Ross Barnett had finally capitulated to federal authority; had, in fact, selected Sunday for the admission of Meredith—that was the word.

The hour before eight was filled with apprehension and foreboding as demonstrations and violence increased, and once the tear gas was fired we moved slowly back, comfortably out of range, past the flag pole to the old Science Building. When the army cars came by, we were sitting on the edge of the Cardinal Club memorial; I was nursing a couple of cracked-open knees, having been accidentally tripped and knocked to the concrete crosswalk by a large Confederate flagstaff carried by a young man in more of a hurry than we. Already the students were yelling about regrouping to attack and about keeping up the attack on the marshals until their ammunition ran out.

It is not my purpose to recount the frightening events of that unbelievable night of passion and fury. Separated more often than not, my wife and I were once more together between two and three o'clock in the morning of October first, at the side of the Chancellor's house, facing the Grove. Two contingents of federal troops, about a hundred men in each, newly arrived from the airport, marched by in full battle dress. As they turned the Circle, away from the pre-Civil War "Y" building and toward the Fine Arts Center, these American soldiers were assailed with fire bombs. We saw two sheets of flame about the size of our small house fall among the troops. They hardly got out of step. Only a miracle kept any number from catching on fire. Their colonel later said that if a single man had been seriously burned, both squads would have wheeled and turned their guns on the rioters in the smoke-filled Circle. By this time the student insurrectionists were far outnumbered by other Mississippians, to whom had been added a few unsavory out-of-state volunteers.

There were other occasions that night when a tragic event lacked only a hair of expanding into a holocaust—when, for instance, the marshals' supply of tear gas was twice almost miraculously saved from exhaustion by a daring truck driver who ran gauntlets of stones and gasoline-fueled fire. Disciplined as they proved themselves to be, the marshals would not have submitted to savage personal beatings without resorting to their firearms.

As it was, the manly bearing of the hastily gathered marshals fighting for their lives and the exemplary conduct of the Mississippi National Guardsmen and the regular soldiers are matters for great American pride. Like many observers, I was alternately enraged and heartsick that my fellow Mississippians, particularly the students, felt called upon to engage in a mad insurrection against their own government. To me it was and still is nothing less than incredible. Later, when the state of Mississippi was being flooded from within by malignant propaganda about what had happened at Ole Miss that fateful night, I felt a growing compulsion to try to tell the truth, to relate in plain fashion what had taken place, and then to put it all in historical perspective. For more than a year and a half this has been in my mind and in my heart—my wife says that I am obsessed with the subject. The result of my thought and study and research is in this book.

I have tried to approach an intensely emotional subject without sentimentality. I am no longer angry with anyone. I have found it necessary to criticize the conduct of certain individuals, some of whom have been my friends. While names have been kept to a minimum and language has been restrained, and while nothing has been put down in malice, I am quite sure that the feelings of some will be hurt by these pages. I will be deeply sorry for such an outcome, but the need for telling the story is greater than the importance of protecting personal feelings, whether those of fellow Mississippians or my own.

It has been suggested to me by well-meaning people that we ought to forget the recent nightmare, to put it in the past where bad dreams belong. And go on from there. The sad truth is that within minutes of the start of the insurrection such a course became impossible for me. For what was happening was distorted with passionate and deliberate speed and was made into the inspiration for some future insanity, an insanity just as inevitable as the bloodshed at Ole Miss. The point is that when people are told from every public rostrum in the state on every day of their lives—and such is the case with the undergraduates who assaulted the marshals—that no authority on earth can legally or morally require any change in the traditional terms of Mississippi social life, this very process generates conditions that will explode into riot and insurrection.

Less than a week after the murder of four Negro children in a Birmingham church, the Mississippi State Sovereignty Commission, that curious arm of the state legislature, unanimously endorsed the behavior of Alabama's Governor George C. Wallace in "standing in the schoolhouse door" to oppose the admission of two qualified Negroes to the University of Alabama, a masquerade of resistance to the will of the nation as expressed by the federal courts. In the summer of 1963 both the Sovereignty Commission and the State Building Commission were willing to risk the accreditation of every state college and university by holding up the diploma of James Meredith. Such actions not only indicate that Mississippi has officially learned nothing; they may well be considered to foreshadow future disaster. Some day Mississippians are going to have to grow up, to accept the judgments of civilization. Else we are doomed to many September 30ths to come.

I am reminded, perhaps presumptuously, of Lucius Quintus Cincinnatus Lamar. In another time of stress that distinguished Mississippian, a man who knew how to serve first his state and then his state and nation in the reunited republic, said: "Upon the youth of my state it has been my privilege to assist in education I have always endeavored to impress the belief that truth was better than falsehood, honesty better than policy, courage better than cowardice."

In more than a quarter of a century at the University, it has been my good fortune to know some truly remarkable native Mississippians, among them David L. Cohn, Robert J. Farley, James P. Coleman, James Howard Meredith, Aaron Henry, and William Faulkner. These six men, beyond all others, have influenced my thought and action.

After several months' pleading on my part, Bill Faulkner agreed to participate in what turned out to be the most exciting meeting in the history of the Southern Historical Association: a discussion of the Supreme Court's 1954 segregation decisions with Benjamin Mays, president of Morehouse College, and Cecil Sims, an eminent Nashville lawyer. The occasion was an integrated dinner in the Peabody Hotel in Memphis, in early November, 1955, at the very time that white supremacists were congratulating themselves on the outcome of the trial of two white men accused of kidnaping and murdering Emmett Till. In a way this session revealed, as Bell Wiley has pointed out in his introduction to the published transcript of the proceedings, "the existence of another and a liberal South—soft-spoken and restrained, but articulate and powerful—that is earnestly pledged to moderation and reason."

My purpose in bringing up the Memphis meeting is not to recall Sims' calm and judicial analysis of the legal implications of the segregation decisions, or Mays' impassioned commentary on the immorality of segregation, or even Faulkner's admonition that "To live anywhere in the world of A.D. 1955 and be against equality because of race or color, is like living in Alaska and being against snow." It is to remind myself that less than ten years ago, when it was decided to publish *Three Views of the Segregation Decisions,* my friends and I were in agreement that if my connection with the pamphlet were known my job as chairman of the department of history at the University of Mississippi would be jeopardized. This at a time when the Citizens Council was in the "town meeting" stage of its infancy! A *Clarion-Ledger* columnist from the state capitol in Jackson made his customary assault on the publication when it came out, though he apparently never learned of my connection with it. A year or so later an indignant alumnus formally protested to the Board of Trustees that I had presided over the "Faulkner" meeting, which, of course, I could deny, inasmuch as the chairman and toastmaster had been well known Mississippi expatriates, one the head of the history department at the University of Kentucky, and the other the president of the University of Louisville.

In a more lasting if less amusing way, this meeting profoundly influenced my own thinking and subsequent conduct. Emphasizing his hope that the speeches would be printed and distributed by "southern amateurs," Faulkner readily consented to the use of his own talk. On December 1, 1955, on my request for a short statement that might be added to the introduction to the pamphlet, Faulkner slipped a rather soiled sheet of yellow scrap paper into his battered old typewriter and, as if he had been musing over the matter all morning, quickly tapped out these words:

The question is no longer of white against black. It is no longer whether or not white blood shall remain pure, it is whether or not white people shall remain free.

We accept contumely and the risk of violence because we will not sit quietly by and see our native land, the South, not just Mississippi but all the South, wreck and ruin itself twice in less than a hundred years, over the Negro question.

We speak now against the day when our Southern people who will resist to the last these inevitable changes in social relations, will, when they have been forced to accept what they at one time might have accepted with dignity and goodwill, will say, "Why didn't someone tell us this before? Tell us this in time."

This message from William Faulkner is one of my most prized possessions. Add to it a few words from *Intruder in the Dust* and one has a firm basis for "standing up to be counted" when the proper time arises: "Some things you must always be unable to bear. Some things you must never stop refusing to bear. Injustice and outrage and dishonor and shame. No matter how young you are or how old you have got. Not for kudos and not for cash; your picture in the paper nor money in the bank either. Just refuse to bear them."

In spite of a few statements to the contrary, sometimes by people who should have known better, and in spite of a general confusion in the mind of the public, there never has been any real uncertainty about Faulkner's long view on the question of Negro equality. He was sure, as he said in his speech to the Southern Historical Association, that the Negro "knows there is no such thing as equality *per se,* but only equality *to:* equal right and opportunity to make the best one can of one's life within one's capability, without fear of injustice or oppression or threat of violence."

William Faulkner assisted in a minor way in the publication, in 1956, of the only issue of the *Southern Reposure,* a modest satire on white supremacy which never once mentioned the colored man. Thousands of copies were mailed out in Mississippi but the "southern amateurs" involved were unable to pool their resources for another number. In his own home that fall, Faulkner met three or four times with a handful of Oxonians, including a minister, a bank president, an editor, a prominent businessman, and a couple of professors, to talk over the prospect of setting up a "moderate" organization to counter the Citizens Council. He was greatly perturbed over the growing strength and arrogance of the radical right. I remember with clarity one evening in particular in which he sat on a straight chair to the right of the glowing fireplace in his library. He never was one for extended conversation, but he said over and over, as if to himself, "We are sitting on top of a powder keg." After a slight survey of sentiment among the men doing business on the Oxford Square, it was concluded that the local Citizens Council would never get off the ground if it were ignored. In general this has been the case, for the Council chapter in Lafayette County has neither gained respectability nor attracted intelligent leadership. Whether the little band of moderates gathered in the Faulkner home could have helped forestall the amazing Council development in the rest of Mississippi is now anyone's guess.

Never an activist, and in his last years spending more and more time in Virginia, William Faulkner made few further pronouncements on the race question. Neither did he change his mind, as some have indicated. The last time I talked with him about the Mississippi situation—or anything else—was on the day he voted enthusiastically for the moderate, Frank Smith, for Congress, on June 5, 1962. A month later he was dead.

The South and the state of Mississippi are not my native land. I have lived in the South for forty-four years and in Mississippi for twenty-eight. I have taught, not too successfully, about five thousand students at Ole Miss. There must be a former student of mine in almost every town in the state. Time and again a few of them, both those who have agreed and those who did not agree with my views, have spoken up in my behalf—as in 1950 when I was called a Communist in the legislature. None of this have I ever solicited. I would be surprised if a single former student would say that he had ever been penalized in any way in his academic work because he held opinions contrary to mine. A number who have been in my classes, I regret to say, have attained places of leadership in the white Citizens Council. It is my conviction that men such as these will find in time that they cannot set the clock back.

I was educated in the South. My wife comes from Alabama and has her degree from Ole Miss. Our three children were born in Mississippi. Our two daughters are eligible, I have been told, for membership in the United Daughters of the Confederacy and the Daughters of the American Revolution. A long time ago, when my yearly income at Ole Miss was $2300, I could have gone to a northern school paying almost twice as much, and only last year I turned down an out-of-state offer of a very substantial increase in salary. The facts are very simple: we came to Mississippi in 1936 as a result of the luck of the draw, we have liked it all these years, and we intend to stay here.

In many ways Mississippi is the most exciting place in America to live. I don't say this because Mississippi is all we have seen. For the past six or seven years I have taught in summer schools from New England to the Pacific, from Georgia to mid-America. My family lived in Scotland in 1949–50 and in Massachusetts in 1951–52, while I was a Ford Fellow at Harvard. But we have always been glad to return to Mississippi.

At the University I helped recruit a history faculty that for ten years ranked well with the best in the South. For a few seasons I coached the Ole Miss tennis team, assisted as faculty adviser for intramural athletics, traveled with the football team to take slow motion pictures for the coaches. For fifteen years I directed speakers programs which brought to the campus people in many fields, including in particular those who had distinguished themselves in American history. I helped re-establish the Mississippi Historical Society and worked like a yeoman on the Mississippi Historical Commission. Two years of my spare time were devoted to collecting and editing materials for one of the two volumes in *Mississippi in the Confederacy,* a state publication which has been highly praised as a serious contribution to the commemoration of the Civil War. I was instrumental in beginning the lumber-industry archives in the Ole Miss Library and in securing the papers and other priceless treasures of the late David L. Cohn for the University. Perhaps immodestly, I list some of these "constructive" things I have tried to do for the University and the state of Mississippi for no other reason than to counteract the current rumor that my life has been absorbed in carping criticism. In these years my wife did more valuable work in tutoring athletes than any other person. Her efforts in counseling sororities on the campus are well known and appreciated. These sundry activities, along with excellent fishing lakes and a good golf course and convivial companions for bridge and poker, help explain why we like

Mississippi. Besides, when they are not riled, Mississippians in general are a demonstrably hospitable and friendly people.

To those who do not believe in a critical attitude toward our social order, I reply that while a great many things are *right* about Mississippi and its customs, many things need to be changed. They need to be changed exactly as slavery needed to be eradicated in the 1850's, even though no one in Mississippi's closed society of that day could speak to that effect. And what may be more to the point at the present moment, Mississippi has no more chance of retaining her present folkways, including outmoded segregation and the conscious debasement of the Negro, than she once had of holding on to slavery. *The only option Mississippians have is whether to make an inevitable transition peaceable or bloody.* Whatever the choice may be, these changes will come. By all that's right and just, they *must* come because posterity will demand it. Mississippians are little different, basically, from other Americans, except that they have been victimized, more than others, by the terrible toll exacted by the closed society. There are many educators, businessmen, clergymen, newspapermen, in fact leaders in all areas in Mississippi's social order, who have been aware of the implications of the closed society and who yearn to break loose from it. Most people of good will are afraid, fearful of the results of their speaking out, their saying what they know needs to be said, what must be said.

It is my notion that one should do his job well. I hope the reader—I am mainly concerned with the reader in Mississippi —who may look at these few pages will do so with an open mind and will be willing to allow that I wrote this book because I felt it the right thing to do. For those who will insist on assailing my integrity and my purpose (there is some question as to whether I qualify as a carpetbagger or scalawag), I offer the words carved in granite over the entrance to the ancestral home of Lord Aberdeen, where my family was fortunate enough to live for a year: "THEY HAVE SAID. WHAT SAY THEY? LET THEM SAY."

I have tried to be extremely careful with my sources. I have read many books and more articles, have consulted newspapers with great care, have examined court records and official reports of all kinds, and, most importantly, have talked and corresponded with hundreds of people who hold a variety of opinions. In many of the quotations I have left out, mainly in order to save space, the normal academic paraphernalia, the *sics* and marks of elision, but I have been most scrupulous about not taking anything out of context. I am sure that I have made mistakes but it is my hope that even those who will disagree with my conclusions will not consider them intentional. Like Mr. George Raymond Kerciu, the Ole Miss art instructor who, when accused of desecrating the Confederate flag, replied that he was only painting what he saw on the night of the insurrection, I contend that I did not cause or create the closed society, I am only describing it.

In a very real sense the insurrection at the University freed me, released me from whatever obligation I might theretofore have assumed of maintaining silence for fear of possibly hurting the institution to which I had devoted most of my adult life. The University has been so badly hurt that it will take many years for it to recover—and the blame rests on Governor Barnett and his henchmen. In any case, to have "gone along" with certain frauds that are described in some depth in this book would have been indecent beyond measure.

By the spring of 1963, I had planned to publish, in pamphlet form, a much longer version of the speech I was determined to give in November, as retiring president of the Southern Historical Association. This document was to have been directed mainly to members of the closed society of Mississippi. A Mississippi editor offered to publish it, but in the early summer of 1963, while I was teaching at Emory University in Atlanta, the editor sold his printing establishment, and I had to look elsewhere. Leslie Dunbar, director of the Southern Regional Council, came to my rescue with a similar proposal of publication. In September the first draft was completed, double the size that had been contemplated. This was sent to about twenty-five historians and others with knowledge about Mississippi, for correction and suggestions. During October I put together the speech made in Asheville, North Carolina, on November 7, 1963. In the meantime some friends, including Mr. Dunbar of the SRC, convinced me that a more effective and lasting presentation could be made in a book, and a contract was signed with Harcourt, Brace & World, Inc. For three months after the Asheville speech, I worked night and day to prepare the manuscript.

Literally hundreds of Mississippians have contributed to this volume. Without their assistance I would have been lost. But for reasons inherent in the meaning of the closed society, I shall not list their names. Beyond these and Mr. Dunbar, my greatest obligation and appreciation go to C. Vann Woodward, professor of history, Yale University; David M. Potter, professor of history, Stanford University; Bell I. Wiley, professor of history, Emory University; William H. Willis, professor of classics, Duke University; Robert J. Farley, professor of law, University of Florida; Hector Currie, professor of law, Louisiana State University; William P. Murphy, professor of law, University of Missouri; James S. Ferguson, dean of the Graduate School, University of North Carolina at Greensboro; Enoch Mitchell, professor of history, Memphis State University; Lawrence Noble, professor of political science, Drew University; Joseph J. Mathews, professor of history, Emory University; Thomas D. Clark, professor of history, University of Kentucky; David Donald, professor of history, The Johns Hopkins University; Albert D. Kirwan, professor of history, University of Kentucky; Robert L. Rands, professor of anthropology, University of North Carolina; George H. Gibson, The Hagley Museum, Wilmington, Delaware; Pete Kyle McCarter, vice-president, University of Oklahoma; Ray Marshall, professor of economics, University of Texas; Frank E. Smith, director, Tennessee Valley Authority; Staige Blackford, research director, Southern Regional Council; Claude Sitton, southern correspondent, New York *Times;* Karl Fleming, Houston Bureau, *Newsweek;* Rabbi Charles Mantinband, Temple Emanu-El, Longview, Texas;

Carvel Collins, professor of humanities, Massachusetts Institute of Technology; Philip F. Detweiler, managing editor, *Journal of Southern History;* William Peters, CBS News, New York City; John Emmerich, Baltimore *Sun;* Edward H. Harrison, rector, St. Simon's-on-the-Sound Episcopal Church, Fort Walton Beach, Florida; Summer L. Walters, associate minister, Roberts Park Methodist Church, Indianapolis, Indiana; Roy C. Clark, pastor, St. John's Methodist Church, Memphis, Tennessee; J. W. Holston, minister, Asbury Methodist Church, Tulsa, Oklahoma; Wilton C. Carter, associate minister, First Methodist Church, Lakeland, Florida; Benjamin Muse, author, *Massive Resistance in Virginia,* Manassas, Virginia; Easton King, New Orleans, Louisiana; Hodding Carter, New Orleans, Louisiana; James H. Meredith, Washington, D.C.; John H. Griffin, Mansfield, Texas; A. E. Cox, Memphis, Tennessee; Mrs. Henry Tracy, Memphis, Tennessee; Neal Gregory, Memphis, Tennessee; and my son, Lt. James William Silver, U.S. Army, Washington, D.C. None of these is responsible in any way for what I have written here.

Quite unexpectedly, the Asheville speech prompted a considerable publicity and brought me more than seven hundred letters from throughout the United States and indeed the world. These letters have been overwhelmingly favorable to my position, including about a hundred from historians and another hundred from Mississippians.

Regrettably there has been some exaggeration in the press as to the plight of my family and me. We do not walk alone, we are not completely ostracized (though we may have swapped some friends around), I am not "the most hated man in Mississippi," and I do not practice with a shotgun on my afternoons off. Claude Sitton's quote, "Hell, I like it here," still applies. It is true that we were somewhat apprehensive on our return to Mississippi, but dire predictions about our reception have not materialized.

The off-the-cuff statement of Governor Barnett that I should have been fired long ago, Congressman Williams' call for a fumigation of college staffs and his criticism of me for biting the hand that has fed me, and a black-out in my home-town paper, were predictable. The Jackson *Clarion-Ledger* ignored the Associated Press Asheville dispatch, which most papers in the United States carried, but two days after the speech was made it mustered a rare coverage. The entire story, buried in the middle of the paper, with the heading, "Dr. Silver Talks Again," requires not a great deal of space: "Dr. Jim Silver, longtime history professor at Ole Miss, spoke in Asheville, N.C., Thursday night. Press wire reports he abused the state of Mississippi, its people, officials and newspapers in the same fashion he has in previous speeches in Atlanta, Memphis, and other points."

As this is written on February 3, 1964, a few nasty telephone calls are still coming in and there is a continuous trickle of derogatory mail. Two or three patriotic organizations have lethargically adopted resolutions denouncing me. One of my old-time friends lent a bit of excitement to a Board of Directors meeting of the Mississippi Historical Society by proposing a "vicious" resolution condemning me as a historian and as a man, but the matter was tabled when it was discovered that no one had read my Asheville speech.

While this book was in the process of being written, the racist Ross Barnett was governor. On January 21, 1964, he was succeeded in office by Paul B. Johnson, who had been elected after three strenuous campaigns in 1963 during which he claimed he had "stood tall" in his opposition to the federal invaders in the Ole Miss integration imbroglio. But in his inaugural address he reminded his listeners that "we are Americans as well as Mississippians." (I do not intend to charge him with plagiarism.) Although he vowed to fight "with every fiber of my being" against any authority which he considered morally or constitutionally wrong, Johnson also declared, "Hate, or prejudice, or ignorance will not lead Mississippi while I sit in the Governor's chair." Obviously the new administration was out to change Mississippi's national image. Could a latter-day Paul or another Thomas à Becket have come on the scene?

An image, no matter how professionally conjured up, would not be enough. The time had come for reality.

Veteran reporter Kenneth Toler wrote for the Memphis *Commercial Appeal* of January 31, 1964:

Gov. Paul B. Johnson's determination to improve Mississippi's national image gained Senate endorsement Thursday when members were admonished to "give serious thought to the after-effects" of hasty actions in the touchy racial field.

The subject arose when Senator Noel Monaghan of Tupelo, speaking on a point of "privilege of the whole Senate," recommended that only in extreme emergencies should measures be considered on the floor without first being cleared through committees.

Earlier, Senator Talmadge Littlejohn of New Albany had questioned wording in the resolution which commends a Brookfield, Mass. school committee for its "courageous and defiant stand against the atheistic, unlawful decision of the Warren court which attempts to outlaw prayer and Bible reading in public schools."

Senator Littlejohn had the resolution amended by striking the words "Warren court" and substituting "Supreme Court."

The resolution had been offered by Representative Charles Blackwell [the Ole Miss law student who parlayed the arrest of Assistant Professor Kerciu and his own membership in three Citizens Councils into a seat in the House of Representatives] of Laurel and unanimously adopted by the House.

Taking his cue from the Governor's pronouncement, Senator William Burgin of Columbus, defense attorney in Federal-instituted voter registration cases, said, "Some of the legislative actions in the past have given ammunition to those who are attacking our efforts to preserve our way of life.

"When Mississippians are called into Federal court, these aggressors throw back in our faces these actions when we seek to establish as constitutional the acts of the Legislature.

"One of their strongest points is statements made when these matters are discussed in the Legislature which tend to show they have as their purpose the maintenance of segregation or discrimination on a basis of race.

"I do not say we should stand silent, but we should give serious thought to the after-effects of our actions."

Senator William J. Caraway of Leland said one of the most important duties of the Senate "is the improving of our image in the eyes of the nation without giving up any of our positions."

The prospects for an acknowledgment of reality do not look good. It does seem, though, that the men in the legislature as well as the new governor have repudiated Barnett's open intransigence and will for some time amuse themselves in an attempt to convince the rest of the country that Mississippi's spots have changed. Necessity however is a sterner master. The explosive pressures building up within the state cannot be contained by sweetening the old rhetoric. What hope there is for the opening of the closed society—and I feel some—lies in the fact that not all Mississippians continue to believe that nothing need be changed.

James W. Silver
University of Mississippi
February 3, 1964

Preface to
the New Enlarged Edition

This preface was begun at Paris Landing State Park, on the Tennessee-Kentucky border, on Sunday, September 19, 1965. Three nights before, I had made what may well be considered my valedictory talk as a Mississippian to about 300 people in the Victory Room of the Heidelberg Hotel in Jackson, Mississippi. At least half of the audience was Negro. A dozen or so coatless whites came, they said, to heckle, but for some reason decided against it. My clearest memory of the trip from Oxford to Jackson was the insistence of the close friend who accompanied me that we go in his car instead of my 1957 white Cadillac (according to local rumor, a gift of the NAACP). The reason, I later discovered, was an automatic shotgun hidden in the back seat. At the meeting, another friend sat behind my would-be hecklers with a loaded pistol in his brief case. There was also a second shotgun available for immediate service.

Melodramatic? Maybe so, but on the next morning I visited Donald Thompson, Unitarian minister and secretary of the Mississippi Council on Human Relations, who a month before had been gunned down one block from where we stayed in Jackson that night. From his bed in Baptist Hospital, Mr. Thompson told me that city detectives had just been in to inform him of their three best guesses about his attempted assassination: 1) it really wasn't a white man, but a Negro Thompson had seen that night with a gun; 2) chances were that a member of his own congregation had tried to kill him; 3) if the Ku Klux Klan had been involved, Thompson would have been shot dead on the spot. The gentle minister, who had taken a full blast from a shotgun in his shoulder and chest, seemed more bemused by the curious condition of the mental equipment of the sleuths than appalled by the results of their investigation.

Moderates who have left Mississippi in the past few years have given many reasons. Except for those who fled before physical and/or economic reprisal, most have rationalized their leaving as did Wofford Smith, crusading Episcopal chaplain at Ole Miss, who felt that his departure would help heal the malaise in Oxford's St. Peter's congregation. I have never questioned my own expendability, nor did I miss the evident certainty of the administration at the University of Mississippi that it could dispense with my services during the rebuilding process made necessary by the excesses of the Barnett reign of ignorance. The latter, in fact, impressed me more than anything else. Not long ago, a former colleague wrote: "The Ole Miss history department these days is like a Bureau of Missing Persons." It is indeed true that most of my friends of 1962 are now gone from the University. Just how much this has affected me is hard to tell. As a matter of fact, I don't pretend any longer fully to understand my own motivation. It is, in any case, too complex and personal to be put on paper. I do know I feel no bitterness toward those at the mercy of an untenable situation in a world they did not make.

Some members of the Mississippi legislature and of the Board of Trustees of the Institutions of Higher Learning—and even the governor at times—have affirmed their belief that the University would be a healthier and saner place without me. With such thinking I am not in agreement, though I cannot see that mere opposition to the wishes of the headhunters is cause enough in itself to spend the rest of one's days in Yoknapatawpha, even with the lovely prospect of burial in St. Peter's cemetery. I taught my last class as a member of the faculty of the University of Mississippi during the summer session of 1965. In September 1965, I became a permanent member of the Department of History at the University of Notre Dame.

Looking back over the years, I am disposed to conclude that certain legislators have gotten themselves needlessly flustered in their random harangues against Old Silver, based, as such have been, on fantasy and exhibitive of a rather low level of emotionalism. Board members, on the other hand, have normally evidenced a somewhat higher degree of prudence, with an occasional flair for genuine shrewdness. An intermittent and always insufficient concern for those standards of intellectual liberty and academic freedom without which higher (or any) learning is impossible has usually characterized the Board. Until the Board, and those who appoint and influence it, understand the causes and nature of the decline of the University and are willing to do what must be done to restore it, there is little hope for the revival at Oxford of those standards that support and sustain genuine learning. Such a revival cannot be initiated or sustained by gestures in public relations.

In general, I am pleased with the reception of my book in Mississippi. With the criticism that little in it is unknown to the informed citizen, I am in agreement, though it does not follow that the story were better left untold. Papers in Greenville, Vicksburg, Clarksdale, McComb, and Tupelo carried reviews of the book, either favorable or noncommittal. The editor of my home-town paper explained the absence of any reference to *Mississippi: The Closed Society* with the happy revelation that I had been seriously ill some years before and had never been quite the same since; the inevitable comment in the *Clarion-Ledger* came from the pen of Tom Ethridge, that Silver "is feathering his nest via the Hate-Mississippi craze." At the University, the *Mississippian* noticed editorially that *Mississippi: The Closed Society* could be purchased at Leslie's Drug Store and, furthermore, was available in the library, "located about 150 feet southeast of the Grill." At Delta State College in Cleveland, the editor of the school paper was removed, according to the irreverent *Mississippian,* for commending a religious group for discussing the Silver book and for printing a movie headline: " 'Pussy Galore' Typical of James Bond's Girls."

In some reviews I have been denounced for being an activist, and in others, for not being an activist. If the author of *Mississippi: The Closed Society* ever got to heaven (an unlikely event) he would have it in an uproar in two weeks, claimed a writer in the Richmond *News-Leader* who implied that he had read the book. In 1965, the same paper, reacting to a speech I made in New York City on receiving a Sidney Hillman award, nominated me for an Uncle Tom prize. Some of my radical nephews in SNCC had used such a term as long ago as 1963.

A Gulf Coast lawyer suggested that "Mississippians in the years to come will only have to read your book to understand what it was to be alive at this tragic time." Not all of my former friends among historians in the state will now recognize me on the street, but one wrote from Jackson: "Local bookstores report that sales are continuing and I feel that this has been one of the reasons for change throughout the state." An ex-Mississippi newspaper woman confessed: "It is my hope that Mississippians will read the book (for *any* purpose) and find there a *truly* mirrored, if unlovely, image of themselves in the raw— naked without their cloak of illusion that not only conceals but flatters and even enhances a delusion that the reflected image is all that is desired." A professor in the medical school apologized for having criticized my 1963 speech (widely circulated in Mississippi): ". . . then I thought it would stir the opposition into a frenzy at about the time they would have to start a retreat. I believe I was wrong just as the University was wrong to strain itself so hard to accommodate the extreme segregationists."

There are always amusing aspects of being controversial. One coffeehouse moderate was most effectively squelched: "You sound like you came straight out of Silver's book." A Clarksdale segregationist wrote the Catholic Boston *Pilot* that my existence in Mississippi proved the high degree of tolerance in the state. In the same town, an Ole Miss co-ed was told by her angry mother that she need not return home if she visited the Silver family. Immunity from economic reprisal did not keep a very wealthy, widely traveled woman from taking to her bed when it was suggested her home might be a suitable place for a television interview involving Silver. After the interview had taken place on the University of Mississippi campus, the film was kept off the Memphis educational channel, partly because the director did not know "to what extent the program would come under the FCC's fairness doctrine. These are not matters that can be decided in a few hours without counsel." In August 1964, a Jackson would-be Anglo-Saxon, apparently ashamed of his eastern Mediterranean origins, declared me a suitable delegate to the Democratic National Convention, now the "National Negro Party."

An office-holder whom I do not know wrote from Jackson that my leaving the state was "received with a certain amount of shock and dismay . . . you have done incalculable good . . . you have not outlived your usefulness." He had met a friend at the Little Theater. Their conversation turned to my book. "My friend asked if I had read *The Closed Society*. I had. 'How did you like it?' he asked in a low voice. 'How did *you* like it?' I parried quietly. 'I asked you first.' 'Great book,' I said, feeling very brave. He looked at me frantically, and whispered, 'You said that too loud. Keep your voice down. I'm a lawyer and have to earn a living in this town.' 'You,' I said, 'what kind of position do you think I'm in?' "

The *Christian Conservative Communique* reported in April 1965 that I would soon return, after "lecturing in northern universities," to my duties at Ole Miss. "The extent to which socialist negrophile Dr. Silver directs the integration move within Mississippi is unknown. Evidence indicates that he plays a larger part than is realized. In addition to recruiting students, he is in very close contact with leading businessmen in Jackson and throughout the state. Dr. Silver . . . has stated that the whole white population of Mississippi is 'paranoid.' " The stake in the old conspiracy mentality is as deep as ever.

A friend of mine inquired in my behalf about the purchase of a house in South Bend, Indiana. After consulting with his wife, the owner called back to find out whether this was the Jim Silver connected with civil rights. So informed, the man asked a logical question: "Is he a Negro?" Prejudice is where you find it.

The most remarkable and unamusing citation of my book was

made by a Baptist minister of Tylertown, Mississippi. In a *Saturday Evening Post* article, Dr. Clayton Sullivan defended segregation as a social necessity in the rural South on the basis of the appalling "behavior gap" separating whites and blacks. He was somehow able to describe in revolting terms the degrading living conditions of rural Negroes and to use these as an excuse for the maintenance of segregation.

There are many minor points the writer wishes he had known in time for the first edition. In the heyday of the Citizens Council, for instance, Bill Simmons drove from Jackson to Oxford but failed to get the endorsement of Professor Irwin C. Kitchin, chairman of the biology department, for a racist pamphlet whose contents Simmons had assembled. On the night of the insurrection, University officials requested every Mississippi congressman and senator to come to the state to help, but none responded. In the last year or so, two libel suits, amounting to $40,000, against Aaron Henry have been dismissed by the Mississippi Supreme Court, acting under mandate from the U.S. Supreme Court. Criminal contempt charges against Ross Barnett and Paul Johnson have been dismissed by the Fifth Circuit Court of Appeals as no longer needed "for the purpose of deterring others. . . ." The Mississippi Freedom Rider "breach of peace" convictions of 1961 have been overturned by the Mississippi Supreme Court, again acting under mandate. That court also dismissed a similar conviction of Bob Moses for having led a racial demonstration in McComb four years before. The charge of the Lafayette County grand jury against Chief Marshal James P. McShane, of conduct that caused the riot, was ruled by Judge Claude Clayton to be one for which the Marshal was not answerable to Mississippi law. Also, it might be noted, a man convicted under the Mississippi statute making it a felony to use obscene language over the telephone was given a new trial because the lady victim had delicately been allowed to write the offensive words on paper rather than be forced to speak them to the jury.

I would like to add the name of Duncan M. Gray, Jr., to the list of illustrious Mississippians who have most influenced my thought and action. Which reminds me of an impassioned telegram sent to the Reverend Mr. Gray by an old friend and parishioner who, after lengthy denunciation, severed their relationship for all time. In true Mississippi fashion, the correspondent ended the message: "Please give my love to Ruthie."

This edition of *Mississippi: The Closed Society* reproduces the full text of the original edition. Nothing has been changed. What is new, besides this preface, is Part Three, "Revolution Begins in the Closed Society."

> James W. Silver
> University of Notre Dame
> Notre Dame, Indiana
> November 15, 1965

PART ONE

1.

The Establishment of Orthodoxy

The insurrection against the armed forces of the United States at the University of Mississippi on September 30–October 1, 1962, was the inevitable response of the closed society of Mississippi to a law outside itself. It made no difference that the law involved was the superior law of the United States—and that Mississippi was one of those United States. The violent response was inevitable because the United States is slowly, painfully, and self-consciously changing from a white society to a multi-racial society. This is happening not because Christianity has suddenly been overwhelmed with success but because the imperatives of the American dream have been demanded by a growing and sizable number of American Negroes who refuse to accept their traditional place at the bottom of American society. In Mississippi this slowly accelerating historic change is seen not as a legitimate outcome of classic American values but as a criminal conspiracy against sanctified institutions. This conspiracy was perfectly symbolized for Mississippians in the threat of the enrollment of James Howard Meredith, a qualified Negro, at the University of Mississippi in the fall of 1962. When the state had exhausted all the delay the law could provide and the Fifth Circuit Court of Appeals in New Orleans ordered the immediate enrollment of Mr. Meredith, all hell had to break loose. It did. The aftermath has been as fated as the

3

insurrection itself. The future, except for the exact turn and
timing of events, is not difficult to discern. In the following
pages will be found an attempt to explain how the closed society
came about, what its meaning is, and the certainty of its eventual
passing.

The Closed Society Embraces Disaster

The Institute for Research in Social Science at the University
of North Carolina not long ago documented what many had
suspected, that about two-thirds of southern whites want segregation and that Negroes in the same proportion desire integration. In Mississippi the proportions would be considerably
higher for the whites and somewhat lower for the blacks.

The melancholy truth is that neither race has been able to
perceive clearly the attitude of the other. In the South as a
whole, a scant few whites recognize that most Negroes simply
do not accept the white concept of proper race relations. It is
notoriously true that in Mississippi the lack of communication
has permitted the dominant group to indulge in what the North
Carolina Institute calls "the luxury of ignorance about the wishes
of those who are dominated." Hence the constant refrain from
city and state officials that there is no racial problem in a social
order where segregation is voluntary and where, they would
have it believed, a peaceful, happy, and care-free citizenry is
occasionally stirred to angry protest only by outside agitators.

"The strict segregationist majority among the southern
states," the report continues, "has the most idyllic image of
the past and the greatest sense of doom for the future. White
integrationists, on the other hand, join the Negroes in low rat-
ings of southern race relations for the past and present and in
high expectation for the future." The authors of the study conclude that only a significant change in the racial attitudes of
white Southerners can insure the survival of political democracy
in the South.[1] That this change is already under way is at best

―――――――――

1. Donald R. Matthews and James W. Prothro, "Southern Racial Atti-

a well-kept secret in the land of the magnolia and the mocking-bird.

Like other Southerners, Mississippians are obsessed by their sense of the past, but this does not insure the accuracy of their historical picture; they see legend rather than history. It is no accident that in Faulkner's *Light in August* the Reverend Gail Hightower's life is shaped by his vision of galloping horses and slanted lances, whereas his Confederate grandfather had been in fact killed by a shotgun blast while raiding a henhouse. Even for the average citizen, patriotic societies make up an integral part of his social life. It is in the life of these organizations, in the accounts in the press, and in the common routines of political oratory that the romanticism of the Old South as well as the cult of the Confederacy flourish—always renewed by bitter stories of Reconstruction.

In their hot pursuit of interposition (see p. 134) neither the Governor nor the Legislature of Mississippi has shown any awareness that in the past of the Jacksonian period Magnolia State legislators resolved that "the doctrine of Nullification is contrary to the letter and spirit of the Constitution," nor that an 1851 political convention, originally called to consider secession, instead heaped ridicule on "the asserted right of secession" as being "utterly unsanctioned by the Constitution." Mississippians have long since forgotten that they were Americans before they were Southerners, and that in a quarter of a century the people of Mississippi moved from a belief that nullification was not only unconstitutional, but also morally and politically wrong, to a decision to secede from the Union. In its earliest days Mississippi was part of the West, not the Old South, and its attitudes and policies were nationalistic. Not until the middle 1850's did the prevailing sentiment of the state's leaders move toward southern separatism.

There are parallels between the 1850's and the 1950's which

---

tudes: Conflict, Awareness, and Political Change," *Annals of the American Academy of Political and Social Science,* Vol. 344 (November, 1962), pp. 108–121.

remind us that Mississippi has been on the defensive against inexorable change for more than a century, and that by the time of the Civil War it had developed a closed society with an orthodoxy accepted by nearly everybody in the state. The all-pervading doctrine, then and now, has been white supremacy, whether achieved through slavery or segregation, rationalized by a professed belief in state rights and bolstered by religious fundamentalism. In such a society a never-ceasing propagation of the "true faith" must go on relentlessly, with a constantly reiterated demand for loyalty to the united front, requiring that non-conformists and dissenters from the code be silenced, or, in a crisis, driven from the community. Violence and the threat of violence have confirmed and enforced the image of un-animity.

This, then, is the essence of the closed society. For whatever reason, the community sets up the orthodox view. Its people are constantly indoctrinated—not a difficult task, since they are inclined to the accepted creed by circumstance. When there is no effective challenge to the code, a mild toleration of dissent is evident, provided the non-conformist is tactful and does not go far. But with a substantial challenge from the outside—to slavery in the 1850's and to segregation in the 1950's—the society tightly closes its ranks, becomes inflexible and stubborn, and lets no scruple, legal or ethical, stand in the way of the enforcement of the orthodoxy. The voice of reason is stilled and the moderate either goes along or is eliminated. Those in control during such times of crisis are certain to be extremists whose decisions are determined by their conformity to the orthodoxy. The likelihood of intelligent decisions is thus being reduced, and eventual disaster is predictable. It in no way washes out the essentials of my analysis to add that there is no contention in this essay that Mississippi society has been *uniformly* closed during the past hundred and ten years. The period of Reconstruction, for example, would be one exception. During the period from the depression of the 1930's through World War II and its aftermath, three Mississippi professors (Rainwater, Bettersworth, Wharton) published scholarly volumes stressing the poverty-stricken quality of Mississippi leadership in the period of secession, the Civil War, and from Reconstruction to 1890. During these years (1938–1947), there was no great attack on the Mississippi creed—and, in any case, Mississippians were rather thoroughly occupied with other problems. If these same volumes of history were to be published today, in the closed society made exceedingly sensitive by massive assault on her innermost bastions of orthodoxy, it is quite likely that the three authors would be run out of the state.

Sooner or later in every discussion of southern politics the issue of state rights is brought up. In practical application, state rights may be defined in terms of local autonomy, diminution of federal power, and interposition of state authority between the citizen and supposed excesses of the national government. From the introduction of the Wilmot Proviso (1846) to the election of Lincoln (1860), the southern position not only *denied* these characteristics of localism but *insisted* on the exercise of whatever national force was necessary to implement southern "rights" in the territories and in all the states. Thus it is somewhat confusing for Mississippians, who have absorbed from youth the mythology concerning the doctrinal sanctity of state rights, to learn that in the 1850's Mississippi Democrats, with their friends in control in Washington, demanded that the power of the federal government be used to destroy local self-determination in the territories and to thwart nullification of the national fugitive slave law by northern states. This historical situation is comparable to the paradoxical reluctance of those who today cry "state rights" but refuse to forego the luxury of federal funds for everything from farm subsidies to the financing, on the Mississippi Gulf Coast, of the longest man-made sand beach in the world. It would at least clear the air if Mississippians would replace the hypocritical slogan of "state rights" with the honest cry of "self-interest."

Having largely missed the era of the extended apology for slavery, ante-bellum Mississippians accepted the institution without question and used it to generate great wealth. In both the 1850's and 1950's, white citizens were completely enamored of their social and economic system. These were the decades of the state's greatest prosperity (though fantasy still prevails about the state's riches in 1860), with God and nature—and more lately the Mississippi State Sovereignty Commission [2]—apparently sanctioning a structure of society that is advantageous to those in control. The harmony of the social order has rested politically on a one-party system, with no serious disagreement on fundamental philosophy.

---

2. Created by the Mississippi Legislature in 1956 and generously supported since, the State Sovereignty Commission, "the watchdog of segregation," 1) operates a public relations department to publicize the Mississippi version of the southern way of life, 2) employs trained investigators to inquire into subversive activities (conduct thought detrimental to the Mississippi image), and 3) makes periodic financial contributions to the Citizens Council.

For the purpose of keeping its special file on potential agitators up to date, the Sovereignty Commission maintains a "network of Negro informers blanketing Mississippi." The Commission dispatches to all parts of the United States patriotic speakers who are uniformly "triumphant" in selling the Mississippi line partly at least because reports of their successes originate with the Commission itself. Also, the Commission brings into Mississippi carefully selected and usually well paid professional anti-Communist speakers, of whom Myers Lowman is representative, and sometimes protests the appearance of such men as Justice Tom Clark at the University of Mississippi. In 1961 the Sovereignty Commission produced, at a cost of $29,000, its movie, *Message from Mississippi,* which contained the expected bromides, like Governor Barnett's deadpan utterance, "No student can get a better education than is offered the Negro children in Mississippi." In the summer of 1963 the Commission contributed $20,000 toward the lobbying activities of the Coordinating Committee for Fundamental American Freedoms, organized in Washington to oppose the Democratic administration's civil rights bill. By the end of 1963 this donation had grown to $120,000.

In speaking in Connecticut for the Commission, one of Mississippi's less gifted judges was asked whether he thought the lynchers of Mack Parker would ever be apprehended. The judge allowed as how he didn't think so, really—"Besides, three of them are already dead."

In spite of its sometimes inadvertent bungling, some instances of which are noted later in this volume, the State Sovereignty Commission, according to the Jackson *Daily News,* "could easily turn the tide of public opinion about the race issue in the North."

All the forces that influence public opinion were harnessed so effectively in the earlier period that after the shock of John Brown's fiasco had been exploited and by the time of Lincoln's election, the people were primed for rash and heedless action. It wasn't called propagandizing in those days, and the modern totalitarians hadn't refined and classified the Big Lie technique, but ante-bellum Mississippians had swallowed a remarkably unstable mixture of noxious home brews. Cotton was king, the South was solid, the money-grubbing Yankee wouldn't fight, and in "the last great bulwark of Christianity" God would not let his chosen people down. It was generally believed that secession, being perfectly legal, would take place "without a jostle or a jar." Politicians vied with each other in their determination to sanctify all the blood that might be spilled, and Governor John Pettus (1859–1863) was making plans of an evening to ambush invaders of his realm as his grandfather had successfully ambushed the Indians. There was slight comprehension of the fierce devotion to the Union of millions of Americans in the rest of the country, nor of the North's enormous industrial potential. Once out of the Union, the southern states were convinced they would be in a fat bargaining position for a triumphant return to it—on their own conditions. Mississippians remembered Lincoln only for his "house-divided" speech, being ignorant of his express determination not to interfere with established slavery in the states.

For a full year before secession Mississippi was flooded by rumors of slave insurrections and incendiary plots (directed, of course, by "outside agitators"). An irresponsible press encouraged local bully boys, organized into vigilance committees, in the performance of their chores of intimidation. It was quickly forgotten that as late as May, 1860, Congress, when prompted by Jefferson Davis, had explicitly resolved, with Republican concurrence, that it had no right to interfere with slavery where it was protected by the Constitution. Senator Davis might have reminded his people that without secession the Democrats would control the federal House and Senate, and that minority President Lincoln would be hard pressed to control his own divided party, let alone transform a Supreme Court that had already awarded the South its last inch of demand in the territories. When Mississippians finally discovered that Lincoln was not the rogue they had been taught to believe, it was too late to do anything except mourn him.

The people of Mississippi had been thoroughly prepared for secession by their politicians, their chauvinistic press, their politicalized preachers, and their local philosophers. Tragically in the dark, caught up in the hysteria of the moment, plagued with a rigid society which looked to authority instead of to reason, Mississippi made a terrible decision, which its citizens have been paying for, and publicly *eulogizing,* even to the present generation. Jefferson Davis claimed that the people "were in advance of their representatives throughout," which was true enough, but he failed to add that the emotional climax of secession was the perfectly predictable result of an authoritarianism which left no alternative. By such means had Mississippi society, closed in the months after the passage of the Kansas-Nebraska Law in 1854, embraced disaster.

What has been said so far about Mississippi could, of course, be said generally about the six other deep-southern states that joined it to form the Confederacy in February, 1861. Our problem today is to try to understand why Mississippi has clung so much more desperately to its closed society: why, indeed, it has drawn into itself more than any other American state.

The Traditional View of Reconstruction Is Exploited

According to the Citizens Council,[3] Mississippi is now the innocent victim of a second vicious Reconstruction from which

---

3. The startling growth of the Citizens Council, the country's leading segregation organization, is chronicled in part in Chapter 2. A native Mississippian, William J. Simmons (no relation to the founder of the twentieth-century Ku Klux Klan), has welded a remarkable group of spoiled intellectuals and loyal ward heelers into a smooth-running, extremely effective propaganda machine. It is generally acknowledged that

the stalwart citizenry will at long last emerge triumphant, as it did in 1875. It is perfectly true that for nearly ninety years Mississippi has grimly nullified the federal Constitution, but that it will convert the rest of the country to its present position is only a wild gleam in the eye of William J. Simmons.⁴ The key to the success of the "redeemers" was the apathy of the federal government, today or in the future an unlikely ally of the Citizens Council. Meanwhile the traditional view of Reconstruction has been thoroughly exploited, with embellishments, for its emotional impact on proud Mississippians. Once more, illiterate Negroes are pictured as demanding integration of the schools and hordes of carpetbaggers and scalawags are seen as poised to drive black legislators into gross corruption and extravagance. As redrawn in today's Council literature, Reconstruction Negroes "were precisely at the same level" of civilization as the terror-inspiring blacks of the Congo in 1962. "Men

---

since the inauguration of Governor Ross Barnett in 1960, W. J. Simmons and his machine have exercised a position of power and prestige seldom if ever achieved before by any extralegal group in the history of Mississippi. (See Hodding Carter, III, *The South Strikes Back,* New York, 1959.)

4. History is not likely to repeat itself, Mr. Simmons notwithstanding. During and after Reconstruction, northern pressure for Negro rights was withdrawn as the Republicans and Democrats channeled their energies into economic development. It may be well to remember that except in New York and New England Negro suffrage came in the North as a result of the Fifteenth Amendment. Northern commitment to the Negro at any time in the nineteenth century is a difficult thing to ascertain, though we know that many Abolitionists, content with the paper victory of the Emancipation Proclamation and the Civil War amendments, turned to other causes. Regardless of the reasons, the North did abandon its colored wards to the mercies of southern whites who quickly grasped the implications of the White Man's Burden and Social Darwinism. But today half the country's Negroes live outside the South and many belong to legitimate, efficiently organized, and effective groups: conservative as the American people may be, the federal government, now and in the future, will continue to press for the elimination of second-class citizenship.

were castrated, women raped, young girls ravished and muti-
lated, homes burned and pillaged, the very earth scorched and
barren." In the light of the Council's propaganda imperatives,
the "ghastly horrors" of Reconstruction become even more sickening, and finally the best white people in the state, their patience exhausted, rise up in their wrath (in 1875 as perhaps
they will tomorrow) to put down for all time such licentious
behavior.

The Mississippi Negro of 1860 was looked upon as a finished
product: he had gone about as far as he was to be allowed to
go. One argument for secession had been that freedom for slaves
would bring demands for social equality, which would in time
lead to intermarriage and amalgamation. It is one of the ironies
of ante-bellum history that slavery had in fact partially prepared the Negro for freedom, inasmuch as he had worked under
the ablest agriculturalists and on the best land. When emancipation did come, many conservatives, such as James L. Alcorn,
were willing to work along with the black man in economics
and politics. But white majority views prevailed, and the racial
code of the poor whites became public policy. The early orthodoxy, soon to be cherished as an irrevocable creed, contended
that the Negro, member of an inferior race, unmoved by the
ambition and aspiration that motivated the white man, would
labor only under compulsion and was incapable of living without a master. This position was institutionalized in law by the
Mississippi Black Code, which in turn helped to bring on Radical Reconstruction and to drive the Negro into the Republican
party.

Until 1870 the Negro's position was uncertain. The "Black
and Tan" constitution was defeated in 1868 as Mississippians
responded to the cry of the Meridian *Mercury:* "This is a White
Man's Government; and trusting in our firm purpose, our good
right arms and God of Right, we will maintain it so." Even after
Grant's election the Mississippi Democrats in convention called
upon the people "to vindicate the superiority of their race over
the negro"; but with the war hero's inauguration and the successful resubmission of the new constitution, Black Reconstruc-

tion was under way, although it was not to last the ten or twelve years usually attributed to it, but was to be overthrown by violence in less than six.

Like the planters who began to see a violation of virtue in the New Deal farm program when the federal government diverted some of its benefits to the tenants, the majority of whom were Negroes, Mississippi white farmers quickly directed their animosity toward the Freedmen's Bureau. Not only was the Bureau a constant reminder of defeat but its activities in behalf of Negroes ran counter to the social and economic code. There were, it is true, many prominent whites who had been ready to allow the Negro his basic rights according to the war amendments and to work with him for mutual benefit, but once given the assurance that Washington would not intervene, these moderates were willing to join the mass of white Democrats in the use of violence to drive the Negro from his new privileges, from what offices he held, and from the polls.

Those Mississippi leaders who inspired the University riot of 1962 made the absurd mistake of challenging the power of the federal government, as Governor Pettus had done in 1861. The veterans of the Civil War had found such a course impractical, and had bided their time until the rest of the country was occupied with its own problems. Meanwhile economic pressure, ostracism, sporadic violence, the enrolling of Republicans in "dead books," and the formation of militia companies and Democratic clubs armed with repeating rifles, were but preparation for the "Mississippi plan"—the use of the riot as a political instrument.

The ending of Republican rule in Meridian in 1871 by means of a more or less spontaneous riot was never to be forgotten in Mississippi. The lesson, as seen by Vernon Wharton, was that "Negroes, largely unarmed, and timid and unresourceful after generations of servitude, would offer no effective resistance to violence." A later explosion in Vicksburg in 1874, in which 36 Negroes were killed, led that city's *Monitor* to predict: *"The same tactics . . . will surely save the State, and no other will."*

And so, on election day in 1875 the presence of rifles and cannons brought an end to Reconstruction in Mississippi.[5]

The orthodox picture of the Reconstruction government thus exaggerates its fearfulness and underestimates its constructiveness, all the while assuming "true" Mississippi leaders to be blameless. In its publications, there is not a single word from the Citizens Council about Mississippi having lost the war, about the Black Code, or about the state's refusal to provide the slightest suffrage or education for the ex-slaves. Nor is any mention made, for that matter, of the fact that in the 1870's Mississippi, as an agricultural state, would have been in economic distress regardless of Reconstruction. On the contrary, the political redemption of Mississippi in 1875 is recounted in one Council version with the following tender concern for the truth:

> During the campaign which preceded the election the Federal commander of troops in Mississippi loaned a number of cannons to the Democrats which were fired by them in advance of their political meetings as was the custom in those days. The carpetbaggers and negroes, or Republicans, had none. This appeared to intimidate the negroes and apparently induced many of them to remain away from the polls on election day.

---

5. Twenty years later, former Governor Adelbert Ames took stock in judicious fashion:

"There was a time when policy made it advisable for the white men of Mississippi to advance 'corruption,' 'negro mobs,' anything and everything but the true reason for their conduct. They are white men, Anglo-Saxons—a dominant race—educated to believe in negro slavery. To perpetuate the then existing order of things they ventured everything and lost. An unjust and tyrannical power (from their standpoint) had filled their state with mourning, beggared them, freed their slaves and as a last insult and injury made the ex-slave a political equal. They resisted by intimidation, violence and murder. Excuses by the way of justification were given while the powerful hand of the national government was to be feared. Soon the national government and public opinion ceased to be dreaded. They then announced boldly that this is a white man's government and that the negro and ex-slave should, forever, form no part of it." (Quoted in Vernon Wharton, *The Negro in Mississippi. 1865–1890*, Chapel Hill, N.C., 1947, pp. 197–198.)

The election . . . resulted in an over-whelming victory for the Democrats.

Inequality Was Effected by Force and Regularized by Law

One of today's recurring little sophistries has it that equality must be earned and can never be achieved by force or law. The historic fact is that in Mississippi, between 1875 and 1890, inequality was effected by force and finally regularized by law, that is, by the constitution under which the state still operates. By 1890 Negroes had long since learned that Mississippi freedom included neither political nor any other kind of equality. Since that date "special privilege" has been the birthright of every white Mississippian in his relation to the Negro.

In those 15 years in which the Democrats cocked a wary eye on northern opinion, Negroes were deprived of their constitutional rights by violence, intimidation, and fraud. All the social and economic sanctions available were applied with savagery. Independent whites who challenged the new business leadership were cried down as traitors to their race. When agrarian distress in the late 1880's seriously threatened the one-party white-supremacy control, "whippings, mutilations, robberies, rapes, and murders by bands of men" became the order of the day. The citizen who protested against such barbarism found himself threatened with reprisal.

Negroes, outside the protection that comes from political and economic power, were cut down in the fierce competitive struggle for existence. It was a matter, as suggested by the Jackson *Weekly Clarion,* of stamping out the black man's "lust for blood." The record includes a species of savagery unknown in the days of slavery when the black man, as property, was not subject to lynching. For two decades after the redemption of Mississippi, Negro blood was coined into white gold through a convict-leasing system which, according to J. H. Jones, a Mississippi historian of sixty years ago, "left its trail of dishonor and of death which could only find a parallel in the persecution of the Middle Ages." Theft of more than ten dollars was declared grand larceny, with a penalty upon conviction of up to five years. The prison population quickly trebled. Statistically, a five-year sentence meant a 50–50 chance of death, because the annual mortality rate among leased convicts ran well over ten per cent (as compared with one per cent among other American convicts). Slavery had been mild compared to this new dispensation. In 1887 a Hinds County grand jury described inmates of the penitentiary hospital as having "the stamp of manhood almost blotted out of their faces." Lest this be considered sentimentality, in the following year the same jury, having examined a camp of leased convicts, reported the comforting discovery that the leathers used in tying up prisoners by the thumbs "are remarkably soft and pliant, so that the only pain inflicted is from the attitude the prisoner is forced to maintain." Public shame brought convict leasing to an end, but not until the new constitution forbade it after 1894.

On the floor of the 1890 constitutional convention, Judge J. J. Chrisman declared: ". . . it is no secret that there has not been a full vote and a fair count in Mississippi since 1875—that we have been preserving the ascendancy of the white people by revolutionary methods. In plain words we have been stuffing the ballot boxes, committing perjury, and . . . carrying the elections by *fraud* and violence until the whole machinery was about to rot down. No man can be in favor of the election methods which have prevailed . . . who is not a moral idiot."

The convention's presiding officer, Judge S. S. Calhoon, who admitted that the 1868 constitution had worked reasonably well, openly acknowledged that after the overthrow of Reconstruction by revolution, enormous evil had resulted from chronic fraud and political juggling. According to the judge, patriotic citizens saw the need for "purifying" the ballot box. More succinctly, the *Clarion-Ledger* summed it up: "If every colored man in Mississippi were a graduate of Yale College, the two races would remain just as widely separated as they are now in all political and social matters." A letter to the editor held that "If every negro in Mississippi was a graduate of Harvard, and had been elected as class orator . . . he would not be as well fitted to exercise the right of suffrage as the Anglo-Saxon farm laborer. . . ." The implication was simple: a white idiot was superior to a Negro genius. As for counting the votes, fifty years later a sensitive and highly intelligent Mississippian, William Alexander Percy, would be able to look back on ballot thievery with moral satisfaction, as a necessity.[6]

An official pronouncement of the Democratic party made it clear that all issues except white supremacy must be obliterated. This was literally done to the only Republican outside the river counties who was audacious enough to make a campaign in 1890. The *Clarion-Ledger* congratulated Jasper County when his body was found riddled with bullets. Not that assassination was the right answer; there was a better method. Colonel B. F. Jones put it this way: "The old men of the present generation can't afford to die and leave their children with shot-guns in their hands, a lie in their mouths and perjury in their souls, in order to defeat the negroes. The constitution can be made so this will not be necessary."

And so, according to the editor of the Port Gibson *Reveille,* "it was reserved for the State of Mississippi to make its very Constitution the instrument and shield of fraud." Through poll tax, residence, registration, and literacy and "understanding" clauses, the Negro was effectively eliminated from participation in politics. The voting rolls of 1892 showed 8,615 Negro registrants and these were soon to be almost wiped out by that shrewd stroke of political mechanics called the white primary. "Foreign and uncongenial to the spirit of popular liberty and representative government" though such an arrangement was, as seen by conservative Mississippi historian J. S. McNeilly, the Negro "was the gainer by the removal from the distraction of a sphere for which he was neither fit nor needful. The con-

---

6. Alfred H. Stone, noted Mississippi sociologist and state official who attended the constitutional convention of 1890, once told the writer that its purpose was to eliminate the corruption involved in competition for Negro votes.

stitution of 1890 brought rest to the plantations." It was a demonstration "of the negro's incapacity and unworthiness for the equipment of political equality."

William D. McCain, former state archivist and now president of Mississippi Southern University, has described the situation with great accuracy: "White supremacy had been gained at a terrible cost. The people of Mississippi would have undoubtedly preferred an inefficient and even corrupt government in the hands of white men, than a perfect government in which there was a danger of Negro control." They got both inefficiency and corruption. In 1876, immediately after redemption, the state debt came to $830,750, only a little more than twice the amount embezzled by a single Democratic state treasurer in 1890.

Political disfranchisement may not have been the key part of the story. An unwritten law had been devised to replace the slave code of 1857. "Few of its provisions could be found in the statute books. Its application was at times capricious and unpredictable. But, in general, members of both races understood and observed its content. In almost any conceivable contact with a white man, there were certain forms of behavior which the black man must observe. The Negro, at last, was 'in his place.' " [7] The caste system had been substituted for slavery. Mississippi's society was closed and the terms of its closure were sacrosanct and beyond ·debate.

In the twentieth century there has yet to be a real challenge in Mississippi to white supremacy in any of its manifestations.

There Is No Issue Beyond the Supremacy of the White Man

The Citizens Council has not actually strayed far from the imperishable wisdom of its spiritual father, Governor James K. Vardaman (1904–1908), Mississippi's greatest white supremacist. Education of the Negro was the real threat. If educated, the

---

7. Wharton, *The Negro in Mississippi,* p. 233.

Negro would become dissatisfied. Inasmuch as he "will not be permitted to rise above the station he now fills," said Vardaman, "education would be a positive unkindness to him. It simply renders him unfit for the work which the white man has prescribed, and which he will be forced to perform." Why "squander money on his education when the only effect is to spoil a good field hand and make an insolent cook?" The Negro, Vardaman continued, was "a lazy, lying, lustful animal which no conceivable amount of training can transform into a tolerable citizen." To prosper he "must avoid politics and maintain the relation which he now occupies to white folks." On the grounds of expediency (with some regard for the federal courts, perhaps), school funds should be divided according to what each race paid in taxes. "No white man in public life in Mississippi proposed doing anything constructive for the Negro," says Albert D. Kirwan.[8] In 1904 fewer than two thousand Negroes were permitted to vote.

Off and on for four decades Mississippi politics was dominated by Theodore G. Bilbo, pronounced by the state senate in 1911 "as unfit to sit with honest, upright men in a respectable legislative body," and described more pungently by his admirers as "a slick little bastard." Bilbo reminded W. A. Percy of the man who picked a yellow-striped caterpillar out of the dust and, swallowing it, said: "It is not my regular diet, I just wanted to see how strong my stomach was."

Whether Governor Bilbo (1916–1920, 1928–1932) "stands for nothing that is high or constructive, represents nothing save passion, prejudice, and hatred, advocates nothing that is worthy," as stated in 1915 by Fred Sullens, long-time vitriolic editor of the Jackson *Daily News,* depends on one's point of view. To the student of government, Bilbo remains symptomatic of the chaos and bankruptcy of Mississippi's one-party system. For more than a century, according to the political scientist V. O.

---

8. For an excellent study of Mississippi politics, see Albert D. Kirwan, *Revolt of the Rednecks: Mississippi Politics, 1876–1925,* Lexington, Ky., 1951.

Key, white supremacy has dictated multi-factional arrangements
in which the voter is "confronted with new faces, new choices,
and must function in a sort of state of nature." There can be no
real debate on issues for *there is no issue beyond the supremacy
of the white man,* no continuity in the existence even of factions, no competition between recognizable groups. Each leader
is for himself. All this "places a high premium on demagogic
qualities of personality which attract voter attention." Any
challenge to the equilibrium in race relations is likely to cause a
Bilbonic plague or a Barnett blight. Historically, the race question "first crushed and then prevented the rebirth of political
parties." [9]

With no qualification for high office except the desire to
serve, Ross Barnett required two expensive campaigns before
he learned the tricks of the demagogue. No clearer instance than
Mississippi's gubernatorial election of 1963 can be found to
illustrate Key's description of "transient and amorphous political factions ill designed to meet the necessities of self government . . . fortuitous groupings of individuals . . . spectacular demagogues odd enough to control the attention of considerable numbers of voters." There is no way to check the wild-
eyed, no deterrent to unscrupulous and spectacular person-
alities, no power to carry out sustained programs of action.
Great negative power accrues to those able to invest their dollars in legislative candidates. Business and finance skillfully
manipulate the one-party system to the greater glory of *laissez-
faire* which, ironically, leads to the much damned but inevitable
transfer of state functions to the federal government and to a
diminution of state rights.

Historical parallels are notoriously dangerous. Mississippi
had no large city in 1860 and none a century later. But in the
20 years after 1940 Jackson had jumped in population from
60,000 to almost 150,000. This highly prosperous metropolitan
area was filled with "new men," bold entrepreneurs as enamored

---

9. For a monumental work, see V. O. Key, Jr., *Southern Politics in
State and Nation,* New York, 1949.

of the satisfying status quo as their forefathers had been. The pursuit of riches and all that money will buy required the talents and energies of the Jackson business leadership to the point that, except for the obvious "good works" done with Rotary fanfare, there was little time devoted to thinking about the inevitable social and political changes bound to accompany economic progress. If there was an aristocracy, its leadership impact was negative and negligible. The right-to-work law was imbedded in the constitution, a colossal program of state socialism (using state and local credit to "balance agriculture with industry" by erecting factory buildings) was set up to entice the Yankee industrialist, and white Mississippi men and women were made available for the subsidized factories at minimum wages. The fruits of this economic revolution were "for whites only," and when it appeared that the caste-ridden Negroes, kept in idleness on relief, were restless, their case was turned over to the Citizens Council for interpretation. As if this were not enough, Council extremists gradually took over the minds of an otherwise capable people, whose feebly-expressed opinions bore no relationship to the independence, the nationalism, and the democracy of their patron saint, Andrew Jackson.

No one has better described mid-century Mississippi politics than Professor Key: "The almost overwhelming temptation, especially in areas with many Negroes, is to take advantage of the short-run opportunity to maintain the status-quo by using the race issue to blot up the discontents of the lesser whites. By this means the governing classes can kill off or minimize pressures for improved governmental services from whites and find support for low public outlays for the benefit of the Negro. . . . With a high degree of regularity those of the top economic groups—particularly the new industrialists—are to be found in communion with the strident advocates of white supremacy. In the political chaos and demoralization that ensue alert men with a sharp eye for immediate advantage take and count their gains. The requirements are for a remarkably enlightened leadership that is at the same time tough enough to maintain a hard-boiled discipline within its own ranks. Only by such means can a social situation with volcanic potentialities be kept under control." As Key was writing, some fifteen years ago, a southern Secretary of the Army, Kenneth C. Royall, was saying in Jackson: "There will always be some who will hearken to the arguments of bitterness and bigotry, but the fundamental common sense and the essential spirit of fairness of the American people will ultimately bring failure to any class party or any party of intolerance." That "fundamental common sense" and "essential spirit of fairness" are at present on leave from Mississippi.

The Sanctions for White Supremacy Have Been Destroyed

Today the closed society of Mississippi imposes on all its people acceptance of and obedience to an official orthodoxy almost identical with the one developed in the middle of the nineteenth century. In fact the philosophical basis for slavery has become the substance of the catechism of white supremacy. Though lacking the considerable intellectual integrity of the ante-bellum pro-slavery argument, the segregation creed assumes 1) the biological inferiority of the Negro, 2) the sanction of the Bible and Christianity, 3) the aptitude of the Negro for menial labor only, 4) racial separation as an absolute requirement for social stability, and 5) the necessity of the Negro earning his way to a higher and more responsible citizenship.

To Mississippians the doctrine of state sovereignty is as much a cornerstone of the American republic as it was in the days of secessionist John A. Quitman, and every Mississippi politician is adept at intoning the sacred liturgy of the Tenth Amendment. An erroneous conception of the political conservatism of the founding fathers is worshipped with such abandon that one may conclude that Mississippi leaders not only deny the constitutionality of the Fourteenth Amendment, but seriously question the legal adoption of the Constitution itself. They have refused to acknowledge the origins of the Constitution as a means to escape from the state supremacy embodied in the Articles of

Confederation. In the ceaseless declaiming of constitutional principles, Mississippi orators show no comprehension that the essence of the American Constitution is the "complete and compulsive operation of the central government upon the individual citizen." Mississippi once exercised its right to secede, lost the war but won the Reconstruction, and every patriot must be ready to do it all over again. Turn-of-the-century shibboleths taken from Social Darwinism, imperialism, and hallowed Anglo-Saxonism, deepen the bankruptcy of today's rationalization in Mississippi.

Whatever sanction white supremacy may have had in the minds of the enlightened in the days of William McKinley has long since been destroyed. It has been routed by the new anthropology, by the abandonment of tortuous scriptural interpretations, by the mechanized assault on mud-sill (menial) labor, by the lessening of the fear of race conflict, and by recognition of the fact that the Negro, when given the chance, has indeed been capable of earning his way. The American dream can no longer be seen as countenancing the idea that some people are more entitled to opportunity than others. Modern notions have even seeped into Mississippi, notwithstanding strident denials by those living in the past; and while they have been discussed only furtively, it is possible to foresee a day when a new and more intelligent patriotism will not assume that every black Mississippian must be an inferior Mississippian.

For reasons that shift from crisis to crisis, "vicious, unfair, slanderous, and deadly propaganda" (to quote the Jackson press) is constantly directed at good, Christian Mississippi from the outside. This is easily believed by Mississippians whose Scots-Irish pedigree carries an aura of persecution. Despite the interminable barrage of Communist-inspired lies, according to Judge Sebe Dale, "there is no ill feeling between the races in Mississippi." "Here in Mississippi," Governor Ross Barnett tells a Negro audience, "we are enjoying a wonderful and peaceful relationship." Senator James O. Eastland is even more reassuring: "There is no discrimination in the South." A former president of the Mississippi Bar says, "The Mississippi Negro is smart enough to know that he is being well treated. They [*sic*] do not like the attitude or actions of the NAACP." As the late Senator W. B. Alexander saw it, "the colored people of Mississippi do not want integration," for the black-white relationship is "that of utter friendship, harmony, trust, peace, and good will." On national television, Mayor Allen Thompson rates his city of Jackson the "nearest thing to Heaven on this earth," and claims in federal court that it has no official segregation policy—which technically may be true.[10] (A few months after the mayor's television appearance, the city fathers purchased an armored truck—quickly nicknamed "Thompson's Tank"— capable of shooting tear gas in all directions.) Attorney General Joe Patterson is sure "the dual system of education is working to the complete satisfaction of both races." A private citizen of Shaw, race unknown, thinks "the colored people of Mississippi have a great privilege to live in a state where the white people will build churches and schools for them." Besides, according to Charles Hills, *Clarion-Ledger* columnist, Negroes have had "a free ride" for more than a hundred years. Congressman Jamie Whitten is confident that he enjoys "the warm love and respect of the Negro citizens." Mississippians refuse to recognize that there is an indigenous race problem: they have surrounded themselves with an atmosphere called by one state lawyer a "cesspool of sanctity."

As instructed by a Citizens Council intellectual, the Mississippian is duty-bound to defy an unconstitutional decision of the United States Supreme Court; otherwise nine men could "succeed in putting themselves above the constitution itself." The Fourteenth Amendment, even though it is the basis for the accepted "separate but equal" doctrine (*Plessy* v *Ferguson,* 1896), is "a false instrument, never ratified." Judge M. M. McGowan clinches the matter: "No court decision is 'the law of the

---

10. In June, 1963, however, Mayor Thompson declared that "nothing the President, Congress, or the courts do is going to change Jackson's policy of separation of the races."

land.' No court decision is the law of the case if based upon an amendment which was illegally placed in the constitution." All court decisions, according to Governor Barnett, must comply with *his* view of state rights, without which "human rights, liberty and freedom will perish."

"*They Are Not and Never Can Be Equal*"

"If we start off with the self-evident proposition," Governor Barnett has remarked, "that the whites and colored are different, we will not experience any difficulty in reaching the conclusion that they are not and never can be equal." For more than a century, no Mississippian in public office has questioned this reasoning. With Vardaman out of the way, Bilbo had reigned supreme as the high priest of the doctrine of inequality, with its horror of amalgamation: ". . . if the blood of our white race should become corrupted with the blood of Africa, then the present greatness of the United States of America would be destroyed and all hope for the future would be forever gone." Today Barnett wipes out ancient Egyptian civilization with an injection of Negro blood.[11]

After the 1954 Brown desegregation decision, Judge Tom Brady, a Yale graduate and now a Barnett appointee to the Mississippi Supreme Court, became for a while the metaphysician of the master racists, following the publication of his hastily written and unscholarly volume *Black Monday*. This was outmoded overnight by the current gospel of Mississippi white supremacy, *Race and Reason*, by Carleton Putnam, a Princeton graduate, a Roosevelt biographer, and an airlines executive. Putnam became, by his own efforts, an expert

---

11. Obviously Negro blood *is* a powerful substance inasmuch as in Mississippi the possession of one-eighth Negro blood defines a person as colored even though the other seven-eighths are white. With little or no knowledge of ancient history, the racists frighten their listeners with the threat of deterioration of our civilization, as they claim has happened before in the case of Egypt—which went under because of "blood mixing."

theologian, psychologist, and anthropologist. To the enchantment of Mississippians, he exposed the conspiracy of the late Franz Boas (Columbia University anthropologist) which, he asserted, had held the scientific world in a climate of terror and fear of reprisal and persecution for a generation. For those unconcerned with the spectacle of academic buffoonery, what more could be asked than the endorsement of *Race and Reason* by the Memphis *Commercial Appeal,* the Charleston *News and Courier,* John Temple Graves (widely syndicated columnist), and the Jackson *Daily News?* Mississippians did not read the book (they just sent it to their friends, as instructed by the Citizens Council), else they would have discovered that, even by Putnam's illogic, the white race was already doomed, since more than half the country's Negroes lived in integrated situations. But who would argue with the new messiah? He was brought to Jackson on October 26, 1961 (proclaimed by the governor as "Race and Reason Day") and feted at a twenty-five-dollar-a-plate dinner attended by more than 500 patriots: the civic and business leadership, the state's "people of education, culture, and high position."

There was no Charles Dickens to point out that there never had been another such day in Mississippi. It could, Barnett believed, "mark the turning point in the South's struggle to preserve the integrity of the white race." Putnam had, said Congressman John Bell Williams, "enunciated an ideology around which the entire movement for racial integrity can be consolidated." Putnam had indeed provided an article of faith Mississippians could live by. Denouncing the "left-wing pseudo-scientists" for creating the fallacy which "has gained complete possession of the Northern and Western mind," he designated Mississippi as "the heartland of the struggle for racial integrity," and in his best William Jennings Bryan manner exclaimed: "You don't crucify the South on a cross of equalitarian propaganda." Calling on the South to produce more Barnetts, Putnam identified equalitarianism with Communism and segregation with Christianity, which, of course, Barnett had been doing long before he ever heard of the word anthropology.

Now, the executive director of the Jackson Citizens Council jubilantly declared, "hard work by good men, armed with a noble and just cause," would enable southern patriots to "get through" to the rest of the nation. Perhaps they did get through. Less than a month later, the American Anthropological Association unanimously repudiated Putnam in a down-to-earth declaration which concluded: "The basic principle of equality of opportunity and equality before the law is compatible with all that is known about human biology. All races possess the abilities needed to participate fully in the democratic way of life and in modern technological civilization."

On March 13, 1963, William L. Gilbert of Utica announced his candidacy for the state House of Representatives, Hinds County post number nine. His stated principles were complete and unassailable, a kind of shorter catechism of the Mississippi ideology:

I am a Mississippi Democrat with conservative political views. I supported the unpledged elector movement in 1960. I am a staunch believer in constitutional government, states rights, the southern way of life, and separation of the races.

The forces of socialism and communism outside our borders are advancing and spreading rapidly over the world while within our borders, the dictatorial Kennedys, socialistic Supreme Court, politicalized federal courts, power-seizing pressure groups are gradually and certainly undermining and destroying the principals [sic] upon which this great nation was founded.

Since Mississippi and the Southland has [sic] inherited the task of making the last great stand for constitutional government, states rights, individual freedom and democracy, we must cast aside our personal and political ambitions, close our ranks, unite and solidify our beliefs and convictions and advance and achieve our destiny by handing down to our children and descendants the greatest gift that one can give or receive—a free Christian, Democratic nation and world.

2.

The Voices of Militancy

"Few Mississippians Believe Anything They See or Hear"

According to the Jackson *Daily News* "there is nothing new in the tactics of propagandists smearing the South. This has been a trait for well over a century. The current crop of hate peddlers simply drum up new accusations and the bias has become so stereotyped only the most gullible fall for this odd-ball thunder." Honorable people all across the nation are beginning to "see through the trashy social and political gunk," and, as might be expected, "damned few Mississippians believe anything they see or hear on a national newscast any more." In the *Clarion-Ledger*, Charles Hills wrote an illuminating historical comparison: "The South has been and is being subjected to such a barrage of hate-mongering and bias from the Yankee press as the world has never seen before. Never was Hitler, nor Mussolini, nor the Mikado, nor even Kaiser Wilhelm attacked so venomously under the caption of 'free reporting.'" Mr. Hills ascribes the reason for this outside malice to northern "jealousy because of Mississippi's industrial expansion." There being no way to excuse the vast loss of American wealth overseas, "the administration tried to camouflage our own national weakness by throwing off on the South." "We are changing from the richest nation to the poorest," and the "Kennedys came along and did away with truth and decency" while using the Negro as a "patsy" and blaming it all on the South. In such neurotic writing, Mississippi invariably represents the South, and the South is always regarded as a solid unit.

Mississippians have long been made conscious of their image both within and without the state. In April, 1962, the UPI reporter John Herbers described the difficulties imposed on newsmen by Mississippi city officials suspicious of potential troublemakers from the press. In one case a bystander was bitten by police dogs used to break up a demonstration protesting segregation at the state fair. An enterprising reporter found the victim in a Jackson hospital, with a new pair of trousers bought by the city and an apology from Mayor Allen Thompson. But the mayor, upset by the story, denied that he had apologized to anyone and said the man should have moved if he had not wanted to be bitten. Winona and Grenada agreed to comply with an Interstate Commerce Commission ruling against segregated travel facilities but quickly reversed themselves upon Citizens Council prompting. "The mayor of Winona explained he thought he had been talking to an ICC agent rather than to a reporter," and the mayor of Grenada charged he had been misquoted, while the local chamber of commerce and city council adopted resolutions against "false" news reporting. A United Press International story on integrated Memphis schools describing white and black children skipping rope together drew this comment from a Mississippi subscriber, "Why can't you report the facts without romancing the Negro race?"

When Medgar Evers, the Mississippi NAACP field secretary, was killed from ambush on the night of June 11, 1963, state officials and the press made perfunctory comments about the "regrettable" incident before launching into diatribes about outside agitators. To Congressman William Colmer the murder was "the inevitable result of agitation by politicians, do-gooders and those who sail under the false flag of liberalism." The *Clarion-Ledger* columnists suggested that "a paid assassin might have done the job. There are rumors that the man was expendable." Moreover ". . . it is barely possible that desperately ruthless forces may have used him as a sacrificial offering, to rekindle the flames of unrest here and spur their drive for 'victory' everywhere." The governor duly notified the Highway Patrol to be on special alert for non-resident vehicles "inasmuch as we have had several agitators in our state in the past several weeks." When Byron de La Beckwith, scion of an old Delta family, born on the Pacific coast but a resident in Mississippi for 38 years, was apprehended, the *Clarion-Ledger* flashed what may remain its most imaginative headline of all time: CALIFORNIAN IS CHARGED WITH MURDER OF EVERS.

The Mississippi press mounts vigilant guard over the racial, economic, political, and religious orthodoxy of the closed society. Despite varying degrees of moderation expressed in the daily papers of Greenville, Tupelo, McComb, and, until recently, Pascagoula, and in an occasional rural weekly, the extremist Jackson *Clarion-Ledger* and the *Daily News* dominate Mississippi thought. Hodding Carter once described the Hedermans (who own both papers) as motivated, at least in part, by a mixture of racism and fundamentalism. To read the Hederman press day after day is to understand what the people of the state believe and are prepared to defend.

The news director of a Jackson television station, fed up with the constant tirade against alleged distortions of the national news media, recently commented on the lack of factual reporting in Mississippi: "We aren't getting the full truth," he said; "too many political officials and too many controlling business leaders are too happy with their home grown version of news management." Only a constant and critical reader of the capital press would believe the extent to which news is manipulated. Negro crime and immorality in the North, Negro complicity in Communism, and even Negro support of the present Governor are given the headlines day after day. The inspiration for Negro demands becomes the Communist Manifesto, not the Declaration of Independence. Shotgun blasts fired into Negro homes become an NAACP plot. The Oxford minis-

The Clarion-Ledger

Mississippi's Leading Newspaper For More Than A Century

Established 1837   AP and UPI Leased Wires   JACKSON, MISSISSIPPI, MONDAY, JUNE 24, 1963   VOL. CXXV.   NO. 135   20 PAGES   PRICE 5c

WEATHER

Monday — Partly cloudy and warm, scattered thundershowers, mainly in afternoon. Low 70, high 90. Tuesday — Little change, low 70. Sunday — High 96, low 61, Pearl River at Jackson 2.9 feet, no change.

BOYCOTT

Mrs. Jackie Kennedy, Mrs. Lady Bird Johnson and an aunt's wives have refused to help sponsor Washington Premiere of "Cleopatra" for the benefit of a very worthy charity. For reason see Drew Pearson on Page 4.

Californian Is Charged With Murder Of Evers

Suspect Transferred To Jail In Jackson

By DUDLEY LEHEW
Associated Press Staff Writer

Byron de La Beckwith, a 42-year-old salesman from the Mississippi Delta city of Greenwood and a native Californian, was charged with murder Sunday in the sniping slaying of Negro leader Medgar W. Evers.

The Federal Bureau of Investigation took Beckwith into custody at Greenwood late Saturday night.

Beckwith's attorney said he turned himself in after bearing FBI agents were watching his house.

A time and date for a court appearance has not yet been set.

Dist. Attorney Bill Waller expects to present the case to the Hinds County Grand Jury July 1, unless Beckwith first would ask for a preliminary hearing.

Beckwith, a salesman for a chemical fertilizer company, was brought here by FBI agents Saturday night, and lodged in the city jail.

FBI IDENTIFIES AS RIFLE USED IN SLAYING — The FBI Sunday released this photograph in Washington and said it shows views of the rifle with telescopic sight used in June 12 slaying of Medgar Evers. The FBI said the circle and arrow on telescopic sight in upper show where Jackson police found fingerprint leading to arrest of Byron de La Beckwith. — Clarion-Ledger AP Wirephoto.

GREENWOOD SHOCKED

Neighbors Recall Beckwith As Outspoken Marine Vet

By JANE RIGGERS
Clarion-Ledger Correspondent

tioticn if you were her tomorrow; about his father, but he did is | he would be for yesterday.. | hert a common interest that has

CHARGED IN MURDER—Byron De La Beckwith, 42, obviously weary from questioning and events leading up to his arrest for the murder of Negro NAACP Field Secretary Medgar Evers, pauses long enough for a photographer to take his picture at the Municipal Court Building, Sunday afternoon. Moments later he was led away with his lawyer, Hardy Lott, left, of Greenwood. Beckwith was taken into custody by FBI agents late Saturday night, and brought to Jackson, where charges were filed against him Sunday.—Photo by Kim Scuberland.

AGREES TO POSE — Byron de La Beckwith first declined to pose for photographers, then agreed to do so when they reported they were doing their job. — Photo by Kim Sutherland.

SURRENDERS

at a means to keep Beckwith in

terial association's moderate statement calling for penitence after the Ole Miss riot is ignored. The accounts of Governor Barnett's reception outside the state are highly colored. The only pictures of the Negro march on Washington of August 28, 1963, show the litter left by 200,000 marchers, and one news story in the *Clarion-Ledger* is captioned, "Washington Is Clean Again With Negro Trash Removed." Reports in September, 1962, of cross burnings on the University campus are both exaggerated and fabricated. The rest of the country is about to come around to the Mississippi way of life, partly due to the missionary efforts of Sovereignty Commission publicists (who write up the reports of their own speeches). Special correspondents in Washington send back political and racial copy to order. Much of the distortion is trivial but its cumulative effect is overpowering.

In time of trial the Jackson papers lose all semblance of perspective. For example, on the day that Judge Sidney Mize ordered James Meredith enrolled in the University, the *Daily News* front page carried these headlines:

> ROSS RISKS JAIL TO HALT MIXING
> Note Bares Negro Plan to Agitate
> Hattiesburg Agitation Order (photostat)
> We Support Gov. Barnett (editorial)
> Negroes Purchased Shot, Says Mayor
> President Deplores Shooting in State
> Judge Mize Issues Permanent Injunction (bulletin)
> Meredith Effigy Hanged at Oxford
> Barnett During and After Broadcast (pictures)
> Moses' Automobile (picture)
> *Crossroads* (column of Editor Jimmy Ward): Barnett—
>   "All Loyal Mississippians Support Him."

There was still room on the front page for a small cartoon about a Mississippi College football game and the index.

On November 28, 1962, the day the Southern Association of Colleges and Schools (SACS) was deciding on the accreditation of the University of Mississippi, the *Clarion-Ledger* contained the following stories:

1. Gov.-elect Wallace of Alabama hits SACS power in Jackson addresses to legislature and Citizens Council.
2. Judge McGowan blasts SACS policy.
3. Speech of Dr. Medford Evans, Citizens Council consultant, at Indianola, identifying communism with integration and denouncing academic freedom.
4. Negroes plead "Fifth" in probe of Muslims.
5. Secretary of State Ladner praises "Women for Constitutional Government," calls for revitalization of 10th amendment.
6. Lt. Governor Johnson declares Mississippi officials innocent of guilt for Ole Miss riot.
7. Ethridge column: "Pastor Says Oxford Clergy Wrong to Urge State People Repent."
8. Justice Percy Lee Says JFK overstepping bounds—Congress must reassert itself.
9. Ole Miss Beauty Enters Maid of Cotton Contest.
10. Mississippi ranks among top 5 in broiler production—and Vice Chancellor Bryant defends SACS.

To heavy-handed Hederman writers, the Fifth Circuit Court of Appeals becomes "the nine judicial baboons in New Orleans," President Kennedy "regards himself as a new Jesus whose infinite wisdom represents mankind's only real hope of salvation," and Ross Barnett is twisted into a modern combination of David, Horatius, and Leonidas. Tougaloo College, a center of Negro activity, is rechristened "Cancer College," with a new summer course in "Rapid Hate." The anonymous *Rebel Underground,* which on January 6, 1963, recommended the execution of "the Marxist Monster," the President of the United States, is characterized as "an innocuous handbill" calling on Ole Miss students "to continue their resistance to integration." By March, 1963, the *Daily News* adds up the "price tag" on the federal invasion of Mississippi as coming to $14 million because of a bonus of 130 accidental deaths on the state's highways, attributed to "a frame of mind, an atmosphere of anger, a period of bayonet-point frustration" which lowered the morale of the Highway Patrol. For University faculty members with the temerity to treat Meredith as a human being, editor Jimmy Ward predicts crushed spirits, bitterness, even self-

imposed tragedy. "It would appear apparent by now that prudent people will not wantonly toy with tradition or tamper with
the soul of a civilized society."

Such blatant irresponsibility is favorably received by an
anxious, fearful, frustrated group of marginal white men, who
exist in every Mississippi community. It makes no difference
whether these people are suffering from their own personal
inadequacies or whether they are overwhelmed by circumstances: they escape from their troubles periodically into the
excitement of racial conflict. They are impelled to keep the
Negro down in order to look up to themselves. They may even
work for the betterment of the Negro *up to a point,* to prove
their lack of basic prejudice. Of course, "when a Negro obtains
a good pair of shoes and learns to write a literate letter, some
whites think he wants to marry their sister," [1] and such a de-
duction is widespread in a state whose white inhabitants assume
that they and only they can understand the black man. Racial
bigotry transcends reason in Mississippi because, for varying
motives, so many leaders are willing to exploit the nameless
dreads and alarms that have taken possession of most white
people. The poor whites may not raise their low standard of
living by blaming it on Negroes, but they do release an aggressive energy upon a socially accepted scapegoat. Themselves last
in everything else, they can still rejoice in having the "nigger"
beneath them. At least in the short run, nearly every white man
does stand to derive economic, political, or social status from
keeping Negroes in their place.

According to Judge Brady, the NAACP is driving toward
"a revolution in the bedroom" to mongrelize the country before
turning it over to the Communists. The judge was willing to
"give the Negro in good conscience all that he is justly entitled
to and what we in good conscience can afford." Council literature from the start specialized in African horror stories.

A coarse speech allegedly made to a Mississippi colored

---

1. Gordon W. Allport, *The Nature of Prejudice,* New York, 1958,
p. 354.

audience by a Howard University faculty member and widely distributed by way of the mimeograph machine was exposed as a hoax. The lurid story reported a Professor Roosevelt Williams as elaborating on the secret craving for white women of Negroes and implying that the day was just around the corner when the blackest male could satisfy his most salacious desires. This crude little jewel was traced to the Attorney General of Georgia, who said he got it from the Mississippi Citizens Council. Executive Secretary Robert Patterson at first shamefacedly declared that "we never claimed it to be authentic," but later boldly challenged the NAACP to prove it wasn't so. Anyway, he countered, the unsuspecting dupe "will wake up some day just in time to see some sloe-eyed, pigeon-toed Red, and a blue gum Detroit black, come up and take his car and his bottle . . . and perhaps his wife and daughter."

In Mississippi the techniques of arousing hopes and fears have long been the source of lucrative rackets and success in politics. An impenetrable rigidity in the face of a deliberately manufactured outside enemy, plus appropriate and pious obeisance to the church, patriotism, and the heritage—a situation in which all can see the demagogue "stand up and be counted" —has been the surest road to political reward. For the most recent example one has only to check the 1963 gubernatorial campaign.

The Citizens Council Creates a Juggernaut

The Citizens Council's conquest of Mississippi was neither assured nor easy, despite a favorable climate and the undeniable organizational talents of its early leaders. Under Governors Hugh White (1952–1956) and J. P. Coleman (1956–1960), these extremists of the right were kept at arm's length while peddling their clan as a law-abiding "modern version of the old-time town meeting." Congressman John Bell Williams had observed that the Council stood for "equality for the Negro under the law, and when the time comes that peaceful and legal means is failing to halt integration it's time for the coun-

cils to disband." For some years after the Supreme Court
segregation decisions, while the Council was gathering strength,
it was possible for a moderate such as Frank Smith to hold out
and to remain in Congress representing the Mississippi Delta.
Though openly advocating the use of economic reprisal and
social pressure to maintain segregation, the Council decried
violence and declared its own respectability. If it was another
Ku Klux Klan, at least it was, in the words of Hodding Carter,
Senior, an "uptown Klan."

The Citizens Council takes little action officially or openly.
Boycotts of the products of Falstaff, Ford, and Philip Morris
just happened—the automatic response of indignant citizens
to the inept public relations of the companies involved. Economic reprisals against Greenville, Laurel, Pascagoula, and
Lexington newspapers were nothing more than the spontaneous
outbursts of an enraged people. When in May, 1955, the
NAACP president blamed the murder of the Reverend George
Lee on the Citizens Council, the secretary of the Humphreys
County chapter emphatically denied that any member could
have shot down the voter registration worker since "violence is
against our constitution and by-laws." On the other hand, it *was*
the Council which kept blacklists of Mississippi professors who
were not *right* on segregation; which circulated a document
showing the gross treason of the dean of the Ole Miss Law
School in signing a statement urging respect for Supreme Court
decisions; which attempted a showdown at Millsaps College that
led the *Delta Democrat-Times* to suggest that "the undertaker
who is president of the Jackson Citizens Council is prepared to
embalm and bury the remains of academic freedom in Mississippi."

For twelve years Eugene Cox and Dr. David Minter, both
Southerners, had worked closely together as manager and
physician for the white and black families making up the Providence Cooperative, a 2700-acre farm near Tchula in Holmes
County. On September 27, 1955, at a mass meeting called by
leading members of the Citizens Council, Cox and Minter were
ordered out of the community, mainly on the basis of testimony

recorded on tape in two hours of questioning by Council and county officials of four Negro boys accused of making obscene remarks about a white girl. Cox and Minter denied allegations of intermingling of the races at the farm, though it was conceded freely that white and Negro patrons did attend meetings of the co-op's credit union together. Threats of violence were made against both men and their families and, his patients having been intimidated, Minter's medical practice fell off about 50 per cent. An economic boycott was less effective. Professional segregationist Edwin White, who had helped make the original tape, said: "We just can't afford to have them up there teaching what they are teaching—which will lead to violence unless it is stopped." At the September meeting, Cox admitted his belief that segregation is un-Christian. A planter, whose father had been a minister, spoke out, "This isn't a Christian meeting." Cox and Minter continued to deny assorted accusations and offered to make their records available for investigation. White commented: "I do not say these men are Communists, but I do say they are following the Communist line." With threats of arson increasing, and a dubious roadblock arranged by the sheriff, Cox sat up, a rifle across his knees, from midnight to dawn for ten straight nights. Minter stuck it out until July, 1956. Cox left for Memphis a month later. Their joint Christmas greeting that year recalled: "Only two members of our church wrote to us. A few others have voiced their faith in us, but above these small voices is the frightening SILENCE. It is frightening—not only for us, but for any Christian and American who may wake up some morning to find himself persecuted because of his beliefs, or for unfounded rumors and 'guilt by association.' "

The Reverend Marsh Calloway, an avowed segregationist who tried to face down the mass meeting and persuade it of its undemocratic procedure, was ousted eight days later by unanimous vote of his Presbyterian church in Durant.

In 1957 it was impossible to find a suitable person to serve as president of the newly-formed Mississippi Council on Human Relations. The acting president, a highly respected woman from the Delta, resigned just before a bullet was put through her back window. The Human Relations Council was inactive for more than four years. In the fall of 1961 it was reactivated by more than 50 people who appointed a committee to select a slate of officers. In May, 1962, plans again went awry upon the discovery that three of the four prospective officers (all of whom had accepted)—a bishop, a rabbi, and a retired businessman— had been pressured into backing down. A. D. Beittel, president of Tougaloo College, was then persuaded to assume the headship of the revived organization notwithstanding the assurance of the Jackson Citizens Council that it would "know how to deal with this threat to our community," which "could serve only to create undermining from within our peacefully segregated social structure." Despite enormous opposition, the Mississippi Council on Human Relations is still alive and functioning, though somewhat furtively.

In late 1954, Hazel Brannon Smith, Mississippi newspaperwoman for a quarter of a century, was found guilty of libel against the Holmes County sheriff for her account of his shooting of a Negro. The $10,000 county court award was thrown out by the state supreme court. But troubles were just beginning for the crusading editor, whose sins piled up. Those sins included refusals to attack President Eisenhower for his conduct in the Little Rock imbroglio, to condemn Governor Coleman for his moderation, and to go along generally with the powerful local Citizens Council. Accused by Council workers of favoring integration and criticized for taking national awards from Communist-infiltrated organizations, Hazel Smith had to fight for her economic existence. In 1958, moreover, she saw a rival paper started by the same persons who had persecuted Cox and Minter. As Hodding Carter put it, in the St. Louis *Post-Dispatch* for November 26, 1961, ". . . in 1958 her enemies organized a new weekly paper at a meeting at which an officer of the local citizens council presided and asked for stock subscriptions from those present—mostly council members. The new weekly, *The Holmes County Herald,* has been subsidized from the beginning by well-to-do council leaders. It couldn't have lasted three months without pressure on its behalf from county politicians and White Citizen Council leaders, generally the same persons and all of the same readily recognizable stripe." Since then Hazel Smith has outsmarted three editors in Lexington while publishing three other papers, but her dogged struggle for survival has been grim indeed. Her magnificent courage may be found in a thousand editorials, such as: "Today we live in fear in Holmes County and in Mississippi. It hangs like a dark cloud over us, dominating every facet of public and private life. None speaks freely without being afraid of being misunderstood. Almost every man and woman is afraid to try to do anything to promote good will and harmony between the races, afraid he or she will be taken as a mixer, as an integrationist or worse, if there is anything worse by southern standards." The Lexington *Advertiser* has, she said in the teeth of her opposition, "recorded your triumphs and sorrows, the good and evil for 121 years and it will still be around to carry your obituary." The state legislature, in the spring of 1962, passed a reprisal law, allowing a town (in Holmes County only) to publish its proceedings outside the municipality. The House committee chairman understood the law "concerned a woman editor who has been writing things which don't go along with the feelings in the community." In October, 1962, the editor of the rival sheet called on all citizens to refuse to accept the Smith paper, which he considered a menace "dedicated to the destruction of those high principles which have motivated our state's resistance at Oxford." Rival editor Jack Shearer was probably right.

In the somber Smith story there is occasional merriment. The director of the State Sovereignty Commission and one of his trusted investigators swore before the secretary of state that at 8:20 on the night of December 15, 1961, they had observed a meeting at 1072 Lynch Street, Jackson, the home of the *Mississippi Free Press*. In attendance were William L. Higgs, Hazel B. Smith, Mr. Smith, Medgar Evers, and two or three other Negroes. Mrs. Smith was seen through a window conversing with a Negro. The Smith car was parked nearby, but "affiants were unable to verify the ownership due to the fact that a green tree, apparently a cedar Christmas tree, was in the trunk thereof and was tied to the rear bumper over the tag, making identification difficult." (The Smiths printed the *Free Press,* and were delivering that week's papers on the night they were spied upon.) The Citizens Council mailed the Sovereignty Commission affidavit to the news media, all legislators, and the white citizens of Holmes County. Somewhat later, Senator T. M. Williams of Lexington rose in all his dignity in the Mississippi upper chamber to announce that although Hazel Brannon Smith, once respected, was now "shrewd and scheming," neither he nor the Sovereignty Commission intended to prosecute. For what crime, he did not say.

By 1958 the Council claimed to have distributed eight million pieces of "literature," much of it reprinted from the Hederman press. A small but select stable of malcontent speakers had been available from the beginning and the Council showed no reluctance in bringing in "outside agitators," especially professional anti-Communists who invariably implied that those lukewarm on segregation were members or tools of the Red apparatus. Scare and atrocity fabrications impressed people nursed on nightmares.

After Barnett's election, the Council felt strong enough to list as subversive to the Mississippi way of life the American Red Cross, Federal Bureau of Investigation, Benevolent Protective Order of Elks, Jewish War Veterans, Methodist Church, National Lutheran Council, Department of the Air Force, Interstate Commerce Commission, and the Young Women's Christian Association. It was never explained what fate would befall the native Mississippian who belonged to the YWCA *and* the women's auxiliary of the Citizens Council.

The Council also circulated lists of "hate" magazines, some of them anti-Semitic; "exposed" a plot of Allan Nevins to bring about intermarriage of the races; and inspired petitions demanding that office holders go to jail rather than submit to federal court decisions ("This is a matter of constitutional government," said Judge Russell Moore); it set up organizations of "Minute

Men" made up of the "finest white citizenry," to assemble peaceably on short notice "to demonstrate a protest against any invasion of our institutions." This last device never seemed to operate, even though each group sported seven colonels, five captains, and five lieutenants. In no case was violence planned (and if it was, who would admit it?), at least as long as the status quo prevailed. Still, as Louis Hollis, executive secretary of the Citizens Councils of America, once bluntly insisted, "there is a point beyond which even the most judicious restraint becomes cowardice. Violence is an unpleasant remedy to which people resort only in a desperate extremity when all else has failed." Up to the present moment the Citizens Council has largely had its way. In the spring of 1963, according to the *Daily News,* the Council justly took credit for "avoiding violence and bloodshed" in Greenwood. An organization that can prevent violence may have the capacity and even the desire, under some circumstances, to cause violence. It makes one wonder how the Council defines "a desperate extremity when all else has failed."

In the beginning, W. J. Simmons (now national administrator of the Citizens Councils of America) had called for "organization . . . and *more* organization." The Jackson chapter built up a card file containing the racial views of nearly every white person in the city. A candid Mississippian wrote the now defunct Jackson *State-Times:* "If a group of serious-minded individuals, armed with pencils and a known philosophy of 'you're either with us or against us,' comes around to your door, demands to know your personal views and applies the pressure, only a Mongolian idiot would fail to give the right answers and pay the $5.00." Block by block surveys of Jackson, Greenwood, and McComb turned up the unstartling findings that 98 per cent of the white people not only supported school segregation but promised to support the Citizens Council in any crisis.

As one astute observer saw it, the Council had, by 1959, "created a climate of fear that has strait-jacketed the white community in a thought control enforced by financial sanctions, and has undone most of the improvements in race relations made over the last 30 years." By 1962, even Erle Johnston, public relations director for the Sovereignty Commission, as well as editor of the Forest *Scott County Times,* was shaken by the immensity of the CC's power. He spoke against "rabble-rousing leaders of the Citizens Council—more interested in agitating the racial problem than solving it," and thought the Council purpose "now appears to be making white people hate each other." As once anticipated by their own paper, the leaders in the Council had indeed created a juggernaut.

Statements from two legislators illustrate the power of the Citizens Council:

> It's hard for us sometimes to consider a bill on its merits, if there is any way Bill Simmons can attach an integration tag. For instance, a resolution was introduced in the House to urge a boycott of Memphis stores because some of them have desegregated. I knew it was ridiculous and would merely amuse North Mississippians who habitually shop in Memphis. The resolution came in the same week that four Negroes were fined in court for boycotting Clarksdale stores. Yet the hot eyes of Bill Simmons were watching. If we had voted against the resolution he would have branded us. So there we were, approving a boycott while a Mississippi court was convicting Negroes for doing what we lawmakers were advocating. It just didn't make sense.

> When the bill came up in the House to give cities and counties authority to make donations to the Citizens Councils, I thought it was unconstitutional. But I voted for it because if I had voted against the Councils, Bill Simmons would brand me as an integrationist.

"Stand Up and Be Counted"

In January, 1960, Ross Barnett moved into the governor's mansion and turned over a considerable degree of the influence of his office to Mr. Simmons. This suave, sophisticated zealot was ready to prove himself a genius at indoctrination on a massive scale. He was to call the tune on interposition, direct the unpledged electors in 1960, and huddle with Barnett in

Jackson and Oxford. His outfit, the Citizens Council, would henceforth receive a generous slice of the state funds ($160,000 by the summer of 1963) allotted to the Sovereignty Commission.

In 1950, Ross Barnett, having made a considerable fortune as the state's leading damage-suit lawyer, decided to crown his successful career with four years in the governor's chair. In 1951 and again in 1955 the people resoundingly said, "No." Shortly after his second defeat, Barnett emerged as a bellowing champion of white supremacy through loudly proclaimed though futile (and, in fact, detrimental) assistance in the legal defense of the terrorists who had wrecked the Clinton, Tennessee, schoolhouse. Already a long-time Sunday School teacher firm in the knowledge that "God was the original segregationist," in 1959 he pulled out all the emotional stops in his third and what he realized was his final try for the prize he coveted. He defeated two ineffectual opponents and the following January came into office militantly stubborn, more negative than conservative, an inflexible racist with a mind relatively innocent of history, constitutional law, and the processes of government.

As governor, Barnett was soon in deep trouble, his administration beset by corruption, inefficiency, and a chronic inability to find enough jobs to fulfill the candidate's promises. His ridiculous posturing—he returned from an extended South American junket pleased with the universal segregation he found there, and he coined an imperishable lamentation upon learning that a favored inmate of the penitentiary had vanished: "If you can't trust a trusty, who can you trust?" [2]—soon

---

2. After three mistrials for murder, Cowboy Dale Morris, one of Mississippi's more vicious though personable criminals, was sentenced to the state penitentiary (at Parchman) for manslaughter. Partly due to his personal charm, he was allowed to go to Arkansas to secure a walking horse for stud purposes. What use the huge state cotton plantation would have for walking horses has yet to be explained. In any case, Trusty Morris, having secured the horse, convinced his two guards that he merited some time off to visit a lady friend. The next thing official Mississippi knew of his whereabouts, the gay cowboy had been

made it difficult to find a person who would admit that he had ever voted for Old Ross.

This simple and blatantly pious man, who had declared during the 1959 campaign that "Hodding Carter is a moderate by his own admission," even before his inauguration called on the faithful to "stand up and be counted" so that the "gentlemen burglars," the moderates, could be driven from the state. His copy of the Constitution was somewhat the worse for age—it stopped with the Tenth Amendment. The new governor was shortly to create, to no one's surprise, what amounted to an office of prime minister for racial integrity and confer it upon Bill Simmons.

"We've Trained Our Politicians to Be Hypocrites"

In the 1963 Democratic primary a high school basketball coach ousted a Rhodes scholar from his seat in the legislature by a two to one vote. Mississippi has long been known for putting first things first, and in its weird system of personality politics practically anyone who can scrape together a hundred thousand dollars can have a fair go at the governorship. Both Governor Ross Barnett and Lieutenant Governor Paul Johnson had no reluctance about starting at the top, Johnson's great stroke of fortune coming when, because of bad flying weather, Barnett got to Oxford too late to block James Meredith at the gate of the University. Thus Johnson, as a later opponent put it, "bellied up to McShane," the chief federal marshal, and into the governor's mansion.

Mississippi politicians talk interminably about the sacred Constitution and spend a great deal of their time trying to find ways to twist it to meet the demands of their closed society. As admitted by Charles Sullivan, gubernatorial candidate in Mississippi in 1955 and 1959, "We've trained our politicians to be hypocrites; we've trained them to be dishonest." Thus,

---

picked up in Oklahoma City for another crime. Hence the Governor's lament.

when Barnett calls on Congress to "let the people decide" whether they want their schools under control of the federal government, or declares that "a state that loses the right to exercise exclusive jurisdiction over its own local affairs loses its political soul," or prepares a "share the Negroes" plan for the country, or categorically states, "There is no hate in Mississippi," he is either parroting the words of cunning speech writers or unwittingly revealing the fact that he is a simple, appallingly ignorant man who seems totally unaware of the ultimate implications of what he says or does. Asked at Harvard whether he believed all citizens should participate in the management of state affairs, Barnett answered: "I don't know what you are driving at. Let me say this about Negroes in Mississippi. There is harmony there, they work side by side with us, we're good to them." This is as good an example as need be found to underscore the characteristic disregard for the true nature of the social conditions in Mississippi which the closed society requires of its exemplars.

Some people may still wonder why eighteen-year-old freshmen charged through tear gas at United States marshals and later compared themselves to Hungarian freedom fighters. The answer is that they had been listening to Mississippi politicians from the time they were ten years old. Rubel Phillips, who became the 1963 Republican candidate for governor, told them that "our [national] government is to a great extent being run by incompetents and communist sympathizers." "That incompetent little juvenile," Attorney General Robert Kennedy, "has declared war on Mississippi and he will demand unconditional surrender." Barnett has asserted to the youngsters, "If you and I and all Mississippians had the courage of our old daddies and grand-daddies, we could perpetuate our ideals and way of life forever." Congressman Williams described President Eisenhower as "the most contemptible liar since Ananias," and declared that Mississippians could not "afford the luxury of moderation, complacency or timidity." State Senator Billy Mitts, in a single letter to the *Clarion-Ledger,* called for "a wholesale firing of members of the faculty at the University," the replacement of every member of the "Educational Board of Higher Learning," [sic] and the impeachment of both Kennedys "for openly defying the Constitution." Another State Senator, John McLaurin, spoke often of the "Kennedy conspiracy" to "crush the freedom-minded people of this once great nation," and of "the grisly gang that works its wicked will," and acts "in wanton disregard of the Constitution and rights of the people."

As early as 1955, Senator Eastland must have impressed the youth of the state when he told them they were obligated to defy the Supreme Court. "The choice is between victory and defeat. Defeat means death, the death of Southern culture and our aspirations as an Anglo-Saxon people. We of the South have seen the tides rise before. We know what it is to fight. We will carry the fight to victory." As Chancellor John D. Williams so plaintively put it, the average Mississippian had heard little else than this sort of talk from his political leaders. "So Mississippians believed about integration in their State—'Folks just wouldn't stand for it'—and I am convinced that much of the fury of our campus that black September night sprang from frustration, from a kind of intellectual outrage that comes when one is forced to believe what he could not believe was possible."

In this environment many youngsters have been "gripped by a poignant loyalty to the precarious present," a fealty that Margaret Long sees to be "uncorrupted by alien facts and ideas from the tight and turbulent little world of Mississippi." One such teen-ager, now an Ole Miss freshman, watched but did not participate in the University insurrection. Governor Barnett, as he saw it, had made a mistake. "That Sunday, if he'd issued a call to white males of Mississippi to stand firm . . . you'd have seen 600,000 men mustered at the gate." The young man continued: "We hate violence but we are determined to keep our way of life. Nobody can take it away from us, and I would die for it. I expect there'll have to be an occupation before there'll be integration in Mississippi, and the Kennedy twins are ruthless enough to do it without batting an eye if they're re-elected. It would probably be the most tragic thing that could happen to our beloved state. But afterward, when the troops leave . . . everything would be just like before, only the poor Nigras would lose all the friendship and goodwill they had."

The new legislature, convening in January, 1962, was met by a request from the governor to 1) outlaw the Communist party (years before, the FBI had found one Communist in Mississippi), 2) pass "an enforceable sedition act," and 3) compel state employees to take an oath of allegiance to the United States and Mississippi. (Barnett didn't explain whether this could be accomplished in a single oath.) When Mississippi legislators get together, their herd instinct drives them to resolve the fate of the world. If they hate Hodding Carter or the Kennedys, or love Elvis Presley, Dizzy Dean, the Mississippi State basketball team, or South Africa, or feel that a former Miss America is a fine actress, they are not inhibited from saying so. Sometimes they think big. Senator Hugh Bailey, who had ridden a mule from Canton to Jackson to fulfill a campaign promise, offered a resolution urging the United States to substitute turnip seed for cash in the foreign aid program. Such action "would relieve pressure in this country's economy and give the world's population necessary vitamins, minerals, and bulk." A mere handful of seed would feed a hundred people and could be mailed overseas for planting. (Senator Flavous Lambert was not amused. "We have," he said, "made big enough fools of ourselves already.") Somewhat more majestically, the legislature resolved "its complete, entire and utter contempt for the Kennedy administration and its puppet courts," and called on the country to rid itself of "the Kennedy family dynasty and to join our State in its defiance to all who would destroy our freedoms, heritage and constitutional rights." In November, 1962, the Senate passed a resolution calling for the impeachment of President Kennedy on four counts, including incitement to insurrection at Ole Miss and betrayal of his inaugural oath.

Legislators spend much of their time devising legal subterfuges to keep the Negro in his place. When it appeared that "smart alecks calling white ladies" on the telephone had reached "epidemic stages," the House voted a $10,000 fine and five years' imprisonment for cursing into that instrument. It was generally conceded that the intended law was aimed at (or to scare) the assumed Negro perpetrators of such outrage against the sensibilities of "white ladies." Some objection to the vagueness of the bill and the severity of the proposed penalties brought the assurance that Mississippi judges would know how to interpret and apply both. When the House had before it seven bills to restrict Negro voting, the chairman of the Judiciary Committee soberly announced, "I think everyone should be reading this bill and should avoid asking questions not absolutely necessary." The House unanimously adopted a resolution calling for a constitutional amendment barring from voting persons guilty of vagrancy, perjury, and child desertion, and concurred in the addition of adultery, fornication, larceny, gambling, and crimes committed with a deadly weapon. A still further addition of habitual drunkenness was defeated when a member suggested that it "might even get some of us." There was some objection, also, to the inclusion of adultery.

Reprisal legislation is common. The legislature, for example, passed a bill condemning land belonging to troublesome Campbell College, a Negro school in Jackson, in order that it could be annexed by state-controlled Jackson State College when Representative McClellan stated, "Jackson has had a cancer in its midst long enough." The cancerous college, seventy-four years old, will be removed to Mound Bayou in 1964.

The legislature's deference to the right wing is notorious. When the constitutionality of a House bill permitting counties to donate funds to the Citizens Council was questioned, Representative Buddie Newman retorted that the measure had been prepared by the president of the American Bar Association, John Satterfield. Two months after the Mississippi riot, Speaker Walter Sillers presented, for an address to the House, former general Edwin Walker, then still charged with violation of federal criminal statutes, as "a great military hero who upholds the principles of states' rights and constitutional government." Walker "has been making speeches advocating the same things you and I stand for" and had gone to Oxford "in an effort to be helpful."

"State Law Must Bow to Federal Law"

There seems to be considerable confusion in the minds not only of Mississippi legislators but also of lawyers and jurists as to whether the state's citizens must obey the law of the land as interpreted by the federal courts. Since 1954 only an occasional Mississippian—Robert J. Farley,[3] former dean of the Ole Miss Law School, or Karl Wiesenburg, ex-legislator from Pascagoula—has raised a lonely voice to suggest that individualistic Mississippians may not select the court decisions they will observe. Dean Farley has repeatedly declared in public that lawyers in the state were acting irresponsibly when by their silence they permitted the Citizens Council and irreconcilable politicians to interpret the law for them. Not that anyone had to agree with the decisions of the Supreme Court—*the dereliction of professional responsibility was in allowing the people of Mississippi to believe that they could get away with an outright defiance of the courts.*

Mississippi's lawyers are not necessarily contemptuous of the Supreme Court but they are members of a closed social order. Queried by a University of Michigan law professor, a number of them "without exception, repudiated the governor's right to defy the federal courts." They also blamed the newspapers for not "presenting the law behind the news," as if this might absolve lawyers of their own duty. Though Governor Coleman in 1955 declared interposition to be "legal poppycock," as indeed it has ever been, he signed an interposition law a few months later.

On the whole, Coleman's record was relatively clear of demagoguery. In 1955 he said that appeal to "police power is worthless. The Supreme Court has said time and time again

---

3. Farley's subsequent story will be found on pages 113–114.

the state law must bow to federal law." (Not only was the use
of police power "so much foolishness," but an attempt in 1958
to allow counties and cities to contribute funds to the Citizens
Council, thwarted by threat of veto by Coleman, was termed
by him a "first step to disaster," aimed at the governor for
"refusing to set fire to everything in the state.") One of the
"law day" speakers in Greenville in May, 1963, dared to say
that the state leadership "took us outside the law in defiance of
the Federal government" during the Ole Miss debacle. "We
courted violence, some of our people advocated it, and we got
it." Such utterances have been the exception.

Most of Mississippi's lawyers and judges who have spoken
out have by their own statements belied their declared belief
in the law. Judge Brady has for a long time set the public tone
for the legal philosophers of the closed society. "We as Mississippians," he stated in 1959, "will not bow down to a court of
nine old men whose hearts are as black as their robes." Brady
labeled Coleman a moderate—by his definition, "a man who is
going to let a little sewage under the door"—and charged he
was "in league with integrationists and has refused to oppose
left-wing elements in the Democratic party in order to advance
his chance for national office." To Brady, Sam Rayburn was
"that egg-headed man from Texas who is arch-traitor to the
South." The Mississippi jurist waxed most eloquent in *Black
Monday*. After disposing of the CIO and NAACP as Communist fronts, and of a half dozen civilizations by infusions of
Negro blood, Brady cried out in frenzy:

Oh, High Priests of Washington, blow again and stronger upon
the dying embers of racial hate, distrust and envy. Pour a little
coal oil of political expediency and hope of racial amalgamation
upon the flickering blaze which you have created and you will
start a conflagration in the South which all of Neptune's mighty
ocean cannot quench. The decision which you have handed down
on Black Monday has arrested and retarded the economic and
political and, yes, the social status of the Negro in the South for
at least one hundred years.

In like manner former district attorney J. O. Day of Lincoln County tore into the Supreme Court. Justice Frankfurter, he insisted, "did not even read the constitution of the United States until after he was appointed to the Supreme Court bench. He was not even native-born. We have turned our country over to a bunch of foreigners and minority groups."

The classic statement regarding law and order came from the very top of Mount Olympus. Indignant over the "sickening" conduct of Negro parents and ministers in Birmingham in permitting boys and girls to "run afoul" of the law by "using these children for ignoble and loathesome ends and deliberately and contemptuously inciting them to become juvenile delinquents," Governor Barnett lost his temper: "What do these degenerates know of freedom? True freedom consists of and is founded upon the observance of law and the power of law to make those who would break the law, conform to it. History tells us that freedom can exist only under the protection of constitutional law. These agitators seek to defy constitutional law under the name of freedom." But in the governor's state, the situation had deteriorated to the point that a federal judge is reputed to have called into his quarters several prominent Mississippi lawyers to admonish them that they were in danger of losing their federal practice if they continued to inform the public that the courts could be defied.

When the Association of American Law Schools decided to take a look at the accreditation of the University of Mississippi Law School, Judge M. M. McGowan condemned the "new pressure group raised up and joined to the pack of those who seem determined to harass and debase the University. Undoubtedly its inspiration could be traced to Washington, D.C. and the political commissars who followed the army into Oxford. There they have since remained in complete and arrogant defiance of the wishes and sentiments of the people of Mississippi attempting to indoctrinate our students in theories repugnant to us. The roster of the association's committee which is now breathing dire threats against Mississippi, is studded with theorists most if not all of whom never earned a dollar in the courtroom."

"It is time," he continued, "for the people of Mississippi to stop cringing shamelessly before these dictators, and assert their sovereign dignity and invite them to keep their meddling hands off our affairs. The vengeance of those who would destroy us seems insatiable."

As Lenoir Chambers, former editor of the Norfolk *Virginian-Pilot,* has written, "It is a serious matter under the American system to violate, systematically derogate, continually belittle, publicly defy, and thereby encourage wholesale disobedience to clearly established judicial rulings." Many Mississippi lawyers and judges have been engaged in a serious matter.

3.

The Voices of Acquiescence

"You Make a Travesty of Our Message"

The church in Mississippi played a principal role in the formu-
lation of the orthodox view in the 1850's, helped stimulate
secession, and sustained civilian morale during the life of the
Confederacy. In the desegregation emergency after 1954, the
course of the clergy has been more difficult to assess, in view
of a general call by the Mississippi Diocese of the Episcopal
Church for support of the Supreme Court's decision and
eventual integration. In the past year or two, many individual
preachers and a few ministerial groups have made courageous
stands, but the church as a whole has placed its banner with the
status quo. Ministers who did most of the talking about segregation were for it, prompted no doubt by "an echo from the
pew," and perhaps by the fear of being branded as "Red-
tinged" radicals. The Citizens Council sponsored "A Christian
View on Segregation," "A Jewish View of Segregation," and
"Is Segregation Unchristian?"—pamphlets filled with Bible
quotations to sustain the weary.

"Letters to the Editor" from Olive Branch to Moss Point
and from Corinth to Natchez—place names which box the
Mississippi compass—reflect the traditional southern formal
reverence for the Bible and the influence of a negatively morali-
stic fundamentalism on the race question. Unfortunately,

scriptural interpretation by the most ignorant reader (the "intellectual" assuages his guilt by allusion to *Race and Reason*) is placed on the same footing as that of eminent Bible scholars in interpreting such passages as:

Genesis 9:25 "And he [Noah] said, Cursed be Canaan; a servant of servants shall he be unto his brethren."

Genesis 28:1 "And Isaac called Jacob, and blessed him, and charged him, and said unto him, Thou shalt not take a wife of the daughters of Canaan."

Leviticus 19:19 "Ye shall keep my statutes. Thou shalt not let thy cattle gender with a diverse kind: thou shalt not sow thy field with mingled seed: neither shall a garment mingled of linen and woolen come upon thee."

Mississippians torture the Scriptures into sacred sanction for inequality and inhumanity.

In order to warn and discipline the Methodist hierarchy (chiefly), the legislature passed a measure permitting an individual church to secede from its central organization and keep its property. During its consideration, Senator Edgar Lee insisted that if the law were not passed, "one of these days you are going to awake to the cries or screams of a mulatto grandchild." Not long after the Oxford riot, the Mississippi Baptist Convention defeated a series of resolutions reaffirming "our intelligent good will toward all men" and calling upon Christians to pray "that we may live consistent with Christian citizenship." It was urged to do so by a Grenada preacher who thought it would be most unwise to take action at that time since any resolution must be open to all kinds of interpretations. This moral gap between creed and deed had little appeal for a Baptist missionary, a second cousin of Governor Barnett, who wrote to *The Baptist Record* from Nigeria that Mississippians were making her work more difficult: "You send us out here to preach that Christ died for all men. Then you make a travesty of our message by refusing to associate with some of them because of the color of their skin. You are supposed to be holding the lifelines for us, and you are twisting them into a noose of racism to strangle our message. Communists do not need to work against the preaching of the Gospel here; you are doing it quite adequately." The missionary's mother expressed regret over the letter: "Antonina doesn't understand that Ross has been doing the best he can. She's been over there and doesn't know about the situation here." Before the insurrection, Billy Graham cabled the governor from South America, urging caution, but somehow this communication never got into the Hederman papers.

The focal point of the furor enveloping the Reverend Edward Harrison, self-admitted "racial moderate" and Rector of Jackson's St. Andrews Episcopal Church, was a telegram he supposedly sent requesting a Texas clergyman not to speak before the "bigots" and "religious renegades" of the local Citizens Council. Before the Texas minister spoke on "Why Integration is Anti-Christian," the forged telegram was read over a local television station, and the whipped-up Council audience, as well as all members of the legislature, received photostatic copies of the message, which said in part: "I urge you not to besmirch the good name of our beloved church by linking your name with the dying cause of white supremacy." A St. Andrews vestryman was promised, but was later denied, time at the Council meeting to read a brief statement from Mr. Harrison. Council President John Wright said he had changed his mind, having no reason to doubt the authenticity of the telegram. Though it was never publicly announced by the church, which obviously has different moral standards from those of the Council, the fake message had been concocted and sent by Elmore D. Greaves, the author of a noxious pamphlet called *The Blackamoor of Oxford,* as well as a chief planner of the resistance after the insurrection at the University.[1]

After four years in Mississippi, Mr. Harrison, winner of the

---

1. Toward the end of October, 1962, when serious disturbances were an everyday affair at the University of Mississippi, the following hand-bill, copied from the *Gulf Coast Gazette,* then edited by Greaves, was distributed on the campus:

Distinguished Service Cross in World War II, moved to another pastorate, out of the state. Later he wrote that while there never had been a lack of real support from many friends, "I felt

---

STRATEGY FOR THE STUDENTS AT OXFORD

There are three steps in the process of integration, and all three must be completed before the NAACP can arrive at its ultimate goal:

Step I. Physical proximity, which is brought about by court-ordered desegregation. The NAACP wants that to lead to

Step II. Social acceptance. Once social acceptance has been achieved, that should lead to

Step III. Biological amalgamation of the races, which is the ultimate goal.

Step I has been forced upon the students of Ole Miss by military might, but only the students can decide whether Step II shall take place. In other words, all the military power in the world cannot force a Southerner to accept a colored person socially. If the tragic situation at Ole Miss can be kept within the strict limits of Step I, the NAACP will have failed in its ultimate purpose. If integration means physical proximity only, Ole Miss has been "integrated" for more than one hundred years by its colored help. I feel quite certain that the students at Ole Miss have more daily contact with janitors, servant girls, and general handymen than can be remembered; yet, there is no social acceptance, and that makes all the difference in the world. In other words, by keeping race-relations within the boundaries of Step I, integration, in the NAACP meaning of the word, never takes place. It is necessary, therefore, to keep the colored boy in a state of constant isolation. He should be avoided for the NAACP leper that he is. Let no student speak to him, and let his attempt to "make friends" fall upon cold, unfriendly faces. In addition, the students should banish from their midst any white student who tries to move from Step I to Step II. There should be no place at Ole Miss for social miscegenation, and those who are foolish enough to cross the barrier should be ostracized. This is a war that can be won, and it is a war over which the armed forces are powerless. Perhaps pledge cards could be printed, and a student movement could be organized. The students would promise to avoid the colored boy completely; he would be unwanted and would be treated as if he were a piece of furniture of no value. That much can be done, and the psychological lift would be tremendous. Such warfare, which is of the mind and of the spirit, is far beyond the control of the U.S. Supreme Court. Such warfare was used by the South during Reconstruction, and the South eventually triumphed.

LET US STRIKE WHILE THE IRON IS HOT!

that the very things I held dear for the future would be more readily accomplished by another Rector. The great disappointment was that persons of prominence who would give you to understand they never paid dues to the Citizens Council gave all the support the CC could hope for by their silence. When the pressure was on, there were the not-so-prominent, who could have been hurt economically and otherwise, who stood firm and courageous."

A remarkable churchman, Rabbi Charles Mantinband, challenged the closed society for 16 years while pastoring his congregation in Hattiesburg. During this time he maintained membership on the Board of the Southern Regional Council, and was active in the Mississippi Council on Human Relations. In May, 1962, he wrote: "Life can be very placid and gracious in this part of the country—if one runs with the herd. The South is turbulent and sullen and sometimes noisy, but there is a conspiracy of silence in respectable middle-class society. Sensitive souls, with vision and the courage of the Hebrew prophets, are drowned out. Timid souls, complacent and indifferent, seldom articulate their protests." "Come weal, come woe, my status is quo," he added, sadly.

In 1958, while Mantinband was abroad, the Citizens Council suggested to his temple that this was a good time to get rid of the "mischief-making rabbi," else "we cannot be responsible for the consequences." With probable misgivings, the temple stood by its pastor, who later commented that ". . . in an atmosphere where emotions are strained and people are hardly rational, there is little place for logic and appeal to reason. Instead, we must resort to 'chochma,' that shrewd combination of wisdom and subtle humor." Mantinband found himself unable to distinguish between God's children or to sit silently in the presence of bigotry. "Ultimately victory must come," he believed. "The time is past when a Jew dare be neutral."

On Washington's birthday, 1963, Rabbi Mantinband wrote in obvious distress: "The 'why' of Mississippi is anybody's guess. I suspect we are lacking in courage and in true spiritual-

ity. Some of us are very lonely." Four months later he moved
to Texas.

"You've Messed Yourself Up Good, Boy"

Feeling that they had "a particular obligation to speak," 28
young Methodist ministers, in *The Mississippi Methodist
Advocate* of January, 1963, issued a "Born of Conviction"
statement which still has the state and the church in an uproar.
They affirmed their belief in the freedom of the pulpit and the
brotherhood of man, an unalterable opposition to the closing
of the public schools, and an unflinching antagonism toward
Communism. Within two weeks the Mississippi Association of
Methodist Ministers and Laymen, displaying more churchman-
ship than religious zeal, had repudiated the "Born of Conviction" pastors, submitted its own "declaration of conscience on
racial matters" (drawn up by professional anti-Communist and
Citizens Council consultant Medford Evans and published in
the January issue of *The Citizen*), and called for a secret
referendum on whether or not Methodists wanted their church
integrated. Later these conservatives declared integration a
"crime against God." The lament of one of the young ministers,
that "The power clique which dominates the conference has
aligned itself with the Methodist Ministers and Laymen and
with the Citizens Council," was further corroborated by subsequent events.

The closed society battered the outspoken young preachers
upon the anvil of public opinion. By summer, ten had left the
state, and at least half a dozen more were kicked upstairs to
less demanding urban pulpits. A few reported only slight
harassment, but the majority was made to feel the displeasure
of congregations and community. At least half volunteered the
feeling that they had not been sufficiently supported by their
superintendents and their bishop.

Methodists in general, with professional assistance, were
reflecting an opinion that had driven from Mississippi 68
of their seminary-trained men since 1954. By a close vote,

the conference "discontinued its connection" with Edwin King, crusading integrationist chaplain at Tougaloo College. Dr. W. B. Selah, for 18 years pastor of the largest Methodist congregation in the state, who had supported the "Born of Conviction" statement and had declared "there can be no color bar in a Christian church," resigned in protest when five Negroes were refused admission to his Jackson church. (By October, 1963, the association of ministers and laymen was preparing legal action against integration groups who hoped to desegregate the city's churches. The president of the association spoke of "the man in the pew demanding his day in court. Either John Wesley's principles will triumph or the radicals will take over and our Church will disintegrate.")

Here is a fair sample of quotations from letters received from 19 of the 28 ministers: "It is tragic that hate not love, ignorance not reason, insanity not sanity, both rule and populate our state." "I see many reasons for optimism in 1963." "A few 'quiet' meetings and some hurt feelings comprise the extent of our situation." "A CC member strode into my office, newspaper in hand, and said, 'You've messed yourself up good, boy!' " "In Mississippi a Christian minister is free only as long as he is willing to run and bay with the pack." "The only pressures have been very subtle, intangible ones that are not subject to measurement." "I never had freedom of the pulpit except in so far as I avoided mention of Race." "The main expressions were that if everyone would leave these problems alone they would soon die away." "I do not think it will hurt my church." "The boycott against the church was used as to attendance and support." "Today the church is stronger than ever." One minister, writing in June, had not answered a January inquiry because "at that time I was trying to stay in Mississippi and I knew that any correspondence with you would not enhance my position." Another wrote:

Pressure was begun in my case when I taught for a week in a local school before the riot. I denounced the numerous intentions toward Mr. Meredith and nearly lost my parish then. It blew over but when the statement was signed it caught me by surprise that people could react so violently. A meeting was held but I got to the leaders first and thought I had it squashed and no action was taken. During my absence one Sunday a man dropped by the parsonage and was so vocally abusive to my wife that it resulted in her being hospitalized and if that was not enough, another "gentleman of the old south" went to the hospital and took fiendish delight in doing the same, resulting in her continuation in the hospital unable to retain food on her stomach from sheer terror (she is from another southern state, not deep South, but free [*sic*]).

Even still I felt that the thing would blow over but the following Friday night due to the hard work of several hate spreaders a secret meeting was held, called by the immediate superior of the church but I found out and went anyway, much to all's consternation. I have never been in such a vicious group in all my life. First they tried heaping vile [*sic*] on me—nigger lover, your wife and a nigger, taunts of "get him a nigger church" and "bet his son marries a nigger," etc. I smiled, then followed the—you were probably duped phase of the meeting. "We know that all the rest of the men are nuts and you were innocently dragged in." Then I was offered the opportunity of a public, later to be published, recantation, with strong emphasis on the fact that I would lose my home and job if I did not follow. I looked them in the eye and flatly refused. Then a vote was allowed by the church official contrary to the policy of the church and I was fired and strongly urged never to show my face in that pulpit again. At present I am living at home and have a very uncertain future in this state, which does not bother me in the least as 53 young men have left the Mississippi conference in the last three years and so can I.

No Forthright Challenge Is Tolerated

To perpetuate itself the closed society must keep a firm control over what goes into the minds of its young people. The alien influence of the national news media scarcely disturbs the mentality of the tens of thousands of youngsters whose aspirations at an early age are focused on football stardom and beauty crowns, with baton twirling championships and band scholarships for the less talented. The intellectually curious, on the other hand, may need to be persuaded to accept the virtues of the Mississippi way of life.

Having been brought up in the system, most teachers are either sympathetic to it or are impressed by the healthy wisdom of not rocking the boat. Surprisingly enough, the State Department of Education has, over the years, retained a remarkable degree of sanity despite constant outside pressure, although in 1963 a veteran superintendent of education barely escaped being ousted because of his professional relationship with the integrated National Education Association. In classroom teaching, at the University at least, there has been very little interference. But woe to the professor who forgets, as Citizens Council Secretary Robert "Tut" Patterson ever so delicately points out, that while "he has a right to say what he thinks, he also has a responsibility to accept the results of what he says." The plain fact is that no forthright challenge of the society is tolerated for long and that repercussions are quick and sure. After a while the sensitive, able, dedicated college teacher either leaves the profession, or the state, or takes out his frustrations in bird-watching or administration.

The care with which an ambitious man must choose his words from the vocabulary of the orthodoxy may be illustrated by a 1963 address of William D. McCain, the president of the University of Southern Mississippi. Dr. McCain praised the early colonists who came to America because of a desire for liberty and freedom, "but the liberals would have us believe otherwise." Our greatest danger today, he said, is the "poisoning of the American mind." Communists are highly successful in their manipulation of the race problem. Federal fiscal policy is dangerous to liberty, for "No man or nation can continue to spend more than he makes indefinitely." The Kennedy administration has discarded the Monroe Doctrine and, he concluded, acted in the Cuban crisis because of its unpopularity after the Oxford incident. Another educator, also with a Ph.D. in history, sponsored a pre-law club which not long ago resolved a hearty commendation of Barnett for "acting resolutely and courageously" in opposing federal encroachment and defending the

basic rights of Mississippi (white) citizens. The resolution
framers may well be on their way to their legislative seats,
though it should be added that their mentor, Dr. Willie Caskey,
rejected by the voters, has gone back to calling down God's
blessings on gatherings of the Citizens Council.

In the spring of 1963 the state faced what a Barnett appointee
to the Board of Trustees called "the greatest challenge to our
way of life since Reconstruction." Three times Mississippi State
University had won the Southeastern Conference basketball
championship and had foregone, because of the "unwritten
law," the pleasures of the National Collegiate Athletic Association tournament, in which its victory gave it the right to compete. Now, the team having triumphed once again, the new and
untried university president, D. W. Colvard, said it might participate. Representative Russell Fox was fearful lest the decision
be interpreted "as a sign of weakness in our stand for segregation." Representative Walter Hester bemoaned the lack of judgment involved, suggesting, "It is no safer to mix with Negroes
on the ball courts than in the classroom. Mississippi State has
capitulated and is willing for Negroes to move into that school
en masse." As a former State cheerleader, Senator Billy Mitts
found it difficult to recover from such "a low blow." "I advocate
a substantial decrease in the financial appropriations for every
university of this great state that encourages integration." He
added that only native sons should be trusted to occupy the
college presidencies so as never again to risk "a similar tragedy
of this sort." The Meridian *Star* sadly predicted integrated
athletics and mixed "after game social affairs"—"dear as the
athletic prestige may be, our Southern way of life is infinitely
more precious."

To meet the challenge Mississippians came out of the huddle
with a pressure defense. The Jackson papers kept up a barrage
of slanted news stories and editorials urging the Board to over-
rule President Colvard. A wire photograph of State's opponents,
Loyola of Chicago, was blown up for the front page as the
editor apologized to the University with tongue in cheek: "A
study of the photo indicates strongly that only four of the five

starters are Negroes." In its spellbound wrath the *Daily News* was somehow reduced to quoting the *Clarion-Ledger*. A temporary injunction was secured from Chancery Judge L. B. Porter against the Board of Trustees, whose vote (9–3 to send the team) was considered "contrary to public policy." In the meantime a cloak-and-dagger farce was begun and carried on for days with the coaches, athletic director, university president, trainer, and first and second teams "disappearing," setting up decoy airplane flights, and dodging subpoenas from deputy sheriffs until, finally, a supreme court justice stayed the temporary injunction. In any case, the game was played, the low blow was struck, and whether Mississippi will recover only the future can tell.

Mississippi's honor was retrieved a couple of months later. Ole Miss band director Lyle Babcock announced the selection of new, non-Confederate uniforms and a decision to abandon use of the world's largest Confederate flag. A horrified student wrote *Clarion-Ledger* columnist Tom Ethridge, "I'm not ashamed but proud of the rebel nickname. It is one of the reasons I came to Ole Miss." In his column, Ethridge capitalized his topic for the day: IS THE REBEL IMAGE EMBARRASSING? Evidently the governor did not think so, for he leaped into the fray with the assurance, "We're the Rebels and I don't think it can be over-emphasized. I had a pleasant talk with Mr. Babcock and understand there will be no change in the color of the uniform. I think that the people would hate to see a change." The Ole Miss *Mississippian* headlined its story, "Ross Against Change." Successfully so, it might have added.

"*Mississippi Is Going Down the Road to Thought Control*"

The day will inevitably come when a handful of colored children, with a court order for admission in their hands, will walk into a grammar school somewhere in Mississippi. With every legal subterfuge out of the way, Mississippi will be faced with the alternative of complying with the will of the court or of closing the school. Although the legislature has the power to shut down the public schools (now delegated to the governor), and this has been advocated from one end of the state to the other by the likes of Commissioner of Public Welfare Fred Ross,[2] it is doubtful that such an extreme course will be followed for long. Be that as it may, the time for decision is not far away; Mississippi is the last state left with complete public school segregation.

The publication of an anonymous pamphlet, distributed by the Citizens Council, which blandly pleaded neutrality, proposed the closing of the University and its reopening as a private school. The document produced a considerable outcry. "It is not necessary," said Representative Joe Wroten, "for the Legislature to dance the fiddlers' tune every time the Citizens Council calls for the next foolish medley of legislation." (In relatively liberal Washington County Mr. Wroten was retired from office at the next election.) About the same time Vice-Chancellor Alton Bryant charged "nameless individuals" with creating incidents to force the closing of the University. The Mississippi Economic Council refused to be intimidated. It urged then and continued to urge that all schools be kept open, regardless of integration, and that their integrity, quality of instruction standards, and full accreditation be maintained.

Aside from the fact that the Mississippi classroom teacher's salary is $2125 lower than the national average, the greatest cause of mediocre teaching, especially in the social sciences, is

---

2. For years Commissioner Ross has been making the same speech, sometimes entitled, "Racial Amalgamation Propaganda Versus Segregation and Racial Cooperation." On at least one occasion he authorized the mailing of excerpts from a newspaper column (containing a letter from a Negro woman commending white persons for their treatment of Negroes in the South) with 160,000 monthly welfare checks. In the late fall of 1963, Ross used public funds to publish and distribute his address (a 12-page pamphlet with his picture on the title page) with the added notation that he would "accept invitations to speak on this subject."

probably the frenetic concern with instructional materials shown by the Citizens Council, the American Legion, and the patriotic ladies. A case in point of what teachers have to face was the withdrawal of a film called *The High Wall,* donated to the state by the Anti-Defamation League and shown in Mississippi schools for more than six years. The Citizens Council interpreted the film as teaching "children to pity their prejudiced parents who did not enjoy the enriching experience of intermingling with persons of different racial, ethnic and cultural backgrounds." At the end of the film, the Council was scandalized to find, "Americans and Poles walk arm-in-arm into the setting sun." An "alert state senator" sounded the alarm, a private showing was given Council and Sovereignty Commission officials who agreed that *The High Wall* was "unfit for showing to Mississippi school children," and the menace was removed.

Since 1942, grammar and high school texts have been furnished to students without charge by the state of Mississippi. According to law, the rating committees "shall be of competent, professionally trained educators in the fields in which text books are considered for adoption." In more than 20 years there has been no scandal attached to the selection of books in the state. But the casual observer, listening to the oratorical outbursts and reading the fuming reports of the Daughters of the American Revolution, might easily think otherwise. In 1962 the Mississippi Farm Bureau supported the good ladies by snorting that some texts did not teach "states' rights, racial integrity, free enterprise and Americanism." There seems to be a high correlation between state "patriotism" and ignorance of Mississippi history.

The DAR works round the clock at rooting out undesirable books. Its bible is *Brainwashing in the Schools,* written by E. Merrill Root, contributor to *American Opinion, American Mercury,* and *Human Events.* A professor of English at Earlham College (now retired), able to identify Jefferson with the Birch Society, fluoridation with Communism, book-burning with Americanism, and to condemn out of hand Henry Steele Com-

mager, Allan Nevins, Walter Lippmann, Merle Curti, Claude
Bowers, the Arthur Schlesingers, Carl Sandburg, and Stuart
Chase, Root is adept at brainwashing, himself. According to
this "unimpeachable source as an expert in the field of subversion writing," Mississippians were told, U.S. history books
were responsible for the disaffection in Communist prison
camps, when as a matter of fact a high percentage of the American defectors in Korea never went to high school and 18 of 21
did not graduate. No "outside agitator," Root has unique distinction among those who see a fellow traveler in front of every
history classroom in that he has been hired by both the legislature and the DAR in Mississippi.

The state DAR, somewhat frustrated in its efforts to purge
about 40 books from the school lists, went directly to the legislature. Predictably, the patriots were encouraged by the governor, who came down hard for cleaning up the books "so that
children can be truly informed of the southern way of life."
The *Daily News* was not only concerned with the lack of attention given in the books to labor union "coercion upon management," but was sorely disturbed by such "oblique propaganda as 'gives evidence that Negro people have done much
to develop themselves.'" Joe Wroten sadly acknowledged that
"Mississippi is going down the road to thought control," but
when the wholesale book-burning failed to materialize, a lady
Communist- and integrationist-hunter wailed that "Patriotic
Americans seem to have no voice. Our side is never heard."
How strange for these zealots to complain about the increasing
loss of personal freedoms because of dictatorship in Washington, when they do their level best to circumscribe freedom of
speech, thought, and inquiry in their home communities.[3]

---

3. By the end of 1963 the Citizens' Educational Association had been
formed (with Elmore Greaves as publicity director) to combat subversion in Mississippi school books and to eliminate standard guidance and
testing programs. The State Textbook Purchasing Board was warned
that a continuation of its policy would mean that "atheists and communists take over." Specific books were criticized for furthering a "belief
in the brotherhood of all people," and for suggesting that "prejudice is

The Daughters of the American Revolution are understandably unhappy when first graders are no longer exposed to "the story of the squirrel storing nuts [which] helped to make America a great nation populated by men and women steadfast in their ability to put into effect their early training for adult life." All but the headiest Keynesian deficit spenders may look upon such a lament with a bit of sympathy. But listen to what the Citizens Council officially recommends for the third and fourth grades:

God wanted the white people to live alone. And He wanted colored people to live alone. The white men built America for you. White men built the United States so they could make the rules. George Washington was a brave and honest white man. It is not easy to build a new country. The white men cut away big forests. The white man has always been kind to the Negro. We must keep things as God made them. We do not believe that God wants us to live together. Negro people like to live by themselves. They like to go to Negro doctors. They like to go to Negro schools. Negroes use their own bathrooms. They do not use the white people's bathroom. The Negro has his own part of town to live in. This is called our Southern Way of Life. Do you know that some people want the Negroes to live with the white people? These people want us to be unhappy. They say we must go to school together. They say we must swim together and use the bathrooms together. God has made us different. And God knows best. They want to make our country weak. Did you know that our country will grow weak if we mix the races? It will. White men worked hard to build our country. We want to keep it strong and free.

From the manual for the fifth and sixth grades:

Our forefathers were willing to stand up to the enemy because their freedom meant very much to them. Our Constitution is a

---

illogical." The end result of the guidance and testing program "was to erase traits of religion, patriotism, morality and character" instilled in children by their parents. Although this new organization was making no appreciable progress, despite vocal assistance from Governor Barnett, it was planning seminars throughout the state in 1964 to warn Mississippians of the need to "do something to save young America."

contract. The states gave the federal government in Washington, D.C. some powers. But they kept most of the power for themselves. No other part of the United States is more American than the South. America was built by white men. King George wanted his merchants to make money. So the Americans were made to buy the Negro slaves. Americans did not want slaves. Americans never did like slavery. They would like to have helped the Negro build his own country. The Negro is happy among his own race, but two races feel strange around each other. Russia has white slaves today.

The Southern white man has always helped the Negro whenever he could. Southerners were always their best friends. The South went to war to prevent the races from race-mixing. If God had wanted all men to be one color and to be alike, He would not have made the different races. One of the main lessons in the Old Testament of our Bible is that your race should be kept pure. God made different races and put them in different lands. He knew that races must live apart so they won't mix. He was satisfied with pure races so man should keep the races pure and be satisfied. BIRDS DO NOT MIX. CHICKENS DO NOT MIX. A friend had 100 white chickens and 100 reds. All the white chickens got to one side of the house, and all the red chickens got on the other side of the house. You probably feel the same way these chickens did whenever you are with people of a different race. God meant it to be that way.

After the Civil War the Negroes moved off to themselves and the white people did the same thing. We knew every one would be happier just with his own race. Both Negro and white have been satisfied living apart from each other. The Negro is not just a sun-burned white man. You are probably surprised to learn a Negro is really different from a white man. Famous scientists say races are very different. The white man is very civilized, while the pure Negro in Africa is still living as a savage. Race-mixers want to change the Southern Way of Life. They do not let the truth about race be printed in the papers or in your books. Instead of telling you the truth, they tell you pretty stories about how much fun it would be to live together. Our government is forcing us to do things we know are not right. Who wants to dance with a boy or girl of another race? Could you enjoy a party where black and white children are mixed? The race-mixers even want Negroes and whites to date each other. White children can learn faster than Negroes can. When the races are mixed in school, the white children do not get as much education as they usually get. The whites have to wait for the Negroes to catch up.[4]

Additional sections of the manual are introduced with such captions as: YOU CAN'T BELIEVE RACE-MIXERS; GEORGE WASHINGTON WOULDN'T LIKE RACE-MIXERS; RACE-MIXERS HELP COMMUNISTS; MIXING THE RACES WILL MAKE AMERICA WEAK; GOD SEPARATED THE RACES; SEGREGATION IS CHRISTIAN; RACE-MIXERS DON'T WANT YOU TO KNOW ANYTHING; RACE-MIXERS MADE INDIA WEAK; WHITE PEOPLE BUILT GREECE; SOUTHERNERS WON'T LET RACE-MIXERS RUIN THEIR COUNTRY. With such tidbits for the tots in print, the Council discontinued its efforts in historical indoctrination, whether from the thought that the child is saved by the time he reaches junior high school, or because the writer of the new history had reached the end of his inventiveness, has never been disclosed.

Not that such efforts fail to pay off. In winning a Citizens Council essay contest, a young high school student came up with these sentiments: "We in the South do not intend to obey men, however exalted their seats or black their robes and hearts. We intend to obey the laws of God and the laws of this country which are made in accordance with the Constitution. As long as we live, so long shall we be segregated."

Refresher courses for historically-minded senior citizens were not neglected, either. In the fall of 1957 the Council paper announced "The New Federalist," a Birch-like column allegedly designed to help the faltering return to the nationalism of Hamilton and Madison. (Curiously, in Mississippi political theory both "nationalism" and "state rights" are valued highly.) Its message was that since World War I the country had been tricked into "doing something" for the world, surely a dilution of patriotism which had taken the United States "from one debauch of international participation to another."

---

4. Taken from several issues of *The Citizens Council* (1957).

Modern political leaders have taken to feeding our people on the apertifs and aphrodisiacs of human greed. The wisdom that flows from truly representative government is too often replaced by political auctioneering. Personal freedoms of enterprise and individualism are traded away for what is now disgustingly called "security." It is an imposter-word which stands for the creature comforts and bodily desires supplied by the government—the full belly, the cozy quarters, the certified medicine, the loose credit for looser living, the license that turns into lawlessness.

The big siege guns of the closed society were brought to bear on the Southern Association of Colleges and Schools when it placed the University of Mississippi on a kind of academic probation. Judge McGowan recommended that the "self-annointed" [sic] accrediting group be abolished by law and replaced by a state agency which "will more nearly meet the needs of the people and the students. Are we to be beaten to our knees by this so-called 'powerful' organization that vaulted up from nowhere and has thrown its weight with the equality cultists?" The Southern Association of Colleges and Schools had overlooked the fact that neither the governor nor the legislature, nor any other official, "has ever interfered in any wise" with the University and should realize that all the trouble had been stirred up by the Communists and the chieftains in the Democratic party. Association members "as well as the socialist professors they so zealously seek to protect, are all living in cloistered ease in the cultural surroundings furnished by the taxpayers," and, surely, had never met a payroll.

Senator Eastland assailed the Southern Association as a "group of little Caesars, a labor union to protect professors" who were "covering up Marxism in the colleges." The blackmailing organization was "lined up with liberals and Reds." A Clarksdale superintendent of schools took the occasion to charge college professors with being left-wing, off-center, maladjusted individuals, who were undermining family, school, and church. Governor-elect George C. Wallace of Alabama gave little indication of his later prowess with a sharp tongue when he addressed the Mississippi legislature to denounce SACS as a "petty dictatorship" and the federals as scalawags and liars. But a Senate resolution, drawn up by Judge McGowan, declaring an intent to ignore "bold, arrogant and unbecoming" threats of SACS, was returned to committee by a close vote after Senator Jolly had pleaded, "Let's keep two-bit politics out of our schools." Sheriff Jonathan Edwards of Rankin County struck a wholesome note when he wondered what all the hubbub was about. The sometime school teacher and principal reminisced: "I was at Mississippi State College when Bilbo took charge of the schools and accreditation was withdrawn. But I never was refused a job nor have I lost a job because I graduated from Mississippi State."

With varying degrees of enthusiasm, the makers of the orthodoxy—the press, the clergy, businessmen, labor leaders, lawyers, judges, politicians, educators, and patriots—have in critical moments rushed to the successful defense of their closed society.

The Old Way and Industrialization Are Mutually Exclusive

The industrialist, kingpin of the power structure in Mississippi and the man most likely to crack open the closed society, has hesitated to exert his strength in the growing crisis of the past decade. As judged by long-time capitalist L. O. Crosby, Jr., "We have splendid leadership in Mississippi but we have some of the worst demagoguery that can be found. The business man can be more successful and happier in a state that does not have continued problems of ignorance, poverty, demagoguery and emotionalism."

Why, then, does the business elite tolerate a Barnett or a Paul Johnson? It is in part the old alliance between conservative businessmen, defending a 1925 brand of free enterprise, and opportunistic politicians, who would keep this power over the populace, black and white. It is in part fear—fear of upsetting the apple-cart, fear of economic pressure from the Citizens Council, which complacent industrialists allowed to grow into a monster. Also, there is an element of truth in Barnett's diagnosis: Mississippi has made manufacturing progress, and some of it has unquestionably come from the increased state socialism (balancing agriculture with industry) sponsored by his administration.

In 1929 Mississippi had a per capita personal income of $510, only 40.5% of the national average. By 1960 this personal income had grown to $1173, or 52.8% of the national average. Most of the gain came during World War II, income having doubled between 1929 and 1945 but having increased only 17% between the end of the war and 1960. Much of this apparent improvement is the result of a substantial migration from the state. Since 1940 the labor force has actually decreased by 65,000, and the number of those engaged in agriculture dropped from 58% of the total at the earliest date to 21% at the latter. Manufacturing employment rose from 67,000 in 1940 to 131,000 in 1960. "Experience since the end of World War II gives little basis for projecting that per capita income in Mississippi will increase at a faster pace than in the nation as a whole," says the state's own Economic Council. "The gap between Mississippi's per capita income and the national average has not been reduced. Mississippi appears to have marked time during the fifteen-year period from 1945 to 1960."

Fifty per cent of the adults over 25 in Mississippi have less than nine years of schooling; in 1940 the average figure was 7.2 years. In 1960 the median for whites was 11 years and for Negroes six years. Increased educational opportunity for skilled workers is imperative, provided they can be kept in the state. High-productivity industries are desperately needed. A low-productivity pants factory does the state's economy far less good, for example, than a high-productivity electronics plant. In the past, manufacturing has not been built upon industrial innovation. Mississippi stands at the bottom of the list of states in number of patents held per capita.

During the very month of the Oxford riot the Mississippi Economic Council declared that "somehow the economic community must find the means of moving more to the forefront of industrial innovation. In its human resources Mississippi does not lack the raw material of economic progress, but this material must be mobilized and adapted to the changing industrial society which has replaced agriculture. The crucial catalyst is leadership, both from those in public office and those in private business. The future economic course of the State will require that as new leadership emerges it brings new dedication, new boldness, and new imagination to meet the new problems of directing Mississippi's progress in a dynamic ever-changing economy."

In 1960, at Barnett's request, the legislature passed 39 "specific laws designed to make Mississippi more competitive," and three years later the governor claimed "the long-promised tomorrow is here, now. It is here today. We are at the dawn of Mississippi's brightest economic day." At least half the people of the state would have found this difficult to believe, had they heard it, but, according to the governor, 416 new industries and plant expansions would provide 31,000 new jobs, and meant that Mississippi was leading the country in percentage industrial growth.[5]

Although Mississippi has made progress industrially (along with the entire country), no one can take Barnett's numbers game very seriously. By the same reasoning, Robert Mason would have won the Democratic nomination for governor in the first primary in 1963, for his vote, as compared with that of 1959, had increased by a whopping 29%—it went from 2704 to 3485. The speculation as to new jobs created was taken by

---

5. Toward the end of the Barnett administration the figure for new and expanded industries was placed at 555. (At the opening of number 546, the Goldkist pecan processing plant in Canton, the Governor claimed that it was Mississippi "which made the pecan the world famous nut it has become." The state produces slightly less than 10% of the nation's pecans.) Much more exciting was the claim that about 40,000 new jobs had been created. Perhaps so, but the Mississippi Employment Security Commission lists employment in manufacturing and selected non-manufacturing industries in Mississippi as: 1960—119,900; 1961—118,-700; 1962—127,500; Jan.–Nov., 1963—132,900.

Barnett from the optimistic estimates of firms coming into the
state. Jobs lost are left out of the calculations. Even the industries themselves are sometimes shadowy. A picture-frame plant,
for instance, opened in Greenwood in 1959 and stopped production in 1962. A "new industry" was announced in 1963,
one which in reality signified a switch in firms but not the addition of a single job. In January, 1963, Barnett dedicated a
building of the Mississippi Surplus Property Procurement Commission, set up to acquire and store federal surplus property,
and certified it as "a new industry, the 418th since I became
governor."

This indulgence in Soviet-style statistics could be forgiven
an ambitious governor were it not that many people are tricked
into believing his administration responsible for industrial development like the great new oil refinery at Pascagoula. According
to its manager, Standard Oil of Kentucky came to Mississippi
because of geographic considerations, the excellent work record
experience of other industries in the region, and the leadership
of county supervisors and businessmen in developing the Bayou
Casotte area. At first Barnett jubilantly announced that Standard Oil chose Mississippi because industrialists throughout the
nation favored segregation. "Who says that segregation doesn't
pay?" he roared to a Citizens Council meeting. When Standard
Oil's president rebuked him, Barnett switched to Mississippi's
right-to-work provision in the constitution, and when challenged on that, to Mississippi's "favorable political climate,"
adding that the state could expect industry to flock in because
of Mississippi's "image of invincibility," built on a last-ditch
stand for segregation. The truth seems to be that Barnett had no
more to do with securing the refinery than the menial chore
of obtaining legislative approval for the sale of 16th section
school land. Standard Oil's need to build a new refinery grew
out of a federal anti-trust proceeding. Governor Barnett has yet
to credit Attorney General Robert Kennedy for his inadvertent
assistance.

The governor's assertion that "Our state is making more gain
in economic development than any other state in the southeast

or southwest" appears somewhat perplexing in view of the
Mississippi wages-salary income for 1962 of $1.74 billion as
compared with Alabama, $3.55 billion; Florida, $6.77 billion;
Georgia, $4.95 billion; Louisiana, $3.74 billion; North Carolina, $5.42 billion; South Carolina, $2.62 billion; Tennessee,
$4.16 billion; and Virginia, $6.16 billion.[6] Even in percentage
of gain over 1961, Mississippi falls below Florida, Georgia,
North Carolina, and South Carolina. Mississippi has, however,
out-distanced her sister states in the tens of millions of dollars
worth of city and county bonds sold to build plants to entice
new industry.[7] A pants factory expansion may well be Barnett's
most enduring industrial monument—or perhaps the Westing-
house Air Brake Company plant, which went to South Carolina
rather than Oxford after the riot.

It is unlikely that even a Barnett or a Johnson would have
the gall to suggest that it has been their influence which will
bring about the spending of several hundred million dollars in
Mississippi by the National Aeronautics and Space Administration. But they should recognize the implications of the fact
that for years a substantially greater flow of federal funds has
poured into Mississippi than the residents of the state have paid
into the federal treasury. Mississippi, among the states, pays
the lowest per capita federal tax and the lowest percentage of
its personal income in federal taxes. In 1959–61, according
to the Library of Congress Legislative Reference Service, per
capita payment to the United States from Mississippi was $218
as compared with $327 going from the federal government into
the state. Of every thousand dollars in Mississippi income,
$286 came from the federal government. It may be argued
that, financially, Mississippi has contributed nothing since

---

6. In 1962 personal income amounted to the following (in billions of
dollars): Mississippi, 2.89; Alabama, 5.26; Georgia, 7.21; North Carolina, 8.20; South Carolina, 3.76; Tennessee, 6.19; Florida, 11.16; Louisiana, 5.68; Virginia, 8.43.
7. According to *Mississippi Magic* (December, 1963) the Agricultural
and Industrial Board approved, during the Barnett administration, the
issuance of $62,514,000 in industrial development bonds.

World War II to the defense or even the running expenses of the national government.

Whether there is enough enlightened leadership in industrial Mississippi to bring the state into tune with mid-twentieth-century progress is doubtful.[8] But the situation is not hopeless. The Mississippi Economic Council has demonstrated that some members are fully aware of the needs for the future. But it will take more courage, intelligence, and unselfish devotion to Mississippi's interest (as well as the national interest) than has been in evidence since World War II. It will require more than a few businessmen scurrying around secretly, as if they were plotting revolution rather than dealing with urgent social problems. It is partly a matter of attitude and instinct. In December, 1962, the publisher of the Kosciusko *Star-Herald* called for fair play toward James Meredith and his family in their home town (where Meredith had been harassed by police and his folks by hoodlums). The gesture was prompted by fine instinct and a sense of justice, but the closed society prompted publisher Billy McMillan a week later to explain that he had written the

---

8. Historical precedent is not encouraging. Despite the prevailing emotionalism in 1861, the conservative men of large property holdings considered secession a doubtful though perfectly legal remedy for their troubles. As Rainwater has shown, it was a much larger group of active, restless, and politically ambitious lawyer-politicians, petty planters, and small-town editors—the "new men," successful enterprisers on the make, but without the restraint of large vested interests—who took Mississippi out of the Union. These partisans, "the hot-spur secessionists in wild frenzy, and madness, bore down upon the halting and bewildered groups, sweeping them along with the angry current of precipitate secession and leaving unmoved and adamant only the most stalwart. This small and loyal union group found itself isolated and, under the pressure of the radical forces, utterly unable to stay the current of secession which was rushing on to war and the ruin of the system which both groups desired to perpetuate at all costs." For those few who attempted to stand fast, the president of the secession convention had a remedy—"a stiff limb and a strong rope vigorously applied will prove a panacea for the infection." Percy Lee Rainwater, *Mississippi: Storm Center of Secession, 1856–1861,* Baton Rouge, La., 1938, p. 221.

original editorial in the hope that "industries would not be afraid to locate here."

Governor Barnett has never indicated any comprehension of the truth that Mississippi's old way of life and industrialization are mutually exclusive. Neither he nor anyone else is magician enough to freeze the social status quo while revolutionizing the economic order. Business leaders should understand that a healthy modern industrial structure cannot be raised upon the sands of segregation, minimum wages, poor schools, anti-intellectualism, Negrophobia, meager social services, anti-unionism, and a general policy of "hate the federal government." The pressing requirement is that a substantial number of prudent and imaginative representatives of the power structure—which has, until this moment, failed the state—will have been aroused sufficiently by recent events to band together for the purpose of crushing for all time Mississippi's self-inflicted closed society.[9]

The Economic Council Need Have No Fear

Next to the anxiety over the future of race relations, the still rurally-oriented Mississippian is most alarmed by the prospect of a successful invasion of the state by organized labor. In fact the firmness of the national unions on integration has become the most grevious cross southern union organizers have had to bear, and it has been the chief reason for the failure of most operations in the deep South. The workers will understand some day that like the white small farmers before them, they are being exploited via the race issue.

To hear Vaughn Watkins, outgoing president of the Mississippi Economic Council, tell it, one would assume that some fifty thousand organized workers were about to capture the

9. Mississippi has for some time allowed freedom in vocational and professional education—in these areas it may even be said that the social order has been moving in the same direction as the rest of the country—but in the province of ideas there is sublime distrust of, and, if possible, elimination of, findings that clash with the prevailing wisdom.

state and deliver it to the enemy. In the spring of 1963 he warned that unless effective counter action were taken, "the plan of the AFL-CIO to take control of politics in Mississippi will succeed." "The danger is real, the time is now," he said. He was referring, of course, not to the fine people who are the workers in Mississippi but to out-of-state dues collectors who "despise the conservatism of the South," and seek "even further liberalism than has been manifested by the national government." Mr. Watkins urged financial backing and organization to prevent "domination by those who are unfriendly to us and our way of life."

The Economic Council need have no fear of organized labor capturing one of the very few states with the right-to-work principle firmly inserted into its constitution. Even moderates on the race question are impressed by the propaganda of the *Clarion-Ledger* that such legislation protects the working man, and they apparently do not question the fake statistics that seek to prove that right-to-work states are the industrial giants of the country. For a long time Mississippi manufacturers will continue to bleed their hearts away before legislative committees for the rights of the laboring man.

It has ever been thus. In 1946 the whole community of Grenada was successfully rallied to keep the Congress of Industrial Organizations out of a local plant. City officials, church leaders, professional men, bankers, and the press set up a citizens' committee which identified the CIO with communism, world government, poll tax repeal and brutality, "all of which are against American and Southern principles." The Grenada *Sentinel-Star* was quite frank: "Should the majority [of workers] favor surrendering their rights to the CIO, it is believed by many that the Industry will cease operation." The election, as the editor looked at it, had been arranged in the first place under "Communist-influenced national laws," and the union had "championed damnable legislation—all that is detestable to Southern manhood and Southern womanhood." This particular edition of the paper went free to all the workers, who voted 297–122 to maintain their happy southern individuality.

There is no need here to recount the vigilante methods used to keep Mississippi society insulated from outside labor influence. After the pistol whipping of an Amalgamated Clothing Workers organizer—which was ignored by law enforcement officials—the prosecuting attorney announced that "The good people of Benton County have always managed to take care of their own affairs without the assistance of an outside organization and we shall continue to do so." A notorious letter, sent in 1954 by the mayor of Pelahatchie to a New Haven manufacturer, indicates how such affairs would be managed in another Mississippi community. It concluded:

Then our wonderful labor, 98% native born, mostly high school graduates, will lower average hourly industrial wage rates 6 cents to 49 cents below other Southern States, and from 50 cents to 95 cents below Northern States. You will also get a much higher average man production, some Plants even getting double what they got in Northern Plants. This labor is truly American, not inflicted with the "Something for Nothing" idea and works together joyously with Management for the success of both.

The more conservative craft unions are themselves often lined up with the status quo. In 1963, Jackson city officials received firm support from a resolution of the Steamfitters and Plumbers local for their handling of "racial agitators." A deeper sense of the intolerance of organized workers may be found in a mournful memorandum of a union official who dared join a colleague, a white lawyer, and a Negro to challenge in court the legality of Sovereignty Commission tax money subsidies to the Citizens Council:

Jan 7:   filed suit.
Jan 8–12:   received reports of upset members, threatening phone calls to family.
Jan 13:   intense opposition to my involvement with Negro in action.
Jan 14:   no calls of threatening nature to family today. Reports from Greenwood and Hattiesburg of intense opposition and petitions being circulated.

Jan 16:   visited by relative with request to withdraw, refused.
             Shaffer [the official's colleague] under extreme pres-
             sure (and me too). Gave him pep talk. Elected presi-
             dent of Central Labor Union.
Jan 17:   Shaffer made public announcement of withdrawal.
             Petitions asking my withdrawal, resignation or trans-
             fer gaining speed in Jackson.
Jan 19:   drove to Hattiesburg. Controversial meeting. Voted
             29 to 6 to recommend I be fired.
Jan 20:   withdrew from suit.

Majority membership in a half dozen locals signed petitions
requesting the dismissal of the labor leader, and the Jackson
local printed a resolution stating: ". . . and may this action
constantly serve as a reminder to all who hold positions of authority that such actions will be strongly met and dealt with in
a determined manner by the membership with or without approval of local officers or officers of higher authority." The time
is coming, the petition continued, "when we must choose between a union principle and a principle of our southern way of
life." It was the understanding of the man who had stirred up
this hornet's nest that the resolution was the work of the Citizens Council.

Industrial workers in Mississippi, in many cases not long
removed from submarginal farms, will not be immune forever
to the call of their own self-interest. In the state's largest
single plant, the Storkline Corporation in Jackson, the workers
were constantly besieged by every propaganda device that could
be thrown against them by business leaders, civic clubs, politicians, company management, and the press. Twice they voted
down the Carpenters and Joiners Union, and twice the election
was thrown out by the National Labor Relations Board because
of intimidation, a "community atmosphere" not conducive to
fair elections, company surveillance and promises of benefits for
anti-union activity, and a last-minute patronizing harangue by
Governor Barnett on company time the day before the second
election. When in the summer of 1963 the employees finally decided for the union 806 to 586, the *Clarion-Ledger,* which had

devoted columns of editorial space to fierce condemnation of the union, announced its victory in two short paragraphs deep inside the paper.

The Exiles Have Achieved Places of Eminence

The best of Mississippi's men born between 1820 and 1845 were lost on the field of battle. Many of the more ambitious who survived went north and west, and they have been going ever since. Between 1940 and 1960 Mississippi gave up two Congressmen because of loss of population (and would lose at least another if the Fourteenth Amendment were enforced). In fact, ex-Mississippians today play a role similar to that once performed by migrants from poverty-stricken Scotland—to a surprising degree they have achieved positions of eminence in all phases of American life. The only native to reach the pinnacle of renown while remaining in the state was William Faulkner, and I have personal reason to believe that he would have completed his removal to Virginia if he had lived another year.

Unquestionably, the primary motive for the exodus of the young people is economic. A survey now being made at Mississippi State University indicates that while over a five-year period only 21% to 35% of the engineering graduates were able to find their first jobs within the state, 97% said they would have remained if job opportunities had been equal, and 93% stated a desire to return, although that figure may have been influenced by potential employment with NASA. In any case, a high degree of loyalty to the way of life is shown among engineers. During the same years only 57.8% of the state's education graduates found first jobs in Mississippi. Negro teachers have a tendency to remain where they monopolize segregated positions (even though the average Negro salary remains about $500 less than the white). No whites teach in Negro primary and secondary schools, and very few in colleges.

The exiles are among the most ambitious, the ablest, and the most adaptable to change of all Mississippians. Such constant attrition of potential leadership is generally regarded as

one of Mississippi's great unsolved problems and must be a
major cause for the state's unwillingness to give up its ancient
folkways. Among the membership of the Southern Historical
Association, at least 25 native Mississippians, most of whom
have done well and profess great affection for the state, are
quite unwilling to go back under present circumstances. After
the Ole Miss integration in the fall of 1962, I received at least
100 communications from former students living outside the
state, and their common sentiment was a willingness to do whatever was necessary to help—except return. It is my considered
belief that, for whatever reason, Mississippi has for more than a
century been driving away a substantial proportion of its brightest young people who might otherwise have played a leading
part in bringing the state abreast of the times. The professor
who sorrowfully departed from the University in 1963 as a protest against the workings of the closed society was in effect
banished from the community, as surely as the sensitive young-
ster who, having had his eyes opened to the outside world by
an inspiring teacher, decides that he would prefer to live in that
world.

Though it is idle speculation, one cannot but wonder to what
degree Mississippi's story would have been different if a sizable
number of those thousands of bright, perceptive natural leaders
among the men and women who have been forced from the
state had in some way found it possible to remain.

4.

The Closed Society
and the Negro

You Can't Trust Negroes Any More

In the first half of the present century there was no serious challenge to the caste system in Mississippi, even though the Negro spoke the same language and subscribed to the same religion as the white, and accepted, presumably, the same universal American goals. In this period, it is true, the Negro also played a proper part in two world wars and heard, ever so faintly, the siren call of Franklin Roosevelt. The white man responded with a more urgent sense of his need to be constantly alert against any crack in the wall of white supremacy.

As elsewhere in the South, there was widespread fear in Mississippi that the Negro would come home from World War I expecting to continue the slightly increased enjoyment of rights and prerogatives he found in the army. But the aims of the Negro were not then particularly high. The "do-gooder" of that day fought for the Negro's right not to be burned alive, for his recognition as a human being, for a greater moral awareness among white people. But the closed society—bolstered by a general apathy, a lethargic federal government, a widespread agricultural distress, an emigration of the most dissatisfied, and the burgeoning power of the modern Ku Klux Klan—was barely challenged. When it became apparent in the middle 1930's that the New Deal might insist on really doing something about tenant farming and thereby would aid the Negro, a rigorous contest might have developed. Before this could happen, World War II intervened. As it was, Eleanor Roosevelt bore the brunt of the closed-society offensive against federal meddling in Mississippi. During the war, the Fair Employment Practices Committee had no impact on the state. The walk-out of the Mississippi delegation from the Democratic National Convention in 1948 proved that Dixiecrats would have none of Harry Truman's playing politics with the race question. There was no evidence in these years that the closed society was in any danger from within: the only potential threat to its way of life was from the outside, most likely from the federal government itself, and this threat seemed infinitesimal.

At the very time when the Negro was engaged in the lengthy process of attempting to raise himself to the common American standard, he appeared to be and demonstrably was culturally inferior. He could not be anything but culturally inferior, for he had been so trained by every controllable factor in his environment. There had been little essential change since Jefferson had commented in his *Notes on Virginia* on the Negro child learning "degraded submission"; it was still true that the black Mississippi infant was born into drudgery. Faulkner has the Mississippian say, "We got to make him a nigger first. He's got to admit that he's a nigger." And in "That Evening Sun," Nancy apologizes: "I just a nigger. It ain't none of my fault." From birth to death the Negro was exposed to an irresistible pressure toward deferential behavior. When he failed to conform he was driven out or even killed. He was regarded by most whites, and possibly by himself, as being shiftless, apathetic, capricious, untrustworthy, lacking in initiative, unstable, insensitive, and, for the most part, an amiable and happy beast perfectly adapted to his wretched position. By and large he played the role of Sambo well, giving little visible indication of a conviction that life could be better, or any apparent hope or desire to share in the white man's privileges.

With half the twentieth century gone, the Mississippi Negro

did not vote, did not serve on juries, held no slightest office in local government. He attended inferior schools, lived in slum housing, received unequal treatment in the courts, sat in the back of the bus, and was "segregated in his illness, his worship, and even in his death." The only integrated chair was located in the state penitentiary. The "good" Negro was the least likely to be maltreated for he had learned that militancy against the code would bring swift reprisal. Resistance in any way, except perhaps through the tricks and cunning of deferential subterfuge, was not tolerated.[1]

There is no need to recount here much of the shameful story of the use of violence to keep the black man "in his place." Every knowledgeable Mississippian can, if so disposed, recall deeds of varying degrees of horror which he has witnessed or has had told to him in moments of confidence or bravado. A decade or so ago, I myself interviewed more than a score of lumbermen in their 70's or 80's, each of whom related tales of the brutality and bestiality of the white man in the hardwood forests of the Delta after the turn of the century. Forty years after the event, a kindly old gentleman remembered with pride how quickly he had solved a "labor problem" at his Charleston (Miss.) mill when the colored crew walked off just because one of the Negro workers had been hanged for talking back to the boss. From the record, one may wonder which race has been living nearer to the law of the jungle.

A classic example of lynching as a means of social control was reported by the Jackson *Daily News* in December, 1928. Before escaping from the state penitentiary at Parchman, a Negro lifer named Charley Sheppard murdered the prison carpenter and kidnaped his 18-year-old daughter, whom he took on a wild 24-hour flight through the swamps. He allegedly raped the girl. Several thousand men, including units of the

---

1. Such open subservience is popularly and incorrectly called "Uncle Tomism" by militant Negroes but, as a matter of fact, the original Uncle Tom died under the lash rather than submit to dishonor. See Harriet Beecher Stowe, *Uncle Tom's Cabin* (1852).

National Guard, aided by bloodhounds, failed to catch Sheppard, who finally turned himself in to a woman plantation owner. A mob, skillfully and purposely directed, then seized him. After being displayed in front of a store, Sheppard was taken on a seven-hour tour of the main roads, the cross roads, and the back roads. Several prison camps were visited. As word of the affair spread through the Delta some 3000 cars and 6000 whites, according to the reporter, converged on the scene of the revelry.

Here, with the same methodical precision which had marked all their actions, mob leaders unloaded dried wood for the cremation, built their pyre, bound and strapped the negro and poured upon him gasoline which had been carried along for the occasion.

Before the match was touched to him Sheppard's mouth and nose were partly filled with mud to prevent him from inhaling gas fumes which might cause his instant death.

As the fire blazed up, "a wild-eyed member of the mob, intent on further torture, leaped atop the pile of wood, straddled the negro's body and cut his ears off with a pocket knife." Like a knock-out in the third round, the sacrifice itself took only a few minutes but not before the shrieks of the victim had been mingled with the screams of a hundred female spectators. Sheppard "twisted and rolled in the flames, and finally rolled off the pile of flaming stavewood." He was immediately seized and thrown back, and more gasoline was applied. The orgy finished, a leg bone and the skull were claimed as souvenirs. Later the ears were exhibited at a filling station. The coroner's verdict: "Death from causes unknown."

During the twentieth century never as much as 10%, and normally less than 5%, of the Negro voting population has been allowed to register. In 1899, 82% of the white voting population was registered, as compared with 9% of the Negroes. In 1954 the figures were 63% and 5%, and in 1960, 67% and 5%. In 1963, 3295 of a voting population of 4449 whites were registered in Amite County, as compared with one registered Negro out of 2560. In Coahoma County, next to Washington the most liberal of the Delta counties, the whites had registered 8376 of a potential 8708, while the Negroes had enrolled 1371 of 14,604. (Even so, more than 1000 Negroes signed affidavits that they had been denied the right to register in the county.) In Lowndes County the white figures were 5869 of 16,460, the Negro figures 95 of 8362. In 1962 there were five counties with Negro majorities in which there was not a single Negro registrant. In January, 1964, Andrew P. Smith admitted in U.S. District Court that he had not allowed Negroes to pay poll taxes (a prerequisite to voting) in Holmes County for eight years (four of which he served as sheriff and four as deputy while his wife was sheriff). The only Negro allowed to pay his tax had sent the money in by mail. But Smith denied the testimony of the editor of the Lexington *Advertiser* that he had told the Holmes County Board of Supervisors that Negroes would never be allowed to vote as long as he was sheriff.

Governor Barnett has repeatedly claimed that Negroes in Mississippi just do not wish to vote, that they could if they so desired. Actually, since 1954 the Mississippi legislature has required the voter applicant to read and write *and* interpret any section of the state constitution, and it has required since 1960 that he be of good moral character and have his name and address published in a local newspaper for two weeks. Applicants may now be challenged as to moral character by any qualified elector, and in a context where the discretion of the county registrar approaches infinity. At the moment, politics remains "white folks' business." A substantial Negro vote would embarrass any white candidate in Mississippi today. But it is well to remember Senator Bilbo's remark to an organizer for the Amalgamated Clothing Workers: "Son, when you can show me that you control any sizable number of voters, I'll be the damnedest champion you've ever had."

Gradual improvement of the state's white schools was shared by the Negroes in their schools only to a slight degree. But, as Governor Vardaman had understood, *any* Negro education spelled the doom of the caste system. There may have been rumblings before, but the summer of 1954 brought a shock from which the Old Guard will never recover. Having talked with a small number of conservative colored men, Governor Hugh White called in a hundred Negroes to get their endorsement for "separate but equal" school facilities. An error was made in sending out invitations a month in advance, for this gave the younger men time in which to maneuver. They arranged for a caucus the night before the big meeting and after heated debate carried the more timid along with them.

Speaker Walter Sillers opened the momentous conference. Governor White spoke of the amicable race relations of the past. As planned in the caucus, Charlie Banks got the floor and argued for the abolition of segregation. Five or six others quickly followed suit. A conservative Negro publisher made a last stand for the old regime, but was roundly denounced by a woman delegate as being a classic example of the effects of segregation. In desperation, Sillers called on another known friend of the white man, the Reverend H. H. Humes. The minister was the center of all attention. "Gentlemen," he began, "you all should not be mad at us. Those were nine *white* men that rendered that decision. Not one colored man had anything to do with it. The real trouble is that you have given us schools too long in which we could study the earth through the floor and the stars through the roof."

At this point, Governor White, mumbling that you couldn't trust Negroes any more, called the meeting to an end. It was also the end of an era. As one of the untrustworthy related almost a decade later: "For the first time I was really proud to be a Negro in Mississippi."

Since that day Mississippi has watched other Negroes "whose courage, intelligence, and integrity fill many with awe and inspiration." In June, 1963, an English instructor at the University of Mississippi wrote to the *Clarion-Ledger:* "Mississippi, after all, did produce Medgar Evers, a man who would not learn to be 'practical' or 'shrewd,' would not learn to serve whimsical

Time and brutal Circumstance, would not accept a definition of his 'place' laid down by someone else (the kind of someone who would skulk in a thicket and shoot him in the back for disagreeing). Here was a man who knew precisely how much he was risking and why, and who had the courage and ultimate intelligence to do so; and I, witnessing his conduct . . . have felt myself grow a dimension in aspiration and resolution. . . ." The instructor is not alone. Mississippi has long had a military tradition that has placed a high premium on valor. The day must yet come when great moral and physical courage will be recognized as having nothing at all to do with color.

When Robert L. T. Smith, a Negro minister, announced his availability for Congress in 1962, his candidacy was treated as a joke. WJTV in Jackson offered him time for six television appearances, but after his first program the others were canceled. Neither Jackson station would do further business with the minister, who protested to the Federal Communications Commission. After some prodding, station manager Fred Beard offered Smith time on WLBT, suggesting however that if he took it, "they" would blow up the station, shatter the plate glass and topple the broadcasting tower, and that if the Negro actually appeared, the bodies of both Beard and Smith would be found floating in the Pearl River. Smith didn't scare easily, made speeches on both stations, and no one got hurt. Mr. Smith didn't go to Washington but he did win the right to run.

The son of the Congressional aspirant owns a prosperous super-market. When asked for proof of harassment, he tossed on the desk a letter from his insurance agency showing the actual cost ($298.22) of replacing plate glass windows broken "by pistol shots" on the night of February 9–10, 1963, and paid by the American Insurance Company. The communication was addressed to "Robert L. T. Smith, 1253 Valley Street, Jackson, Miss." There was no "mister"; in fact, there was no salutation at all. Smith hadn't noticed.

Mississippi Is Famous for Its Justice

While life in Mississippi can be languid and pleasant, certain hazards confront the dissenter who would disparage the local customs. Mississippi is famous for a past of police brutality, and for the sure harassment, even to death, of those who defy the code. The state still retains some of the frontier abandon and recklessness toward human life found by William Howard Russel, the Civil War correspondent of the London *Times,* who observed that casual Mississippi conversations had "a smack of manslaughter about them." Today the press has learned to be even less bothered about reporting brutality than it was shown to be by a down-played news story in the Raymond *Gazette* on July 18, 1885: "Four negroes were lynched at Grenada last week: also one at Oxford."

Because segregation is the cornerstone of the society, the victim of the perverted use of legal processes is likely to be the Negro, whose "lot," the historian A. D. Kirwan noted in 1951, "did not change throughout the period" from Reconstruction to the New Deal. "No one," Professor Kirwan continued, "thought of him save to hold him down. No one sought to improve him. Whether race baiters like Vardaman were in power, or whether 'respectable' politicians governed, he fared the same—no better, no worse. He was and is the neglected man in Mississippi, though not the forgotten man."

An estimated 22,000 Negro voters in the state in 1952 had dwindled to about 8000 by 1958.[2] According to the president of the National Agricultural Workers Union, hundreds of Negroes have been forced to leave their jobs and homes by threats of violence. On August 13, 1955, Negro Lemar Smith, who had been "messing around" in politics, was shot to death at mid-

---

2. There is nothing available beyond a loose estimate of the level of Negro registration in Mississippi, except for the few counties reported on by the Department of Justice and a few more for which the United States Commission on Civil Rights has hard figures. For 1958 some estimates for the state run as high as 27,000.

day in front of a courthouse. Three whites, indicted for murder, were never brought to trial. Judge Brady gave the reason: no white man would testify against another for murder of a black man. Dr. T. R. M. Howard, founder of the Regional Council of Negro Leadership, sold out his holdings in Mound Bayou and left the state, because, he said, of Citizens Council pressure. A young Negro doctor was run out of Indianola in 1957. Gus Courts, colored grocer in Belzoni, refusing to withdraw his name from voter registration rolls, was told by a local banker that if he didn't back down, "we'll force you out of business." Courts led 22 Negroes to the polls that fall (their votes were voided) and a couple of weeks later he was critically wounded. The sheriff professed irritation because the injured man had impeded an official investigation by allowing himself to be driven 75 miles to a Mound Bayou hospital, but must have borne up well when Courts moved to Chicago. In 1955 four Negroes were killed by white men in Mississippi. There were trials of a sort but no convictions. It would almost seem that when these atrocities had served their purpose, murder, as an instrument of public policy, was then put aside for a time.

In federal court, Sheriff Edwards testified that he had indeed beaten D. M. Grim, Negro voter registration worker, in the Rankin County courthouse. He contended that Grim refused to move outside, impudently saying, "I got just as much right in there as you." "I hit him as many times as I could," admitted Edwards. "If he hadn't have run, I'd have kept on hitting him." As Grim recalled the scene, Edwards "came in and started hittin' me. Only thing I did was try to get out of there. They grabbed me. The sheriff pulled me from behind, on my sweater. He backed me against the building. He was hitting me." There is no disagreement about the beating, and not a great deal about the cause and severity.

Stories of alleged brutality against those who risk their lives in voter registration drives must come as a surprise to Senator Eastland, who says, "All who are qualified to vote, both black and white, exercise the right of suffrage." On the contrary, Wiley Branton, director of the Voter Education Project, sponsored by the Southern Regional Council, in March, 1963, charged that Mississippi had thrown down the gauntlet to would-be Negro voters by "discriminatory practices of the registrars—by economic pressures, threats, coercion, physical violence and death." A registration drive had been begun in Leflore County in the summer of 1962. In September the county supervisors abandoned distribution of federal surplus foods, at least in part to coincide with the cotton picking season. (Civil rights agitation probably weighted public opinion against the relief program, whereas before this emergency the landowners had favored it and merchants had led the opposition.) In March, 1963, three registration workers were fired on, one hit in the neck. There were 13 bullet holes in his car. Their headquarters was burned and the records destroyed. Two shotgun blasts were fired into the home of a Negro whose son had applied for admission to the University. Barnett put the finger of blame on "hired outside agitators, as dangerous to the community as a loaded bomb resting in the street in the heart of a city. I am a strong advocate of local self government." By this time the mayor of Greenwood was certain that Negroes had set fire to their own headquarters. Anyway, he shrugged, the injury to the wounded man was minor—"he was just in the hospital for a few days." People in the North should come "to see the wonderful race relations that white and colored have" in Greenwood. (They saw some of it on television.) Finally, the mayor and commissioners officially charged the Negro registration workers with shooting themselves.

Early in 1963, the Voter Education Project released a chronological list of 64 acts of violence and intimidation against Negroes in Mississippi since January, 1961. The thirty-page indictment of man's inhumanity to man, with its accusations of whippings, shootings, murder, and outrageous debasement of the courts admittedly came from an interested party, but it is characterized by understatement rather than by flamboyance. It has not been contradicted.

Nothing would be gained here in the retelling of the murder of the boy Emmett Till, the lynching of Mack Parker, or other

Mississippi outrages against justice that have been so publicized, some beyond their merit, throughout the world. But I would like to examine briefly a few cases of recent years. They all remind me of the time, some 15 years ago, when a colored skilled craftsman employed by the University of Mississippi was indicted for attempted rape of a white woman. For months, while kept in the Holly Springs jail, he maintained his innocence, but with the court already in session, he dramatically changed his plea to guilty. I was present at the conference where the accused was told in positive terms that his family would be placed in great physical danger if he went to trial, but that if he admitted his guilt he would be given a two-year sentence and pardoned in twelve months. He *was* sentenced to the state penitentiary for three years, all of which he served, and when released he left the state. (I was also present at an informal hearing in mayor's court of a former University professor accused of driving while intoxicated. The city attorney began the inquiry with these words: "Mr. Mayor, before we proceed with this trial, I think we ought to clear up the rumor that Professor ＿＿＿＿＿＿＿ intends to sell his house to a nigger." The rumor was cleared up and the problem was quickly adjusted among the white folks.)

"A Negro in Mississippi Receives Less Than His Due"

When James Howard Meredith made his painful entry into Ole Miss, Clyde Kennard, the "forgotten man" who had tried to break down the Mississippi education racial barrier alone and without federal aid, was languishing in the state penitentiary. He had been sentenced to a seven-year term for stealing by proxy $25 worth of chicken feed. Much of the evidence points to the conclusion that Clyde Kennard was "framed" into Parchman penitentiary, though no one seems to know who the guilty person was. Born in Hattiesburg, Kennard moved to Chicago at 12; discharged from paratroop service in Korea and Germany in 1952, he attended the University of Chicago meritoriously for three years. Upon the death of his step-father, he returned to Mississippi to help his mother run a chicken farm in Forrest County. For several years he discussed with the president of the University of Southern Mississippi his possible admission on a voluntary basis. In 1958 he turned down Governor Coleman's offer of education outside the state, but obligingly agreed to delay his formal application until after the 1959 Democratic primary. On September 15, he was officially refused admission in a fifteen-minute interview witnessed by the chief investigator for the Sovereignty Commission. Within minutes Kennard was arrested for speeding, then fined for possession of liquor (probably planted) in his car. By 1961, when the Mississippi Supreme Court set aside this summary justice, Kennard had been convicted as an accessory in the theft of three bags of chicken feed and sentenced to one year's imprisonment for each $3.57 worth of feed allegedly stolen. Assuming guilt, the penalty for such a crime would normally have been 90 days at most. The illiterate boy who had allegedly transported the chicken feed from the cooperative to Kennard's farm (and who had done the actual stealing, if there was any) did not even lose his job.

Though President McCain refused Kennard's application on the grounds of "irregularities" and "questionable" moral character, and is alleged to have said that he could do more to "develop honesty, culture, and individual integrity as president of Mississippi Southern than he can in a silly martyrdom for one Negro," Kennard himself trustingly refused to believe that McCain "had anything to do with what happened to me." The subsequent career of Clyde Kennard is a sad one. It includes surgery for cancer at the University Hospital in Jackson in June, 1962; unconscionable treatment at Parchman in the months following his operation when he was refused periodic checkups recommended by University doctors; the rapid development of his malignancy; an eight-hour operation in the Billings Hospital at the University of Chicago; and his death in the early summer of 1963. Not long before he died, Kennard was planning to return to his chicken farm and to help, as he saw it, Mississippi "coordinate" her race relations. One of his last statements was: "I still think there are a few white people of good will in the state and we have to do something to bring this out."

Of all the hypocrisy indulged in by those who help to perpetuate the closed society, some of the most insidious appeared at the expense of the gentle Kennard in the January 28, 1963, *Clarion-Ledger* column of Charles Hills: "Gov. Ross Barnett hastened admission of a negro convict suffering from cancer, into University Hospital here the other day. At the time, he reported he didn't know the man was in serious condition. That is true. Now, the case of Clyde Kennard, the negro who once tried to enter Mississippi Southern University, we understand that the man has not been neglected. Hugh Boren [assistant to Governor Barnett] tells me that Supt. C. E. Breazeale and doctors at Parchman have been fully aware of and have been closely watching the Kennard case. Apparently, outsiders were more worried about Kennard than the authorities who actually knew the man's illness and were attending to it as appeared necessary. Boren says that the negro is not nearly so bad off, prison doctors think, as news stories have pictured."

Early in May, 1963, the home of Hartman Turnbow, voter registration leader in Holmes County, was fire-bombed with three Molotov cocktails (quart beer cans filled with gasoline) thrown into the living room and kitchen while the family slept. Turnbow asserted that some 30 shots were exchanged with the white assailants, after which the fire was put out. While taking pictures of the damage next morning, Robert Moses, of the Student Nonviolent Coordinating Committee, was arrested for "impeding an official investigation of the fire." Later, Turnbow, Moses and three other Negroes were bound to the Holmes County grand jury and charged with setting fire to the house in hopes of increasing racial tension in the Delta. The victims of violence in Mississippi are often accused by white officials of creating the disorder themselves. Thus Deputy Sheriff Andrew P. Smith said his investigation showed the fire was designed "to get the colored population excited," that it was unlikely no one would have been wounded in the alleged exchange of shots, and that the house would have been burned more severely "if Turnbow had fought a gun-battle before extinguishing the blaze." The *Clarion-Ledger*'s headline for the day: NEGRO SAYS HIS HOUSE WAS BOMBED. Six months later the charges were dropped for lack of evidence.

President J. H. Germany set aside 150 of his 500 acres near Philadelphia for the campus of Bay Ridge Christian College, an institution intended to train Negro ministers for the Church of God. The school was to have a two-story classroom building, an integrated faculty of 5, and 30 colored students. In the summer of 1960, trouble began. A county grand jury investigated but "did not consider it advisable to set out the findings." Germany claimed the Citizens Council had put pressure on Attorney General Patterson, who refused a charter on the basis that it "would not be in the best interest of the state." Germany was beaten up several times. A UPI correspondent interviewed a businessman of Union, designated as the opposition leader. He knew nothing about the beatings. "But somebody down at the barbershop told me this afternoon that a brick wall fell on Germany." The chief of police added: "I don't have any news for you. I did not see anything." On August 22, about 1000 people gathered in a Baptist church to resolve that the founders of the college were stirring up racial trouble for their own personal gain. One participant wanted "it definitely understood that this is no mob." Other groups at various times marched on Germany's home and demanded that "out-of-state Negro people" be sent away within 48 hours and the college disbanded. Unable to defend his people, Germany stated that "it has been made clear the Citizens Council will be free to act with violence and annihilate me." Shortly before the abandonment of the project, he was reported "resting comfortably under police protection" in the Meridian hospital. Today his college is operating in Texas.

William L. Higgs, native white Mississippian and avowed integrationist, after graduation from Ole Miss and the Harvard

Law School, where he specialized in federal procedure, had returned to Mississippi to engage in politics and the civil rights movement. He had originated a suit against the Sovereignty Commission for donating state money to the Citizens Council, had represented several out-of-state ministers in legal action against the Jackson police, and had assisted in the Meredith case. Just before the New Year, 1963, and three hours after he had asked the federal court to order the enrollment of another Negro at the University, Higgs was arrested and charged with contributing to the delinquency of a minor, a runaway boy from Montgomery County, Pennsylvania, whom the young lawyer had befriended. Jackson Detective Chief M. B. Pierce emphatically denied that the arrest was connected with Higgs' civil rights activities. "Nobody can claim we framed him [Higgs], because this was a Northern boy instead of a Southern boy," said Pierce. In February Higgs left Mississippi to receive an award from the New York Civil Liberties Union. He failed to return (saying that he feared for his life), was convicted in absentia by an all-white jury, and was given the maximum sentence. In July, 1963, he was disbarred from further practice in the state of Mississippi because of his lack "of good moral character."

This is not quite the end of the story. Higgs is now in possession of a signed, sworn affidavit taken at the Juvenile Detention Home, Montgomery County, Pennsylvania, on March 20, 1963, in the presence of Peter J. Franscino, chief juvenile probation officer, and his assistant, Charles H. Hitman. In the statement William McKinley Daywalt, the 16-year-old boy in question, swears that during the whole time he knew Higgs, there was nothing unnatural in their relationship. Here is the pertinent part of the testimony:

Q. What else did the detective ask?
A. Did you ever have unnatural relations with him. He asked me if Mr. Higgs ever messed around me or used me as a girl. The first two times I said NO. Then they said they could put me up in reform school for four or five years on different charges. Then the detective asked me again what went on at

night and about unnatural relations. THAT IS WHEN I TOLD
THEM THAT HE HAD UNNATURAL RELATIONS.

Q.   Why did you tell him that?

A.   They kept saying that they would put me in reform school
     and that stuff.

Q.   Why did you think if you said this they wouldn't put you in
     reform school?

A.   For me living with Mr. Higgs I knew the police were trying
     to get him on something.

Q.   Did they suggest to you in any way if you told this story
     things would go easier with you?

A.   YES and again NO. They didn't come right out and say it.
     I had an idea and as it went on they started feeding me good,
     chicken and all that stuff and taking me out for rides and
     stuff like that there. Then I started putting two and two to-
     gether and found out they were using me to get something
     against Mr. Higgs.

Thomas E. Johnson, ordained as a minister by the Southern
Baptist Convention and later employed by the American Sunday School Union, moved to Canton, Mississippi, in 1956, as a
white missionary among rural Negroes. His special project was
starting Sunday Schools, but he and his wife also distributed
much free, used clothing (which they collected) and some food,
as well as aiding in charity medical work. Johnson reported:
"Some families have such low incomes that the smallest
emergency would unbalance their budgets completely. Hungry
children are no novelty. 'It's hard to hear a hungry baby cry
hisself to sleep,' young mothers would often tell us." His wife,
Marcella Johnson, took a job as secretary to the dean at
Tougaloo College. The three children were ostracized before
long, and when the oldest girl (eleven) required psychiatric
treatment, the family moved to Jackson.

In the meantime the missionary had joined the Mississippi
Advisory Committee on Civil Rights, an official agency of the
United States government. After an unduly heavy barrage of
stones and eggs on Halloween night, 1962, Johnson took a
neighbor into court for breaking the peace. Upon the neighbor's

acquittal Johnson was charged and convicted of perjury. As shown in the justice of peace trial record, Johnson interrogated ten witnesses, who by their testimony indicated the climate of neighborhood feeling: "We don't want any nigger lovers." "Go back to Tougaloo." "Johnson should live with the blacks if he works with them." "We were all talking about getting the Johnsons out of the neighborhood." "Like to blow his house up. We can't do that." "We would like to do it without violence." "He had some niggers in his house Saturday." "Your white children went to church with colored people." "You belong to the NAACP." (The Johnsons *had* entertained two East Indians, at the request of the federal government.) The testimony brought out that the unlettered conspirators had attended Citizens Council meetings, had met with Council President Wright, and had been trying "to get a fellow from the Citizens Council out here." They were enraged with investigations of violations of civil rights. Throughout the hearing, Johnson protested that he had come into the community as a missionary, had acted within the segregation pattern, and had not tried to change the rules.

In January, 1963, Hinds County District Attorney William Waller dropped the charges against Johnson, convinced that he had been unduly persecuted and that, in any case, a federal court would not sustain such frivolity. An eminent Mississippi attorney who went exhaustively into the record wrote with some emotion: "If an instance such as this occurred to an American citizen in one of the Iron Curtain countries, all of us would rise up in righteous indignation. When it occurs right at our front door, we blithely turn our backs because the racial problem is involved."

The most likely candidate in Mississippi for the next Medgar Evers treatment is the personable president of the state NAACP, Aaron Henry, one-time porter and shoe-shine boy in the old Cotton Bowl Court Hotel in Clarksdale and now owner of a drugstore on Fourth Street. He walks the earth with the sure step and upright carriage of a younger version of another Mississippian, Archie Moore, and he is not likely to be run out of Coahoma County. He does not know how many times the windows of his store have been smashed, but the last time, in March, 1963, he left for all to see the bricks, the broken glass, and the displays—one of the Declaration of Independence and the other of the Emancipation Proclamation. In 1962 he was convicted of leading a boycott of Clarksdale stores (at the same moment the Mississippi House was calling for identical treatment of Memphis business houses) after it had been announced that there would be no Negro float in the Christmas parade.

In March, 1962, Henry was fined $500 and sentenced to six months in jail by an eighty-year-old justice of the peace, for allegedly molesting a white hitch-hiker. According to the *Daily News* reporter, the Bolivar County attorney "during the final arguments, took the Mississippi statute and read to Judge Rowe the disturbing the peace law, explained it to him and told him the maximum sentence and fine." Before sentence, the judge said, "The evidence shows this young man could not have described the interior of the defendant's car unless he was in it." There was no other witness.

When Henry accused the county attorney and police chief of plotting this charge against him, they countered with a libel suit in the Coahoma Circuit Court, where the jury awarded them damages of $25,000 and $15,000. All these cases are still in the higher courts, the case involving the hitch-hiker having been accepted by the U.S. Supreme Court in February, 1964. On March 13, 1963, Henry's living room picture window was demolished and his home set afire at two in the morning by gasoline bombs thrown by two young thugs who said they were "just having fun" and were not aware of being in the Negro section of town. Not only did they admit the bombing but were heard by a filling station attendant planning the attack and commenting afterward that Henry "was lucky to be alive." The first man tried was acquitted of arson by an all-white jury, which deliberated for 15 minutes. An identical charge against the other man was dropped. One of those involved later asked

Henry's forgiveness, saying he had been tricked into the nasty business.

In May, 1963, the Henry drugstore was rocked by an explosion which ripped a hole in the roof. Sheriff Ross and Deputy State Fire Marshal Hopkins investigated and found that the blast "was caused by a bolt of lightning." Henry wrote, "I am not really sure as to the cause. The hole on top of the roof is much smaller than the rupture in the ceiling. The experts I have talked with contend that lightning does not act that way." It would appear that Henry is not only courageous but a scholar and a gentleman.

The Mississippi Advisory Committee to the United States Commission on Civil Rights made a report in January, 1963, on the administration of justice within the state. In a period of 14 months it had held six open meetings in which 100 or so Mississippians had testified, though "actively opposed by agents and instrumentalities of the State Government." In 1960, the legislature "passed an act," the Committee noted, "to intimidate persons who might wish to assert their rights as citizens by altering the requirements of proof for prosecution of perjury solely in cases where the defendant has testified before this Committee."

In its published findings, the Committee declared that "in all important areas of citizenship, a Negro in Mississippi receives substantially less than his due consideration as an American and as a Mississippian. This denial extends from the time he is denied the right to be born in a non-segregated hospital, through his segregated and inferior school years and his productive years when jobs for which he can qualify are refused, to the day he dies and is laid to rest in a cemetery for Negroes only."

"We do believe that a pattern exists in our State that leads to the denial of Constitutional rights and, in some instances, to brutality and terror. From the moment a Negro adult is hailed as 'boy' or 'girl' by a police officer, through his arrest, detention, trial—during which his Negro lawyer is treated with contemptu-

ous familiarity by the judge and other officers of the court—
and eventual imprisonment, he is treated with a pernicious
difference. This difference is incompatible with Christian ideals
about the dignity of man and with principles of Anglo-Saxon
criminal law. . . . Justice under law is not guaranteed for the
Negro in Mississippi in the way that it is for the white man . . .
42.3% of the citizens of this State must either accept an inferior
station in life and an attitude of servility or endanger themselves and their families by protesting. We find that terror hangs
over the Negro in Mississippi and is an expectancy for those
who refuse to accept their color as a badge of inferiority; and
terrorism has no proper place in the American form of government." "In general the press is failing to meet its obligation to
our society. The people of Mississippi are largely unaware of
the extent of illegal official violence and the press is partly
to blame." "When a State disregards a large segment of its
population, the Federal Government is compelled to intervene
in behalf of the victims."

And so in 1964 Mississippi is the only state in which not a
single school is desegregated, where voter registration drives
have brought meager results, and where even the U.S. Department of Justice has been largely baffled. Here is a revealing
"special" news story:

CITIZENS NOT OBLIGATED TO ANSWER RIGHTS QUERIES

Greenwood, Miss. Members of the Leflore County Bar Association have announced that in view of recent inquiries, they felt it
appropriate to reiterate the following resolution passed by the organization.

"In view of the public interest in possible investigations under
Civil Rights legislation of various local affairs by the Attorney
General of the United States, the Leflore County Bar Association
feels that as a public service it should inform local citizens of
their individual rights if they should be approached or questioned
with such investigations.

"A citizen is under no legal obligation at any time to answer any
question asked by any investigator about anything except in a court
hearing or at a court connected proceeding.

"For example, if an FBI agent or other investigator contacts a citizen at home, at work, on the street, or elsewhere, such citizen can, if he wishes, advise the investigator that he does not wish to answer any questions and can legally refuse to do so.

"In expressing that opinion, the Bar Association does not imply that information in any real criminal investigation should be withheld from any investigating officer. The FBI is a very efficient and honorable law enforcement organization, and the Bar Association urges that all citizens cooperate with it fully in its endeavors against crime and subversion.

"On the other hand, we do point out that when the FBI or another agency is ordered to make an investigation, not against a criminal or against a subversionist, but under Federal Civil Rights legislation, a citizen can legally stand silent and refuse to assist in that investigation by refusing to answer any questions of any kind, harmless as such questions may appear, about voting, schools, employment, or anything whatsoever."

The Civil Rights Advisory Committee proclaims unsavory facts with indignation but also with despair. With a highly effective Citizens Council always in the background and a racist in the governor's chair, there is no indication of any serious breach in the utter intransigence with which white supremacy is embraced.

Until exactly ten years ago Mississippi had been able to keep her own house in order, while those Negroes who wanted to be fully endowed as Americans had to get out. But some, like Evers and Henry and Meredith, who discovered freedom in the armed forces of the nation, came back to their home determined to challenge their allotted position in the basement. With leadership developed from their own ranks, with increasing awareness of the civil rights movement, and with solid help from outside sources, both private and governmental, the patience of many Negroes is wearing thin.

More than four of every ten Mississippians are Negroes and in some areas the black-white ratio is still more than two to one. The anguished cry is that Negroes will take over all local offices if allowed to vote freely. This is primarily a scare tactic for there is no danger of a Negro take-over and the whites know it. What they firmly resist is the placing of one Negro in any office. A substantial Negro suffrage might upset the caste system. In any case, a registered voter is more likely to receive the full protection of the law, especially the federal law. Scare tactics by intransigent whites lead to force, terrorism, and violence. It hardly softens the nature of such acts to understand that those who inspire or take part in them are frightened themselves. The white supremacist who encourages riot, who slays an opponent from ambush, or who inflames a crowd with his own hysteria is haunted by a palpable terror. Violence in Mississippi today has shifted from the random terrorizing of ordinary Negroes to specific extraordinary targets. It is aimed at the Negro leaders like Evers, Meredith, and Henry, who would show their people the way to a better, unclosed society.

In Jackson, whites still profess officially to believe that selective buying campaigns directed at downtown merchants, the Negro boycotts of 1963 and 1964, and publicly segregated Christmas festivities and decorations, are the evil machinations of a few agitators who themselves threaten violence. The whites fail to acknowledge that what Charles Evers calls the "Freedom organizations" are "expressly and in fact non-violent." But Mr. Evers, who fills the position his slain brother held, claims that self-respecting Negroes "have decided, of their own free will, that they will not spend their hard earned money with merchants who treat them as second class citizens," and that the segregationists cannot do anything about it. He may be right, even in the short run.

What one can see as the result of the showdown of these two forces—the first all-powerful at the moment but weakening, and the other presently weak by comparison but growing in strength—is only the distant future where the new society will be established. Perhaps it can be seen only as a matter of faith, as something beyond a temporal Jordan. It is in the middle distance that the terror will be worked out, that the convulsive imperatives required by the doctrine of white supremacy will wreak carnage.

APPENDIX: *On Voting in the Closed Society*

Negroes and whites agree in Mississippi that if Negroes were given full and free access to the ballot, the lot of the Negro would have to change for the better. Politics is perhaps the most popular of the southern arts. It is an art, however, to which the Negro has not been allowed to contribute much in Mississippi. If Negro suffrage were ever permitted to become widespread, there is little doubt that the white supremacists would be in serious trouble. It is no surprise therefore that every effort is made by the minions of the closed society, whatever their level of office, to keep the Negro away from the polls. The essential technique of Negro exclusion from the polls is a matter of some interest. There are two devices involved. The first is the poll tax—now forbidden by the Twenty-fourth Amendment to the Constitution as a qualification for voting in national elections, but still in force in local and state-wide contests. The second is the requirement that a voter applicant appear before the county Registrar. In this proceeding the citizen applies to vote by filling out a rather long application. In one section of the application the applicant is asked to interpret in writing a section of the Mississippi constitution. The Registrar, whose discretionary powers are virtually without limit, then decides whether the applicant is qualified to vote. The Registrar is under no legal obligation to defend, explain, or state how he has reached his decision. An appeal may be taken to the County Election Commission and thence to the appropriate Mississippi circuit court, but the more effective resort is in the federal courts, in a suit brought by the Department of Justice under the Civil Rights Act of 1960.

Copies of two voter application forms from Forrest County, Mississippi, which were admitted into evidence at the contempt hearing of *United States* v. *Theron C. Lynd,* No. 19576 (Court of Appeals for the Fifth Circuit), and thus are public records, are reproduced at the right. The forms were filed by Dale Bryant, a white applicant, and Carrie Magee, a Negro applicant. Both applied after an injunction pending an appeal had been entered by the United States Court of Appeals for the Fifth Circuit restraining Theron C. Lynd, the Registrar of Forrest County, from discriminating against Negro applicants and both applied after the same court had ordered Mr. Lynd to show cause why he should not be held in contempt of court for disobeying its injunction. Both applicants received Section 10 of the Mississippi constitution to interpret. Dale Bryant, a white truck driver, testified that Mr. Lynd told him to erase "2"—the answer he had given as his election district in Question 21—and write "Rawls Springs" instead. Dale Bryant did as Mr. Lynd told him and then Mr. Lynd registered him. Carrie Magee, a Negro school teacher, was rejected for registration but Mr. Lynd did not tell her why. He rejected her because he knew from her address in answer to Question 9 that she resided in the "Eaton" election district and not the "Walthall" election district. Nothing is to be gained from a microscopic comparison of these two documents, though they do exude the unmistakable aroma of the closed society. The thing to keep firmly in mind is that in precisely similar situations, Registrar Lynd registered a white citizen and disqualified a black one. He knew exactly what he was doing.

DEMENT-MERIDIAN Form 2139

No._____

SWORN WRITTEN APPLICATION FOR REGISTRATION

By reason of the provisions of Section 244 of the Constitution of Mississippi and House Bill No. 95, approved March 24, 1955, the applicant for registration, if not physically disabled, is required to fill in this form in his own handwriting in the presence of the registrar and without assistance or suggestion of any other person or memorandum.

1. Write the date of this application: *May 24, 1962*

2. What is your full name? *Carrie Mae Magee*

3. State your age and date of birth: *31 yrs. Nov. 12, 1930*

4. What is your occupation? *Teacher*

5. Where is your business carried on? *In Hattiesburg, Mississippi L. J. Rowan High School*

6. By whom are you employed? *Hattiesburg City School System*

7. Are you a citizen of the United States and an inhabitant of Mississippi? *Yes*

8. For how long have you resided in Mississippi? *31 years — (all my life)*

9. Where is your place of residence in the district? *1214 Hall Avenue Hattiesburg, Mississippi*

10. Specify the date when such residence began: *August, 1956*

11. State your prior place of residence, if any: *Route 2, Box 14 Utica, Mississippi*

12. Check which oath you desire to take: (1) General *✓* (2) Minister's_____ (3) Minister's Wife_____ (4) If under 21 years at present, but 21 years by date of general election_____

13. If there is more than one person of your same name in the precinct, by what name do you wish to be called? *Carrie Mae Magee*

14. Have you ever been convicted of any of the following crimes: bribery, theft, arson, obtaining money or goods under false pretenses, perjury, forgery, embezzlement, or bigamy? *no*

15. If your answer to Question 14 is "Yes", name the crime or crimes of which you have been convicted, and the date and place of such conviction or convictions._____

16. Are you a minister of the gospel in charge of an organized church, or the wife of such minister? *no*

17. If your answer to Question 16 is "Yes", state the length of your residence in the election district.

Carrie Magee—Plaintiff's Exhibit 5905 admitted into evidence at the contempt hearing of *United States* v. *Theron C. Lynd*, No. 19576 (C.A. 5).

18. Write and copy in the space below, Section _____ 10 _____ of the Constitution of Mississippi.

Instruction to Registrar: You will designate the section of the Constitution and point out same to applicant.

Treason against the State shall
consist only in levying war
against the same or in adhering
to its enemies, giving them aid
and comfort. No person shall
be convicted of treason unless
on the testimony of two witnesses
to the same overt act, or on
confession in open court.

19. Write in the space below a reasonable interpretation (the meaning) of the section of the Constitution of Mississippi which you have just copied:

One may commit treason against
the State by aiding the enemies
or giving them support in time of
war, or starting a war.
A person cannot be punished
for treason unless two persons
witness or testify against him on
the crime, or unless the person
charged with treason confess
openly in court that he did
commit the crime of treason.

20. Write in the space below a statement setting forth your understanding of the duties and obligations of citizenship under a constitutional form of government.

The duties and obligations of citizenship under a constitutional form of government are: Owe the allegiance or loyalty to my country, pay taxes, vote for officers, to support the government, and defend my country in case of war.

21. Sign the oath or affirmation named in Question 12.

NOTE: Registrar give applicant oath selected under question 12. Mark out that portion of oath that is not applicable.

Note:—Registrar. In registering Voters in Cities and Towns not all in one Election District, the Name of such City or Town may be substituted in the Oath for the Election District.

(a)   GENERAL and/or SPECIAL OATH:

I, *Carrie Mae Magee*, do solemnly swear (or affirm) that I am twenty-one years old (or, will be before the next election in this County) and that I will have resided in this State two years, and in _____Election District of _____County one year next preceding the ensuing election, and am now in good faith a resident of the same, and that I am not disqualified from voting by reason of having been convicted of any crime named in the Constitution of this State as a disqualification to be an elector; that I will truly answer all questions propounded to me concerning my antecedents, so far as they relate to my right to vote and also as to my residence before my citizenship in this District; that I will faithfully support the Constitution of the United States and of the State of Mississippi, and will bear true faith and allegiance to the same. So Help Me God.

_____
Carrie Mae Magee
Applicants Signature As To Oath

(b)   OATH OF MINISTER and/or MINISTER'S WIFE:

I,_____, do solemnly swear (or affirm) that I am twenty-one years old, (or will be before the next election in this County) and that I am a Minister or the wife of a Minister of the Gospel in charge of an organized church and I have resided two years in the State and in

_____Election District of_____County six months next preceding the ensuing Election, and am now in good faith a resident of the same, and that I am not disqualified from voting by reason of having been convicted of any crime named in the Constitution of this State as a disqualification to be an elector; that I will truly answer all questions propounded to me concerning my antecedents, so far as they relate to my right to vote and also as to my residence before my citizenship in this District: that I will faithfully support the Constitution of the United States and of the State of Mississippi, and will bear true faith and allegiance to the same. So Help Me God.

_____
Applicants Signature As To Oath

_____
Carrie Mae Magee
The applicant will sign his name here

STATE OF MISSISSIPPI

COUNTY OF_____

Sworn to and subscribed before me by the within named_____

_____ on this the ___ day of ___ May ___, 19 __

_____
County Registrar

GEMENT - MERIDIAN Form 2139

No._____

SWORN WRITTEN APPLICATION FOR REGISTRATION

By reason of the provisions of Section 244 of the Constitution of Mississippi and House Bill No. 95, approved March 24, 1955, the applicant for registration, if not physically disabled, is required to fill in this form in his own handwriting in the presence of the registrar and without assistance or suggestion of any other person or memorandum.

1. Write the date of this application: 18 June 1962

2. What is your full name? Dale Leon Bryant

3. State your age and date of birth: 21 years June 18 1941

4. What is your occupation? Truck Driver

5. Where is your business carried on? Southern Miss

6. By whom are you employed? D J Daly milling co

7. Are you a citizen of the United States and an inhabitant of Mississippi? Yes

8. For how long have you resided in Mississippi? 21 years

9. Where is your place of residence in the district? Rt 4 Box 150 (Beat 2

10. Specify the date when such residence began: June 18 1941

11. State your prior place of residence, if any: NONE

12. Check which oath you desire to take: (1) General __✓__ (2) Minister's _____ (3) Minister's Wife _____ (4) If under 21 years at present, but 21 years by date of general election _____

13. If there is more than one person of your same name in the precinct, by what name do you wish to be called? Dale Bryant

14. Have you ever been convicted of any of the following crimes: bribery, theft, arson, obtaining money or goods under false pretenses, perjury, forgery, embezzlement, or bigamy? NO

15. If your answer to Question 14 is "Yes", name the crime or crimes of which you have been convicted, and the date and place of such conviction or convictions._____

16. Are you a minister of the gospel in charge of an organized church, or the wife of such minister? NO

17. If your answer to Question 16 is "Yes", state the length of your residence in the election district._____

Dale Bryant—Plaintiff's Exhibit 5957 admitted into evidence at the contempt hearing of *United States* v. *Theron C. Lynd*, No. 19576 (C.A. 5).

18. Write and copy in the space below, Section_____10_____of the Constitution of Mississippi.

Instruction to Registrar: You will designate the section of the Constitution and point out same to applicant.

Treason against the state shall consist
only in levying war against the same
or in adhering to its enemys giving them
aid and comfort.

No person shall be convicted of Treason
unless on the testimony of two witnesses
to the same overt act, or on the confession
in open court

19. Write in the space below a reasonable interpretation (the meaning) of the section of the Constitution of Mississippi which you have just copied:

To be gilty of treason you must
commit an act of war against the state
or helping the enemies of the state

No person shall be convicted unless
there are two witness to the act or
in confession in an open court

20. Write in the space below a statement setting forth your understanding of the duties and obligations of citizenship under a constitutional form of government.

To be a citizen is to obey & carry out to the fullest the laws and statutes of the County, State, and nation in which I live & should exercise my rights to vote as I see fit which will be in my opinion for the betterment of my Country

21. Sign the oath or affirmation named in Question 12.

NOTE: Registrar give applicant oath selected under question 12. Mark out that portion of oath that is not applicable.

Note:—Registrar. In registering Voters in Cities and Towns not all in one Election District, the Name of such City or Town may be substituted in the Oath for the Election District.

(a) GENERAL and/or SPECIAL OATH:

I, Dale Leon Bryant , do solemnly swear (or affirm) that I am twenty-one years old (or will be before the next election in this County) and that I will have resided in this State two years, and in Kowba Springs Election District of Forrest County one year next preceding the ensuing election, and am now in good faith a resident of the same, and that I am not disqualified from voting by reason of having been convicted of any crime named in the Constitution of this State as a disqualification to be an elector; that I will truly answer all questions propounded to me concerning my antecedents, so far as they relate to my right to vote and also as to my residence before my citizenship in this District; that I will faithfully support the Constitution of the United States and of the State of Mississippi, and will bear true faith and allegiance to the same. So Help Me God.

Dale Leon Bryant
Applicants Signature As To Oath

(b) OATH OF MINISTER and/or MINISTER'S WIFE:

I, , do solemnly swear (or affirm) that I am twenty-one years old, (or will be before the next election in this County) and that I am a Minister or the wife of a Minister of the Gospel in charge of an organized church and I have resided two years in the State and in

Election District of County six months next preceding the ensuing Election, and am now in good faith a resident of the same, and that I am not disqualified from voting by reason of having been convicted of any crime named in the Constitution of this State as a disqualification to be an elector; that I will truly answer all questions propounded to me concerning my antecedents, so far as they relate to my right to vote and also as to my residence before my citizenship in this District; that I will faithfully support the Constitution of the United States and of the State of Mississippi, and will bear true faith and allegiance to the same. So Help Me God.

Applicants Signature As To Oath

Dale Leon Bryant
The applicant will sign his name here

STATE OF MISSISSIPPI

COUNTY OF_____

    Sworn to and subscribed before me by the within named_____

_____on this the _18th_ day of _____July_____, 19_62_

_____

County Registrar

5.

The Great Confrontation
and Its Aftermath

A Ditch to Die In Was a Whimsical Illusion

The University of Mississippi has had its moments of greatness. Among its faculty and administrators have been men of integrity and virtue, and always at hand has been the familiar fact of genteel poverty. In the presidency of Alfred B. Butts (1935–1946) Ole Miss began a precarious climb from the depths of a depression-caused despair and the shame of the Bilbo spoliation. For at least a decade after World War II, under the leadership of Chancellor John D. Williams, the University seemed on the verge of living up to the dreams and hopes of its founders and directors of exactly a century before. A tremendous building program was under way on the already beautiful, wooded campus; there was an expansion of libraries and laboratories and the addition of new departments, and, most exciting of all, the gathering together of an excellent faculty dedicated to good teaching and solid research. The new chancellor was adept not only at promoting support for the University among the people, but also in making it an integral part of many schemes designed to raise the horizons of a long submerged society. It was good to be alive in those days and if some critic mentioned the abnormal concern of the chairman of the Board of Trustees for the expansion of Hemingway Stadium, the answer quickly came that he was equally solicitous for the new library. Dean Farley discussed calmly with the Board the possibility of seeking out a couple of likely Negro prospective law students in order to avoid court costs and the setting up of a separate law school. Thurman Arnold, Jacob Potofsky, Hodding Carter, and Felix Frankfurter appeared on the campus without any great hue and cry. When a few professors were charged in the legislature with Communist leanings, only the minority of McCarthyites paid much attention.

It was increasingly evident in the middle fifties, however, that changes were taking place in the state that would adversely affect the University. In a series of crises from Kershaw (1955) to Kerciu (1963),[1] the administration became more and more appeasement minded, more and more involved (like a woman constantly professing her virtue) with presenting the Ole Miss story to the state as if it were a bar of soap. "Quality, Integrity, and Progress" somehow became the motto of the University. This advertisement was stamped on all official mail. Captive audiences at football games were saturated with saccharine reports on the greatness of the various colleges. As late as the spring of 1963 an appeal to alumni for gifts still harped on the University's "academic greatness . . . an outstanding faculty which possesses a much higher percentage of Ph.D.'s than the national average." The national average of what was left up to the imagination of the reader while the alumni were praised for their "desire to enhance the Ole Miss image as a truly great University."

More serious was a 1955 edict of the Board of Trustees requiring the screening of all speakers brought to the campus, a ruling steadfastly opposed by the chancellor at its inception but

---

1. George Raymond Kerciu, assistant professor of art, was arrested in the spring of 1963 for having desecrated the Confederate flag when he put on exhibition five paintings depicting the 1962 insurrection, which he had witnessed. Mississippians who were enraged at the paintings failed to understand that the rioters, not Mr. Kerciu (who simply painted what he saw), had profaned the flag. As often before, the administration missed an opportunity to consolidate behind it faculty support by refusing to take a strong stand for Kerciu's academic rights

stoutly defended some years later when he refused even to pass along to the Board a petition of the AAUP calling for an end to the screening. A clergyman, Mr. Alvin Kershaw, was turned away from Religious Emphasis Week when it became known that he had contributed to the NAACP. Though the chairman of the Sociology Department resigned in protest, the faculty as a whole was placated by the chancellor's plea that this "was not the ditch to die in." Professor Joseph J. Mathews, the 1964 president of the Southern Historical Association, was paid his full fee for not delivering a history lecture after the shocking disclosure that his wife had written in the *Saturday Evening Post* of her experiences teaching Negro students in Atlanta.

On the other hand, the handling of absurd charges of apostasy and subversion against fourteen members of the University community was brought off expeditiously and with a flair for public relations. Faculty members involved in this tempest, which was kept going in the press for almost a year, were asked to remain silent (which most of them did) while the chancellor affirmed his belief in the Bible, an omnipotent God, immortality of the soul, state sovereignty, segregation, and the rights of private property. In August, 1959, the Board dismissed the allegations against the chancellor and the faculty and stated its policy that "there should prevail at our universities and colleges an atmosphere of freedom in their research, teaching programs and services and that there should be no political or subversive propagandizing in the academic program." No attempt had been made to educate the general public in the basic necessity for freedom of inquiry and expression in the public schools. University officials and enlightened members of the Board of Trustees well knew that this would not be received tolerantly in the closed society.[2]

---

2. Historians may be amused at the formal accusations leveled at a professor of history by an alumnus whose college training included a total of six hours in history, with grades of C and D: The teacher (1) chaired a meeting where Faulkner denounced the South for its stand on segregation; (2) stated that Mississippi was a backward state; (3) "loves labor unions and curses the South for the War of Independ-

In the past year or so the University of Mississippi has desperately needed the help of all those interested in her welfare, but, far from being consulted, these friends have constantly been told that things were under control, that the situation was returning to normal, that enrollment was holding up in great style, that just a few professors were leaving. On the anniversary of the insurrection of September 30, 1962, the University news director insulted "some few professors" by accusing them of having leveled "bitter attacks" against it to "make national headlines" for the purpose of securing better positions, and it belittled the intelligence of those who remained by stating that "the vast majority" of these had refused more lucrative job offers elsewhere. In the closed society, where higher education also is expendable, this bowing before, and in fact anticipating, every wind may have a soothing effect on the legislature but it also indicates a chronic confusion of the image of the University with its reality. After all, General Ulysses S. Grant has been the only man in history to make a positive decision *not* to destroy the University.

In March, 1961, Ole Miss junior Billy Barton charged that the Sovereignty Commission and the governor had tried to block his election as editor of the *Mississippian* by sending to the University a "confidential" report that Barton had participated in Atlanta sit-ins, was a "left-winger," an integrationist who was "very dangerous," and that he had been planted on the campus by the NAACP. The director of the state commission had indeed been responsible for the "confidential report" which, it appeared, had come to him on Citizens Council stationery signed "Bill." Governor Barnett advised Barton that the rumors had originated on the campus, not in his office, and when confronted with documentary evidence to the contrary, lapsed into silence. The Jackson *Daily News* acknowledged that "the Sov-

---

ence," (4) asserted that southern generals were "numsculls" [*sic*] and the "scum of the earth," (5) stated in class, "I am a socialist and don't give a damn who knows it." (6) admitted he was an integrationist; and (7) went to Vanderbilt, "well known for its integration sentiments."

ereignty Commission and the Citizens Council have pulled a boo-boo."

The case of William P. Murphy, professor of law (1953–62), shows what the closed society can do to an able and innocent man. Within six weeks of the 1954 Supreme Court desegregation decision, Murphy proposed to the Mississippi Legal Educational Advisory Committee, through Dean Farley, a plan under which implementation of the decision would be left initially to the states. He asserted, however, that "it will and should be effectuated," and stated that "the adoption of legal subterfuges in the long run will be of no avail." (About the same time Dean Farley told the Municipal Association that Mississippi could not "outsmart the Supreme Court.") In rebuttal to the Murphy proposal, which was highly commended by many southern senators, William J. Simmons wrote the *Clarion-Ledger* that the Fourteenth Amendment was illegal, that "nine New Deal partisans" had perverted the Constitution, and that the federal government had been captured by "the NAACP, New Dealers, Fellow Travelers, and other left wingers." Murphy and Farley were "racial amalgamationists." Thus was the battle line drawn.

In a 1957 book review for the *Mississippi Law Journal,* Professor Murphy declared interposition to be legal nonsense and state sovereignty a "baseless cause." Then in 1958 came the charges against him of atheism, apostasy, communism, integration, and subversion. Professor Murphy was accused of not being objective in his teaching of constitutional law; he had not presented "the view and arguments of the South and the majority in Mississippi." In the meantime Murphy had joined the American Civil Liberties Union. In 1960 the state senate adopted a rider to an appropriation bill prohibiting the payment of funds to members of the ACLU, the NAACP, and the Communist party. Senator Lee asked the legislature to request "respectfully and militantly" that Murphy be fired. The law professor replied (an unpardonable act to the majority but, to some of those shackled at the University, a heroic act) in a statement to the press that he would not "tailor my teaching to

satisfy any cult of crackpots, fanatics and wilful ignoramuses."
In 1960–61 the controversial Murphy taught at the University
of Kentucky, in 1961–62 at the University of Missouri; his
first leave of absence had nothing to do with the Mississippi
excitement, the second came because of it. In February, 1961,
the Barnett appointees on the Board made an effort to end
Murphy's contract, and when Farley, as a matter of course,
recommended Murphy for summer teaching, certain alumni
suggested they both resign "for the good of the school." The
law faculty backed Murphy solidly, and so, initially, did the
chancellor and the provost. By March the chancellor thought
it might be in Murphy's best interest to resign. In May the
provost telephoned him that the Board (whose action he called
"unprincipled") had approved the summer contract with the
proviso that Murphy not be allowed to teach. No action had
been taken on his appointment for the following year. Murphy
had become a symbol to a small but powerful group of segregationists, including six members of the Board now committed
"beyond persuasion by facts and arguments."

In July, 1961, the chairman of the Board refused to accept
a law faculty petition protesting the ugly situation. But the
office of the attorney general saw a dilemma: if Murphy were
fired because he was an integrationist, would it not prejudice
the state's argument in the pending Meredith case that the University had no policy requiring segregation? In the meantime,
Dean Farley talked with his old classmate, Governor Barnett,
and reported that the governor apparently had never heard of
academic tenure and that he seemed surprised that the law
school might be disaccredited if Murphy were fired. He was
also surprised that Dean Farley would have to report the matter
to the accrediting agencies.

While at Missouri that fall, Murphy inquired about his tenure,
inasmuch as all other law professors had received letters con-
firming theirs. Six weeks later he wrote the provost again. On
December 1, 1961, the chancellor answered: "Dean Farley's
recommendation has not been endorsed by the Provost. Moreover, I wish to make it clear that even if the Provost should

decide to add his endorsement at this time and forward the recommendation to me, I would not approve it. In brief, your appointment has not been and will not be established on a tenure basis." On December 9, Murphy wrote the chancellor, "Your present denial is at complete variance with the position you took at our meeting last April." He asked for an explanation. There was no further correspondence and Murphy resigned in March, 1962, to accept a permanent appointment at Missouri. In slight anticlimax, he was allowed to teach in the summer of 1962 because the Board feared disaccreditation of all of the state colleges. The Committee on Academic Freedom and Tenure of the American Association of Law Schools stated in December, 1962, that "the University of Mississippi administration and its governing board persisted in violating Professor Murphy's rights."

Robert J. Farley would reach the retirement age of sixty-five in December, 1963. Assuming good health, a retiring dean normally continues on the faculty until 70, on a year-by-year arrangement. In the spring of 1963 the chancellor advised Farley that in his opinion appointment by the Board on any basis after his retirement was unlikely. Gentleman that he is, Farley went quietly. About the first of June he resigned because, as he told a friend, he did not want the law school involved in further controversy and because of the need for "my own economic self-preservation."

Dean Farley had enriched the Law School academically and physically, had by the force of his own remarkable personality saved its accreditation. He was of pioneer Mississippi stock; his grandfather had been in the class of 1854, and both of his grandfathers were killed in action in the Civil War; his father was a former dean of the Law School. This giant of a man had given up a career of distinction at Tulane University to return to Mississippi at a sacrifice of several thousand dollars in yearly salary. Largely because he had insisted that even Mississippi could not forever defy the Supreme Court, he had been brought down by the conformists who abound in the land

of orthodoxy. His departure clearly demonstrated that the call
of the chancellor in the Kershaw case to discover the right
ditch to die in was no more than a whimsical illusion. The
chancellor too was the victim of the closed society.

The Defense Would Have Been a Credit to Quintus Fabius Maximus

Almost exactly 18 months after he had first written to the
registrar, James Howard Meredith, the "man with a mission
and with a nervous stomach," was on June 26, 1962, ordered
admitted to the University of Mississippi. Speaking for the
Fifth Circuit Court in New Orleans, Judge John Minor Wisdom
announced that "A full review of the record leads the Court
inescapably to the conclusion that from the moment the defendants discovered Meredith was a Negro they engaged in a
carefully calculated campaign of delay, harassment, and mas-
terly inactivity. It was a defense designed to discourage and
defeat by evasion tactics which would have been a credit to
Quintus Fabius Maximus."

Tartly reprimanding Judge Sidney Mize of the U.S. District
Court for the Southern District of Mississippi for "continuances
of doubtful propriety and unreasonably long delays," Judge
Wisdom viewed the case as one "tried below and argued here
in the eerie atmosphere of never-never land." He might have
added, "of the closed society." The contention of the Board
of Trustees and of University officials, accepted as fact by
Judge Mize, "that the University is not a racially segregated
institution," and that "the state has no policy of segregation,"
"defies history and common knowledge." There was nothing
in the case "reaching the dignity of proof" to make the court
think otherwise.

The University refusal to accept credits from Jackson State
College "demonstrates a conscious pattern of unlawful discrimination." In any case, it had been indefensible to ignore
Meredith's credits from Maryland, Kansas, and Washburn,
which would have entitled him to admission as a sophomore.

(One evidence of alleged bad faith was Meredith's failure to mention Wayne University in the list of all colleges attended; he had gone to Wayne for two weeks.) Judge Wisdom noted that the assertion of Meredith's supposed "false swearing" in making application to vote in Hinds County was not only frivolous but had been thrown out by Judge Mize, "since these facts were not known to the Registrar at the time the application was made." "The defendants are scraping the bottom of the barrel in asserting that the University should not now admit Meredith because he is a bad character risk. The defendants fail the test. There are none so blind as those that will not see. We find that James Meredith's application for transfer to the University of Mississippi was turned down solely because he was a Negro."

Members of the Board of Trustees of the Institutions of Higher Learning are political appointees and may be expected to act as such. University administrators, however, are professional educators who, in matters of high policy concerning non-academic affairs, act only as agents of the Board. Many members of the faculty expressed dismay when Ole Miss officials made uncalled-for affirmations which the court deemed frivolous and "in the teeth of statutes," followed "a determined policy of discrimination by harassment," and assigned as a reason for rejecting Meredith "a trumped-up excuse without any basis except to discriminate." These same faculty members were hard put to comprehend why an administrator would deny that "he understands and interprets the policy of the State of Mississippi as being that Negroes and whites are educated in separate institutions of higher learning." More than a hundred years before, Chancellor Barnard had declared that the University's destiny was "to stamp upon the intellectual character of Mississippi the impress it is to wear. . . ."

"We Will Not Yield an Inch"

The pertinent Meredith chronology after the June 25, 1962, Fifth Circuit Court of Appeals decision is as follows:

July 17, 27, August 4:   Fifth Circuit Court orders District Court to issue injunction requested by Meredith (4 successive stays by Judge Ben Cameron).

September 4:   Board reserves decision on Meredith to itself, taking it away from University administrators.

September 10:   Justice Hugo Black issues injunction against interference with mandate of Fifth Circuit Court (having set aside Judge Cameron's stays).

September 13:   Judge Mize issues sweeping injunction against Board and University officials.

September 13:   Governor Barnett reads interposition proclamation.

September 19:   Chancellor L. B. Porter, Jones County, issues injunction prohibiting admission of Meredith.

September 20:   Registration of new students at University.

September 20:   Meredith found guilty in absentia in Justice of Peace Court, Hinds County, of false voter registration, fined $100 and costs, sentenced to one year in Hinds County jail.

September 20:   Senate Bill 1501 passes legislature, prohibiting person guilty of criminal offense or charged with moral turpitude from enrolling in state institution of higher learning.

September 20:   Barnett appointed registrar of the University. Rejects Meredith at University.

September 20:   Fifth Circuit Court restrains arrest of Meredith and any person enrolling Meredith.

September 21:   University officials cleared of civil contempt by Judge Mize.

September 22: In Fifth Circuit Court, Board and University officials agree to register Meredith.

September 25: Board rescinds appointment of Barnett as registrar, orders Meredith registered.

September 25: Barnett stops Meredith in Jackson (from appearing before Board).

September 26: Lt. Governor Johnson stops Meredith in Oxford.

September 28: Meredith turns back from within 30 miles of Oxford.

September 29: Ole Miss versus Kentucky in Jackson (football).

September 30: Meredith arrives on campus. Insurrection.

October   1: Meredith registered at University.

October   1: U.S. Supreme Court formally refuses to review June 25 decision of Fifth Circuit Court.

From September 13, when Mississippi's long court battle against Meredith reached "the end of the road" in Judge Mize's sweeping injunction, and Governor Barnett read his antiquarian interposition proclamation, it was evident to all that a showdown was imminent. In those last hectic days the "power structure" of the state made a rather impressive attempt to control the Barnett juggernaut, but it was too late, and most people were largely unaware of the effort.[3] Moderate statements by Oxford ministers appeared in the Memphis but not the Jackson papers. There was heavier than routine thunder in the Jackson press, which threatened to take note "of those who stand with

---

3. Frantic wires were dispatched and telephone calls were hurriedly made, meetings were arranged, resolutions and petitions were drawn up, as the elite among the state's business and professional men tried desperately to stave off disaster. The effort came too late, was too meager, and failed miserably.

courage in an hour of crisis." The closed society was operating
efficiently, almost automatically. A malicious Frankenstein was
on a rampage.

On the Ole Miss campus, a broadside, *The Liberty Bulletin,*
was circulated, urging students to "Place yourself under the
direction of Gov. Barnett. Do not engage yourself in force or
violence unless he calls for it . . . do not permit yourself to
be intimidated by any leftist school administrator." In Jackson,
Charles Hills reported that "the governor will watch with a
jaundiced eye any attempt to apply punitive action against
Mississippi's patriots. College presidents are standing ready to
fight alongside the governor, or else." Hills continued in his
Clarion-Ledger column, "The match is in the Kennedys hands.
We have been convicted without trial and punished without
justification. The state of Mississippi is wholly blamed by the
very oppressors who stir up our problems in the hope of creating a negro nation."

In the upper house on September 25, Senator E. K. Collins
arose to remark: "We must win this fight regardless of the cost
in time, effort, money and in human lives." Senator Hayden
Campbell thought "they would have to open the doors to murder
and rape." Senator Hilbun barked that "these are the same
people who won't let our children pray in school." The *Clarion-
Ledger* joked uneasily: "You can get a law passed in the halls
of the New Capitol at the drop of a hat. Of course, the federal
courts can nullify them and will, at coffee break." In Washington, Senator Eastland was sure that the next few days would
"determine whether a judicial tyranny as black and hideous
as any in history exists in the United States."

On Thursday, the 27th, the *Clarion-Ledger* took an unusual
glance at history. David had "interposed" himself between his
people and Goliath. Harotius had "interposed" himself between
his people and Xerxes. "And Ross Barnett has 'interposed'
himself between his people and the cheap effort of the Kennedy
crowd to force the deep South to pay his political debts to the
Northern Negro." Music for Mississippi's new battle cry, the
"Never, No Never Song," was printed in the *Daily News* with

the suggestion that it be clipped and taken to the Ole Miss-Kentucky football game.

Never, Never, Never, Never, No-o-o Never Never Never
We will not yield an inch of any field
Fix us another toddy, ain't yieldin' to no-body
Ross's standin' like Gibraltar, he shall never falter
Ask us what we say, it's to hell with Bobby K
Never shall our emblem go from Colonel Reb to Old Black Jo.

That same day the *Clarion-Ledger* carried a sensational headline to the effect that a "gunbattle" was possible at the University. Representative Walter Hester told the UPI it was "likely" that state officials would attempt to fight off the marshals if they tried to enroll Meredith, but he did not prophesy an all-out insurrection. The situation was "extremely tense and there are some people who don't mind dying for an honorable cause." [4]

Barnett talked about jailing any federal officer attempting to arrest a state official. The *Daily News* was accused by the campus paper, the *Mississippian,* of distortion, fabrication, "screaming and sensational stories." On the day of the football game the hysteria whipped up in Jackson was unbelievable. The press and radio added their bluster to the normal uproar of a conference game. At the half-time ceremonies that night, when he still might have turned the populace aside from its madness, the governor achieved his greatest triumph of oratorical lunacy: "I love Mississippi! I love her people! I love

---

4. Emotions sometimes lead individuals to give the closed society away. In a heated legislature debate after the riot, Senator Flavous Lambert charged that he had been told by either Senator McLaurin or Senator Yarbrough that "they were going to provoke the Kennedys into sending troops into Mississippi." And months later, Attorney General Patterson called McLaurin, the "CC & Co. . . . a little band of would-be ruthless dictators seeking to promote all-out riot and bloodshed on the campus by encouraging the people of Mississippi to pick up their rifles, shotguns and slingshots and go to fight it out with the armed forces of the United States." This, he said, could result only "in bloodshed, death, destruction and heartaches."

her customs!" Understandably, the man was overcome by his
own hoarse eloquence and the reasonless, incoherent, delirious
response. He could not go on. The people were bewildered.
Television carried the infection statewide and former General
Edwin Walker was on his way to Oxford to lend such aid and
comfort to intransigence as was in his power to bestow.

The propaganda machine never faltered. The next day, September 30, the Sunday that began so peacefully, a joint legislative committee pronounced nine frivolous reasons for denying
Meredith admission. It also cunningly announced that his registration would jeopardize the accreditation of the University
to the point of expulsion from the Southern Association of
Colleges and Schools, an exact reversal of the logic of the
situation, for which a certain wry admiration is perhaps due.
In the afternoon and early evening, weary students were driving
back to the campus, listening to their blaring radios tuned to
the appeals of the Citizens Council to "form a human wall
around the mansion" to protect the governor from arrest by
federal marshals. Thousands of citizens swarmed the streets
of Jackson. Few knew that the governor, whom Episcopal priest
Duncan Gray called the "living symbol of lawlessness," had
already sold out his closest advisers by making deals with Washington to surrender, while seeming to stand firmly against overwhelming federal power. Word came that planeloads of marshals
had been flown out of Memphis. For some time their destination
was in doubt. Unknown to most Mississippians, Meredith was,
before supper, unpacking his bag in his room in Baxter Hall
on the Ole Miss campus.

The Admission of Meredith Was Not Negotiable

When Mississippi officials on four separate occasions blocked
by physical might the court-ordered enrollment of James Meredith in the University, and the Fifth Circuit Court wearily acknowledged that it had come to the end of its resources, President Kennedy was faced with the alternatives of the acceptance
of the breakdown of law or the employment of force. A nation

guided by the rule of law cannot permit fear of mob violence to dictate its policy. The admission of Meredith was not negotiable. Kennedy performed his constitutional obligation in the same spirit George Washington had exhibited in the Whiskey Rebellion. Having apparently learned the lesson of Little Rock, he insisted upon the use of civilian federal marshals rather than paratroopers, and Mississippi politicians, who talk endlessly about "principle," had voiced no objections to marshals accompanying Meredith as long as they had been so few in number as to be overcome by superior state power. Whatever "deals" he may have made with the governor behind the scenes, the President gently and eloquently appealed to the patriotism and sense of sportsmanship of Mississippi citizens in asking them to obey the unpopular court decrees. But given General Walker's incendiary bravado in calling for 10,000 volunteers to go to the aid of Barnett, and given its being known that hundreds and perhaps thousands of inflamed Mississippians (plus out-of-state irregulars) were converging on Oxford, it would have been a serious evasion of responsibility had the army high command not prepared for a real emergency. Thousands of troops were moved to Memphis. The President earnestly hoped that the job could be done by civilians and the United States Army was not ordered to the University of Mississippi until it became evident that the marshals were fighting for their lives. The plain truth is that the army's first contingent arrived just in time to prevent a disaster.

From the arrival of the marshals at the Lyceum Building shortly before five o'clock, until the firing of the tear gas at eight, it became increasingly apparent that there was a serious lack of liaison between federal and state officials on the scene. At six the chancellor (at this time not much more than a spectator himself) believed the deal had been made and the game would have to be played out, and many of the gathering students and faculty were so informed. By seven, all observers knew that, for whatever reason, the Mississippi Highway Patrol (from the beginning its use by the governor had been illegal) had abandoned its enforcement of law and order and was in fact in some cases encouraging the restless crowd to demonstrate against the marshals. Between seven-thirty and eight, one professor noted 11 acts of violence against news photographers, faculty, army personnel and equipment, and, of course, the marshals. Twice, these agents of the federal government donned their masks as the crowd closed in. The campus chief of police and four highway patrolmen had moved back part of the surly crowd (which promptly surged forward again when the officers left that part of the scene) and were achieving some little success in front of the Lyceum Building when the marshals opened fire with gas and drove what almost instantly became a howling mob back to the Confederate monument.

Whether Chief Marshal James P. McShane was justified in giving the order to fire at precisely the moment he did is a question for the professionals to answer. It is relevant, however, that between 40 and 50 faculty members and their wives later testified that the marshals had undergone for at least an hour a constant harassment of obscene language and a minute-by-minute heavier barrage of lighted cigarette butts, stones, bottles, pieces of pipe, and even acid. It is a small matter whether the gas should have come fifteen minutes earlier or later, but it is rather ironic that a full-scale insurrection should get under way at the exact moment that the President was appealing to Mississippians on radio and television for fair play, in the name of Lucius Quintus Cincinnatus Lamar.

The Record Is True for All the World Except Mississippi

The night of insurrection at Ole Miss has been called the most explosive federal-state clash since the Civil War. Before the work was done, the Army brought more troops to Mississippi than General Washington had ever commanded at one time, and almost as many as General Sherman had had in the environs of Oxford exactly 100 years before. Several hundred reporters from all news and interpretative media concentrated on the Mississippi campus to ferret out the facts about what had actually taken place and to inquire into the background of the state's turmoil. By and large the reporting was accurate and the interpretation sound and temperate. Those who wished to know have had spread before them a reasonably trustworthy record of events.

This is true for all the world except Mississippi. With their long history of being on the defensive against outside criticism, and with their predisposition to believe their own leaders can do no wrong, the people have been almost completely deceived. The closed society intuitively and immediately projected (in fact, it had foreshadowed) the orthodox version that the insurrection came as the inevitable result of federal encroachment, deliberately planned by the Kennedys and callously incited by McShane when he called for tear gas. What did happen in front of the Lyceum Building in that crucial hour before eight o'clock on the night of September 30? Truth cries out that the orthodox Mississippi view is false, that cleverness in shifting the culpability for defiance of law from those creating the violence to those enforcing the law could only succeed among a people suffering from a touch of paranoia.

The genesis of the deception [5] that shifted the blame for the insurrection from Mississippians to federal officials came from the University administration, attempting both to justify its own

---

5. It has been brought to my attention by knowledgeable individuals, as this volume is going to press, that within minutes of the firing of the tear gas the Barnett men in Jackson had been alerted to the possibilities of charges against the marshals and quickly responded to their opportunity. Thus the "genesis of the deception," in the strict sense of the phrase, came from state politicians rather than from the University administration. There is also confusion about the exact time when Eastland's office was reached in Washington, some evidence pointing to between nine and ten o'clock the night of the insurrection, other testimony suggesting that it was two o'clock in the morning of October 1, and one report putting it as late as six that morning. Whatever may be the exact chronology, my general thesis is in no material way impaired. The exaggerations in Senator Eastland's account of the event are still apparent in his speech to the Senate and in his October 1 press release, which was offered as the "official" view of the University in the David Lawrence column of October 2.

conduct and to appease the political powers in Jackson and
(the Mississippi delegation in) Washington. A singularly in-
accurate story blaming the "trigger-happy, amateurish, incompetent" marshals, and suggesting examples of diabolical brutality toward male and female students, was in the hands of Barnett
and Eastland within an hour or so of the firing of the gas.
These opportunists took up and grossly exaggerated the cry and
called for state and federal investigations. Within 30 hours
David Lawrence was to devote his whole syndicated column
to the "official" view of the University. Long after it was made
abundantly clear that many faculty members and their wives
had witnessed the inception of the riot and knew for a certainty
about the fraud against the federal government, the University
administration did not deviate from its original position but,
on the contrary, continued to search for evidence condemning
the marshals. The Department of Justice of the United States,
in answer to a query from me, had this to say regarding the
conduct of federal marshals and troops in Mississippi:

Many false and unwarranted criticisms are leveled at the conduct of the federal marshals and troops during the riot on Ole
Miss campus. It is strange indeed that none of the so-called brutalities were reported by the several hundred newsmen, including
many from Southern newspapers, radio and television stations, who
witnessed the riot and its aftermath. Far from criticizing the marshals, the newsmen praised their courage and calmness under fire.

Many of the marshals were injured and 27 were wounded by
gunfire, but they did not return this fire. The marshals apprehended about 30 youths and adults who were attacking them and
held them under guard in a basement room in the Lyceum Building. There was no place else to put them. The conditions were not
the best, but were not nearly so bad as those the marshals had to
undergo. Many of the marshals went without food and sleep far
longer than any of the prisoners.

Members of the mob also attacked the soldiers of the National
Guard and the Regular Army as they arrived on the scene and a
number were injured.

In all, about 300 persons were taken into custody ranging in
age from 14 to 57. The adults came from as far away as Los

Angeles, California and Decatur, Georgia. A large number of shotguns, high-powered rifles, knives, blackjacks, clubs and other weapons were temporarily taken from these persons.

On October 1, the prisoners were removed from the Lyceum Building to the airport. Some were kept in a garage building. By the afternoon of October 2, all but a handful had been released.

Before being released, the prisoners were questioned by agents of the Federal Bureau of Investigation and complaints were filed against 13 men. Four of these subsequently were indicted by a federal grand jury of Mississippians on charges of interfering with U.S. Marshals in the performance of their duties and obstructing orders of the United States courts.

On the morning of October 1, shortly after the mayor of Oxford turned to U.S. soldiers to save the town from rioters, having been refused help by the Highway Patrol, Governor Barnett ordered the Mississippi flag at half mast because "there had been an invasion of our state resulting in blood." The riot, he said, had been touched off by those "inexperienced, nervous and trigger-happy" marshals who had "deliberately inflamed" the people "in order that the resulting resistance can be cited as justification for military force against a sovereign state." Next day the *Clarion-Ledger* headline, "EASTLAND, OTHERS CHARGE [⅜ inch] Marshals Set Off Ole Miss Rioting [⅞ inch]," was serenity itself compared to featured columns which elaborated the official view: "Our state is labeled insurrectionist because it does not care to be negroid in totality," and "The grapevine has it that the NAACP paid Meredith a flat sum between $20,000 and $50,000 to serve as guinea pig in this experiment." Columnist Hills did admit a temporary defeat: "So watch the peace-lovers come to the fore, grab a nigger-neck and start bellowing brother love."

There was more comic relief. The Memphis *Commercial Appeal* presumptuously complained of Mississippi demagoguery; a man named Walter Bailey announced the disbanding of the state Ku Klux Klan because nobody showed up for a council of war. Representative Tom Gibson berated Oxford's mayor for not supporting Barnett: "Sending to Kennedy, your enemy who would mongrelize the Anglo-Saxons of the Southland, to police your town, brings to the fore that you are a most undesirable citizen." [6] (For the moment the citizens had been more afraid of physical destruction than mongrelization.) Judge McGowan underwent a spasm of joy because Barnett, he was sure, had electrified the nation, had broken through the glacial complacency of the masses, who would now rally around the saviour of our country from communism, bureaucracy, bankruptcy, atheism, and the United Nations.

In the more than a year since then, politicians, editors, judges, lawyers, educators, churchmen—all the makers of public opinion—have continued the hypocritical tirade of misrepresentation and deceit. It does impress people who are attuned to hearing nothing else and want to hear nothing else. In the 1963 campaign, every gubernatorial candidate started out with a deep hatred for the Kennedys, and the man who screamed the loudest is now Mississippi's governor. While warming up in Florida for the main event, Paul Johnson, then lieutenant gov-

---

6. Apparently Mr. Gibson's anger was not easily appeased, for a month later he wrote the following letter on House of Representatives stationery:

Mr. Henry A. Fly
P. O. Box 561
Jackson, Mississippi

My dear Mr. Fly:

I see by the Citizens Council report that you are quite pro-Meredith and quite anti-white. After reading the articles about you as given by Tom Etheridge [sic] it would give me a good deal of pleasure as a member of the Legislature and as a citizen of the state of Mississippi to have some respectable white people call on you some evening.

We wonder where you came from, Mr. Fly. You are certainly not a Southerner and we feel like you are not a fly yet but probably a maggot.

Anytime any body wants to call on me to give you a party, it will tickle me to death. I was raised out in New Mexico where we did that every now and then to undesirables.

Yours very truly,
Tom L. Gibson

ernor, spoke on the subject, "The Cause of Freedom Won at Oxford and We Have Just Begun to Fight." President Kennedy, it would seem, had tried "to subvert the foundation pillars of this great government," backed by a "kept segment" of national press, television, and radio grinding out "its slanted story, half truths and prejudiced propaganda." Mr. Johnson continued:

"Shall the people be subject to search and seizure by spies and inquisitors who haunt the land?

"Shall men speak of public affairs only in whispers?

"Is the right of criticism denied?

"Shall a man go to jail or an asylum for voicing honest opinion?

"Shall the safeguards of justice in trial or imprisonment be set aside?

"Is there no right in one's own home which our government respects?"

This kind of talk prompted a University graduate of 1904 to write, "During my life span all of the Old Miss Darks [*sic*] were shadows cast from the occupants of 'the Mansion.' "

The Mississippi Junior Chamber of Commerce distributed almost a half-million copies of a 24-page pamphlet entitled: *Oxford: A Warning for Americans,*[7] which put the blame for the insurrection squarely on the shoulders of John and Robert Kennedy. By the following summer the Jay Cees claimed to have received 16,000 letters, all but 200 praising the work, which was judged to be the second most worthy Junior Chamber of Commerce project in the nation for the year. The most specious implication of the pamphlet was that Meredith would have been allowed to enroll peacefully if only the Attorney General had awaited "the completion of the judicial processes," a most unlikely result in a state which had already indulged in so much legal quackery and whose governor had made it so

---

7. For views on legal questions involved, see the appendix at the end of chapter, pp. 134–140. As one of 12 "outstanding young Jackson men" considered for the annual Distinguished Service Award of the Junior Chamber of Commerce in 1964, W. Swan Yerger, 31, was designated as the "chief writer" of the pamphlet.

evident that he would never accept the desegregation of the University. John Satterfield, probable contributor to the *Warning* and certainly an intimate counselor of Barnett, was now defending his own bad advice, which in part came straight from John C. Calhoun. The President did not use "unauthorized and illegal armed force," but, on the contrary, had specific authorization in the U.S. Code for its use. In addition, Kennedy did not even call the troops into action to enforce the registration of Meredith, but to protect the marshals from extinction. Whether Barnett was bound by the Meredith suit was not at issue; the governor committed a crime when he prevented the marshals from carrying out a court order. The President had no alternative except the use of federal power when the execution of the order was prevented by state force. All in all, it would seem that Satterfield has been trying to place the mantle of respectability on Barnett's unlawful conduct and to cast doubt on the legality and propriety of the federal government's actions by suggesting that it had used force without exhausting legal processes. He threw his weight as past president of the American Bar Association and a prime mover in the Citizens Council into the intellectual propaganda barrage directed at Mississippians, who were unlikely to pay any attention to the statement made on October 2 by the incumbent president of the ABA: "The paramount issue was whether or not the judgment of the court was to be upheld. The executive branch had a clear duty to see that the courts were sustained."

Mr. Satterfield maintained an Olympian judicial composure compared to Judge W. M. O'Barr who, in his charge to the Lafayette County grand jury investigating the death of two persons on the night of the insurrection, spoke of the U.S. Attorney General as "stupid little brother," and described the U.S. Supreme Court as made up of "political greedy old men" who "together with the hungry, mad, ruthless, ungodly, power-mad men [in Washington] would change this government from a democracy to a totalitarian dictatorship." The grand jury responded appropriately with an indictment of McShane for precipitating the riot, and for good measure castigated University professors (who had previously defended the marshals) for talking too much.

Exactly one month after the insurrection the "Women for Constitutional Government" were assembled in Jackson by the sister of the speaker of the House of Representatives to adopt a "bill of grievances" against the "unwarranted and unlawful use of military force" and the alleged violations of Mississippians' civil rights resulting from "the collusion of the President of the United States, the Justice Department, and the Federal courts." The high-flown language of "the thousand angry women" obscured, for Mississippians at least, their exquisitely imaginative account of what had taken place at the University.

Politically-minded educators swarmed into the breach. The President of Mississippi Southern University rendered for the *Mississippi Educational Advance* the historical justification for the state's orthodox position, pointing out that the recent troubles had begun with Franklin Roosevelt, and concluding that with the assistance of the Supreme Court, "the time is near when there will be little to choose between our system and communism." This little treasury of historical interpretation, a veritable patriotic primer, was reprinted in *The Citizen* about the time that its creator was telling a college audience: "We must not stand still. Beware of little men with little minds in little ruts, men who resist change and progress."

In the months after the insurrection, speculation was rampant as to whether the governor was at the moment taking instruction from the "resistance to the death" counselors (the White Muslim clique in the Citizens Council) or from the more cautious who, as one observer put it, had planned only a little riot, who didn't really want to see anybody killed. The Council sent up trial balloons suggesting the closing of the University, called upon faculty moderates (to Simmons, "gutless liberals") to accept segregation or resign, and conducted a postcard campaign directing the Board to fire "quislings and scalawags [who] betray our state and our people in the time of crisis." Whether the Council was more than covertly responsible for the open defiance of University authorities by extremist students, who returned from weekends at home with suitcases filled with cherry bombs and minds filled with rebellion, is still an open question. The Oxford Council, whose leaders were dedicated if not brilliant, distributed a mimeographed list of faculty members who were to be harassed with anonymous telephone calls—which did cause some little inconvenience because the sleeping habits of the daring dialers did not mesh with those of their victims.

Mississippi requires only one license plate and for many years extroverts have used the empty front space for metal signs carrying such messages as: MISSISSIPPI: THE LAND OF BEAUTIFUL WOMEN and MISSISSIPPI: THE MOST LIED ABOUT STATE IN THE UNION (which is probably true). So it was natural for thousands of cars to blossom forth with bumper stickers shouting the new belligerency: I'M WITH ROSS; BEAT LIL BROTHER; FEDERALLY OCCUPIED MISSISSIPPI; KENNEDY'S HUNGARY; BROTHERHOOD BY BAYONET; and BROTHERS CASTRO. A traffic hazard may have been created in Mendenhall, where citizens, the chief of police, and state troopers stopped cars on Highway 49 to offer stickers to the drivers. Negroes were not excepted. In Jackson a state senator sacrificed hours from his legislative duties to paste the emblems of defiance on other people's bumpers. One Oxford friend of freedom did a land-office business: he bought stickers for $15.00 a thousand and sold them for a quarter each.

The Mississippi Municipal Association, whose members are apparently not at their mental best when on their feet, prepared a model speech to be used in winning friends and thwarting enemies. After touching lightly on the notion that, after all, court decisions are not the law of the land, and warning of the dangers of centralization, the orator would rise with eloquence to the defense of Mississippi's official conduct. "This action is not a defiance of the law or the courts. Such action is an exercise of the heritage of freedom and liberty under the law preserved for us by our fathers." Although it was not suggested, the ambassadors might also have been prompted to sing the "Ballad of the Ole Miss Invasion." One verse read:

They came rolling down from Memphis and dropping from the
 skies
With bayonets for our bellies and tear gas for our eyes
Some resisted them with brickbats, while others ran and hid,
Some tangled with the marshals—who can blame them if they did?

With a few clergymen in modest rebellion against the status
quo, the Citizens Council eagerly grasped to its bosom a strange
new reinforcement in the person of Rabbi Benjamin Schultz.
Not long after his arrival from New York, the Clarksdale rabbi
laid down the "principles" which could save America:

> If Mississippi had its way, Castro would not be in Cuba now.
> Washington would not have installed him there.
> If Mississippi had prevailed, the Berlin Wall would have been
> torn down as soon as it went up. But then, the Russians
> would not have been there in the first place.
> If Mississippi had prevailed, pro-Communists would be off
> American college faculties. Corruption of our youth
> would stop.
> If Mississippi with its States' Rights philosophy had its way,
> big government, provocative dictatorship and eventual
> national bankruptcy would be thrown out the window.
> If Mississippi had its way, "red-baiter" would not be a dirty
> word. Traditional patriotism would sweep the land to
> strengthen our people inwardly, and insure victory in
> the international crisis. As it is, America is losing,
> mostly because of decay among its own intellectuals.

Such a statement did nothing to prevent Mr. Schultz from
being elected in 1964 as president of the Coahoma Ministerial
Association.

The Mississippi Society of the Sons of the American Revolution vigorously protested the enforced enrollment of Meredith
and called on every citizen to intensify efforts to bring a halt
to federal interference. The man who had faked the telegram
to the Texas Episcopal minister (see p. 55) devised, from his
study of Reconstruction, a plan by which "complete segregation
will again be the law of the land." Faculty and chancellor,
Elmore Greaves told Ole Miss students, were left-wing but

"weak—contemptibly weak," and could be overcome with ostracism, indoctrination, and obstructionism. "We know from Jefferson that resistance to tyranny is obedience to God."

For months the innocent-minded University professors of social science believed that the General Legislative Investigating Committee would quietly abandon its inquiry into the insurrection as it ran into more and more unpalatable facts. Having sent investigators to Oxford from Washington to look into the sensational accusations, Senator Stennis made no report and Senator Eastland shifted his effort to the collection of tall tales by disgruntled students against their instructors. The Mississippi Senate of course didn't need facts to resolve its contempt for the Kennedys nor to plead with the country to "join our State in defiance of all who would destroy our freedoms, heritage and constitutional rights." Only one senator called for secession, a few more demanded Kennedy's impeachment, while others galloped up and down the land to warn their countrymen of the coming of the orangejackets, those federal fiends whose savage brutalities at Oxford had "stopped short of Nazi atrocities only in that there were no deaths." In all this bombast the real casualty was *truth,* as in the fabrications of a senator who tried to lead an audience in New Orleans to believe that because Paul Guihard, the dead French newspaperman, "was on our side," he had been liquidated by the marshals.

The General Legislative Investigating Committee of the state was, however, to be heard from. The committee took over six months to put together, from the sworn statements of more than 90 witnesses, its masterpiece of sententious fiction. For reasons never explained, faculty witnesses and even legislators who had been at Ole Miss with the federalized national guard had not been called upon to testify. There was no minority report. How scores upon scores of the world's crack reporters had been kept from seeing the blundering and the repeated brutalities and "planned physical torture" by the marshals, the women students hit by projectiles fired at point-blank range, the deliberate gassing of seven dormitories, the "torture slab," the army truck set on fire by "a folded paper airplane," and dozens of other Alice-in-Wonderland concoctions will remain one of the mysteries of twentieth-century journalism. One eyewitness sadly commented that the "young gentlemen of the New Confederacy," who were able to glorify insurrectionist conduct in the "Brick and Bottle Brigade"—attacking the armed forces of their own country—would have small compunction about lying to a legislative investigating committee, especially one that made perfectly clear what it wanted to hear.

The legislative report was "verified" in advance by a documentary film, *Oxford, U.S.A.*, depicting "how the federal government violated the Constitution in the invasion of Mississippi last fall." Just before he sold three copies to the Sovereignty Commission for almost $7,000, the producer asserted the picture was "based strictly on the Constitution," and had been endorsed by Governors Barnett and Wallace. According to billboard advertising, it EXPOSES FEDERAL ATROCITIES. Actually, about half of the fifty-minute extravaganza is taken up with poorly filmed statements from Barnett, Johnson, Attorney General Patterson, Chief of the Highway Patrol Birdsong, and a legislator who makes some disparaging and untrue remarks about the University and Meredith. The opening action shot shows motorized troops moving into Oxford, which they did—about eight hours after the beginning of the insurrection. By implication, the viewer gets the impression that marshals had fired shotguns (which they didn't have) at innocent students and even that they had killed the French reporter. Altogether the film is a shabbily-put-together conglomeration of falsehood, distortion, and political dissemblance unlikely to convince any of the fair-minded who may be left in the membership of the Citizens Council.

The people of Mississippi have thus once again been victimized, this time by a palpable and cynical hoax, perpetrated on them by their own time-serving leaders whose sense of loyalty is only to the false orthodoxy of the closed society.

APPENDIX: *On Reading the Constitution in the Closed Society*

Printed below are the views of a well-known professor of constitutional law, born in the South and a long-time resident of Mississippi, on the constitutional questions raised in the Junior Chamber of Commerce pamphlet, *Oxford: A Warning for Americans.*

In October, 1962, the Mississippi Junior Chamber of Commerce distributed a 24-page pamphlet entitled *Oxford: A Warning for Americans,* which put the blame for the insurrection on the University campus squarely upon John and Robert Kennedy. In November, John Satterfield, past president of the American Bar Association, Citizens Council leader and intimate counselor of Barnett, delivered an address to the Jackson Rotary Club which was later published and circulated in pamphlet form under the title *Due Process of Law or Government by Intimidation.* Both pamphlets advanced legal arguments that cast a mantle of respectability on Barnett's unlawful conduct and challenged the validity of the federal government's actions throughout the Meredith affair. These legal arguments, however plausible to credulous Mississippians, are specious and untenable. The most important legal distortions and misrepresentations are as follows:

1. *Interposition.* After Meredith was ordered admitted to the University, Barnett issued a so-called declaration of state sovereignty in which he "interposed" the rights of the state of Mississippi between the people of Mississippi and the federal

government. The pamphlets assert that this declaration raised legal issues not previously decided. This is false. Interposition is but another name for defiance of federal law. It is not a new doctrine. As long ago as 1809 (in *United States* v *Peters*) and as recently as 1960 (in *Bush* v *Orleans Parish*) the Supreme Court expressly repudiated interposition as a valid constitutional doctrine. Interposition is squarely in conflict with the Supremacy Clause of the Constitution (Article VI). Obviously, if each state were free to determine to its own satisfaction and with finality what the Constitution means in any given instance, the decision of each state, rather than the Constitution itself, would be the "supreme law of the land."

2. *The Tenth Amendment.* Barnett maintained that operation of the public school system is not one of the powers delegated to the United States by the Constitution, and therefore is one of the powers reserved to the states by the Tenth Amendment. The pamphlets assert that this position raised legal issues not previously decided. This is false. The Tenth Amendment on its face states that certain powers are prohibited to the states and are therefore not reserved. One of these is the power of a state to deny to persons within its jurisdiction the equal protection of the law, which is prohibited by the Fourteenth Amendment. It is a denial of equal protection to deny admission of a qualified Negro to a public school solely because of his race, which is the very thing Mississippi was seeking to do to James Meredith. Thus, by its own terms, the Tenth Amendment affords no basis upon which Meredith could have been barred from admission.

3. *The Fourteenth Amendment.* The pamphlets also suggest that the Fourteenth Amendment, on which the desegregation decisions were based, was never validly ratified. The circumstances surrounding the adoption of the Amendment are discussed by the Supreme Court in considerable detail in the 1939 decision of *Coleman* v *Miller*. These circumstances afford no sound basis for concluding that the Amendment is not a valid part of the Constitution. Furthermore, since its adoption in 1868, the Amendment has been accepted as an integral part

of the Constitution by every President, every Congress, and every state. It has been applied by the Supreme Court, the lower federal courts, and the state courts in thousands of cases. The assertion of its invalidity does not raise a debatable question.

4. *The "Law of the Land."* The court order to admit Meredith to the University was based on the 1954 landmark case of *Brown* v *Board of Education,* which in turn was based on earlier cases prohibiting discrimination against Negroes in state-supported institutions of higher learning. The pamphlets attack the decision in *Brown* v *Board of Education* on the ground that it is not "the law of the land" but merely the "law of the case" binding only upon the parties in that lawsuit. This is false. Because our basic law, the Constitution, is necessarily couched in general terms, some person or some institution must have the task of authoritatively interpreting its meaning and applying its provisions to contemporary society. The founding fathers delegated this task to the federal courts, of which the Supreme Court is the final arbiter. Thus, the rulings of the Supreme Court interpreting and applying the Constitution are, unless they are later overruled by that same tribunal, the law of the land. This is true of the decisions of the Supreme Court in the field of school desegregation, involving the interpretation and application of the Fourteenth Amendment. Mr. Satterfield's "law of the case" theory completely disregards the doctrine of precedent, under which the rule of law declared in one case is applicable to all other like cases arising thereafter, unless and until the law is changed. Thus, if the Supreme Court should decide in a given case that a certain kind of income is not taxable, presumably Mr. Satterfield would countenance the federal government's regarding the decision as being only the law of the case, taxing all citizens on such income notwithstanding the decision, and thus forcing every taxpayer in the country to litigate the matter all over again. Subsequent Supreme Court decisions since 1954 have reiterated the ruling in *Brown* and applied it in other areas of racial discrimination. There is absolutely no doubt that *Brown* is what the Court

expressly declared it to be in the 1957 decision in *Cooper* v *Aaron*—the law of the land.

5. *Justice Black's Order.* Judge Ben Cameron of Meridian, Mississippi, was not a member of the Fifth Circuit panel of three judges that issued the order to admit Meredith to the University. Nevertheless, he promptly issued a stay of the order. The panel which decided the Meredith case then set aside Judge Cameron's stay, thus putting the admission order back into effect. Again Judge Cameron issued a stay. Three times this happened, until finally Supreme Court Justice Black issued an order vacating Judge Cameron's stays. The pamphlets maintain that there was procedural irregularity in Justice Black's action. This is completely erroneous. In the first place, stays are normally issued by the same panel of judges who issued the original order. It was most unusual for a single judge of the court of appeals, who had not even participated in the case, to attempt to render inoperative the order of the other judges of the court who had heard the case and ordered Meredith admitted. After Judge Cameron's three attempts to thwart the order of his colleagues, Justice Black simply restored the status quo by setting aside Judge Cameron's stays. Although it is clearly within the proper prerogative of a single Supreme Court Justice to issue such an order, Justice Black nevertheless consulted all of his colleagues on the Court and they unanimously concurred in his action. If anyone was guilty of procedural irregularity, it was Judge Cameron and not Justice Black.

Furthermore, it must be realized that stays are not normally issued pending an appeal. They are issued only upon a showing that, if the stay is not issued, the party against whom the original order runs will suffer irreparable damage and also that issuance of the stay will not cause irreparable damage to the beneficiary of the original order. There must also be a showing that the appeal raises such questions of substance that there is some possibility that the case may be reversed. No such showings could possibly be made in the Meredith case, as the Fifth Circuit pointed out. First, there was no possibility that the Court would reverse (or even review the case) since the petition for certiorari raised no arguable questions of fact or law. The Court on October 9 did refuse to review the case. Thus, issuance of the stay would have done Meredith irreparable injury, since it would have kept him out of classes for several weeks after school commenced. Second, even on the assumption that the Court would review the case and reverse the decision, not issuing the stay would not cause the University any irreparable damage, since it would only have matriculated for a few weeks an ineligible student.

6. *Conviction in absentia.* Barnett and Johnson were found guilty of civil contempt by the Fifth Circuit on September 28 for violating a court order restraining them from interfering with Meredith's admission. The pamphlets suggest that the contempt proceedings were improper because neither Barnett nor Johnson was present. This is false. Barnett and Johnson were absent from the proceedings by their own choice. They had ample notice and opportunity to appear and defend themselves. For reasons of their own, they refused to do so. Mr. Satterfield seems to be saying that Barnett and Johnson had a right to defeat the court's jurisdiction by refusing to appear. But, of course, court proceedings are not annulled simply because the defendant refuses to show up.

7. *Completion of Judicial Process.* The pamphlets charge that the government did not await the completion of judicial processes before using military force to enforce the court order to admit Meredith. Federal marshals and troops were sent to the University campus on September 30–October 1, 1962, to quell the civil disorders that arose because of Barnett's defiance of the federal court order. But well before this date Meredith's right to enter the University had been definitely established. After more than a year of litigation the Fifth Circuit Court of Appeals in June, 1962, had ordered that Meredith be admitted. On September 10, 1962, Justice Black had ordered Meredith's admission in September by setting aside the stays which would have delayed his right to enter pending disposition of the state's petition for Supreme Court review. After this action, Meredith had an absolute legal right to enter the University, and no fur-

ther judicial proceedings were necessary to perfect that right. The only legal proceedings which were uncompleted on September 30 were the contempt proceedings against Barnett and Johnson, who had on September 25 been restrained by a Fifth Circuit order from blocking Meredith's admission, and who had thereafter violated that order. But these contempt actions had no bearing whatever on Meredith's right to enter the University. The validity of the earlier order to admit Meredith was not in issue in the contempt proceedings, and therefore the outcome of that proceeding could in no way affect his right to enter. That right had already been finally established.

8. *Use of Troops.* The pamphlets charge that President Kennedy's use of troops was contrary to the Second Amendment of the Constitution and also to Article IV, Section 4. The Second Amendment provides that the right of the states to maintain a militia shall not be infringed. But Article I, Section 8 of the Constitution confers upon Congress the power "to provide for organizing, arming, and disciplining the militia" and also "to provide for calling forth the militia to execute the laws of the Union," and to "suppress insurrections." Article II, Section 2, of the Constitution imposes upon the President the duty to "take care that the laws be faithfully executed." This includes the "law of the land" as set forth in the decisions of the Supreme Court. Sections 332 and 333 of Title 10 of the United States Code expressly authorize the President to use both the militia of any state (National Guard) and the armed forces of the United States in certain described situations, such as obstruction of the authority of the federal government. This was exactly the situation at the University of Mississippi on September 30, 1962. The basic statute authorizing the President to call out the militia was enacted in 1795 and was upheld by the Supreme Court as early as 1827.

Nor was there any violation of Article IV, Section 4 of the Constitution, which requires the United States to protect the states, upon application of the legislature or governor, against domestic violence. Clearly, this provision must contemplate domestic violence against a state which the state by itself is unable to quell. It is equally clear that the provision does not apply when the domestic violence is against the federal government and is precipitated by state officials. This was the situation at the University on September 30. Mr. Satterfield's position is that, under these conditions, the federal government has no right to protect itself unless it is requested to do so by the very officials who are responsible for the obstruction of federal authority. Obviously, this is nonsense.

In 1895, in the case of *In re Debs,* the Supreme Court upheld the use of the Army by President Cleveland to enforce a federal court injunction against a strike by railway workers which interfered with interstate commerce and the transportation of U.S. mail. The Court stated in that case: "The entire strength of the nation may be used to enforce in any part of the land the full and free exercise of all national powers and the security of all rights entrusted by the Constitution to its care. . . . If the emergency arises, the army of the Nation, and all its militia, are at the service of the Nation to compel obedience to its laws." In the Debs case, the violence and the riots were not directed at the federal government as such, nor were the state officials engaged in the obstruction of federal law. The Mississippi situation was therefore a much stronger case for the use of troops than was *Debs.*

6.

The Voices of Dissent and the Future of the Closed Society

"It Was Just a Matter of an Oath I Took"

The closed society is never absolutely closed. There always have been and there always will be dissenters, doubters who will point to the road not taken. They are the hope of the present and the future, and even when they are wrong, their presence is required if the social order is to avoid intellectual stagnation and to escape the excessive belligerence of totalitarianism. A chronic weakness of democracy is the lack of assurance that the majority can come up, at any one time, with the right answers, or with answers sufficiently right to ensure the continuance of democracy. The majority in Mississippi was wrong in 1861, and the minority—perhaps thirty per cent—was right. The majority has been wrong many times since. This has been due in part to ignorance, lack of good leadership, and also to the exclusion of the non-conformist. For Mississippi to make correct decisions, it must have an enlightened electorate and a leadership intelligent enough to summon that enlightenment to save the state. For more than a century neither of these grounds for correct decision has been present in Mississippi, because freedom of inquiry and expression have not been tolerated. Criticism of the reigning orthodoxy has resulted in expulsion of the critic and the imposition of the smothering hand of conformity on the society. As long as this remains true, Mississippi will be left in her mental poverty and in her low social and economic state.

In the year after September 30, 1962, more than fifty professors left the University of Mississippi. Many of them were literally forced from the state. The best of them, particularly the native Mississippians, would have remained if there had been any prospect of an atmosphere of freedom or a decent chance to fight for one. Forced to leave the University of North Carolina in 1857, a professor fired a parting salvo that is still relevant: "You may eliminate all the suspicious men from your institutions of learning, you may establish any number of new colleges which will relieve you of sending your sons to free institutions. But as long as people study, and read, and think among you, the absurdity of your system will be discovered and there will always be found some courageous intelligence to protest against your hateful tyranny." True enough, but as long as the next "intelligence" and the one after him are carefully eliminated, the tyranny remains and the society stays closed.

In early 1963 a professor of the University of Mississippi (no longer on the faculty) wrote a letter to an editor, who chose not to publish it. Perhaps it was too long. In any case it deserves quotation:

> Men of good will who are content to sit on their hands silently hoping that nothing will rock the boat are seemingly unaware that the use of their oars might stay the foundering craft; these men are not leaders, nor are they followers.
>
> Leadership nurtures on controversy, it matures on intellectual dissension, it mellows on the free exchange of provocative ideas. A controversial, dissenting, and provocative faculty is therefore essential in developing a university-trained leader. Muzzle the faculty, restrict them to the "areas of competency," keep from the classrooms discussions of problems which are "out of our hands," don't talk of subjects offensive to people in Jackson. Follow these directions and students with no leaders of their own will find leaders as they found them on the night of September 30.
>
> But don't stop here, for leadership nurtures on controversy. And this controversy has stiffened a few faculty backbones. Previously

quiescent souls are speaking out, implanting ideas alien to the plantocratic dogma. A few open-minded students are listening and realizing that perhaps daddy's "Never" view is extreme. These students are the nascent leaders. Silence them! Ostracize those who seek to know more of their first Negro classmate. Censure those who question the existing order. Vandalize their quarters. Make them shape up or ship out. Then get to the heart of the problem. Harass the faculty members who inspire this sort of thinking. Work assiduously to be rid of them, to move them and their ideas away from here. Have no fear—the University will not lose its teaching staff. The inactive and the inept will still be around. Offers of employment elsewhere are made only to the competent, so only they will leave. A few good teachers unconcerned with the integration issue will leave solely because of the side effects of the harassment campaign and the pathetic gestures of a feeble administration which fears both the legislature and the "men of good will."

These measures will go far, but not far enough in ridding the University of controversy, of breeding ground for leadership. For there is a small faculty group that genuinely concerns itself with making this university a fountainhead of leadership. They will remain not for money and not for notoriety, but through an unappreciated sense of loyalty to the University and the state. And they will not be silenced. They will continue to search for the reasons leading to the development of the September 30 society. As long as this group is here, there can be no tranquillity, no peace. There will be controversy.

Use fair measures and foul and all forms of harassment to rid the campus of these elements. For only then are we assured that our sons will enjoy September 30ths yet to come. Only in this way have we guaranteed that our leaderless sons will be just as ignorant as we.

No, the closed society is not absolute. In Mississippi there are legislators, editors, lawyers, labor leaders, educators, and ordinary citizens who sometimes protest against the prevailing orthodoxy. The day that Governor Barnett let loose his interposition blast, Ira Harkey pointed out in the Pascagoula *Chronicle* that it wasn't the Kennedys but "the United States of America, democracy itself, the whole of humanity" that was making demands upon Mississippi. In a series of five short, magnificently logical articles, Representative Karl Wiesenburg demonstrated conclusively that Barnett's course was "the road to riot," that the governor had violated his oath of office, that the bloodshed on September 30 was the "price of defiance," and that states have responsibilities as well as rights. *The Mississippi Methodist Advocate* accepted part of the guilt for the riot: "We have known for eight years that there were pressure groups who boasted that if the people did not conform and cooperate with them, they would use social, political, and economic pressures. In the name of patriotism, the groups thrived until they had control of our social, political, and law-making forces. Yes, the church is partly responsible. By choosing to do nothing, we have permitted political pressure groups to chart our course and have allowed the voice of moderation and good will to be completely ignored."

An "ordinary citizen" wrote the *Daily News* in June, 1963, of her disgust at "the picture of grinning white spectators standing idly by while one of their cohorts stomps on the head of a bleeding Negro. Surely you know that there are thousands of us who are sickened by a policy that has brought this about. We yearn for a spokesman who will let the world know that there are many Jacksonians who feel degraded and disgraced by this unyielding adherence to segregation at any cost."

Three days after the insurrection, the Ole Miss chapter of the American Association of University Professors adopted a ringing statement protesting the fraud against the marshals. Without a campaign in its favor almost 70 faculty members signed the document as their way of "standing up to be counted." A professor of anthropology made his protest by putting into writing the conclusions of those in his profession concerning the validity of Putnam's *Race and Reason,* and this was serialized in the Pascagoula *Chronicle.* The exemplary conduct of more than 3000 federalized Mississippi national guardsmen is worth the scrutiny and praise of all Americans. General W. P. Wilson, adjutant of the Mississippi National Guard, said: "There were absolutely no incidents of any individual wilfully refusing to report for mobilization." George Fielding Eliot paid high tribute to the state guard: "In its ranks are men who, as citizens, share some of the views and even the prejudices of their fellow Mississippians. But when the call to duty came, they laid all else aside. After that they were soldiers of the United States, summoned by the President to aid in enforcing the laws of the Union, as the Constitution provides." One guardsman, who had suffered rough treatment at the hands of the hoodlums, went right to the heart of the matter: "It was just a matter of an oath I took."

Men of Good Will Are Not Enough

There are many thousands of "men of good will" in Mississippi, mild-mannered people for the most part, who in their day-to-day affairs do what they can to ameliorate the difficult conditions imposed upon their fellow men by the closed society. But because of a strong desire to live in peace, or because of one or another kind of fear, these men will not openly protest what they know in their hearts are gross evils. These are the individuals who, when one of their own number speaks out or in some other way defies the orthodoxy and is maliciously pilloried as a result, shrug their shoulders and say, "Well, he asked for it."

Men of good will are not enough. In his article in the *Saturday Evening Post* after the riot, John Faulkner, brother of the novelist, professed surprise at a plea to return to law and order, "this to us, the responsible people of Oxford, who raised no finger against any man." In high indignation he refused to see the need for penitence: "If all the sin I have to answer for is my part in bringing on what happened here Sunday and Monday, then I relinquish my place to someone more needful of forgiveness than I." [1] Perhaps Mr. Faulkner said more than he in-

---

1. The Reverend Albert H. Freundt, Jr., of Forest, Mississippi, also felt that "our people do not care to shoulder the sins of others or . . . to repent for someone else's errors . . . we feel no guilt for a set of circumstances not of our own making."

tended, perhaps he was speaking for all the good men who, to whatever degree, had abandoned the feeling of accountability for the condition of things in Mississippi. These same men were shocked to learn, probably at Leslie's drugstore, the price of defiance, as well as the fact that some of their neighbors were throwing rocks at other neighbors in the uniform of the United States government. But they were not moved by the riot—they were solidified. They had forgotten, if they had ever known, that it was not the lawyer Gavin Stevens who had prevented the lynching of Lucas Beauchamp, in William Faulkner's *Intruder in the Dust,* but Miss Habersham, Chick Mallison, and Aleck Sander.

There are moderates in Mississippi who look upon the future with some degree of optimism because increasing numbers of colored citizens are becoming eligible to vote. Unquestionably the promise of tomorrow has some merit, but not because of the assistance of men of good will. The voter registration drives are all conducted by local Negroes and "outside agitators" of the Student Nonviolent Coordinating Committee, NAACP, and other organizations. In the courts the chief defender of first-class citizenship for colored Mississippians is the U.S. Department of Justice. The Mississippi Civil Rights Advisory Committee, which seeks to protect the rights of all Mississippians, has found it well nigh impossible to recruit members.

The most unreasonable and cruel tirade James Meredith had to endure came from a *Commercial Appeal* columnist. Having, at least privately, expressed some sympathy for a much-maligned individual, this man of good will pounced upon Meredith's first apparent false step (his criticism of the U.S. Army), denouncing him as an "ignoble failure" who had betrayed his race and damaged its reputation beyond calculation. The column was filled with innuendo, falsehood, and bad judgment. Its author, who laid claim to an "overload of grief, compassion and charity," demonstrated he had none of these qualities when he refused to rectify in any way his character assassination of an innocent man. Once again, the pious, self-righteous man of irresponsibility had failed miserably, even in a mild crisis.

A Mississippi Paradox: Barnett's Negro Friend

Sometime during the month before he went out of office, Governor Barnett gave an interview which might well be likened to a Farewell Address, his valedictory word on the closed society. As recalled by Judd Arnett, in a Chicago *Daily News* wire service dispatch, the governor frankly stated his position:

In the early afternoon of the day I came to see him, Gov. Ross Barnett had spent a carefree hour bird hunting on a nearby farm owned by Dorsey Moore.

"Dorsey and I have been friends for 15 years," the governor explained, "and we go hunting together at least once each fall. I call him 'professor' because he trains bird dogs."

Dorsey Moore is a Negro. Further, he is a landowner (70 acres) because a number of years ago his friend, Ross Barnett, loaned him $1,100 to buy the property. Today, it is worth perhaps $14,000.

This same Ross Barnett, to the despair of his staff, is a "soft touch" for at least a platoon of Jackson Negroes. They waylay him in the corridors of the handsome old capitol building, or catch him as he is leaving in the evenings, and say: "Cap'n, I sure could use a dollar." Or five.

He forks it over. Certainly he can afford it. He owns real estate and is the senior partner in one of Jackson's finest law firms, reputed to be "the best trial lawyer in the state of Mississippi." He will never miss the money he gives to the indigent Negroes.

But it is necessary for you to know these few off-beat things about Barnett in order that you may come a bit closer to understanding "The Mississippi Mind."

If you ask a northerner "Who is the leading segregationist in America?," the odds are he would reply—"Ross Barnett."

And then in turn, if you should ask Barnett (as I did), "When will there be racial equality in Mississippi?"—remembering that he is a friend of Dorsey Moore, Negro—you would be a trifle taken back at the vehemence of his answer, "Never!"

He professes to believe we are getting "farther and farther away from race mixing." He agrees with Governor George C. Wallace of Alabama, who told me that "a strong civil rights bill would be unenforceable."

Barnett has not given an inch on civil rights, desegregation, integration, the "socializing" of white and blacks. Even so, he went hunting with Dorsey Moore.

I asked him a personal question: "Governor, would you please try to explain to me what Dorsey Moore means to you? What is it you see in him as a person, as a fellow human being? Why do you like him?"

Perhaps for the first time he attempted to put in words his appraisal of Dorsey Moore, friend but Negro. "Both of us love to hunt and he is very good at training and handling dogs. When we are together we have a good time. We laugh and joke and he gets a kick out of it when I call him 'professor.' There is a lot in our relationship that I can't explain. We are friends, even though we would never mix in social affairs."

"What are 'social affairs,' Governor?"

He replied: "Schools, hotels, restaurants—anything where integration is concerned."

Then he told me a story. Or, rather, he put in "story form" the reason why he has forbidden Mississippi colleges to compete against schools with integrated athletic teams.

"Supposing Ole Miss went somewhere and played a team that uses Negroes," he began. "In a year or two, we would have to have a return game with them in Oxford, or Jackson."

"After the game, there would be a social event. What would the Negroes do? They would attend. All right, supposing there was a dance. What would the Negroes do? Would they dance with the white girls? Not in Mississippi. It wouldn't work and that's why we are staying out of it."

Mixed bird hunting, yes. Or cotton chopping, or being a soft touch, or going down to the jail in the ungodly hours of the night and bailing Ol' Jim—yes to all of these and more. But not "socializing," not in Mississippi.

Barnett is approaching the end of his term as governor (it is once around and out, in Mississippi), and it seems to me that all of the tension has drained out of him and now he is as serene as a politician still under the hammer can get.

Our interview was one of the most "relaxed" of my recollection.

Like what you know of him or not, the fact is that Barnett will leave office on Jan. 21 with the praises of most of his constituents sounding in his ears. He had to run three times to get this office, but in his own way, and in the way of his people, he has made the most of it.

He will be succeeded by his own man, incumbent Lt. Gov. Paul Johnson. He has fit the mood of Mississippi whites during an era when their social structure has been under severe attack from many quarters. What has seemed "shameful" elsewhere, has not seemed so here.

If you are going to indict Barnett, then you must indict a whole state, or the better part of it, for they have been in this thing together, the whites of Mississippi, one the leader, the symbol, but the others the eager partisans.

There are thousands of Barnetts down here, each with his Dorsey Moore, and I doubt if they have changed an iota since the day James Meredith entered Ole Miss to the rattle of small arms fire and the hiss of gas grenades.

The governor told me that under his administration the state income tax has decreased from 6 per cent to 4.5 per cent; that 538 new or expanded industries have created 40,000 direct jobs, not including those in allied or service industries; that population has been increasing whereas it decreased between 1950 and 1960; that unemployment is now 4.2 per cent of the work force, lower than the national average.

The Distinguishing Marks of the Closed Society

The social order that Governor Barnett defends with such satisfaction rests upon the fierce determination of the white population to keep Mississippi a white man's country. The governor and his articulate advisers have refused to acknowledge that any serious challenge to the doctrine and system of white supremacy exists. Their beliefs are sustained by the unconditional and unwavering acceptance of an interlocking sequence of discredited assumptions:

a) the biological and anthropological "proof" of Negro inferiority
b) the presumed sanction of God as extrapolated from the Bible
c) the present state of affairs as one that is desired and endorsed by Negroes and whites alike

    d) the repeated assurance that only through segrega-
       tion can law and order prevail

    e) a view of history which declares that there has been
       a century of satisfactory racial experience in Mis-
       sissippi

    f) a constitutional interpretation which denies the val-
       idity of the Supreme Court desegregation decisions

Nowhere in the prevailing thought is there admission that nearly
everyone in the civilized world has long since abandoned these
premises, premises without which the Mississippi way of life
founders in its own absurdity.

A philosophical foundation, even if intellectually respectable,
would not furnish the massive support necessary for the continuation of the closed society in an antagonistic world. Beyond
its fundamentalist creed, then, the society has two engines designed to insure the maintenance of white supremacy: the distortion of Mississippi's past and the distortion of Mississippi's
present. The first of these is composed of *the ante-bellum myth*
(the Old South as a classical Golden Age), *the Confederate
myth* (the South as a humane society risen in spontaneous self-
defense of its sanctified institutions, its family and country life,
against wanton northern aggression), and *the Reconstruction
myth* (a society laid waste by an unprovoked war, become a
federal garrison, oppressed by an insolent Yankee inquisition;
a society filled with puzzled Negroes, who are forced beyond
their desire or capacity to function as citizens and officials; and
a society that is finally redeemed by virtuous southern patriots—
the intruder is expelled and the Negro is saved from himself by
returning him to his old security through the safety of segregation, and through new and beneficent forms of his old tasks).

The present view of life is distorted by the claim of Negro
contentment, by the notion that all racial troubles originate outside the state, by the politics of segregation (the asserted usurpation of Mississippi's sovereignty by a federal civil-rights-and-
school-desegregation conspiracy based in Washington and not
so obscurely related to the international Communist plot to

destroy America), and by the almost absolute support of the status quo by the makers of public opinion—the press, the pulpit, and the politicians.

With such powerful forces of indoctrination at work it would be strange indeed if whites and blacks alike did not grow up prepared to accept and extol their heritage. But there are still stronger means by which the closed society is entrenched. Every lawmaking body and every law enforcing agency is completely in the hands of those whites who are faithful to the orthodoxy. From governor to constable, from chief justice to justice of the peace, each and every officer of the society is dedicated to upholding and maintaining the status quo by whatever means are necessary. The white man is educated to believe in his superiority and the Negro is educated to accept his position of subservience and inferiority. The civic and service clubs, the educational institutions, the churches, the business and labor organizations, the patriotic, social, and professional fraternities—all individuals who would advance themselves in any of these are oriented from infancy in the direction of loyalty to the accepted code. In times of stress the Legal Educational Advisory Committee, the State Sovereignty Commission, the Citizens Councils, the Women for Constitutional Government, Patriotic American Youth, and dozens of similar new groups spring up to man the ramparts against outside encroachment and internal subversion. The non-conformist learns the advisability of keeping his mouth shut, or is silenced in one way or another, or he finds it expedient to depart the state.

The closed society of Mississippi thus swears allegiance to a prevailing creed with over a hundred years of homage behind it. Based on antique assumptions no longer tenable and on a legendary past, the doctrine of white supremacy is guarded by a bureaucracy, by ceaseless, high-powered, and skillful indoctrination employing both persuasion and fear, and by the elimination, without regard for law or ethics, of those who will not go along. Within its own borders the closed society of Mississippi comes as near to approximating a police state as anything we have yet seen in America.

The Spiritual Secession Has Never Ended

The more embattled the closed society becomes, the more monolithic, the more corrupt, the more willing it is to engage in double-think and double-talk. There is Mississippi's institutionalized hypocrisy that the Negro can freely vote and freely attend the university of his choice. There is the profession of Governor Barnett that he is preserving law and order and upholding the Constitution by physically obstructing the execution of an explicit directive of the Fifth Circuit Court of Appeals of the United States. There is the legislature, passing laws because the judges "will know how to handle" them, or for the purpose of "getting" certain individuals. The idea that this is a nation of laws and not of men, constantly reiterated within the state, has a hollow ring in Mississippi. How few of its leaders can come into court with clean hands!

Hostility to authority and disrespect for law are commonplace in Mississippi. How could it be otherwise in a state that tolerates the cynical disregard of the Mississippi prohibition law and blithely collects a black market tax on liquor? How can anything else be expected when the state itself brazenly tells the world it has achieved "separate but equal" school facilities, although in 1959–60 local school expenditures were $81.86 per capita for the white child as against $21.77 for the colored. Or when, as in 1951, the county superintendents of education, looking greedily toward the allocation of state equalization funds, reported 895,779 children of educable age (6–20) while the United States Census of 1950 listed the number of children from 5 to 19 as only 651,600? What respect can there be for the legal process when one standard of justice prevails when a Negro commits a crime against a Negro, another when a Negro commits a crime against a white, still another when a white commits a crime against a white, and a fourth when a white commits a crime against a Negro?

What about the morality of a social order that sends a teenage colored girl to a long sentence in an institution for delinquents because, by walking from her school to the courthouse, she is held to have violated an injunction against demonstrations? When questioned, the society justifies the exhorbitant penalty on the basis of previous abortions—which, up to the time of her sentence, it had ignored. Which is immoral, the girl or the society?

In spite of the closed society the Negro has made *some* gains since his emancipation a century ago. In the same period, the white man, determined to defend his way of life at all costs, has compromised his old virtues, his integrity, his once unassailable character. He has so corrupted the language itself that he says one thing while meaning another. He no longer has freedom of choice in the realm of ideas because his ideas must first be harmonized with the orthodoxy. He automatically distrusts new currents of thought, and if they clash with the prevailing wisdom, he ruthlessly eliminates them. He cannot allow himself the luxury of thinking about a problem on its merits. In spite of what he claims, the white Mississippian is not even conservative—he is merely negative. He grows up being against most things about which other men at least have the pleasure of arguing. He spends all his life on the defensive. The most he can hope for is to put up a good fight before losing. This is the Mississippi way, this is the Mississippi heritage. It will ever be thus as long as the closed society endures.

Although there have been moments of enlightenment, Mississippi's spiritual secession from modern America has never ended. For more than a century Mississippians have refused to be bound by the will of the national society. Perhaps this recalcitrance could be borne with in the past, as many other excesses of democracy have been. But now that the sanctuary once provided by two oceans is gone and the country is fighting for its survival, the national interest and the instinct for survival demand discipline. They demand also that attitudes or "principles" growing out of racial situations not be allowed to intrude themselves into the country's policy-making decisions. Since Reconstruction Mississippians have had no real reason to believe that they were not free to handle the race question as they wished, without meaningful interference from the federal government; and when they now discover that all their bluster and subterfuge and intransigence will avail them nothing, they have little to fall back on except blind rage and fierce hatred.

In committing itself to the defense of the bi-racial system, Mississippi has erected a totalitarian society which to the present moment has eliminated the ordinary processes by which change may be channeled. Through its police power, coercion and force prevail instead of accommodation, and the result is social paralysis. Thus, the Mississippian who prides himself on his individuality in reality lives in a climate where non-conformity is forbidden, where the white man is not free, where he does not dare to express a deviating opinion without looking over his shoulder. Not only is the black man not allowed to forget that he is a "nigger," but the white moderate must distinctly understand that he is a "nigger-lover."

Mississippi has long been a hyper-orthodox social order in which the individual has no option except to be loyal to the will of the white majority. And the white majority has subscribed to an inflexible philosophy which is not based on fact, logic, or reason. Non-white Mississippians and all others are out-landers. Close contiguity with a large repressed population and fear of what their "inferior" people might do have held the society near the point of unanimity. Especially in times of stress, the orthodoxy becomes more rigid, more removed from reality, and more extreme conformity to it is demanded. Today the advocacy or even the recognition of the inevitability of change becomes a social felony, or worse. Mississippi is the way it is not because of its views on the Negro—here it is simply "the South exaggerated"—but because of its closed society, its refusal to allow freedom of inquiry or to tolerate "error of opinion." The social order that refuses to conform to national standards insists upon strict conformity at home. While complaining of its own persecuted minority station in the United States, it rarely considers the Negro minority as having rights in Mississippi.

Perhaps the greatest tragedy of the closed society is the

refusal of its citizens to believe that there is any view other than the orthodox. In recent years there has been a hardening attitude among college students, who do not want to hear the other side. In such a twilight of non-discussion, minds not only do not grow tough, they do not grow at all. Intelligent men with ideas are isolated from the rest of the community, and what little interracial communication existed in the past is now destroyed. One reason the Ole Miss faculty failed to protest against an ugly situation in the period just before the insurrection was that through one means or another freedom of speech had long since been curtailed. This was at least a partial cause for the resignation of from eight to ten members of the history department in the two years *before* the troubles that followed the September insurrection in 1962. The jolt of the violence on the campus and the obvious fraud against the federal government initiated a spurt of resistance to ignorance and stupidity and conformity. For a moment, many of the faculty developed a healthy scorn for expediency and security. This might have developed into an important pocket of real leadership, if the administration and the Board of Trustees had not succumbed to pressures from the closed social order. In the light of Mississippi's history it was probably already too late to expect anything more than an occasional stand, taken by an individual or small group, such as that put up by the 28 ministers who were willing to count the cost and pay the price. Given the great silence from the men of good will, and the disposition of the good people to let things run their course, there can be little hope for anything constructive in Mississippi in the next few years.

The strongest preservative of the closed society is the closed mind. It has been argued that in the history of the United States democracy has produced great leaders in great crises. Sad as it may be, the opposite has been true in Mississippi. As yet there is little evidence that the closed society will ever possess the moral resources to reform itself, or the capacity for self-examination, or even the tolerance of self-examination. Inasmuch as a nation marching with deliberate speed toward the fulfillment of the promise of the Declaration of Independence and the Emancipation Proclamation is at the same time fighting for survival against communism, it will not much longer indulge the frustration of its will. Nevertheless, it would seem that for the foreseeable future the people of Mississippi will plod along the troubled road of resistance, violence, anguish, and injustice, moving slowly until engulfed in a predictable cataclysm.

And yet, in spite of all that has been presented in these pages, it seems inescapable that Mississippians will one day shed their fantasy of past and present and will resume their obligations as Americans. It is melancholy to contemplate the fact that in the year 1964 there is small reason to believe that they will somehow develop the capacity to do it themselves, to do it, as William Faulkner says, in time. That time is fast running out. It cannot be long before the country, seeing that persuasion alone must fail, and perhaps acting through the power and authority of the federal government, will, with whatever reluctance and sadness, put an end to the closed society in Mississippi.

PART TWO

PART TWO

Some Letters from the
Closed Society

In this brief book I have made no effort to tell the day-by-day story of the events in Mississippi leading up to and since the insurrection of September 30, 1962. This is a story crying to be told, but it would require more time than is at my disposal. Furthermore it would require a thorough search into the files of the United States Department of Justice, the Board of Trustees of Higher Learning, the offices of the governor and attorney general of Mississippi, dozens of newspapers and magazines across the country, and many other agencies and individuals. That would be a mere beginning. Such a project would necessitate above all free access to the minds of major participants, an unlikely prospect now or later. It is extremely doubtful that some of those intimately involved in the various state-federal-local clashes could give an accurate account of their participation even if they were so disposed.

As an on-stage observer of much that happened, I wrote many hundreds of letters, of some of which I made carbons. While these letters may contain errors of fact and perhaps of judgment, they do reveal thoughts and emotions in times of stress in a way which is impossible for me to recapture now. Although I am somewhat doubtful of the wisdom of publishing these bits of evidence so soon after the events described, I have decided to do it in the interest of getting before the public, and particularly the people of Mississippi, a partial narrative of what really happened at Ole Miss. This may encourage others to do the same, and as the testimony piles up, the chances of getting at the whole truth will be measurably enhanced.

Most of these letters were written to my son and daughter, both of whom lived on the campus of the University of Mississippi from infancy. At the time of the correspondence Betty (Virginia Elizabeth) was a twenty-year-old junior at Wellesley College. Bill (James William) had graduated from Harvard University in June, 1962, had been commissioned a 2nd lieutenant in the United States Army in August, and was first home on leave (September–December, 1962), then for a period (December–February, 1963) in France as a civilian, home again for a week or so, and thereafter at Fort Benning, Georgia. Their nine-year-old sister, Gail, frequently mentioned, was at home in Faculty House 6. There are several letters (self-explanatory, I hope) addressed to Mississippi and Tennessee newspapers, and a few to individuals who are identified. For the period involved I have saved well over a thousand letters from people of every frame of mind. I am aware that where two sides to a correspondence exist, it is far better historical practice to disclose both. For obvious reasons, however, only my own letters (and several of William Silver's) are printed here. To be sure, I did not answer every letter I received. Some could not be answered, some I chose not to answer in kind, many I could only answer by writing this book. There are, in addition, a few self-explanatory communications by other hands.

Published in the New York *Times*
October 2, 1962

DISAGREEMENT OF FACULTY

To the Editor of the *New York Times:*

Your coverage of the Meredith case has been generally excellent. It is not true, however, that Governor Barnett had unanimous university support.

The Mississippi professors have never reached consensus on a solution for the race problem; they range from stanch segregationist to integrationist. Hardly one among them, however, has failed to take offense at Governor Barnett's handling of the present crisis.

Education, even to the most advanced degrees, does not guarantee anyone a monopoly on truth. At the same time, men who have spent their lives mastering and teaching the various disciplines guard their "facts" jealously.

So it was when Governor Barnett committed Mississippi to a course which in all its particulars flew in the face of these facts he insulted the Ole Miss faculty's intelligence, and won its passive resistance.

The "never-never land" which the Governor described, in which Mississippi could successfully ignore Federal law, struck even the most confirmed Southerners among the educators as unparalleled folly. Most found it hard to believe that the Governor could seriously propose "interposition" in 1962. Had that not all been settled at Appomattox?

In another section of the country, the outcome of this disagreement would have been easy and predictable. The offended professors would have issued a broadside detailing the legal and historical inaccuracies in the Governor's position, and the press would have duly noted this minority sentiment.

In Mississippi, however, this was impossible, as the expression of minority views by state employed educators is not tolerated here. The faculty, realizing that disagreement with the

orthodox, official position would mean political and social reprisals, kept quiet.

Yet the *Times* should not mistake this silence for concurrence. This only gives credence to the myth of unanimity, and
serves no one but the Governor.

William Silver,
2d Lieutenant, U.S.A.R.
University, Miss., Sept. 28, 1962

University, Mississippi
October 2, 1962

Dear Betty:

Thought I had better write you something about the last few
days before it gets mixed up in my mind or before I read too
much about it all in the papers. It is hard, even now, to remember exactly what I saw on Sunday night. You should read
the various *New York Times* accounts of everything because
they are more informative than everything else together that I
have seen so far.

Sunday afternoon your mother and I drove out to the airport, getting there just after the first batch (about 175) of
marshals had arrived. They were brought to the campus in
army trucks and everyone thought that they were going to
settle down in a camp that had been provided for them, probably in the armory. So we were a little surprised to see them
half surrounding the Lyceum when we got back to the campus.
Your mother let me out by the post office and before I walked
to the Lyceum I saw unloaded at the gym a bunch of mat-
tresses. It looked as though (and this was confirmed by patrolmen) that the Highway Patrol was giving up the U.S. Armory
to the marshals and was moving into the gym. Over by the

library I passed Dr. Cabaniss who seemed a little bitter in saying to me, "I suppose you are now satisfied." My answer was noncommittal. About the time I got back to the Lyceum the other marshals had arrived and the building was completely surrounded, man to man. We all assumed that it had been decided that Meredith would be registered, and soon. There were not more than a hundred and fifty students and other onlookers present.

I talked with the chancellor in front of Peabody and he stated that the game was being played out, that Barnett knew exactly what had happened and that the Highway Patrol was there to help the marshals to keep the peace. The small crowd was curious and somewhat jovial. Certainly at that moment the chancellor thought that it was all going smoothly; in fact, he seemed somewhat amused to see the script adhered to. This must have been about six o'clock.

Then, for two hours nothing happened. That is, Meredith did not put in an appearance and no one seemed to know where he was. Actually he had come to the campus and both the feds and the school authorities had agreed that he would be registered Monday morning, that it would not be proper to register him on the "sabbath." Sometime around seven the rumor had it that Meredith was on the campus and it seemed to reasonable people that he would come to the Lyceum, else there would be no reason for the marshals' presence. But at no time was there made any announcement; in fact, as it turned out, there was not even a loudspeaker at the Lyceum. This was a major error on the part of everyone concerned.

The small crowd was slowly augmented and students began some rather frivolous activity. Yells, catcalls, etc. Two boys showed up in Confederate uniform and waved Confederate flags to the accompanying cheers. The talk got a bit nastier as time went on. A few cigarettes, lighted, were flung toward the marshals but they stood there stoically, with no show of emotion. Then a little violence began to take place, all perpetrated by students. Air was let out of the tires on the army trucks. A newspaper man, over towards the Fine Arts center, was roughed up a bit and the glass in his car smashed. The Highway Patrol, after this happened, did take off the man and his wife. Someone else got the car off by driving it across the grass on the circle. Then I saw a big man (a student, I think) snatch a camera from a newsman and dash it to the ground and stomp on it. With patrolmen looking on students began to slash the tires of the army vehicles. Somehow the canvas top of one was set afire. The driver put it out, without any help from the patrolmen. Then someone threw a rock or a coke bottle which smashed the glass in the cab of one of the trucks. About this time I saw and heard a marshal walk over to a patrolman and ask him if something couldn't be done about the crowd. The patrolman said that he couldn't do anything and walked off. The language being used by students at this time was pretty nasty and then a few rocks and (I did not see this) a piece of lead pipe was thrown from the rear of the crowd at the marshals. This time the marshals donned their gas masks (they may have done this once or twice before).

Your mother and I were on the curb but the crowd had moved up to the army trucks. There was an order, I think by the highway patrol, for the crowd to move back to the curb. A few patrolmen came up and started moving the crowd back a few feet. Your mother and I moved back and were half way to the flagpole when the tear gas shooting started. Exactly what happened is a matter of great controversy and I did not see enough to be able to say categorically what happened. Of these facts I am certain: the marshals for at least an hour had been thoroughly provoked and had taken it all with no show of emotion or movement. And the crowd was entirely student and faculty. The tear gas came in great quantity and the crowd took to its heels. We had a good start and were moving back gingerly in the dark when someone hit me broadside, knocking me to the pavement, tearing my pants, and skinning up my knees and elbow. But this was accidental: the student half apologized—he was just running faster than I was. Most people retreated at least to the Confederate monument. The marshals came about to the flagpole; then I heard them beat their sticks on the sidewalks and they retreated to the Lyceum. The grove was completely filled with tear gas for some minutes. The students were yelling like mad men and were, for the first time, indulging themselves in obscenities.

Then, for the first time, I saw the viciousness of the matter. About a half dozen cars, obviously army sedans and obviously filled with marshals, came up to the Monument and turned up past the Y building. The thought that came to me was that they were bringing in Meredith and that the marshals had simply cleared the Lyceum for the event. (I was wrong on this for Meredith was already in his room in Baxter Hall.) The students picked up bricks at the New Science building and went after the cars which slowed down for the turn. At least 150 stones and bricks were thrown at the cars, at point blank range, and most of the cars had their windows smashed, the glass shattering over the six marshals in each car. This really scared me for I knew then that this was a first class riot.

Then a series of attacks on the Lyceum took place, up through the grove. The marshals would wait and then charge, the students would fall back and then charge. About this time people, many of them pretty rough looking, began to come in from town. After awhile I heard some of them saying that they were going to keep this up till the marshals ran out of gas cartridges. (It was lucky this didn't happen because if it had the marshals would probably have had to defend themselves with their pistols—which they never used.) The reinforcements came with a couple of trucks filled with ammunition.

Gen. Walker, I was told, made a speech at the monument before attacks on the Lyceum broke out. A fire engine was brought up about as far as the flagpole but the boys running it were driven off with tear gas. Much later a bull dozer started for the Lyceum, the drivers being driven off with gas, and so they let it go by itself, aimed for the Lyceum, but it diverted itself and stopped dead. I'm not sure when the rifle fire started but from the vicinity of the old science building and the Engineering building it kept up for most of the night. Mostly twenty-two bullets, but some of much larger caliber. The firing was toward the Lyceum but mostly I think for the purpose of putting out the floodlights which had been placed in front of the Lyceum. Of course the marshals all this time were in deadly danger and, I think, some of them were hit. One marshal was hit (by what I don't know) in the throat and word got out that he was dying. The students were crying that the marshals had killed a co-ed but this turned out to be false. The girl was overcome with gas and that was all.

A few trucks of army men came up past the bridge over the IC track and as they turned the monument a tremendous gasoline fire was started in front of the old library—but the vehicles went right through the fire. This apparently enraged the rioters for, expecting another expedition, they set plans for a bigger and better fire, with cars in the highway covered with gasoline. About this time the rioters started throwing Molotov cocktails, each one of which set off a temporary blaze about the size of our house. The pavement in front of the library was pulled up to be used as obstruction material.

From then on the scene was about the same. The marshals stood their ground. Rifle and shotgun firing came more often. The newsman was shot in the back over by Ricks and was dead when he was found. Apparently the boys who had the blockade set up got tired and set it afire, burning four cars in the road in front of the old library.

I talked with a professional agitator from Atlanta who had a small car with three rifles in it. While I was there a rioter came up, said he needed a more powerful gun and the agitator handed him what he called a 30:06 and told him to bring it back later if he could. He also went to town while I was watching and brought back five gallons of gasoline. He talked to me quite freely about what he called his right wing activities. Next morning I turned his name, car license no., etc., to the marshals who had apparently picked him up already.

I guess it was after two that two squadrons of MP's marched in from the airport. They marched right through the mob to the Lyceum. Your mother and I went home about three a.m. Got to bed (had two Notre Dame students in the house) about

3:30 and was not quite asleep at 4 when a large number of rioters came into the yard. Several threw stones at the house and then the whole place was lighted up, almost like day. The crowd ran down into the gulley between our house and Evelyn Way's and we then saw the reason for their rush. This was the big push undertaken by the military. They were chasing the rioters off the campus and the lights were from their jeeps. I thought maybe the jeeps would be stuck in the little creek but they went over it like it was McAdamized. It wasn't so uneven as you might imagine because the soldiers could not fire and the rioters could throw rocks and use the few guns they had. As late as six in the morning they were still hollering in the distance, towards town.

You can read about the rest of the story in the *Times*. I've been interrupted so much since I started this that I'm quite sure it makes little sense. Today—now about 5 p.m. Tuesday—the campus is ringed with 10,000 soldiers. Meredith has been to his classes for two days. The campus is filled with rumors of students withdrawing, coeds gone hysterical, etc., but most of the rumors are false. I haven't the slightest notion of the next step although I'm sure that there are students dedicated to killing Meredith when the chance arises. I have never known such hysteria or bitterness or hatred. I don't see how it can be tempered down and the Citizen council temperament will keep it going. Barnett last night put on a great show of demagoguery. His (and Eastland's) charges against the marshals are nonsense and there are many faculty who will testify to this when and if the Congressional inquiry comes off. But that is in the future. We are all safe and sound (your mother heats the C-rations for the troops in Evelyn's yard and we have them in for watching television). I'll write more later. We all send our love.

Dad.

Resolution of University of Mississippi AAUP Chapter

October 3, 1962

RESOLVED, that we, the members of the University of Mississippi chapter of the American Association of University Professors, deploring the tragic events centered about this campus during the past few weeks, do declare our belief that:

1. While it is obvious that errors of judgment were made by those in authority on the University campus on Sunday, September 30, we have evidence that the attempt of men in prominent positions to place all the blame for the riot on the United States marshals is not only unfair and reprehensible, but is almost completely false. We encourage an investigation by the proper authorities.

2. Some news media in Mississippi have entertained irresponsible and second-hand stories in distortion of the facts, and have thereby helped to provoke a general state of confusion, alarm, and misdirected wrath. We join with those fellow Mississippians who resolved in Jackson, on October 1, their hopes that all news media would "cooperate with sane, sensible, public utterances and . . . refrain from the publication of inflammatory statements."

3. While all citizens of Mississippi and of the United States of America have the right to disagree in every peaceable and legal way with the law of the land as interpreted by the Supreme Court, it is the duty of every patriotic citizen to obey the law and to encourage others to obey it. We believe in the use of courts and ballot-boxes to state our convictions; we oppose and deplore the useless employment of clubs and missiles against fellow citizens on behalf of any conviction whatsoever.

4. Riots, weapons, and agitators have no place at a university. This university can better carry on its important part in the march toward progress and prosperity in Mississippi without any of these. With the cooperation of the overwhelming major-

ity of law-abiding Mississippi citizens, the University of Mississippi can return in the near future to the normally peaceful conditions essential to education, to Mississippi, to the nation, and to constructive work for the future.

                              Sunday, October 7, 1962
Dear Betty:

This will be short because I *must* get back to the work that I have neglected for more than a week. Inasmuch as I am on leave this year, it is *my* time that I have been "wasting." But I thought that I would write you a few thoughts that come to mind, looking back over the last seven days.

I am convinced that, starting as early as last Sunday night about 11, the University authorities have put on a campaign to blame the riot on the U.S. marshals. You have seen something of this in the papers, I'm sure. Sen. Eastland got his information from the administration and then blew it up a few hundred percent. That information was in large measure false. This is understandable but there is all sorts of evidence that the school policy hasn't changed in spite of the faculty resolutions which came solely because eye-witnesses were indignant that a fraud was being perpetrated on some very brave men. The truth of what happened is to be found in a special edition of the *Mississippian* which came out very early Monday morning. This was written by students who were eye-witnesses and is an extremely accurate statement. I'll enclose a copy of the paper if I can find one. I'll have to admit that in this instance I have been proud of the more than fifty faculty members who have signed the statement of protest.

Did you see Bill's letter in the N.Y. *Times,* on October 2? He sent it in without my knowledge and of course he wrote it before the riot. I was very pleased that he had written it. For about a week Bill has been working for the National Broadcasting Company and in his job went to press conferences, etc. and talked a great deal with federal officials of all kinds. We got word, several days ago, from the campus police and others that Bill was being singled out as an "informer" and that some of the idiots might rough him up a bit. I think that the danger of that is now passed, although he had sense enough not to go to Jackson to the game, as he had planned. (One reason for that may have been that he has been seeing a good deal of Sidna Brower, the editor of the *Mississippian.*) Just in case, we borrowed a shotgun from Bob Farley and have it in the front closet at home. I'm sure we won't have any cause to use it but it does give us a feeling of some security. Actually, I think that except for the hard core of fanatics, the students are beginning to see how foolish they have been. Booing, etc. of Meredith still goes on but my guess is that it will stop this week. Bob Farley has been enraged that the administration makes no effort to control the students and that no effort has been made to discipline those who are known to have taken part in the riot. Of course any disciplining of students would bring the wrath of the people in Jackson but it seems to me that the time has come for the administration to stand up to its obligations in the whole matter.

Troops are still all over the place and it takes a pass from the provost marshal to get into Oxford without a search of the car.—The students on the train to Jackson were apparently quiet and somewhat reflective.—Something over a hundred students have withdrawn but I suppose most will return. One girl wrote on her application for withdrawal, as her reason, "nigger."—Meredith has classes under Bickerstaff [actually, Nolan], Fortenberry, Halstead, and Marquette. No incidents have happened in class as yet.—Meredith has eaten four or five meals in the cafeteria, and has taken books out of the library.— The chancellor issued a fine statement yesterday, to the effect that Meredith would eventually be accepted by the students. Sort of wishful thinking but it may come to pass.—The Jackson papers and the legislature (and the governor) seem to have learned absolutely nothing. Reporting in the Jackson papers is as slanted as ever. The faculty were called "scalybacks" for their resolutions. But I guess some of us are used to this sort of thing.—Right now the campus is very peaceful. I think it will remain this way. Bill will probably take off for France next week, via New Orleans. Gail saw herself on national television. We are in no danger at all now, and I'm looking forward to a peaceful week and will now try to get back to my book. We all send our love.

October 10, 1962

Mr. Arthur Schlesinger
The White House
Washington, D.C.

Dear Arthur:

I hope that the enclosed quote from the President [1] is not accurate, for, as an eye-witness I can say that the events that

---

1. According to the *Allen-Scott Report* (Robert S. Allen and Paul Scott), which appeared in the Jackson *Daily News,* October 9, 1962, the following conversation took place:

"What about Oxford?" asked Senate Democratic Whip Hubert Humphrey, D. Minn.

"It was a tragic chain of events and errors," replied the President. "Gov. Barnett did not keep his word to help us maintain order, and the U.S. marshals were inexperienced and blundered in their use of tear gas. It was a very sad day."

Mr. Schlesinger wrote back and flatly denied that the President had made the statement given in the *Allen-Scott Report.* So did the Attorney General. The important point to keep in mind is that the alleged dialogue between the President and the Senator was quoted in the Junior Chamber of Commerce pamphlet, *Oxford: A Warning for Americans,* and in just about every other piece of propaganda. It is inconceivable that President Kennedy made such a statement.

transpired on Sunday night, September 30, would indicate no blunder on the part of the marshals.

I am not writing of the strategy of government officials nor of the relationship between the federal and state people. I don't know what Barnett and Robert Kennedy had to say over the phone.

But I am sure, because I was there from 5:30 p.m. till three in the morning, that the conduct of the marshals was exemplary. For a good two hours before the first firing of tear gas, the marshals took a great deal of abuse, saw federal property being destroyed in front of them, and were pelted with cigarettes (lighted) as well as a few rocks, bottles, and at least one lead pipe.

There was a conspiracy starting as early as midnight on Sunday, by the administration here and, of course, politicians in Jackson and Washington, to throw all the blame on the marshals. The Justice Department has the testimony of several dozen of us who were eye-witnesses. The faculty was so indignant over this attempted framing of the marshals that it took its most decisive action in twenty-five years.

I heard many people comment, in the period from 6 to 8 p.m. on Sunday, on the unemotionalism, the almost stoic attitude of the marshals—and I don't think that they ought to be let down by anyone. Therefore, I do hope this quote from President Kennedy is wrong.

Sincerely,
James W. Silver

October 10, 1962
University, Mississippi

Dear Betty:

I really did not think that I would be writing you so soon again, but I think that you will be interested in my first impressions of James Meredith. I came over here about 9:30 this morning and was about to go to the cafeteria for my morning cup of coffee when a Justice Department official asked me if I would talk with Meredith. The funny thing was that I had decided already that this was the day to try to get in touch with him. Anyway, Meredith came in and we talked for over an hour, about everything from his professors and courses to his own daily problems.

It was already my opinion that he had handled himself magnificently, that he had said just the right things for the press, etc. Now I feel more than ever that here is a young man, solid in his conviction that this is what he has to do, with no thought of reward that will come to him. He's a small fellow, immaculately dressed (even to a handkerchief in his pocket), reasonably talkative, with a decided mind of his own. He talks slowly with a little trace of his cotton picking days, and he makes a few mistakes in English but not many. When he says that all he wants to do is to sort of fade away from public attention and pursue his studies, I believe him. He says that in all honesty but with the knowledge that he will always be the center of attention, at least as long as he stays here. I saw no evidence that he is particularly put out with the white race; he made no criticism of anyone except for the press who keep questioning him along lines he is unwilling to talk about. I asked him whether he thought that he could keep up his present pace, whether he thought he might give up his crusade, etc., and he gave me a very sensible answer. He admits that anyone can be broken and he won't prophesy what he will do next week, but when he says this, you can see it is with the conviction that he will prevail, that he won't be broken. He is very mild-mannered, talks lowly, and is as completely self-possessed as any human I have ever seen. He is a bit put out because he is in classes which he thinks are not advanced enough for him, but thinks this will be changed in time. Admits that he can't study but thinks that he will be able to in time. He has a considerable knowledge of American history although it is slanted from the point of view of the Negro. But he is not stubborn, he doesn't think he knows it all, and I think he would be a fine person to have in my "Rise of Southern Nationalism." He told me about his plans after graduation but on the condition that I would not pass them on, and I shall not. Anyway, he will be around here a long time if he has his way. He has taken issue, as you may have seen, with both the army and the NAACP and in both cases I think he is right. He is determined not to be exploited by the NAACP and I think he will have his way on this. His chances of ever being accepted here would be blasted if he started making speeches for the NAACP in other sections of the country, or anywhere. Personally, I think he has more judgment by far than those who are handling him. I think he could sell most of the students, even here, if he had a chance to talk with them. Maybe this will come to pass.—Last night Hal Holbrook was here as Mark Twain and he used all the Twain items that had to do with slavery and the closed mind of the South and was very well received and effective, too. Of course the people who were in Fulton Chapel were not the rock-throwing kind. But there have been started a few grass root movements by faculty and students which may help to quiet the local situation somewhat. I have no real reason to be optimistic but I am at the moment from the standpoint of the local people. What the idiots in the state will do is beyond my comprehension. It is obvious that the governor, the *Clarion-Ledger,* etc. have learned nothing.

We all send our love.

                                                        Dad.

October 31, 1962

Editor, *Commercial Appeal*
Memphis, Tennessee

Dear Sir:

I have read with care and not without sympathy the "Bill of Grievances" adopted in Jackson yesterday by the "Women for Constitutional Government." I cannot and do not believe that these ladies of the South would wilfully distort the truth. I can only conclude that they have been misinformed.

Their statement included the following: "Before the marshals fired tear gas into the crowd of unarmed students at the University, not one act of violence had occurred. The students had not attacked the marshals or even threatened violence against them."

I am willing to testify under oath that on the night of September 30, after seven o'clock and *before* the firing of tear gas by the marshals:

a) I saw the beating up of a photographer, who was finally taken to safety by two State Highway Patrolmen. Every window, the headlights and the windshield of the photographer's car were smashed, and other damage was done to it.

b) I saw a young man snatch the camera from another photographer, smash it on the ground, pick it up, and smash it down again, and then jump on it.

c) I saw a faculty member roughed up by students. The professor was taken into the Lyceum Building by marshals.

d) I saw a truck belonging to the United States Army set on fire.

e) I saw the cab window of an army truck smashed with an object thrown from the crowd. Broken glass fell on the driver, a soldier of the United States.

f) I saw a young man, with a state patrolman standing beside him, let the air out of a truck tire of an army truck. I saw tires being slashed by young men from the crowd. I saw a young man putting either grass or dirt into the gas tank of an army truck.

g) I saw numerous objects, including lighted cigarette butts, bottles and stones, thrown toward the U.S. marshals in front of the Lyceum. I saw one soft drink bottle break on the sidewalk directly in front of several marshals and my wife saw what appeared to be a length of lead pipe hurled at the marshals.

h) I witnessed a conversation between a marshal and a patrolman. The marshal asked the patrolman if the patrol could not do something to quiet the crowd. The patrolman smiled, said that they couldn't do anything, and walked off.

i) I saw the marshals don their gas masks twice before they put them on for the third time in anticipation of the firing of the gas.

The events of that tragic night are burned indelibly in my memory. Many who were present that night are willing to testify to their accuracy. There is no question in my mind but that the above statement is incontrovertible.

Sincerely,
James W. Silver
Professor of History (since 1936) and
Vice-President, Southern Historical
Association

University, Miss.
November 1, 1962

Dear Betty:

Yesterday was an exciting day here and I now have the feeling that we have passed some sort of crisis. I wonder if anything like this has ever happened on any university campus; there were dozens—maybe a hundred people in all—of faculty members "patrolling" the campus last night. The Chancellor and the administration, after dragging their feet for almost a month, seem to have caught up with faculty and responsible student opinion. We were told that all we needed to do was to apprehend any student in any sort of action against Meredith or the troops or marshals and he would be summarily expelled. It was made clear that we didn't need evidence that would stand up in court, but proof beyond a reasonable doubt. That is, if two faculty members reported that a student was throwing cherry bombs, out he would go. The rumor had it that there would be a full scale offensive against Meredith last night but it did not materialize. If we can get by tonight and Friday night—with the LSU game Saturday in Baton Rouge, we may have it made.

Had a long talk with [Provost] Haywood yesterday. The administration has it pretty straight that the chief desire now of the extremists is not to *get* Meredith but to provoke an incident such as the violence of the soldiers against a student, and Barnett would use it to close the school. Closing the school is now their aim. Haywood told me that one plan was to get the University to call in the State Patrolmen to handle the trouble on the campus and that Barnett would use that as an excuse to close the university. When your mother saw a dozen patrol cars in the picnic area across from Bob Farley's, we were right suspicious. I called the Chancellor's residence and Mrs. Williams told me that the patrolmen had been called to be ready for trouble. You can see that this led to some little suspicion on our part, but I now believe, particularly in view of the peace on the campus last night, that Williams did it in all good faith.

I talked with him a few minutes early in the evening—he had just returned from Greenville—and I have never seen a more weary man. Today he is talking in convocation to all male students, to really read them the riot act. I really think that everyone involved is going to be tough on the disturbers from now on. Haywood admitted to the AAUP that the administration had not done its job, that it had assumed that things were getting better, and had relaxed.

It is the consensus of the administration, the CIC, the Justice Dept. people, that there is a hard core of not more than twenty-five students who are not here for study but solely to agitate the Meredith business. They are being supplied from the outside with encouragement and with ammunition. For instance, on Monday $200 worth of cherry bombs were handed out from a laundry bag in Mayes, B-37. This room and, in fact, a whole dormitory was searched last night at bayonet point, but nothing much was found. I guess this was yesterday afternoon for Haywood told me that once the administration had decided on the search and the Army had agreed to do it, it wasn't ten minutes before he got a call saying: "Come on up to Lester Hall. You'll find it clean." It is difficult to tell who is on whose side in this business.

I have been right proud of many of the faculty, even though some have gone somewhat hysterical—some advocate telling the State that we shall go out to get qualified Negro students. But the group in the AAUP have really stood up to the administration (and the State) and now the administration at least has come to their point of view. Among other things our group told the chancellor that they never wanted to hear again the statement that he was following such and such a course "to save faculty jobs." The idea was that this was no longer of any real importance, which, I think, is the case.

The Silver family has really been mixed up in all this, except, perhaps, Gail. And even Gail talks about the riot and cherry bombs and soldiers as if they were normal parts of existence, as I suppose they are here. Bill is the regular NBC correspondent here now, and has been on the air a half dozen times lately.

Trouble is that you never know when he will appear. Last night he had fifteen minutes to write his story and read it over the phone to New York where it was taped and then it came back. He's pretty much all aflutter. But he does a good job and is quite superior about it all. He wrote an editorial for the *Mississippian,* on the Gowries (see *Intruder in the Dust*) and how we don't need them in the University. He and Sidna Brower, the very intelligent editor of the paper, from Memphis, are together a good part of each day.

Yesterday's *Clarion-Ledger* carried a little item on the front page about my having breakfast with Meredith, which was part true—I talked with him while he ate breakfast and then he came over to the office where we talked another hour. I'm still enormously impressed with him. I have turned over to him autographed books which were sent to me (at my request) from Frank Freidel, Rembert Patrick, Bell Wiley, Arthur Schlesinger, Dewey Grantham, George Tindall, John Hope Franklin (all five of his), Vann Woodward, Arlin Turner, and several others. The beginning of a right nice library, for an undergraduate. This morning's *Clarion-Ledger* has a UPI quote from "Professor Jim Silver" that many of the faculty now believe that it is just a question as to whether the Citizen's Council can run the University. It is also in today's NY *Times.* About three this morning the NY *Post* called me and the night editor, getting his cue from the early edition of the *Times,* talked about thirty minutes. What he has printed I have no idea. Anyway, this *is* the central problem and the sooner it is out in the open, the better we'll be. The stuff I sent to the *Reporter* ought to be out by now, but I haven't yet seen it. Incidentally, your mother went to the phone last night; we expected to hear the voice of a Delta crackpot but the call turned out to be authentic. Yesterday I sent letters to the *Clarion-Ledger* (which will either not print the letter or will distort it) and the *Commercial* (which, I think, will print the letter), taking off on the inaccuracy (downright lies, actually) of the thousand women who met in Jackson Tuesday to tell the truth, they said, to the world about the crisis up here. Just a bunch of froth and nonsense and I tried to tell them so, in dignified language. Well, we'll see what comes of this. I wrote you, I think, about my talks at Earlham College. Next week I'm to talk at the Southern Historical Assoc. meeting in Miami, with Woodward presiding, at the only special session the Assoc. has ever called, that is, in addition to the regular program.

Last night we locked the house, took Gail down to the Willises, and your mother, Bill, and I were on the campus to see the fun. As I have said, nothing developed and we went home fairly early, about 11:30. In front of the door there was an enormous pumpkin, with grinning teeth, lighted for all marauders to see. Which means that Gail went on her regular course of "trick and treat" and came home with a sackful of what she considers good things to eat. Of course, they will lie around the house for a couple of days and then be thrown away.

There have been some choice communications coming to faculty members. Russell Barrett, for instance, has now joined the "Honorary Nigger" club and has gotten calls practically every night. We have been spared this, as yet. Our lives are considerably more boring than this letter would indicate. I don't think that we are in any danger, though we try to be cautious. I believe this "hard core" will be eliminated or really driven underground in the drive now taking place. Next Wednesday your mother and I are flying to Miami for *five* days. Gail will stay with the Willises. By that time Bill may have gone to France; he hates to leave the excitement here and is still waiting notice of his transfer to Intelligence. (Maybe he will be assigned to the campus, a much more interesting place than Cuba.)

I've *got* to get back to work. We all send our love. For further details, see the NY *Times*.

Box 404
University, Mississippi
November 8, 1962

Mr. Jack Olson
710 Valley Road
Kosciusko, Mississippi

Dear Mr. Olson,

My father, Professor Silver, is out of town this week, presiding as Vice President of the Southern Historical Society. He will want to answer your letter when he returns; but in the meantime let me put your mind to rest about some of your twenty points.

Father was born in upstate New York (a traditionally conservative part of the country), but moved to North Carolina when he was five or six years old. He received his B.A. degree from North Carolina, his M.A. from Peabody (Nashville) and his Ph.D. from Vanderbilt University. He has taught at Ole Miss since 1936.

Father believed in the New Deal, but he is becoming more conservative, I believe, as he grows older. He is certainly not a pacifist, and endorses our efforts in Cuba, South East Asia, etc. I myself am in the Army, and am of course ready to serve in any of these places with his blessing. One thing he does believe strongly is that a State can't be allowed to ignore National laws, as that would make our country weak in its battle against communism.

My army training may clear up one of your points. A tear gas gun does not fire a "bomb," but only gas, and the shell ejects to the side. My mother (Margaret Thompson Silver, from Montgomery), an assistant in the Dean's office here, assures me that no girls were hurt in any way during the riot.

Father's life has been devoted to the teaching of American history, and he knows a lot more about constitutional government than I will ever know. He believes in it firmly. He has a reputation of scrupulous fairness to all his students, and I'm sure that the grades he gives them are based on merit alone.

I have not covered all of your questions, but Father will attend to that when he returns. I hope, however, that the above will be of some use to you.

Sincerely,

/s/   James William Silver

November 15, 1962

Mr. Edgar Shook
Time Bureau Chief
1020 Rhodes-Haverty Building
Atlanta 3, Georgia

Dear Mr. Shook:

Without questioning your motivation nor your integrity, I would like to comment on your article concerning the University of Mississippi.

You say that Chancellor Williams "did nothing to head off the riot." This is true only in the narrowest of senses. The administration, to my certain knowledge, had been making plans for well over a year (1) to keep the University open, and (2) to prevent violence. These plans were based on the certainty that sooner or later James Meredith or someone like him would enter the University. It is impossible for me to delineate these plans but I can assure you that they were intelligent and practical. It is true, I believe, that on the night of September 30, the Chancellor was of the opinion that an agreement had been made between Attorney-General Kennedy and Governor Barnett and that the United States marshals and the Mississippi Highway Patrol would act in concert. So it appeared to those of us who saw the marshals enter the campus and surround the

Lyceum. I agree that from about 6:30 that night until 8:00 p.m. there was a disconcerting lack of liaison between the forces of the State and the federal government and I would be the last person to assess the blame. I also know that the administration thought until the last minute that Mr. Meredith would be brought in on Monday morning and that plans had been made to control the situation as of then—by such means as an edition of the *Mississippian* specially put out to caution students as to their conduct, leaflets to same effect, and radio talks by the Chancellor and student leaders.

Your statement "To hunt down possible integrationists, professors must sign yearly disclaimer affidavits . . ." There were many other reasons for these affidavits—such as the exposing of Communists. We all agree, I think, that these were bad but I have never thought of them as even principally concerned with the integration crisis, although this might have been the case since Meredith's application for admission.

Your statement "the barring of one scholar because he once entertained Negroes in his home." The scholar in this case was Professor Mathews of Emory University and a former history professor here. His wife Marcia teaches at Morehouse College in Atlanta and, as a part of her work, regularly entertains Negroes in her home. She wrote about this in an article for the *Saturday Evening Post* which contained several pictures showing the reception in the Mathews' home for whites and blacks. Our history department here protested strongly against the administration edict. My main criticism of your statement is the inclusion of the word "once."

Your statement "In one two-year period, 25 per cent of the faculty quit." is, I think, questionable. Just what 25 per cent of the faculty would include I do not know. Does this mean professors only? Does it include staff members and graduate students who teach? Does it include people who were hired for one year only, or for a short period? What I'm trying to say is that your 25 per cent is meaningless unless more precisely defined. I still don't quite understand the meaning of the "associate professor syndrome"—but even if this is an accurate description, I

can't see that "an undemanding job in which a man can almost
retire" would necessarily have much connection with the attrac-
tion of "men willing to take low pay . . ." I do not know of
any case in which a man *came here* because of the prospect of
an undemanding job. I think everyone has come here in the
way I came, that is because this University offered at that time
the best I could obtain. Sticking around when a professor has a
chance to leave at a higher salary is something else again but I
shall not go into that.

I think that I did make the exact quotation you attributed to
me—"In a sophomore class of 30, before the end of the first
month I'm talking to only five." I hardly think that I meant it
to be taken literally and I'm afraid the reader may have taken
it so. Even so, I have taught at a good many other institutions
such as Emory, Missouri, Virginia, and Harvard, and I think
that I would make similar though not such strong statements
about those places. To be honest, I can't make the exact comparison because I have not taught sophomore classes at these
institutions and my teaching has been mainly in the summer
schools when students as a whole are not up to the regularly
scheduled ones. I do admit, though, that I did make this statement to you and that I have made it many times to the classes
themselves, but I think in an effort to prod along some of those
who might be "saved."

As to your statement that from Mississippi "good students go
elsewhere," this is only partly true and I think it might be said
about almost any southern or western state. My son attended
Harvard, as you know, and was selected from the State of
Mississippi as a candidate for a Rhodes scholarship. His record
at Harvard was about a "B" average; I do think that if he had
attended the University of Mississippi he might well have obtained a Rhodes scholarship because his record would have been
much better than it was in competition with the obviously better student body that Harvard has. On the other hand, a great
many national merit scholarship winners, who could go to Harvard, do choose the University of Mississippi. The great tragedy
is that many leave the State after having obtained their under-

graduate degree. But that cannot well be blamed on the University.

You mention "scholarly James Meredith." At this very moment Mr. Meredith seems to be on the verge of failing out. Please don't misunderstand me here. I believe honestly that Meredith has many admirable qualities; in fact, I think that he is one of the most remarkable people I have ever met and he has my admiration. But I doubt if he could be called, in the wildest moments of admiration, a scholarly person.

You write that Chancellor Williams has long *served* rather than *led*. This would take a lot of defining. In some ways I agree with you; but it is also true that in a great many areas the Chancellor has been an outstanding leader. As for his being "public-relations-conscious on a statewide basis," this is obviously accurate but it is just as obviously acknowledged to be a requisite for leadership in any state-supported institution. If this were Chancellor Williams' only qualification it would not be enough but this is not the case.

It seems to me that you have some of your key chronology mixed up. You put events in this order: (1) the professors volunteered statements on October 1. (2) They created a committee of nine. . . . (3) The AAUP made its statement about the press of Mississippi. It is true that (1) did occur on October 1. But your third event came two days later on October 3. And your second statement came much later, I would guess about November 1. The patrolling of the campus began either on October 30 or 31, I think the latter. But it really became effective on the most crucial night of all, Thursday, November 1, after the Chancellor had thoroughly endorsed it. It had been supported by Dean Love the night before, when the Chancellor was in Greenville making a very effective speech in an attempt to save the University.

I don't really think that the "committee of nine" has ever *assigned* the night patrols, although it is true, I think, that this may have been done informally. For instance, I was never assigned to do any of this duty, although I did perform it for several nights. It is also true that on the crucial Thursday night, the faculty received tremendous help from the Highway Patrol and more especially from the troops and marshals on the campus. This was indeed a community enterprise with everyone involved. The committee of nine was itself suggested, I believe, by Provost Haywood.

In my second quoted statement I did not mean to imply that the University was *finished* if anyone was fired. I do think that the individual faculty member has had more freedom of action, at least in his own mind, during this whole crucial period after the "Monday night riot."

I don't think that you made it clear that the faculty and administration have been irrevocably bound together since that Thursday night, November 1, and that we had been moving in that direction for some time. Nor that everyone was convinced that things had been quieting down for the two weeks before the "Monday night riot." It seems to me that we were all caught napping in that period of increasing calm. Nor did you mention that the administration was kept from any action from the night of September 30 until the federal forces turned over their evidence to the University. Nor that Chancellor Williams made a major contribution in his effort to line up hundreds of leaders in the State for his policy of cracking down, which did come on November 3. Nor did you mention the gigantic efforts of Dean Love through the whole crisis to bring order to the campus. One other thing: it seems to me that you should have talked with Provost Charles Haywood to get something of the administration story before you printed your article.

Now, please let me reaffirm that I believe that you made an honest and intelligent effort to tell a complicated story in a relatively few words. I don't think that I could have done anything like as good a job, that is if I had come to the campus in a fluid situation which changed dramatically from day to day. Your quotations were accurate. I think that some of your understanding of the situation here was phenomenally good and that your "intuition" was excellent. I do not question your motivation, your honesty, nor your integrity. I feel responsible myself for not having given you more information than I did give you. This whole business has been the most emotional experience of my life and I have gone through a number of crises in my own thinking and action. I'm sure that I have made some incorrect decisions but I also know that at times I did the exact right thing. I don't think that any outsider could have written a story that would be pleasing to us in all aspects. When you were here I was still under the impression that the patrolling of the campus by faculty was not only unique in this country but positively inspiring. I still believe this, for the most part, but there has also been some sober second-thought that has taken a bit of the edge off my earlier convictions.

Please don't think that I have been personally affronted by what you have written. I think that your article has done us more good than harm and I am most certainly not writing you because of any least fear of personal reprisal. But I have read your article at least a half dozen times, and I felt that I should write you as I have above.

Sincerely,
James W. Silver
Professor of History

cc: Chancellor John D. Williams
Provost Charles Haywood
Dr. Gordon Sweet
Dean Leston Love

November 29, 1962

The Editor, *The Clarion-Ledger*
Jackson, Mississippi

Dear Sir:

In the *Dan Smoot Report* for October 15, 1962 may be found the lurid tale by a nameless Ole Miss student whose interview was broadcast over Station KPCN, Grand Prairie, Texas and published in the *Dallas-Park Cities Digest* on Ocober 8.

This alleged student told of a gassed co-ed brought to his fraternity house the night of the riot and hospitalized for two days. Then he really loosened up:

> "The federal marshals . . . shot . . . two of my fra-
> ternity brothers—one of them was shot in the stomach
> with a shotgun, another was shot in the arm. . . . One
> of my brothers had a brick thrown from a jeep—hit
> him in the head—with the possible loss of his eye, and
> 22 stitches above his eye.
>
> "One boy was shot between the eyes in the head by a
> marshal. A fraternity brother saw this. He was carried
> to the hospital and, on arrival, was dead. . . .
>
> "There have been reports that there have been two
> girls shot with guns. They say that one is in critical con-
> dition and the other has died."

A casual reading of the Mississippi press or a simple call to University officials would have demonstrated the incredible fraudulence of the above statement. Mr. Smoot had at least a week in which to verify it. Therefore, it seems logical to assume that he knew what he was doing.

How much of the present anguish of Mississippians may be traced to irresponsible declarations by those who, for whatever motives, have led the people astray? Does any cause, however just or sacred, require a foundation of falsehood, duplicity, and deceit?

Sincerely,
James W. Silver
Professor of History

December 10, 1962

Editor, *The Clarion-Ledger*
Jackson, Mississippi

Dear Sir:

In this morning's paper your columnist Charles M. Hills described and quotes from "a young official of Patriotic American Youth." According to Mr. Hills, the youth "was with the National Guard at Ole Miss, got in the thick of things and personally observed the marshals open fire with tear gas."

"The young man recited that the marshals not only fired, but some of them declared that the resisting students 'ought to be machine-gunned down.' "

Mr. Hills also states that the Kennedys disarmed the state highway patrolmen, something they will be surprised to know.

There was no national guard unit on the Ole Miss campus when the marshals fired the tear gas.

Either the "young official of Patriotic American Youth" has developed a super-enthusiasm about his own conduct on the night of the riot or he has been misquoted by Mr. Hills.

I hesitate to continue to beat a dead horse but, it seems to me, we should be more careful about sticking to facts.

Sincerely,
James W. Silver
Professor of History

Written December 19, 1962
Published in the *Clarion-Ledger*
December 21, 1962

Editor, *The Clarion-Ledger*
Jackson, Mississippi

Dear Sir:

In a genial, holiday mood the Citizens Council's magazine has suggested that it need not be mandatory for University faculty members to sign a new oath of loyalty to the State of Mississippi. The fine gesture is, I am sure, appreciated.

Still, this enlightened policy does not get to the heart of the problem of subversion. I have a suggestion.

By law every state employee is required to make a yearly statement of the organizations to which he belongs. Using state funds for the necessary secretarial help, the Citizens Council can easily check each instructor's membership list with that of the organizations already decreed by the Council (December 6, 1959) to be subversive of the Mississippi Way of Life. These include: American Red Cross, Catholic Welfare Congress, Episcopal Church, Federal Bureau of Investigation, Improved Benevolent and Patriotic Order of Elks of the World, Jewish War Veterans, Methodist Church, National Lutheran Council, Department of the Air Force, Interstate Commerce Commission, and the Young Women's Christian Association.

If a professor admits that he belongs to one of these organizations, off with his head!

There will be difficulties, of course. Let us say that an instructor belongs to the Methodist Church or the Air Force AND the Citizens Council or Patriotic American Youth. Such a confused state of affairs will call for the wisdom of a Solomon. I would suggest, in such a case, that a Supreme War Council, made up of Mr. Simmons, make the necessary judgment. He might verify his findings with a postal card referendum.

I would urge strongly that a professor who has recanted, at least five years ago, and now disavows an organization (i.e., the Y.W.C.A.) to which he has belonged, may well be put on disciplinary probation.

Such a course, with modifications the Council may deem necessary, will bring a consensus of conformity to every college campus in Mississippi by Valentine's Day.

Sincerely,
James W. Silver
Professor of History

December 31, 1962

Mrs. Sam Neill
Leland, Mississippi

Dear Mrs. Neill:

I am not sure that this address (from the *Commercial Appeal*) is complete enough but I hope that you will get this note.

It seems to me that there is and probably should be much disagreement among Mississippians as to the basic causes of our present trouble and particularly the riot at Ole Miss. I'm rather sure that you and I would have considerable disagreement about these things. I would like very much for us to have the chance to talk about Mississippi's problems for I assume that we are both much concerned about the State's future.

On the other hand, I don't feel that I can indulge in an urge to engage in newspaper controversy where motivation, beliefs, etc. are involved, simply because it is so difficult for well-meaning people to get across their ideas in short letters. Also, it is extremely time consuming.

Whether you or anyone can get a casualty list from the De-

partment of Justice (as to the marshals, at least) I don't have
any idea. In my various letters to the editor I have not been
trying to defend the federal government or anyone else—nor
am I concerned with attacking anyone. (This, of course, does
not mean that I do not have convictions—but, again, I think
it fruitless to indulge them in newspaper correspondence.)

As for the Smoot Report, I *know* that the part I criticized
was false. For instance, there were rumors here for days about
a girl who had been killed, etc. I talked at length with Dean
of Women, Katherine Rea, who (also having heard the rumors) made a complete check of every single woman student
on the campus. This took a good deal of time but it demonstrated that there was not a single girl who was hurt, let alone
killed. I talked with Dean Leston Love (who has charge of
the men, here) who made similar checks which demonstrated
the falsity of the Smoot Report. These two deans are the people
in charge and you can get from them a factual statement, if you
wish.

I believe that both you and I are interested in "the hard
light of Truth." Every statement I have made to the papers
is the truth, as I have been permitted to dig it out and understand it.

> Sincerely,
> James W. Silver

January 7, 1963

Mr. Arthur Schlesinger, Jr.
The White House
Washington, D.C.

Dear Arthur:

Though this is written on the spur of the moment I hope that it will make some sense. I have just completed about a two-hour talk with James Meredith and I am convinced, in spite of all his mystical talk, that he will not pull out at the end of this semester. At least he did say flatly that he wouldn't do it without serious consultation with some of his friends here. It is difficult at times to keep up with his reasoning for he is a very involved human being.

I'm sure that there will be all sorts of pressure on him from the outside, especially from the NAACP, etc. Also he is at this moment being confronted with the TV cameras, etc. Meredith is pretty damned stubborn and this pressure may help consolidate within him some of the thoughts he has at the moment about leaving. There isn't much we can do about the pressure, though I believe a half dozen of us here on the campus know more about how to "handle" him than anyone on the outside. At the moment, I am somewhat optimistic.

What I'm writing about is this: If, around the first of February, the situation becomes difficult and if, for any reason, Meredith is still determined to leave the University of Mississippi, I think that I shall try to get in touch with you in the hope that you can arrange a telephone conversation for him with the President. Only as a last resort, Meredith should be told by the President that he must go through with his present year of studies. I am telling no one of this letter and I don't think that my suggestion need ever be carried out, but perhaps it will come to this last ditch effort. Whether this is necessary, it seems to me, should be left to those of us in daily contact with Meredith. I'm not going into the reasoning behind this letter but I do feel compelled to write it. Again, I am hopeful at the moment, but if we need to read the riot act to Meredith, let's do it.

Sincerely,
Jim Silver

University, Mississippi
January 14, 1963

Dear Betty and Bill:

I probably won't get very far with this because there is another AAUP meeting coming up at five o'clock, and while I'm not sure as to what the boys are up to this time, I have a feeling that—well I must have had some sort of feeling, but now it is Tuesday morning (the 15th) and I haven't the slightest idea as to what kind of feeling I had. The meeting took place but not much of anything happened except to call another meeting shortly. The AAUP boys have been resoluting all over the place though, including another indictment of the Chancellor for his lack of control in the cafeteria for most of last week after Meredith's announcement (last Monday) that he might leave if things didn't quiet down. For three days the demonstrations were rather boisterous, some of them being likened to prison demonstrations against certain inmates. Then on Friday night the administration did crack down, with ID cards being necessary for admission to the cafeteria and one student being shipped for some kind of action against Meredith on Thursday. All of this, of course, came out of Meredith's Monday press conference. It was as if he asked for and wanted more trouble; in any case he got it. Since then he has had a tire on his car cut up and has been given a good deal of trouble I'm sure he would otherwise have missed.

Willis, Barrett, and I (with a few other witnesses, including

John Hutcherson) talked with Meredith for a couple of hours last Monday afternoon. I'm afraid that we didn't learn very clearly what Meredith has in mind. Willis kept asking him specifically what he wanted but got no very clear answer. Whether James Howard will leave us I have no idea about but it is still my judgment that this is all a pressure play of his and that he will not leave. I guess the main reason that I think he will not leave is that it isn't in the nature of things for him to do so. It would mean a great victory for the Citizens Council and, more, it would probably strengthen them in their desire and attempt to keep the next Negro out by force. It does seem that there is a qualified Negro who might enter the Law School next September. But with Meredith ousted, for whatever reason, the other fellow would have little chance, it seems to me, of getting in here alive. Paul Flowers had a column yesterday attacking Meredith but Paul's facts, judgments, etc. were pretty sorry. Like so many he equates the injustices of the state and federal governments, which is a rather stupid thing to do. God knows the Washington people have made mistakes but they have been infinitesimal compared to the gross errors coming out of Jackson. Anyway, people act as though they think Meredith ought to behave rationally and as they would when it must be true that if Meredith were an ordinary person he wouldn't have gotten here in the first place. Not that I condone his press conference or his action—I'm as put out with him as the rest, I suppose, but I still think that he has his own reasons for doing as he has done. I still believe in him and think and hope that he will do the right thing when the chips are down. The only right thing, as I see it, for him to do is to return regardless of what it does to him. In other words, it seems to me that he has volunteered for the duration and can't pull out in anything less. The NAACP is very much worried and apparently thinks that he will leave. I still think he will not. I also believe that his grades will be sufficiently high for him to stay here. He is bright but whether he has done or has been able to do any real studying is something I don't know. I have one last power play myself which I'm going to pull if there is an opportunity for it at the last moment, but I can't very well divulge it here.

I have been before the federal grand jury, to tell of the agitator whose activities I witnessed the night of the riot. It seems to me that the jury must indict him on my evidence alone. Whether they or rather some other jury will ever convict him is something else again. Duncan Gray and Nolan Fortenberry testified yesterday and I'm supposed to be called back again. Also, this morning a couple of justice department men were in the office for over an hour, going over my general testimony about the riot, and suggesting that this material might be used in the case against Barnett and Johnson. I can't quite see how it is pertinent but I'm willing to testify wherever it may do some good. Your mother rewrote her testimony and her nine pages make a first class account of the riot, and are especially rough on the State Highway Patrol.

Now, I must get back to work. Bill writes from Florence but may be in Nice by now. We are all well. Had a couple of good parties over the week end. One dinner at Justine's in Memphis. We all send our love.

Dad.

January 16, 1963

Mr. Arthur Schlesinger, Jr.
The White House
Washington, D.C.

Dear Arthur:

I have just had a satisfactory talk with Jim Meredith. He starts taking his examinations on Friday (or maybe tomorrow) and completes them on Tuesday afternoon (the 22nd). He has promised me that he will talk with me again before he leaves.

There is no question in my mind about this: Meredith has not yet made a decision as to whether he is coming back next semester. He has "put it out of his mind" for the duration of the exam period. Yesterday or today he received a letter from his mother telling him that he was on the wrong track (thinking about leaving) and this has shaken him up more than he is willing to admit. He suggested that the two of us might get together during the between-semester period to talk about his objectives, etc. (This comes from the fact that we have never really been able to communicate—it has always seemed to me that his aims are so vague and mystical that he himself doesn't really know what he is thinking—and it may be that I just can't comprehend him.) Anyway, we have never had the chance to sit down and talk for hours, partly because someone is always interrupting and because he is so damned busy all the time. I suppose what I'm trying to say now is that I still believe that he will come back, that I am even more optimistic than when I last wrote you.

On the other hand it would be stupid to take anything for granted in dealing with a man such as Meredith is. If the situation looks black (no pun intended) at any time during the vacation period, I want to feel free, and I do feel free, to get in touch with you to see about taking whatever drastic action may seem required.

Yours,
Jim Silver

January 18, 1963
(not published)

Mr. Paul Flowers
The Commercial Appeal
Memphis, Tennessee

Dear Paul:

Upon seeing your announcement that an official of the University of Mississippi is reprinting your columns of January 14 and 15, I read them once again, and once again I failed to discover the "overload of grief, compassion and charity" you claim for yourself. Instead, I find bitterness, rancour and, what is worse, ignorance.

Your resounding words are at fault, it seems to me, for the following reasons:

1) You equate "Federal stupidity and state demagoguery"— ("irresponsible politicians on state and national levels")— which is nothing less than an intellectually sloppy performance indicating your unwillingness to face the facts. The agents of the Federal government made some mistakes in carrying out their responsibilities; the record of persistent, deliberate, and fundamental irresponsibility on the state level, by contrast, drew headlines and editorials in the *Commercial Appeal* when it came to one of its critical peaks last September 30.

2) Your denunciation of James Meredith's criticism of the U.S. Army conveniently neglects his simultaneous blast at the NAACP. To have included the latter would have blunted your charge that Meredith is merely a tool of the NAACP.

3) As for Meredith having invited "the die-hard opposition to bracket him with all other Negroes who ask for equality of opportunity," it seems clear that a man with a mission would consider this an honor, and would be indifferent to the wishes of the die-hard opposition.

4) Instead of the "inflammatory scripts prepared by the NAACP, each incident calculated to precipitate more strife,"

there is overwhelming evidence that Meredith makes his own plans, usually without script. Furthermore, if you have been able to penetrate his mind to the point of explaining his motivation, you have done something well beyond the capacity of those who are associated with him. Mr. Meredith is a very complicated human being; above all, an individualist.

5) You write of Meredith's "reckless and unfounded charges of harassment and persecution; a weak and cowardly effort to shift responsibility for his academic failure. . . ." This implies, at the present moment, an unwarranted omniscience on your part (regarding his "academic failure"), and is evidence of a colossal misunderstanding of the man's character—commensurate only with your shallow insight into his harassment.

6) It would be difficult for you to specify Meredith's "wild tirades against the university administration." His words have been mild indeed compared with the criticisms of the faculty members in the AAUP. On the contrary, Meredith has been almost unfailing in his favorable comments on the university—administration, faculty and student body.

It seems to me that when you write of Meredith's "ignoble failure and treason to the nobler ideals of a cause," you convict yourself of the very faults you attribute to a man obviously beyond your comprehension. I say this with no malice because I believe that Meredith is beyond the understanding of all of us. Nor do I think his fellow Negroes have reason to be bitter toward him.

Your columns, however well-intentioned and filled with honest, righteous indignation, tend to place you among the "silent multitudes," those pious souls who have kept quiet throughout the storm, waiting patiently with a restless anger to pounce on the first (or the second) false step of a much beleaguered and maligned individual.

Written, I hope, with some compassion and charity:

Yours,
James W. Silver

January 23, 1963

Mr. Arthur Schlesinger, Jr.
The White House
Washington, D.C.

Dear Arthur:

Just before he left yesterday, Jim Meredith came by the office for a last little talk before leaving for the semester break. He was in a fine mood, thinking that he had made the grades required for his readmission on the 30th or 31st. We talked some about a proposal which will, if he returns, enable him to get acquainted with a good many of the majors and graduate students in political science, and this seemed to please him.

Though I am as optimistic as at any time since I started writing you about this, there is still a good deal of doubt about Meredith's coming back here. He told me that he would be in Jackson for about ten days and would not go to Memphis, where I had planned to meet him and talk with him at some length. So, after his departure, I called his lawyer (A. W. Willis, Memphis, Tenn.) who seemed to be as convinced as I am of the necessity for Meredith to return to Ole Miss.

Inasmuch as Mr. Willis plans to go to Jackson to talk with Meredith, I told him about the plan I had suggested to you about the possibility of a last minute plea or "order" from the President, if it were absolutely necessary. And as I will not be in Jackson, I suggested that in the case of a real emergency, he get in touch with you. I earnestly hope that this will not be necessary but don't be too surprised if you get a call from Mr. Willis.

Meredith is staying in Jackson. Just when Mr. Willis will be down there I'm not sure but it seems likely that he will have a good deal to do with Jim's final decision. I still believe that his decision will be to return to the University for at least another semester, but I want to do everything possible to make this necessary decision certain.

If there is anything that occurs to you that I might do, please call on me.

Sincerely,
Jim Silver

January 25, 1963

Mr. James B. Nicholson
Byram, Mississippi

Dear Mr. Nicholson:

I am writing you as one who was greatly heartened by the "Born of Conviction" statement in the January 2 issue of the *Mississippi Methodist Advance*. This resolution was another bit of evidence that there is still some chance for Mississippi to follow the right course, although, frankly, I see no reason for optimism for the near future.

In November of this year I shall deliver as my presidential address to the Southern Historical Association what I hope will be a first rate exposition on what I consider to be Mississippi's "closed society," with particular reference to the control of public opinion.

I have no intention of using the names of people except where they are already in the public domain as the result of newspaper stories, etc. But I am most eager to hear from you, as one of the 28 signers of the statement referred to, as to what pressures have been put on you since the statement was made public. I would not expect you to write me a very long letter but it would be most helpful (in what I consider a very worthwhile cause) if you would send me a sort of outline, listing perhaps quantitatively what your community has done to you since January 2 and relating in some degree how it has affected you. I am concerned, of course, with the kind of pressure you have been subject to, the type of people it has come from, etc.

Again, I want to make it clear that your name will not be connected with any conclusion I may be able to come to from the letters I hope to get from each of the ministers involved. This is a most serious project and its ultimate object is that it will contribute, perhaps someday, toward convincing Mississippians that they must allow ministers, educators, etc. to speak their minds if the State is to make the right decision in any given crisis that may come along.

It may be true that I do not have the right to ask you to take your time for this project but I do hope that you will find it possible to do so.

Most sincerely,
James W. Silver
Professor of History

January 28, 1963

Chancellor John D. Williams
University, Mississippi

Dear Chancellor:

I would like to make it clear, just for the record, that in talking with Ben Thomas of the Associated Press (whose article appeared in yesterday's *Clarion-Ledger*), I did not say some of the things attributed to me.

It was unfortunate that in the printed article the word "protect" came out "protest" and thus changed the meaning of the paragraph—but I think this must have been evident to any discriminating reader.

What made me shudder was the statement: "I'm probably the only white man in Mississippi who will speak up for Meredith himself." This is obviously untrue and if it were true

I think I would be the last person to say so. I did tell Mr. Thomas that I had written Paul Flowers a letter of protest against the errors in his column of January 14. As a matter of fact my protest was quite strong because I thought Flowers had maligned a man's character needlessly. Mr. Flowers did not print the letter nor did the *Commercial Appeal* last Sunday. I showed Mr. Thomas this letter and suggested that if it were printed it would probably be the first time James Meredith had been defended by a white Mississippian, in print that is. As the statement appears in Thomas' column, it is factually wrong and, more important, is really taken out of original context.

When I told Thomas that some of the men leaving were irreplaceable, I not only had in mind but told him specifically I was talking about Bill Willis. I feel the same way about Sam Clark. As you well know, I am less optimistic about the future than you are.

I write this solely for the purpose of letting you know that I feel that Mr. Thomas did not quote me accurately, and I hasten to add that I do not believe that this was from any feeling of malevolence. What he wrote just did not come out the way it should have come out.

Sincerely,
James W. Silver

Graduate 16, University, Mississippi
January 30, 1963   1:12 p.m.

Dear Bill and Betty:

Since the first of last September I have wished so many times that I had kept a diary, not so much because events cannot be recapitulated, but because it is impossible to recover the feelings and emotion and excitement except perhaps in extreme instances. I still, I think, can recapture the anguish I felt on the morning of October 1st when I saw the flaming gasoline thrown on the first contingent of MP's when the men were marching between the Y and the Fine Arts Building.

Not that what I'm going to write you about now is particularly exciting, but there is a lull in the "news" and rumors and maybe I can put down something of the way I feel. This morning Meredith announced in Jackson that he was coming back, which, of course, pleased me. I didn't feel any particular thrill of exhilaration because I have been pretty sure all the way through that the logic of events would force him to come back. But I felt satisfied and thought of how down in the dumps I would have been if his announcement had been the opposite.

Anyway, about noon your mother dashed into the office with the request that I leave town immediately. It was apparent that she was quite upset by news or rumor that she had heard a few minutes before in the Lyceum. This was all hush-hush and I had to promise that I wouldn't reveal the source before she would tell me much of anything. How straight this all is cannot be told at the moment though it seems certain that via phone calls from Jackson it has been learned that the Citizens Council boys and those close to Barnett are damned excited. According to the story there are rowdies already on the way from Jackson who are going to "get" a number of faculty people whose names have been in the paper, etc. These would include Barrett and Farley and Silver and perhaps Willis. At least these were the names used. Who is coming, how many are coming, no one seems to know. Barnett is supposed to have said that the Highway Patrol would not be used to stop anyone coming for the purpose of getting these people. So I guess we cannot depend on help from the Highway Patrol. There have been meetings in the Lyceum about all this but there has been no information leaked, as far as I know. I can't imagine the Silver family getting much protection from the division heads. I have heard that the campus police force has been increased by three men, a fact or rumor that doesn't give me much satisfaction, either. The Governor is reported to have said that there will be blood shed, but whose blood and by whom no one seems to know.

There are some marshals in the vicinity and, I hope, 300 military police. I'm not particularly concerned about our safety as long as these people are in the vicinity. Dutch [Mrs. Silver] has heard, too, that Meredith will be flown in and registered before eight a.m. tomorrow. This also is a rumor. Everything is.

How do I feel about all this? I'll be damned if I know. I do think that there may well be trouble tonight. We plan to have Gail stay out at the Tatums. Beyond that I don't intend to do anything though I rather imagine that we won't get a hell of a lot of sleep. I assume that the Army will be informed. But I have no great feeling of emotion, one way or another. Dutch wanted me to leave town which, I suppose, in some instances I might do. But I'm not going to leave as the result of a rumor . . . and, anyway, I think that my carcass would be safer here than anywhere else. But, again, I don't feel any particular way, except maybe somewhat sad that this sort of thing is allowed in a "civilized" society. I can't believe that the Governor is in on this but he could easily be in on it. We have a shot gun in the house, with five shells, but I don't expect to have to use it and am not sure I could work the damned thing if I had to. I can't imagine that would-be thugs will be allowed near the house but they might be and I'm sure we'll be apprehensive tonight. And if they don't get in tonight, how about tomorrow and the next day? Well, that can take care of itself. Well, this is all for the moment. I won't send this, naturally, until the matter has been somewhat cleared up. I certainly don't have any feeling of being in danger, and God knows your mother doesn't think in terms of danger to herself. At the same time I can realize, just a little bit, the emotion of a "moderate" in a small town Mississippi atmosphere.

Graduate 16, University, Miss.
February 15, 1963

Dear Bill and Betty:

Yesterday, it being Valentine's Day, I helped make a little Mississippi history by asking Jim Meredith to play golf with me. He said that he had been hoping to get in a game or two but his clubs were in Jackson, etc., etc. Anyway, he agreed to meet me at the office at 1:30 and in the meantime I had asked Cliff McKay and Russell Barrett. Only McKay showed up, with Meredith, and we dropped by the club house to talk with June Lovelady who was damned nice to Jim. Instead of paying the fifty cent fee Meredith signed up for five bucks worth of playing, suggesting that he would have to come at least nine times more to get his money's worth. I'm sure that he intends doing just that. As we teed off it was apparent that we had plenty of company, with marshals all over the place, Chief Tatum in a University car up by the Veterans apartments, and a jeep load of soldiers off towards the cemetery. It was cold and windy and we had to wait a good while before each shot. Meredith is apparently a good golfer but completely out of practice. It seems that he played a lot in Japan. As you know he is a slight person, is the most relaxed person I ever saw. He dubbed a good many of his shots, rather topped them because he was trying to play in mid-season form. He did get away a few awfully good shots, particularly his drives on the 5th and 6th holes. We didn't keep score. McKay was in better form than usual and I was in the middle. In spite of the fact that it was cold and drill day for the various service units on the campus, there must have been forty people playing on the course. I was a little apprehensive each time we caught up with some golfers or they caught up with us. Actually, the golfers couldn't have acted better. They weren't exactly over-friendly in their relation to Meredith but neither were they nasty, as I had thought some of them might be. Even with this apparent almost-good will, it was something of a trying experience for me because I was always anticipating trouble which never really came. Standing around was a chore, too. When we got to the second tee it was most apparent that we were being watched by a lot of people, including a couple in an army helicopter. The walkie-talkies used by the marshals and the military weren't exactly conducive to good golf. On the second I went into the ditch with my second shot, then played up near the green and then pitched in for a par (one of two for me). This was the highlight for me. Jim kept getting a little more sure of himself and came through with some good shots besides those off the tees. At the third green and near the fourth tee there was something of a small crowd, over by the apartments, and we could hear occasional loud laughter as though someone were indulging in wise cracks. But no one came near us, at least not near enough so that we could hear them. With the cold and the crowded course, it took us two and a half hours to play seven holes. That part was rather dreary and there were times when, ordinarily, I would have quit and gone back to the club house. But we kept at it and eventually got through. On the 6th someone mentioned that this was our "separate but equal" hole inasmuch as there are two flags on the green because we now have to double back since the course has been torn up. We didn't do the doubling back. I was relieved to get back to the warmth of the house and to a cup of coffee in the grill. This was longer than I had been out in months and I was just damned tired. A lot of it was nervous exhaustion which seemed to hit me but not the others. Meredith was relaxed all the way and we joked and had an all-round good time, in spite of the tension that I was more aware of than anyone else. How this guy keeps up his spirit, having to put up with constant surveillance 24 hours a day, and putting up with the rest of the human race, is beyond my comprehension. I'm sure that I'll play golf some more with Meredith but I doubt whether I'll ever do so with relaxation—not in Mississippi, that is. Anyway, we made it, apparently without incident.—Monday I'm going down to Jackson to have dinner with Rabbi Nussbaum and to talk with a half dozen Jacksonians about why Mississippians behave as they do.

Ole Miss
February 21, 1963

Dear Betty:

It always takes me a day or so to recover from a trip and I'm just back from three days in Jackson. I was a little dubious about getting into the stronghold of the Citizens Council but I ran into no difficulty and felt almost as a Mississippi citizen before I left. You see, I ran into the right people, largely by choice. I'm still working on dope for my talk in November and felt that I ought to get out into the state for a few days. Next week your mother and Gail and I are going to Vicksburg for two or three days, ostensibly to attend the Miss. Hist. Soc. meeting, but mainly so that I can talk some more with people generally. Anyway, in Jackson, as I figured it out on the train coming back, I talked with 19 people at some length and with some result. The 1st night there I was a dinner guest of Rabbi and Mrs. Nussbaum (only a fair meal, which rather surprised me) and after the meal we talked for about four hours with ——————, —————— (Methodist leader, teacher at Millsaps), Roy Clark (pastor, Capitol Heights Methodist Church), ——————, leading businessman and prominent Methodist layman, and ——————. These are all moderates who, believe it or not, have been trying to do something about Barnett. What surprised me most of all was to learn of the feverish activities of a fairly large number of lawyers and businessmen in the week before the riot last September. The boys were too late, obviously, but it seems that they *almost* stopped Barnett and might have in another day or two. No one knows this story; at least it has never appeared in print and I guess it ought not to appear now because it might mean the kiss of death to the activities of these people. Right now they are working through the Mississippi Economic Council (Jack Reed, the president, made a damned good speech on the need for law and order last week) and hope to avoid more bloodshed when there is a bona fide attempt to integrate the Jackson schools. Incidentally, this court action is supposed to be started within a month. Also, I learned, there are now some 200 women engaged in a "Save Our Schools" campaign, but whether this will be able to counteract the idiocies of the "Women for Constitutional Government" I doubt. I *was* a little more hopeful after my Jackson visit than before but not a hell of a lot. Had lunch with ——————————, a prominent lawyer, who gave me a fine transcript regarding a case of harassment against the Rev. Mr. Johnson, who had allowed himself to be placed on the Civil Rights Committee. I'll use these facts in my speech, at least some of them. . . . [I saw] . . . the Smiths, father and son, the leading Negro team in Mississippi, in the fight for Negro rights. These men fought the Sovereignty Commission in its gift to the CC of state money and supported Higgs financially. The father ran for Congress (had spoken at Harvard, where Bill heard him) and is a wonderful, impressive sort of older man. The young fellow isn't attractive physically but is an aggressive soul who is not afraid of anything. He had a picture of Meredith in his store window and the plate glass was shot out by pistols last week. He's very successful in his business career, having a Kroger-like store, an apartment building, etc. He wants me to stay with him the next time I go to Jackson but I told him I wasn't ready for that, as yet. Anyway, I saw a number of other people and gathered enough material for my speech to make the trip worth while.—There is another *Rebel Underground* out but nothing spectacular other than a few adultery charges. Gail says that some of her playmates have told her that I played golf with Meredith (which I did) but she doesn't seem to be upset by it all. We still get a few calls but nothing that matters. Tomorrow night Margaret Mead will be here. I'm anxious to meet her. We are all well. Love.

February 22, 1963

Chancellor John D. Williams
University, Mississippi

Dear Chancellor:

I have just read, carefully I hope, your address to the
Commonwealth Club of California and I find it of the same
high caliber as your Greenville speech.

Being something of the perpetual pedagogue, I have the
desire to make a comment or two. I really do like it; there is
an honesty, an evident sincerity and a reasonableness about it
that ought to convince all except the real die-hards. Yet I
would have changed an item or two. You say, when talking
about the arrival of the marshals: "Their arrival touched off a
bloody riot which provided a Roman holiday. . . ." This, I
think, is slanted. Technically speaking, it wasn't the *arrival* of
the marshals, for the riot started two and a half hours later.
Nor was it even their presence. It was rather a combination
of things, including their presence, but also including the
presence of students and outsiders, the general atmosphere in
the state and among its leadership that you describe so well,
the laxity of the state highway patrolmen, the evident unpre-
paredness of the federal or state officials to take over, etc., etc.
I'm not trying to assess the blame; I am pointing out that your
statement does cause some readers to assume that the marshals
were to blame, something I think not true.

Your statements about the history of the South and the
political climate of Mississippi and the stand that Mississippi
politicians have taken are magnificent. I can find nothing to
complain about here.

The University Greys did include, I think, some townspeople.
I don't think that Reconstruction was quite as savage as you
indicate and yet I know this is what southerners have been
taught to believe. It *was* bad enough. But, I insist, I am not
complaining here. You have done exceedingly well.

I have recently read again *Intruder in the Dust* and I recognize that the quote you have from Gavin Stevens is representative of the thinking of Mississippi. It is also true that Faulkner realized, before his death, that southerners would never really give up segregation without outside force. I am sending to you a copy of the speech Bill Faulkner made (for me) at the Southern Historical Association meeting in Memphis years ago. I would like to call your attention specifically to his statement on page 12, a statement he typed out for me when he agreed to have his talk published. This little quotation has been more influential with me than anything else I have ever read of Faulkner, perhaps because he gave it to me.

Toward the end of your speech, you say: "Many deep South state institutions may maintain a de facto but not de jure segregation. . . ." It would appear to me that you really mean the reverse.

I repeat that I believe this is a magnificent address and I am very pleased indeed that you have made it. It gives me more hope.

Yours,
Jim Silver

University of Mississippi
Saturday, March 9, 1963

Dear Betty:

The lights have gone out in the office but it is a beautiful spring day and when I have finished this I'm going out for a walk. First, though, I want to write you about another adventure of mine which turned out to be rather prosaic. While Bill is here I have been thinking of doing (with him) a number of things among which were a dinner with some friends and Meredith and a trip over to Clarksdale to talk with Aaron

Henry, the head of the NAACP in Mississippi. I had met
Henry a couple of times and had told him I was coming to
see him. During the first part of the week I read through all
the stuff of the Civil Rights Commission about police brutality
and barbarism in general in Mississippi and also went back
over my notes regarding harassment of Negroes, particularly
in the Delta. So by Friday, when I had set the appointment,
I wasn't quite sure that I dared set foot in the Delta. On Wednesday I got Evans Harrington to agree to go with us and then
yesterday I ran into Tom Truss who also wanted to go. Your
mother was somewhat apprehensive about our going at all but
we took off about seven in the Chrysler which was hitting on
about half of its cylinders. Nothing much happened going over
and we arrived in front of the 4th Street Drug Store (in the
colored section) of Clarksdale at 8:15 p.m. Henry was waiting
for us and closed up after handing us some of the NAACP
propaganda. Both plate glass windows in his fairly large store
had been smashed by bricks a night or two before; in the show
cases he had displays portraying the Declaration of Independence and the Emancipation Proclamation. Apparently these
are frowned on in Clarksdale, at least in Negro Drug Stores.
Henry came with us in our car and we drove about a mile to
his house, which is not far from Highway 61. A rather nice
looking frame house with furniture about on a par with ours—
the main difference being that he owns his home. His wife and
13 year old daughter were up but soon disappeared and we
settled down to about three and a half hours of talk. Henry
is exactly 40, what I call a younger replica of Archie Moore—
probably because he bounces around like a boxer—is an easily
met fellow, rather aggressive and certainly very cocksure. You
have a tendency to like him at once. That is, in spite of the fact
that he assumes an intimacy with you that you may find hard
to take, at once that is. He is also a real optimist, thinks that
his troubles will be all over in ten years and that the Negro
will have equal political rights at least by that time. He personally has been about as harassed as the ingenuity of man can
devise—at the moment he has a couple of judgments against

him for $25,000 and $15,000 both of which he expects the
Mississippi Supreme Court to reverse, and then he is now in the
circuit court with his appeal from a sentence of six months and
$500 fine for molesting a white boy he is supposed to have
picked up on the way to Cleveland. He says all these charges,
etc. are simple harassment and the stuff that a worker in Civil
Rights takes as a matter of course. He's quite flip about it and
I believed that he was telling the truth. He went on with all
sorts of statements about how the local sheriff and chief of
police had constantly tried to get local juvenile delinquents to
frame him—how the boys had been promised money, whiskey,
exemption from prosecution, etc. to testify against him. But
somehow he gets by with his activities and runs his prosperous
drug store too. He's away from home a good deal, traveling
mainly in Mississippi, for rallies, etc. He's an expert propa-
gandist, you can be sure of that. I'm certain too that the only
way the enemy can get rid of him is to kill him, which they
may well do. As a man who is in constant danger, he seems
not to be aware of it, and laughs about our hoping to live forever, etc. While we were in his house I heard a couple of times
a number of cars outside, and I firmly believed that we would
be stopped and perhaps molested on our leaving his home. I
had seen to it that there wasn't any liquor or anything else
incriminating in the car, and that none of us touched even beer
while we were there. I just didn't believe that they, the police,
would quite dare try to frame us, though this wasn't outside
the realm of possibility. We left about eleven thirty and got
home about quarter to one, without incident. I had called your
mother about ten from Henry's house and yet she was still
apprehensive when we returned. Seems silly, now. Henry is
coming over tomorrow for a meeting with Meredith, and next
week a couple of faculty carloads are going down to Tougaloo
for a conference with faculty there. Just what will come out
of all of this I'm not sure but it is interesting, getting acquainted
with the state Negro leaders, after not knowing any of them
for so long. Mississippi does have some good Negro leadership
now, certainly on a par with the best of the white and consider-

ably more daring than any of it.—Bill goes to Fort Benning tomorrow. We've enjoyed having him here. We all send our love.

University, Miss.
March 14, 1963

Professor George Carbone
Portland State College
Portland, Oregon

Dear George:
Yesterday was one of my bad days. My skin had been acting up, as it does after a few days of tension (although I'm usually at a loss as to the cause of the tension) and I felt once again that I had been trapped. Frank Howard had asked Evans Harrington and myself over to a steak dinner and I felt obliged to go although I really wasn't up to it. Several of us had visited Aaron Henry (state NAACP head) in Clarksdale last Friday, Henry had come over Sunday to visit Meredith (and the question was unsolved as to where he would eat) and Frank had bought the steaks to be used Sunday—but they weren't. I'm also in the process of getting up a carload of faculty for a visit to Tougaloo. Anyway, I was fed up with the whole damned Negro business and certainly didn't want any more involvement. But you can't well get out. Tuesday night Frank was over at the house for supper and mentioned his up-coming meal and Dutch was rather unhappy about it. I got angry, more, I think, because I was caught than at Dutch's unwillingness to go all the way in this business. (She will not have Meredith down to the house, and I feel that is her business and her right.) On the whole she has come a long ways and has been right reasonable. Actually, she is more sensitive to what little ostracism

we have been subjected to than I am. (We are both concerned, of course, with Gail who has not really been touched as yet.) So yesterday I felt pretty damned bad but was determined to go through with the dinner. Late in the afternoon Chief Tatum (not asked but) told Dutch that Meredith was eating at our house last night. She sort of blew her top, I guess and soon got Tatum, the army, and the marshals straightened out. It seems that everyone is afraid of Meredith and everyone hesitates to get information from him, for fear of affronting him. So there was a mix-up as to the time and the place of his dinner. Our car was in the shop and I walked over to Howard's house about six. Didn't notice any cars or jeeps outside and in the house I found Howard working like hell over the steaks and Harrington and Meredith in deep conversation. So I forgot all my troubles and had a fine dinner along with better conversation. There were about a dozen telephone calls, most of the people hanging up when Howard answered. Some wanted to come over to interview the illustrious assembly while others just asked: "Can James come out to play?" This didn't bother us much. We ate in the kitchen. I still am not sure as to what Meredith is talking about but now it seems to me that he is nothing more than a damned old Mississippi state righter. He really wants to get rid of the marshals and the Army because, he says, it is the duty of the state to protect him or at least to admit that it cannot if it won't. I think he is willing to risk his life to prove his point about state rights. I told him, in my usual subtle way, that he is a damned fool. But he is not a fool. We discussed the possibilities of Negroes running for office in Mississippi and he is against this, except where, in such a place as Hinds County, they might really have a chance of winning. I guess that he doesn't want any token anything. He is most anxious for Negroes to have some little say in the making of decisions in the state and of course he is eager for the terrible restrictions on the Negroes to be dropped. He and I agree pretty well on the necessity for Negroes to get the rights implied in the Declaration of Independence but when he gets much farther than that he is likely to lose me. He's a mystic, all right.

Harrington couldn't get too far with his proposed discussion of James Baldwin because Meredith had read very little of Baldwin and didn't much agree with him, except that he seemed to think Baldwin had a right to make a living by writing anything he wished. Well, our meal went off with no trouble, Meredith was driven back to Baxter by a couple of marshals, and I came home with Harrington. Actually, it was a fine experience even if I did get the thought a time or two that a brick might come through the kitchen window. It is hard to define the tension one feels—at least it is always there with me, because I know there are people who would like to interrupt such sessions. These are the "they" groups who, as Billy thinks, would like to convey the impression that they are about to erupt but who (he thinks) are afraid to. I'm not as sure as he is about their lack of courage but he may be right. It's hard to think so, sometimes late at night. At least it is more sensible to believe that "they" might do something. No calls when I got home and today the world looks peaceful. Maybe it is.

                                                          Yours,

                                              March 14, 1963

Editor, Jackson *Daily News*
Jackson, Mississippi

Dear Sir:

According to the March 14 *Daily News,* "the General Legislative Investigating Committee said yesterday it will hear more testimony before completing its study of the University of Mississippi desegregation crisis."

The committee's report will be completed "as quickly as possible," but it seems certain data must first be processed.

I shall be glad to furnish Representative Russell Fox, chairman, with the names and addresses of at least fifty people who witnessed various phases of the Ole Miss riot, but who, for reasons unknown to me, have not been called on to testify by the committee.

Sincerely,

James W. Silver

Professor of History

Published in *The Mississippian*
March 19, 1963

To the Editor:

Mr. Macdonald was so right when he implied that many of us are hypocritical when it comes to freedom of speech for the other fellow. Academic freedom should not mean immunity to attack on the part of a professor from those who disagree with him. He should expect to take it as well as dish it out. He has the moral responsibility to allow disagreement without penalty, even in the classroom. On the other hand, common decency revolts at the victimization of a professor with unpopular opinions through an anonymous attack based on scurrility.

In the fifteen years that the ODK forums were under my direction, it was my constant hope that the day would arrive when our campus would be open to speakers of all persuasions. There has never been any doubt in my mind about the capacity of students to think for themselves. Unfortunately, for a number of years we have been moving in the direction of complete censorship.

My guess is that Mr. Macdonald is disturbed by an incident that occurred when Circuit-Rider Myers Lowman spoke here. It may be that he was not treated as "academically" as he deserved and I may have been guilty of impoliteness. Mr. Lowman was brought to the campus by the State Sovereignty Commission, the same outfit that got itself involved in a University election through an agent who later worked against several Mississippi citizens who were not present to defend themselves. He refused to answer simple questions. He "proved" that people were disloyal by finding their names on lists drawn up by himself. Even so, the most vigorous attack on Mr. Lowman came from an extremely conservative student. Myers Lowman (admittedly this is a subjective judgment) put on the most anti-intellectual performance of the hundreds I have witnessed in Fulton Chapel since 1936. He was rebuked as he should have been but not before he had been allowed to say his piece, feeble as it was.

Sincerely,
James W. Silver
Professor of History

University, Miss.
Saturday, March 23, 1963

Dear Bill and Betty:

There's not a great deal to write about tonight. This afternoon your mother and Gail and I drove out to Coontown and about sundown got a boat (which we paddled) and a half dozen minnows and went out into water about two feet deep. We also looked for arrowheads but found none. On the way back, Gail caught and I suppose her mother pulled out of Sardis Lake a crappie weighing a good three-quarters of a pound. But I don't think this experience will take me back to fishing. I didn't catch anything.

This is the day of the spring football game and I suppose that someone won and someone lost. Tonight is the big banquet, with tickets at ten bucks a throw. The boys get luggage or something like that and the coaches are suitably rewarded for their fine season. Then everyone listens to George Healy tell about the glories of this and that. I suppose this is all in the cafeteria. This noon we went over there late, almost at 1 p.m. We were about to leave when in walks Meredith with a friend. The friend was about six feet tall and black as he ought to be. The two Negroes calmly went down the line while everyone else in the place was in a dither. The colored help stood at the east end of the big room and watched, apparently mesmerized. The white managers scurried around and finally Woody Bounds came up from the subterranean chambers of the building. Then a cop showed up and another. Tom Tubb, the chairman of the Board had just eaten and I don't know whether he knew Meredith was in the building, with a friend, that is. Then Chief Tatum arrived and a great deal of conferring went on. I didn't know whether the Negro was breaking the law or whether he came under the protection of the Fifth Court. Surely the marshals wouldn't protect him. On the campus and in the cafeteria were numbers of legislators but apparently none of the roughnecks or candidates needing an issue. But there was some scowling, and some laughing. After about fifteen minutes the two Negroes, having finished lunch, walked out and rode off in a car. No incident, but there was a good deal of tenseness. I guess it will always be this way. Actually, I thought the Negro would be arrested when the cops showed up and I kept wondering what I should do. I knew damned well that my influence with anyone was very little and I decided to do nothing. What I would have done if people had started roughing up the Negro I don't know—probably would have left. I can't see how this situation is going to change for a long, long time.

I guess it was last night or maybe Thursday night when, in the midst of a fancy string quartet, a student came in the back of the Fulton Chapel and asked whether it would be all right to throw eggs. The astonished usher said nothing. Whether this guy was a nut, whether he was after Meredith (who happened not to be there) or whether it was just a stunt I don't know. Anyway, he threw two eggs and one splattered all over the stole of Mrs. Doyle the wife of the professor of city planning. The University is having her fur piece washed or renovated or whatever needs being done. The first egg hit the edge of the platform but did no damage. I wasn't there because I had forgotten about the performance. Wish I had been. Apparently the concert stopped a bit and then went on. The egg thrower turns out to be a senior who is now up before the Judicial Council. What they'll do with him is anyone's guess. The Underground will probably reward him with membership in the Brick and Bottle Brigade. But I'm not sure he had anything to do with the local unrest. At least he needs some rest and he may get it.

Tuesday night Mrs. Wallis Schutt, housewife from Jackson, will be here to talk with some of the Save-Our-Schools women. How many I don't know. She is the chairman of the Mississippi Committee which advises the Civil Rights Commission in Washington. I'm going to try to get her to meet with some of the men who are getting interested in the Human Rights Council of Mississippi. But things are moving slowly and I doubt if Mrs. Schutt will have much of a crowd. They are meeting at —————————. I didn't know that his wife is a crusader but maybe she is.—I'm tired and am going home and finish reading *Caste and Class in a Southern Town* (1937). We all send our love.

Published March 27, 1963
Jackson *Daily News*

Editor, *Daily News*

For a moment it seemed, on the first day of spring, as though you, in your usually merry column, were going to get down to serious discussion of what has been termed Mississippi's gravest crisis since Reconstruction.

You lined up an imposing array of big guns aimed at the

Karl Wiesenburg pamphlet, "The Price of Defiance," but you failed to fire them off. The presumption must be that you are holding in reserve the Women for Constitutional Government, President McCain, Professor Caskey, and Judges O'Barr and McGowan. And it won't be long before you will be able to enlist in your battery the report of the Legislative Investigating Committee.

Your own mighty fusillade consists of misspelling the name Wiesenburg five times and a little more or less amusing name-calling. You note that the pamphlet is a "windy dissertation," that Representative Wiesenburg pretends to be a "super expert of some kind," and you wonder who paid the bill for the printing.

"The Price of Defiance" is only twelve pages long. It contains powerful arguments and salient facts. Instead of assuming that the people of Mississippi are a gullible lot who can be taken in by ridicule, why don't you read one of the six copies in your possession and tell us why, point by point, you disagree with it? It would be refreshing to have a real dialogue in our paper.

Back in December LOOK magazine made some rather damaging charges against your favorite administration in Mississippi. Mr. Johnson called the article "scurrilous" and let it go at that. Our governor has said nothing. Don't you think it is time to pull back the rug to let the people see some of the sweepings that have been pushed under it?

Come, come, Mr. Ward. Instead of your light fare of frivolity and innuendo, can't you appease our hunger with a healthier morsel of fact or a more satisfying portion of reason?

James W. Silver
University of Mississippi
University, Mississippi

April 7, 1963

Editor
The Clarion-Ledger
Jackson, Mississippi

Dear Sir:

In last Saturday's paper, Tom Ethridge and his Oxford informant, Mr. Calloway, complained of "an allegedly obscene painting on display at the University," in which the Confederate flag was desecrated and Mississippians were depicted "in a most derogatory light."

"The flag was allegedly inscribed with vulgar four-letter words—the kind dirty minded kids and degenerates scribble on sidewalks, fences and walls of public rest rooms."

Whether our modern Paul Reveres have accurately described the contents of Mr. Kerciu's painting is not for me to say. But Mr. Kerciu did not make up the words and phrases recorded in his painting. They came from the mouths and/or brains of Mississippians, and many of them can be found in the literature of the Citizens Council.

When it sinks into the minds of the local Minute Men that Mr. Kerciu has simply immortalized some Mississippians acting as best they could in defense of what they considered their heritage, they may want to hang his work of art in the chapter room of the local Council.

Mr. Kerciu, a fine young artist, has put us enormously in his debt by recording the activities of some energetic Mississippians, the flag of the Confederacy in hand, at work and play. His dramatic, if symbolic, display of history in the making should be preserved for future generations.

Now that Mr. Calloway has rendered us this fine service, it is to be hoped that he won't rest on his laurels. He should take a large dose of milk of magnesia and return to his leadership in the Oxford Citizens Council, whose members have so gallantly and courageously waged their patriotic campaign of anonymous telephone calls to men and especially to women with whom they disagree.

Sincerely,

James W. Silver

April 8, 1963
University, Mississippi

Dear Bill and Betty:

Inasmuch as I was fined twenty dollars for speeding, in the mayor's court, this morning, it may be that I won't be able to write an unemotional account of what has happened in the past week or so. There is not any way to tell whether this fine was a kind of harassment—it was for "going more than 15 miles an hour" in front of the high school—and you ought to drive less than 15 MPH—so I'll give Mayor Elliott the benefit of the doubt in my mind at the present time.

Anyway, you have seen something in the papers about the Kerciu case. Ray put up six paintings having to do with the riot and subsequent events. Actually, they are more posters, I suppose, than paintings. The big one (which has my name on it) does contain most of the slogans, nasty words, etc. that have been bandied around by the idiots in the last six months. All this is imposed on a mis-colored Confederate battle flag. Frankly, I don't think that the paintings are all that emotional but they seem to be to some people.

Last Thursday (I guess it was) Dick Calloway (the leading racist of Oxford) came out to the gallery where the paintings, along with another hundred of Ray's, had been hanging for almost a week. With the aid of the deputy sheriff, Calloway took some pictures and left. Friday afternoon Ray was called in and after a two hour talk with the Provost, Chuck Noyes, was ordered to take the controversial paintings down. It developed that the Provost had had calls from Citizens Council people and from some UDC biddies. (Most of us think the decision was really made by Hugh Clegg—the Chancellor was out of town all week.) Noyes was apparently naive enough to believe that the story would not get out. It was well "leaked" that night, for one by a woman who called Ben Thomas, AP man in New Orleans. I don't know who she was but I know others who were working on the story getting out; I had nothing to do with it as I had the poker group at the house (won $50). The next morning Ethridge in his nasty *Clarion-Ledger* column had a typical Ethridge statement, pulling out the stops and indulging in his usual innuendo. Said he got his information from Calloway. (I wrote a letter to the *Clarion-Ledger* suggesting that Ethridge was right in his reporting of the four-letter words, etc. but that these came from the mouths and/or brains of Mississippians, but not from Kerciu, who only recorded them. I suppose they will print it.)

Yesterday Liz Willis opened her show at the Buie Museum, and among her paintings are several of the riot and aftermath, one big one especially, of the scene in front of the Lyceum on the night of September 30. Her show hasn't been protested yet. Today some of Kerciu's students have been and I think still are picketing the Fine Arts Center, with placards of "Unfair," "Un-American," etc. Chief Tatum had a slight altercation with a couple of the picketers and with Prof. Hahn, this noon, but I understand that he didn't do much more than take a couple of identification cards. The boys who are the "trouble makers" have written the usual letters to the chancellor. The AAUP has been notified in Washington (but the local chapter hasn't met) and I suppose other things have been going on that I'm not up on. All of this is just another tempest in a teapot and Meredith hardly enters the picture at all. But in this tense atmosphere people get emotional and really mad very easily. This thing isn't over yet. Ray has had offers to show his stuff in the Downtown Gallery in New York City and in Detroit—and this pleases us because he's a nice guy and doesn't have a job for next year. The University administration has goofed on this situation, as it does on most, sooner or later, and I expect we haven't heard the last of it yet.

Now to a history meeting or rather a confrontation of the dept. with the chancellor.

University, Mississippi
April 11, 1963

Dear Betty and Bill:

There have been so many unbelievable things happening around here that I thought I would write a bit before they get completely confused in my mind. Anyway, your mother, Gail and I are leaving in the morning for the Gulf Coast and New Orleans. This is a mixture of pleasure and "business" because I have some talks set up with various people all the way down and back, including what I hope will be a fine talk session at the Longfellow House in Pascagoula with Harkey, Wiesenburg, Ramsay (the labor chief) and others. Of course you will see that I am meeting the "right kind" of people. So I emphasize that I shall talk with Oliver Emmerich in McComb.

I have sent you information about the AAUP resolution on the Kerciu case. It has seemed to me that the time for resolutions has long since passed but I suppose they do some good. Anyway, with the meeting coming up at 5 p.m. I talked with the chancellor (who was quite rude, for the first time in his life, to me) who told me in no uncertain terms that the University would not make any effort to defend Kerciu in court (as a member of the University family), that it could not take issue with the state itself, which of course is prosecuting Kerciu. I couldn't follow his reasoning inasmuch as he had offered services to the rioters who were accused, but I didn't argue with him. His statement to me was very positive. Then the

AAUP, after pausing for a committee to draw up the resolution, passed it, for delivery to the chancellor's office the next morning and to be released to the press by 12 noon. About nine a.m. the chancellor's office announced that the Chancellor had already asked the Board permission to hire a lawyer to defend the University and Kerciu. It seems that this statement was dated the day before it was released and "for immediate release." A lot of skullduggery, it seems to me. My guess is that the Chancellor has been trying to outfigure the AAUP and to keep in with the accrediting agencies at the same time. My guess also is that he knows already what the Board will do, or at least that he has this all figured out with Mr. Jobe. What makes me suspicious of the Chancellor is that the administration is really giving Kerciu a hard time, that it is, or has, in effect been making a liar out of him. I have talked with him all the way through and know him quite well and I am certain that he was sure he had been "ordered" to take down the paintings. Now this is not the administration policy at all. The other night the Provost was explaining to Kerciu that he had not, indeed, ordered the paintings down and Kerciu asked whether they could be put back up. "Absolutely not," said the Provost over the phone. Then Ray asked him if he would put that in writing, and the Provost asked him to be in his office the next morning with his lawyer. At least the Provost is learning fast how to wheel and deal in this administration, and Kerciu is growing up too. He trusts no one any more, and rightly so.

That is about all, except for many rumors and some funny things. In my letter to the *Clarion-Ledger* I suggested that the informant, Mr. Calloway, might well take a large dose of milk of magnesia and go back to leadership in the Oxford Citizens Council (and the rest of this was left out of the paper) "whose members have been engaging in a courageous and patriotic campaign of anonymous telephone calls to men and especially women with whom they disagree." Even with this left out, it seems that Mr. Calloway has received several bottles of magnesia and is not too happy about it. Maybe it is a good thing I am leaving town for a few days. Maybe this is the

Lord's retribution for his having ordered me out of his shop two or three years ago.

Now I've got to get off a quickie article for the *New Mexico Electric News.*

April 25, 1963

Mr. Jack Reed
R. W. Reed Company
Tupelo, Mississippi

Dear Mr. Reed:

I had no intention of answering your letter of March 9, mainly because I know that you are engaged in an enormously worthwhile work and I do not want to interfere with it, even a little bit. I have read your letter over several times and this compels me to suggest that 1) it is the most forthright, honest, intelligent and understanding letter I've ever had from a Mississippi businessman (my correspondence here is not heavy), and 2) I wish that I could think that it was representative of Mississippi business leadership.

In any case, I am not concerned with your answering *this* letter, though I would appreciate your sending me, if you have one, a copy of the last speech you made in Jackson.

Recently I made an eight-day trip through Mississippi to the Coast and talked with thirty to forty people, most of whom, I'm afraid, were on the liberal side, including almost all of the editors in that category. I came back with a much more optimistic view than I left with, and this was tied up with the apparently increasing chance of the election of J. P. Coleman and the leadership shown by the Mississippi Economic Council.

I continue to be frightened by the possibilities of what will happen when four or five Negroes walk into Jackson (or other) schools with court orders for admission. This is, of course, our real, more or less immediate deadline. Probably within two years.

I don't know what you think of our BAWI [Balancing Agriculture with Industry] program, though I think perhaps it has done some good. Eddie Khayat, for instance, reminded me that the Ingalls people had come to Mississippi via BAWI. As far as I can see, though, it is pretty much of a "whites only" program and may deepen the race problem rather than help it.

I have been collecting evidence of police and other kinds of brutality to Negroes and even if most of what you hear is discounted, there remains enough to be frightening. The caste system is still with us, but is most certainly destined to go. The transition here is, it seems to me, the most difficult problem we have. We seem to have failed to teach this to our students or maybe the ones who learn just leave the state.

Yesterday I saw the film made by the Sims Associates (but sponsored, I think, by the Women for Constitutional Government) and I have never seen before such a gross fraud. The same is true of the Legislative Investigative Committee report. We do have gross corruption in very high places.

I agree with you that until recently the Negro has not been a real problem in Mississippi. He was well taken care of during slavery and then there was a flurry for about 25 years until the Negro was put officially into his place. Mississippi has been very successful at nullifying the Constitution and, I suppose, has continued to believe it could defy the federal government if it just stood up to it strongly enough.

You and I may not agree on what is involved in academic freedom but I do think there has been a good deal of irresponsibility on the part of faculty here at the University. I believe, too, that some faculty members believe that this gives them an immunity from attack when they speak out on controversial matters. This, of course, is nonsense. The business leadership in the state could improve matters here by encouraging faculty to speak out and to frown upon the campaigns, mostly underground, to "get" faculty members because they do speak out. The most terrible thing that has happened here since last fall is that at least twenty-five of the best of the faculty will be gone by next fall. These people are of all stripes of thinking and many of them are staunch segregationists. They just won't tolerate abuse forever. Like Hector Currie in the law school, they go quietly. The University administration has been most lax, over the years, in trying to educate the state in the direction of a wholesome academic freedom.—Of course, some of the rumors going about the state concerning statements of faculty in their classrooms have been false. (I am not involved because I'm not teaching this year.)

The long-run future of Mississippi not only looks promising but is inevitably alluring. As for the short run, the next ten years, we are in for bitter strife and really deep trouble. Your own work may be the most crucial in bringing about a return to sanity and a realization among businessmen that we are, right now, in the midst of Mississippi's most significant social revolution. (This is bound to be true because even the Civil War did not upset, for long, the white-black relationship; this revolution is bound to do just that, and we may as well prepare for it.)

I do appreciate very much your March letter. Please don't bother to answer this one.

Sincerely,
James W. Silver

University, Mississippi
May 8, 1963

Dear Betty:

At supper time last night I got a call from Medford Evans, one of the head moguls in the Mississippi Citizens Councils, who said he wanted to talk with me. I arranged to meet him at the office at eight-thirty and then your mother, who seemed to think that Evans had come to town to shoot me, announced that she was going to accompany me to the office. I said in no uncertain terms that she was not, but finally agreed to bring Evans to the house—this being complicated by the fact that Pete McCarter was supposed to show up after his dinner with the Chancellor. (It didn't seem quite right to bring Evans to a home in which Meredith had never trod.) Anyway, I met Evans, took him home—then in came Liz Willis and later Bill. I thought this was a bit of unnecessary collusion on your mother's part but she denies this. Today Evans came by the office and we talked for another two hours. Last night he left about ten.

This is my first chance at long talks with the die-hard opposition. His purpose in coming has something to do with a book which Bill Simmons is apparently writing on the Mississippi-Meredith situation. (Which stimulates my thinking in that direction.) Evans is apparently collecting some of the "facts" which Simmons will use. This afternoon he is over talking with your mother and he has already talked with Barrett and Fortenberry.

This is a strange character. He taught English as an instructor here from 1928 to 1930. Taught in a good many relatively small schools including Chattanooga, the college in Natchitoches, La., was dean at McMurray College, etc. etc. During and after the war he had a job having to do with security at Oak Ridge and here, apparently, he got the notion that most people were likely to be communists. He wrote a report which was not accepted, then started a movement (and wrote a book after getting out of the AEC) which, he says, probably resulted in the attack on Oppenheimer. In the 1950's he worked with *Facts Forum* (H. L. Hunt), was an organizer for the Birch Society, organized local citizens councils in Louisiana and was ousted from the Louisiana school where he taught. He hasn't been in Mississippi long but the only difference between him and good Mississippians, he says, is that he was first anti-Communist and then a segregationist while Mississippians undergo the reverse process.

Fortenberry says he has the eye of a fanatic but I can't see this. He must be about sixty, dresses very well, and talks well. When we were getting acquainted, he even seemed quite charming. He's rather clever in debate and will catch you up on little things until you get wary and then he isn't so clever. He follows most of the cliches and it is interesting to see someone who really believes that Meredith is a Communist (how do you prove he isn't?) and that Martin Luther King is also a Communist. Whether he carries a card seems to be immaterial. These people are not just following the Communist line, they are Communists. Evans seems to think that we have gone down the drain in foreign affairs, that we have lost Cuba and everything else because it was planned that way, that the Kennedys are the dupes of Russia. His picture of the future is dreary except that he is sure the American people are not only basically conservative but are about to join the Citizens Council and will reverse the trend toward Negro emancipation. The Negro is inferior biologically and that is all there is to it. He should be treated in kindly fashion, as you would treat a dog you like. Evans is very emphatic about the patriotism in defying the Supreme Court. It is your duty. These nine men are dupes of Communism and the left wing apparatus that is running the country. What he calls the "academy"—the college professors, etc. especially in the Ivy League, is responsible for what is happening. Businessmen are dupes because most of them have too much respect for the "academy" and will do what the professors say as long as they get honorary degrees, etc. When there is a board in Washington composed of a general, a big businessman, and a professor, the college man always dominates it. We must overthrow all this or the world is going to hell. Bob Welch is a great man but not as great as General Walker for whom Evans worked, as public relations man, for a while. He admits that Walker is not the most articulate man in the world, except at times he is quite eloquent. Well, this went on for hours and I was completely fascinated. Come to think of it, I guess this man does have the look of a fanatic.

June 6, 1963

Mr. Maxie Dunnam
Box 1092
Jackson, Mississippi

Dear Mr. Dunnam:

On January 25 I wrote to each of the twenty-eight Methodist ministers who had signed the "Born of Conviction" statement, asking for information as to what had happened to him, mainly in the way of harassment, since the publication of the resolution.

I heard from fourteen of the twenty-eight but, I am sorry to say, you were not in this list. I appreciate very much the time it takes to answer such queries as mine and that there may be other reasons for not complying with my request.

If you are so inclined, I still would like very much to have from you a statement as to what has happened to you, personally, since the resolution. The composite story will make a very important part of my presidential address before the Southern Historical Association in November, and will be distributed in pamphlet form in Mississippi. I hope that it will have some effect in the making of a more tolerant public opinion.

In any case, there is almost no likelihood that I shall use names in this part of my paper and certainly I shall not do so in cases where such is requested. I am enormously concerned with the real need for freedom of discussion in this state and I hope what I write will contribute somewhat to that end.

Again, I would appreciate very much hearing from you at your convenience. I shall begin writing the speech about the middle of June. I shall be glad to send you a copy of my paper when it is completed.

Sincerely,
James W. Silver
Professor of History

June 10, 1963
University, Mississippi

Dear Betty and Bill:

. . . Intended to write you the day that Cleve McDowell matriculated but there was absolutely nothing worth while to mark the event. This was last Wednesday and it appears that all day Tuesday our estimable governor was in close touch with his advisors who, by this time, had split into two groups, the die-hards and the appeasers. And most of the night it seems he was on the phone. We thought he would show up on Wednesday for one more piece of defiance but he thought better of it, appeared on television in Jackson and let it go at that. So Simmons and company didn't win this one, although everyone still claims that the University is occupied and not integrated. They may have something there. I was in front of the Law Building when McDowell came in. The military and Justice Department were at his heels but he walked in by himself and had no trouble. All the news and television people were here but they didn't have much to do. Apparently McDowell won't be the newsmaker that Meredith is. One strange development; people like Love, Williams, Ellis, etc. who made all sorts of mistakes last fall are now talking about what a nice guy McDowell is, in comparison with Meredith, of course, on the assumption that if only McDowell had come first there wouldn't have been any trouble. Of course, actually, Meredith didn't do a damned thing but keep quiet until long after the riot so it seems that these fair haired boys are engaged in their own specious reasoning. But this does give McDowell a fair start and he intends to stay here for three years. I have yet to meet him. Will probably go up to Baxter tonight to see both of our black boys.

I'm sure that you know each other's address, but here they are, just in case: Betty: 4717 Drummond Avenue, Chevy Chase 15, Maryland—and Lt. James W. Silver, 05014362 Off. Stu, Det. USAINTC, Fort Holabird 19, Maryland. I suppose that you will see each other before you get this. My address for the summer will be: History Department, Emory University, Atlanta 22, Georgia. I'm going over to Atlanta this coming Saturday. Will be back in Oxford about July 1st to testify against one of the rioters. The others up for trial got off free last week— another miscarriage of justice, I presume.

I think that I have about caught up with my notes for the famous paper. I have entirely too many as it is, but still have a half dozen books I want to read before beginning it. How this will work in with two classes every day I don't know, but I won't have anything else to do. Am not even going to take my golf clubs to Georgia. I hope the paper will be finished, first draft at least, by the end of the summer school. If not, I'll come back here and finish it.

Well, now I'll get back to the various and sundry chores awaiting me. We all send our love.—Gail and I are now expert bowlers, though we are not sure as to how to keep the score. But we'll learn.

June 12, 1963
University, Mississippi

Dear Bill and Betty:

Thought that I had written my last "joint" letter to you, but today has furnished its excitement too (I'll be gone Saturday, I'm happy to say). Your mother waked me up about eight saying that she had found a note (in the morning paper) signed "A. P. Willis." It said that the writer had arranged to meet Meredith in my office at 9:30 for a statement on the "assination" of Medgar Evers. I must not have been thinking too well, but I assumed that for some reason the NAACP lawyer in Memphis had come down, and, of course, I knew nothing of the slaying of Evers. "Assination" was crossed out and the word "slaying" written in above. Anyway, I got over here later than 9:30, found no one and went to the cafeteria. Later it turns out that A. P. Willis is Liz Willis and the AP is for Associated Press. Just her little joke inasmuch as Caroline is now working for Ben Thomas and while Caroline is in New Orleans Liz is taking over her summer job, and liking it. Yesterday I got a scoop for her about the army pulling out of town and off the campus. About ten a.m. Meredith finally got to the office with a three page statement about the killing of Evers. (I'm sure that you have already found out about that and so I'll say no more of it.) Meredith's statement you will also have seen, at least in part, by the time you get this. In its original form it was really inflammatory as well as, I suppose, libelous. We talked about it for some time and then he went off. Liz called in the story to New Orleans and I talked with Colonel Lynch, as Meredith had agreed I should do. After thinking it over for a while I talked with Barrett and then went down to the High School Building and got Meredith out of his biology class. The AP had agreed to hold up the wires to give us a chance to talk with him. The upshot of it all was that Meredith, on my suggestion, thought it better to delete the worst two sentences. They were left out, whether justifiably I'll never know. We called the UPI who had the story by this time and they had already deleted the two sentences. Then we got the AP again and they also agreed to kill the sentences. In the meantime I had talked with Colonel Lynch three or four times, telling him, among other things, that I could not get Meredith to change his statement about the Army. For the first time I think that Meredith, in spite of being tremendously emotional (and not showing it a bit) was concerned for his own safety. As I think I wrote you, when I left Baxter Hall the other night I could have gone right up to Meredith's window and could have killed him without anyone detecting me. This has had me worried ever since and, apparently, Meredith, too. There were only two marshals present that night, and both were inside. Col. Lynch said that the Army was keeping better tabs than I had thought, that it knew I was in Baxter. That didn't take much sleuthing for I'm sure the marshals on duty had called the command post, a couple of miles south of town. But, as a result of all this, there will be a couple of marshals at night in the darkened dormitory across from Meredith's room, so I suppose this will make him and McDowell reasonably safe. That is about all there is to it except that I'm going out to the Army post and talk with the Colonel and will try to find out something about Bill. Just what effect the Evers killing will have on the state and especially the Negroes I just don't know. There should be a revulsion everywhere except among the die-hards. At first the people may even rejoice but this will pass, and, incidentally, I think in a few weeks the whole thing will redound to Coleman's benefit. Maybe not. The Negroes may now be more intimidated than ever or they may react violently. I don't know what has happened in Jackson today. There is more evidence than ever now that the whites in control around here have almost taken McDowell under their wing. He's now a "good nigger" and Meredith is responsible for everything. Of course no white could be to blame for anything— it's all due to the "trouble-makers." Well, as I have written before, living in Mississippi may be a nauseating experience but it is also rather exciting. In a way, I'm sorry I'm going to Atlanta but I must get my paper written and I doubt if I could do it here. We all send our love.

Published in *The Clarion-Ledger*
June 17, 1963

Dear Editor:

As I leave for the summer, I wish to offer my heartiest congratulations to Edwin White, who recently expressed to you his fears that "our beloved Ole Miss is doomed." Mr. White has every reason to be proud rather than afraid, for his campaign to purge the University faculty is well on its way to fruition.

Following is a carefully compiled list of Ole Miss faculty members who have fallen before the relentless onslaught of Mr. White and his kind since January of this year:

The Provost

Dean of the Law School

Assistant Dean of the Law School

Director of Institutional Research and professor of psychology

The Law School: 1 professor, 2 associate professors, 1 assistant professor

School of Pharmacy: 1 associate professor

Department of Philosophy: the chairman, 1 associate professor

Chemistry: the chairman, 2 professors, 2 associate professors, 3 assistant professors

Classics: the chairman

Home Economics: 1 associate professor

Economics: 2 associate professors

Physical Education: 1 assistant professor

Civil Engineering: 1 professor, 1 associate professor

Modern Languages: 3 assistant professors

Anthropology: 1 professor, 1 associate professor

Political Science: 2 associate professors

Physics: 2 associate professors

Art: 1 associate professor, 1 assistant professor

History: 1 assistant professor

Mathematics: 1 professor

Instructors have not been listed because they do not have tenure. Scores of our most talented students will not return in September. This is all to the good, of course, because the bright ones are the potential subversives.

There are other vulnerable teachers at Ole Miss, men and women who insist on the right to free inquiry, and I suggest that Mr. White get right after them. And how about those horribly contumacious ministers in Oxford? Once they have

been eliminated, the time will have come for the formal burning
of the library books not endorsed by the Citizens Council.

At the risk of being called premature, I suggest that Edwin
White be considered for the next chancellorship. He could then
preside over the destinies of his great University, an institution
of conformity, complacency, compulsion, and consanguinity.

Yes, Mr. White, as you have put it so well: "We should
pray."

Sincerely,
James W. Silver
Department of History
University of Mississippi

July 2, 1963
University, Mississippi

Dear Bill and Betty:

I have smoked too many cigarettes lately and I'm a little
depressed too—so probably won't write much even though I'd
like to say a few words about MISSISSIPPI JUSTICE. Not
that it has changed. This afternoon a federal jury set one
agitator free. There is no question about his having come from
Atlanta with three rifles in his car, about his bringing at least
one five-gallon can of gasoline to the campus and depositing it
at the site of the cars later set on fire, about his handing a
30:06 rifle to a man who said that he needed it to finish the job
with the marshals and who left to do so. He had been indicted
for obstructing justice which means that all the jury had to
believe was that he had been an accessory to the fact of
obstruction. The jury was out for about an hour.

A similar jury sometime early in June had set free 1) a man
seen throwing a Molotov cocktail at the marshals, and 2)
another who was found in possession of a gun from which

the FBI said at least a dozen shells had been fired from the direction of the Fine Arts Building. The empty shells had been found the next morning by Mr. Joslin. Also a slug fitting the gun had been found in the wall of the Lyceum.

Coming across the campus tonight, one of the campus policemen told me that he and another cop had picked up a rioter about 1 a.m. October 1st whom they *saw* shooting out two campus lights with a .22 rifle. They testified to this effect before the Lafayette Grand Jury last fall (or whenever that was) and were asked whether the shots were fired in the direction of the marshals. They said no. The man was not even indicted.

The reason, or one, that I'm a bit sick about this acquittal today is that I saw the agitator carry the gasoline can to the Circle between the Y and Fine Arts Bldg. and later saw him hand the gun to the man who said he was going to use it on the marshals. Apparently the jury didn't believe me.

Today Beckwith was indicted for the murder of Medgar Evers. Now he will either be sent to Whitfield for a couple of months or will be held for jury trial. When that comes off he will be held incompetent or insane or will be given about eight years or, more likely, will be acquitted.[2]

These things, naturally, remind me of the eight or ten Negroes who have been killed in Mississippi in the past few years, with only one indictment that I can remember (aside from Beckwith) and no convictions. I am reminded of Mack Parker (Judge Sebe Dale later told a New England audience,

---

2. On February 7, 1964, the circuit court jury, after deliberating for eleven hours—an extraordinary length of time in a trial of this sort in Mississippi—reported itself hopelessly deadlocked. Thus the trial ended in a mistrial. As this book goes to press, no date has been set for the next trial and the prisoner has not been allowed bond. Ross Barnett and former general Edwin Walker visited Beckwith in the courtroom. Their visits were of about five minutes each. The two men paid their respects to the prisoner while the jury was out and so could not have affected the jury's decision. The visits were as public as daylight and were commonly interpreted as conferring the sympathy if not approval of the two arch segregationists on the prisoner's cause. The whole state, including the prisoner, was stunned by the mistrial. Everyone had expected acquittal.

inadvertently, that he knew three or four of the mob), Emmett Till, George Lee and several others whose names I can't remember, and the dozens of Negroes shot and shot at, with the sheriffs, in the last cases, usually suggesting that the Negroes did it to themselves or the crimes were done with other Negroes. As a matter of fact, Governor Barnett, a couple of Congressmen, and both Jackson papers intimated that the NAACP or other outside agitators had shot Evers.

Where this will all lead to I just don't know. I know that I can't do a hell of a lot about it. In court both yesterday and today was ——————————, a segregationist now [a student] in the Law School, who saw the agitator freed today hand the gun to the man and who listened to the same conversation that I heard from the agitator. He refused to testify and the U.S. Attorney thought it not much use to subpoena him. He sure would have made a reluctant witness. No doubt about it, he's going to make a lawyer of complete integrity some day.

Also, I got a letter today from the president of Mississippi College telling me that I shouldn't write a paper on "Mississippi, the Closed Society," because the society in Mississippi is not closed, and besides, the history of the world has been filled with racial conflict.

I've got some work that I can do here and won't go back to Atlanta until Sunday. I'll probably fly, as I left my car at the Atlanta airport. When I get back I'll really have to get down to work on my paper. So far have written only eight pages and they aren't too good. Tomorrow night we are having the Harringtons, the Farleys, and the Smiths to dinner—getting ready, I suppose, for the fray in the fall. The *New York Times* wants part of my speech for the Magazine Section the Sunday after it is given and I'm sure I'll go along with them. Now I've got a book to read so that I can get off another piece of genius to the *New Mexico Electric News*. May be a bit more cheerful the next time I write. Bill's letter came tonight. A rather amusing place, apparently, the Intelligence Department of the Army. We all send our love.

October 17, 1963

Mr. Edward J. Bogen
Bogen, Wilkes & McGough
Weinburg Building
Greenville, Mississippi

Dear Mr. Bogen:

Thank you for your letter of October 14. We seem to differ about what may be good for the University and I don't suppose that either is disposed to change his mind.

I have spent most of my adult life here on the campus. This may be hard for you to believe but I have worked hard to make this the place you say it should be, "preeminent" in the educational world. Perhaps it will attain this status in the future, but if so it won't be based on good public relations or on fraud.

It may come as a surprise to you but I think it can be established that I had a good deal to do with the University's keeping its accreditation last year. Or do you consider this important? I don't mean to quarrel with you but I do insist that I am as concerned with the University's future as anyone in the state. And I believe that no university is worth its existence if its faculty isn't free to study, to do research, to make whatever inquiries come to mind, regardless of the outcome.

In any case, if you have the feeling that the University of Mississippi has any preeminent position in the educational field at the present time, you are sadly misinformed.

Sincerely,
James W. Silver

November 16, 1963

Editor, *The Clarion-Ledger*
Jackson, Mississippi

Dear Sir:

Two days after the event you reported a somewhat controversial speech made in Asheville, N.C., under the caption, "Dr.
Silver Talks Again," and stated that "he abused the state of
Mississippi, its people, officials and newspapers in the same
fashion he has in previous speeches in Atlanta, Memphis and
other points."

It is my belief that I have never abused the state of Mississippi, nor do I have any intention of ever doing so. It is true
that before the annual meeting of the Southern Historical Association I presented some facts about Mississippi and made an
honest effort to draw some warrantable conclusions from the
facts. In my audience were some 700 people, most of them
professional historians and most of them Southerners not likely
to be taken in by abuse.

If my conclusions are invalid, they should be and will be
exposed as such. If my conclusions are valid, the people of
Mississippi will do well to take a look at them, to think about
them, to discuss them, and perhaps to act upon them. Or do
we just assume that the *Clarion-Ledger* knows best what should
go into the heads of Mississippians?

It is conceivable that people in Mississippi might want to
decide about the validity or non-validity of a speech the *New
York Times* thought significant enough to devote a whole page
to it. The *Clarion-Ledger* just blasted the document without
satisfying anyone's curiosity as to its contents, thus verifying
my contention that Mississippi is a closed society.

Congressman Williams did the same thing when he implied
that my talk included "foreign ideologies." The only statement
which might be considered as foreign in ideology had to do with
the Mississippi BAWI program of state socialism (of which

I approve). As several southern editors have already noticed, Governor Barnett also confirmed my notion of Mississippi as a closed society.

With my permission, the Southern Regional Council, 5 Forsyth Street, Atlanta, Georgia, ran off some copies of the speech. These are available, as long as they last, just in case anyone in Mississippi would like to find out what it is that has been so roundly condemned. And, at the risk of seeming contentious, I meekly suggest that the editor, the congressman, and the governor might profit from a reading of the document, maybe on their way to my funeral.

Sincerely,
James W. Silver

PART THREE

Revolution Begins
in the Closed Society

Eighteen hectic months and two summers—the long spasm of grim, massive resistance to change in 1964 and the one of grudging, minimal compliance with the national will in 1965— have passed since this indictment of Mississippi as a closed society was published on June 22, 1964. To meet the anticipated horde of barbaric invaders in that first summer, a furious Mississippi legislature enlarged local police powers to the point of legalizing home-grown vigilante committees, doubled the size of the state Highway Patrol and gave it police powers, and lashed out against those miscreants who might engage in the vague and wondrous activity of criminal syndicalism. During the summer of 1965, on the other hand, the quixotic gentlemen in the State House, on direction from the governor, speedily cleared the slate of all laws whose purpose was to frustrate the Negro's exercise of the suffrage and secured the people's assent to the elimination of similar provisions in the state constitution.[1] Thus Mississippi, history having at last caught up with her, has been moving with understandable anguish into

---

1. In 1965 Representative Thompson McClellan asked for the repeal of legislation he had steered to passage in 1962. He told the House that "the whole country is arraigned against a few Southern states" because of voter qualifications Negroes could not meet. "We've got to pay for the discriminations we all know have taken place in the past." Chairman Roy Strickland of the Registration and Elections Committee added:

authentic social revolution. It is a period of organic change, largely compelled from the outside, and one whose end is by no means in sight.

Mississippians will almost certainly look back to the summer of 1964 as the time of troubles. It was then that the cracks first appeared in the pillars that upheld the cruel edifice of their society. As the summer heated up, the cracks widened. Pillars wobbled and fell. The path back through the rubble to the normal national standard, while difficult, was clear. Once set in motion, the process of return and reconciliation was irreversible. The evidence of what took place is largely in and needs no chronological repetition. In the past year or so almost two dozen books have established beyond doubt the real nature of a society on its way to destruction and the course of the revolution that is destroying it. As essential background material two sociological classics have been reissued in paperback, Myrdal's *An American Dilemma* and *Deep South,* the Davis-Gardiner scholarly exposition of violence-scarred southwest Mississippi. Benjamin Muse in his knowledgeable *Ten Years of Prelude* and Anthony Lewis and the New York *Times* in their *Portrait of a Decade: The Second American Revolution* have occasionally observed the Mississippi scene in firsthand accounts of feverish civil rights activity. A pair of sensitive Mississippians has carefully documented the predicament of intellectuals of integrity, who were in effect warned to conform or be driven from their white supremacist society: Frank Smith in *Congressman from Mississippi,* his "story of a politician's failure to bridge the gap between Mississippi and reality," and Robert Canzoneri in his delightfully low-key reminiscence, *I Do So Politely: A Voice from the South. The Hearings before the United States Commission on Civil Rights* and the Commission's *Voting in Mississippi* have blasted for all time the wide-

---

"If you think, under color of law, this nation is going to let you continue to discriminate, you're living in a world of fantasy." It was indeed a sad day when Representative Betty Jane Long sighed, "We are heartsick over what we are doing . . . the federal government is making our voting laws . . . we have little chance to circumvent . . . it is useless."

spread and self-serving rationalization about a dreamily content relationship between inferior and apathetic blacks and a noble race inspired to carry the white man's burden.[2] The incredible last-ditch resistance to federal authority at the University of Mississippi in 1962 has been expertly chronicled by Professor Russell Barrett in *Integration at Ole Miss* and by a master story teller, Walter Lord, in *The Past That Would Not Die*. Liberal and radical viewpoints regarding the course of the federal commitment to the implementation of civil rights in Mississippi have been expressed in Burke Marshall's *Federalism and Civil Rights* and Howard Zinn's *SNCC: The New Abolitionists*. Two of the South's best known novelists have contributed illuminating chapters on Mississippi's racial tensions: Robert Penn Warren in *Who Speaks for the Negro?* and Erskine Caldwell in *In Search of Bisco*.

For the events of the summer of 1964 eight books are now available: an unsensational interpretation of the spectacular Philadelphia murders that shocked the nation, William Bradford Huie's *Three Lives for Mississippi;* a crack reporter's story of what he saw, Nicholas Von Hoffman's *Mississippi Notebook;* a dedicated Stanford University psychologist's memoir, William McCord's *Mississippi: The Long Hot Summer;* a cry of indignation as expressed in Len Holt's *The Summer That Didn't End;* the superb chronicle of a charming liberal adventurer, Sally Belfrage's *Freedom Summer;* and the down-to-earth revelation of the motivation, fears, and trials of civil rights workers as expressed in their own *Letters from Mississippi*. Two large-format paperbacks, *Mississippi from Within* and *Mississippi Black Paper,* contain newspaper and pictorial documentation and the awesome testimony of Negroes and whites as to police brutality, the breakdown of law and order, and the corruption of justice in Mississippi.[3]

---

2. In November 1965, the U.S. Commission on Civil Rights published its incontrovertible *Law Enforcement: A Report on Equal Protection in the South*.
3. Ronald Fair, a Chicagoan whose father was a Mississippian, has responded as a novelist to the folklore of oppression in *Many Thousand*

It is not suggested here that these volumes are of equal merit or that their authors have been unerring in their search for truth. But surely the mass of evidence presented leaves no excuse for the often indicated ignorance of the Mississippian as to what is going on in his own state. Of course, the most revealing of all the proposed accounts of the Mississippi madness may some day be found in a presumably planned but as yet unpublished book, the long-heralded inside story of Citizens Council impresario William J. Simmons. Perhaps Mr. Simmons is overcome with the wisdom of silence or is hung up on the problem of a title. *Failure of a Mission* has the right ring to it. So does *The Emperor's New Clothes*.

The Long, Hot Summer

At the end of the summer of 1964 most of the civil rights workers left Mississippi with no great sense of achievement. Two or three thousand Negroes at best had been registered as voters, many of these as the result of federal court orders, a tiny minority of colored children had been exposed to the freedom schools, and the poor-white project had never got off the ground. Mayor Charles Dorrough of Ruleville, president of the Mississippi Municipal Association, was glad to see the workers go: "I don't believe they have accomplished anything, except to poison the minds of the younger Negroes [who] will now have to be taught the Democratic way of doing things."

On the surface the mayor's analysis seemed to be perceptive, whereas, in fact, his society had been shaken to its foundations. The cold glare of publicity had been on the state all summer in the massive search for the corpses of the three slain civil rights workers and in the quest for evidence against the murderers in a hostile community. Congress responded by breaking a southern filibuster to pass overwhelmingly a civil rights

---

Gone. This short fiction does not belong to the class of books of documentation, reportage, and interpretation given above. Written by someone who has never set foot in the state, it draws from the myths of the closed society a dread logic that white supremacist doctrine permits.

law which established firmly the nation's will on the side of the Negro. The stepped-up federal presence in Mississippi, while notably inconspicuous to those whose bodies were fair game to a large lawless element, was also indicative of a rapidly changing public opinion.

The one affront that Mississippi's caste system could least tolerate and survive was the presence of more than a thousand whites living with and working amiably alongside Negro families. For a while, of course, the society could ignore these mongrel agitators, as it had traditionally refused openly to acknowledge the Caucasian blood present in most of the Negro population, or it could designate them as the lowest kind of white trash. Long apathetic and fearful of retaliation, Mississippi Negroes were hesitant to accept the crusading invaders, but slowly freedom's ferment began to rise, especially among the very young. Even with federal court orders to county registrars to ignore the maze of restrictive red tape in the Mississippi registration process, it required the most persuasive efforts of the civil rights workers to induce rural Negroes to summon the high courage needed to make the trek to the county courthouse.

The mock election of the Freedom Democratic Party, which enrolled some 80,000 would-be voters in the fall of 1963, led directly to the most amazing single propaganda victory of the summer of 1964, the dramatic fight to take over Mississippi's representation at the Democratic Convention in Atlantic City. An otherwise dull convention was enlivened by the eloquent pleading of Fannie Lou Hamer, Aaron Henry, and Bob Moses, and through television the whole country was made emotionally conscious of conditions in Mississippi.

At the same time that Mississippians were informed of the pending positive enforcement of the provisions of the Civil Rights Act, the state's legal resistance to token integration in four elementary school systems came to an end. The Mississippi Economic Council had long taken the stand that public schools must not be closed to prevent desegregation, and now, at last fearful of impending economic chaos resulting from the image of the state as a lawless community, the business establishment exerted its full strength for compliance with federal laws and federal court orders. A gallant group of moderate women calling themselves Mississippians for Public Education waged a spirited and successful campaign to keep the public schools open.[4] The most significant aspect of the campaign was their deliberate defiance, without serious retaliation, of the mandates of the Citizens Council. This emergence of long-dormant moral forces forecast the impending demise of the white supremacy organization which had for a decade suppressed the law-abiding instincts of a supposedly free people. Thus the Citizens Council had at last lost its deathlike grip on the closed society, and, with the presence in September of some sixty Negro children in the previously all-white first grades of Biloxi and Jackson, the moderates forgot to pay their Council dues, while right-wing extremists drifted from the Council into the ranks of the Ku Klux Klan and the Americans for the Preservation of the White Race.

Federal legislation, federal court decisions, and the threat of federal power marked the end of massive resistance in Mississippi. Civil rights workers had created the pressure on Washington in the first place. Local political and business leaders grasped their last chance to change the state's direction. Compared to the anticipated fears of her people in the spring of 1964, the summer had indeed been relatively peaceful. The new harmony had stemmed from the galvanic effect of the Philadelphia murders, the increased federal presence in Mississippi, efficient control of violence by state and local police, and,

---

4. This statewide, nonprofit, independent organization called on thoughtful citizens "to protect our children's heritage by: 1) giving our support to school authorities and other public officials who have been given orders by the Courts which they must obey and are working to make this transition a peaceful one. 2) working to create a community climate in which law and order are respected and in which violence and lawlessness are unacceptable. 3) making the facts about the pitfalls of the tuition grant system known to every parent, to every taxpayer. 4) continuing to upgrade our public schools by securing higher standards, better teachers' pay, and community-wide interest in the schools."

most important of all, the magnificent self-discipline of the civil rights workers.

The revolution was peaceful in a relative sense only. In July Allan Dulles told the business leaders of Jackson that "the FBI has documented over forty crimes ranging from beating to murder to bombing, all against Negro or civil rights leaders, since the first of the year. These do not get in your papers, not a person has been indicted, no arrest has been made, and in most cases no attempts to investigate have been made by local officials. A forty to nothing score is most upsetting. Something is going to explode unless someone begins to move." About the middle of August the Southern Regional Council listed fifty-four instances of major lawlessness in Mississippi in the previous seven months. The Council of Federated Organizations compiled figures of violence to humans and property that included more than fifty beatings and 250 arrests in connection with voter registration. Obviously, the crimes against humanity committed in Mississippi in the summer of 1964 will never be recorded in full.

The accommodations provisions of the new civil rights act were met with a sullen, partial compliance in the larger towns. Even here, private eating clubs and exclusive recreational associations blossomed forth, and in the rural areas, where colored citizens were excluded from all but the segregated honky-tonks by economic necessity, the law had no meaning. In a society where most Negroes were dependent on whites for their livelihood, there was no rush to take advantage of federal legislation. Tallahatchie County Negroes were simply afraid to exercise their rights under a federal court order that they be registered without the application of Mississippi law. There seems to be no way yet to induce a Mississippi white jury to look honestly at the facts in a case of assault on civil rights workers. The degree of resentment built up among Mississippians against outside interference in what they considered their private affairs was vividly shown in the remarkable protest vote for Barry Goldwater in the November presidential election—87.1% of the voters, whose proud heritage had for a century known only the Democratic Party, cast their ballots for the Republican nominee. In a Louis Harris poll published three weeks later, 19% of Mississippi's citizenry approved of Lyndon Johnson's over-all performance as against 58% approval for the South and 74% for the country. When it came to the President's handling of racial outbreaks and civil rights problems, only 2% and 4% of the people of Mississippi responded favorably. They had been forced to accept revolutionary change, but they most assuredly didn't like it.

The Summer Volunteers

Most of the summer volunteers in The Mississippi Project of 1964 were recruited by the Council of Federated Organizations (COFO), made up in the main of the Student Nonviolent Coordinating Committee (SNCC), the Committee on Racial Equality (CORE), the National Association for the Advancement of Colored People (NAACP), and the Southern Christian Leadership Conference (SCLC). Aaron Henry, state head of the NAACP, was also president of COFO, with Robert Parris Moses, the legendary figure who had come into Mississippi with SNCC in 1961, as the chief formulator and director of the project.

In the spring of 1964, the people of Mississippi were led to believe that from 10,000 to 50,000 invaders were coming to take over the state. Aaron Henry estimated there might be as many as two thousand. A Harvard *Crimson* editorial predicting a blood bath was duplicated and widely circulated. Very little if any communication took place between the COFO leadership and responsible state officials. The legislature passed more than twenty laws aimed at the prospective enemy. Auxiliary police in most small towns were given instruction in riot control, and local stockades were made ready for full occupancy. In June, Mississippians could watch on television the Oxford, Ohio, campus where the invaders were being schooled in nonviolent resistance to the police brutality they were warned to expect in the Magnolia State. The disappearance of Michael Schwerner,

Andrew Goodman, and James Chaney on June 21 only heightened the apprehension of both the invaders and the invaded.

Before, during, and after the summer, Mississippi officialdom and white people in general were almost unanimous in their characterization of the summer volunteers as communist-inspired agitators, immoral, filthy, frustrated beatniks whose personal desires were limited to interracial fornication and whose chief political ambition was to see Mississippi occupied by federal troops. These backward children who had declared war on soap and society would inaugurate a second Reconstruction, enough to outrage the sensibilities of all good white and colored Mississippians, who wanted only to be allowed to work out their problems in peace and tranquillity.

One highly informed and somewhat moderate state senator thought the summer project most unfortunate in the creation of "a strong and bitter resentment on the part of the average white Mississippian against outside interference in the state's problems. No other single activity has served more to retard the growth of racial understanding." The summer workers, he added, "appear to be crusaders without any real grasp of our problem. While I would not presume to question their motives or good faith, I do question their tactics and intelligence." A statewide politician who has fought hard against the racists admired the "tremendous idealism that motivated most of the participants," but felt they had set in motion "a massive expression of bitterness and frustration. The poor whites and some not so poor feel somewhat like a brute that has been driven into a corner, and they are lashing out at everything that smacks of integration." Still another leading moderate thought it unfortunate that the passage of the civil rights law and the invasion came simultaneously, for this gave extremists the chance to use COFO and established Freedom Houses as scapegoats and denied responsible leaders the psychological advantage of urging widespread compliance with the federal law in a period of relative calm.

A college-trained housewife whose husband aspires to be a novelist reported that her Negro cook had "mother wit" enough not to join the workers, who had "definitely worsened the relationship between the races." Another woman, of considerable social prominence, was condescendingly pleased that Greenville had accepted the rights workers "without much criticism, or even curiosity." Of course, she added, "without them we might not have the church bombings or the killings." Which is true enough. But, as Jess Brown, one of Mississippi's few Negro lawyers, suggested, accusing the "outside agitators" of causing trouble and therefore jailing or killing them was much like holding a rape victim responsible for the unfortunate incident or arresting a banker when his bank has been robbed.

Over and over one heard that summer a curious attack on the unwelcome visitors. "Who do these beatniks think they are, coming dressed that way? Why, it's insulting, and insulting to the nigras too. They dress worse than the nigras. What kind of sense is that, when you're trying to raise somebody up, to go into his house looking ten times worse than he does? No wonder they're not getting anywhere. It's a disgrace." Such indignation would seem to imply that a few sartorial changes might have revolutionized the campaign and that the native critics were chagrined at COFO's failure. I talked at some length with at least two hundred of the summer workers without noticing more beards or sloppy dress than may be found on an average college campus. It was true, though, that some of the more dedicated, the professional type, mostly in SNCC, did dress in overalls, T-shirt, and sneakers for the purpose of identifying with the Negro poor, with those so poverty-stricken that they possessed no "Sunday clothes."

There were white Mississippians who understood the significance of the presence of the workers. They were awakened to the fact that if moderate people didn't come forward to do something about intolerable conditions, someone from the outside would. One minister saw a big gain in the establishment of a spirit of confidence, a new kind of morale, in the Negro communities, especially among the very young. A sensitive lawyer wrote, "I was surprised at the dedication of the summer workers. They came, despite the known danger. True, they stayed out of some areas but it took guts to come at all. They were young, idealistic and not very well trained. Trained in techniques but very immature in understanding. They probably received more from the experience than they were equipped to give. I am sure something of permanent value came from this but how can you educate half-slave, half-free Mississippi Negroes during a summer? Let's say something was started anyway."

By and large the white people of the state were kept isolated from the summer invaders as they themselves were indoctrinated by their leaders (no difficult feat in the closed society) in what they should believe. But what about these college students who had come to challenge the caste system? They were highly disciplined, superbly courageous, extremely intelligent, indefatigable idealists who would not be turned aside by threats of violence or by violence itself. They were sons and daughters of corporation executives, of reputable lawyers and physicians, of nationally known politicians and educators, and even the children of owners of industrial plants in Mississippi, as well, of course, as children of hundreds of plain American families. They were superior students, many from the best graduate schools of the country, all highly motivated socially, some with a cynical approach to many aspects of American society, all eager to "find themselves" and to make something worth-while of their lives. They were, indeed, a super-Peace Corps willing to move constantly in the shadow of violence and death for nothing more nor less than the implementation of the promise of democracy and equality in the Declaration of Independence.

In thousands of letters written back home, the summer workers spoke for themselves: "The sheriff told us that every Mississippian's blood boiled, that he felt a physical revulsion when he saw us; but he would protect us to the hilt in order to protect the image of his beloved state of Mississippi. . . ." ". . . the omniscient *Meridian Star* has been very instrumental in protecting us from any possible physical violence on the part of the local aristocrats. Besides calling us left-wing fanatics (which I might be . . . who knows?), race-mixers, trash, and a lot of other such things, they have continually gone into full descriptions of our physical appearance. Naturally, besides being dirty, long haired . . . it seems that we all (I'm not sure if the girls are included) have beards. So far, I have yet to meet one person on the project with a beard." "There are Negroes who want to kill whites and many Negroes have much bitterness but still the majority seem to have the quality of being able to look for a future in which whites will love the Negroes." "We have lived under the increasing weight of fear and the struggle to come to terms with the possibility of death consumes much of our emotional energy." "If only the local columnists who are always wise-cracking about trying to smuggle a bar of soap into the Movement could live in the rural area for just a week of 90 degree temperatures and dusty roads and no privacy, they might not only appreciate why we don't go around in evening gowns smelling like magnolias but also why we maintain that living conditions for 'their Nigras' could stand some improvement." "Greenville is certainly a liberal city by Mississippi standards. It has three Negroes on the police force. The town appropriations to white and colored schools have each year come closer to being equal, and the police force watches the Klan as closely as COFO. . . . The Negro and white swimming pools are exactly alike. Greenville does not use terror tactics to maintain segregation."

"Violence hangs overhead like dead air—it hangs there and maybe it'll fall and maybe it won't. Sometimes it's directed at people in the movement, sometimes it's indiscriminate. Cars have been roaming around; seven or eight vigilante trucks with their gun racks and no license plates have been seen meeting at the city dump. What will they do? When? Something is in the air, something is going to happen, somewhere, sometime, to someone. . . . A few nights ago cars roamed the streets, empty bottles flew . . . striking cars and homes. They were empty that night—the next night the bottles were loaded—exploding as they hit the church and setting it afire."

In the spring of 1964, one of the young men who would make the supreme sacrifice in Mississippi was a student in a writing course in Queens College. After a discussion in class of A. E.

Housman's "To an Athlete Dying Young," Andrew Goodman turned in the following poem:

> How dismally the day
> Screams out and blasts the night.
> What disaster you will say,
> To start another fight.
>
> See how heaven shows dismay
> As her stars are scared away;
> As the sun ascends with might
> With his hot and awful light.
>
> He shows us babies crying
> We see the black boy dying
> We close our eyes and choke our sighs
> And look into the dreadful skies.
>
> Then peacefully the night
> Puts out the reddened day
> And the jaws that used to bite
> Are sterile where we lay.[5]

Roommate of my son-in-law at Yale, grandson of a long-time U.S. senator from Connecticut, shy, scholarly, sensitive, intelligent, Steve Bingham put in six weeks at the Freedom House in Mileston, not far from Greenwood. His living quarters were an abandoned sharecropper cabin with no plumbing, a single droplight in each of the three rooms, no telephone, pallets on the floor, constant police surveillance. Steve was twice beaten up, once by Canton police, and when he came to Oxford he looked the part Mississippians had assigned to his kind. After his summer experience, Steve wrote a long letter. He recalled that at Oxford, Ohio, the workers had been told that some would not return from Mississippi—"these students had an extraordinary dedication to an ideal, enabling them to face danger and even death. There was a strong and realistic feeling that only by the death of white northerners would the Nation ever wake up to

---

5. Published in *The Massachusetts Review*, Autumn-Winter, 1964–65.

the horrors of Mississippi . . . they found two bodies in the
Mississippi River whose torsos were severed in half. When it
was determined that they were only local Negroes . . . all
interest in them ceased." "Bob Moses starts from a position that
he is living on borrowed time." "We were an immature group."
It was, Steve thought, truly unfortunate that Mississippi whites
were aggravated. Both sides were to blame. Mississippi officials
should have been informed of the exact COFO program. Governor Johnson should have told his people more of what the
project involved. The workers had no intention of breaking
Mississippi laws, except those patently unconstitutional. Local
whites indicated no sense of responsibility. "Nor did any of
them feel he had any personal obligation to help improve that
society."

Steve recalled the commitment of individuals who could say,
"It seems to me that you get only one chance in your life to do
something really worth while." "I'm ready to die. I can think
of few things in this world that are worth dying for, but this is
one of them." He was amazed at the "calmness, courage, and
compassion" of Mississippi Negroes. They bore "no deep-seated
malice toward the white man." High-school kids were most
effective in the movement. Once a Negro had gone to the courthouse in an attempt to register, had been photographed, had
had his name in the paper and been identified as an "uppity
nigger," he was tied irrevocably to the movement. And then
Bingham had a last word of truth for northerners who could
"not seem to understand how important it is to the southern
white not to lose face completely." It was not valid to say, he
thought, that the country had looked to the white South for a
hundred years to reform itself. *"Until ten years ago, no one
gave a damn."*

The daughter of an eminent Pittsburgh physician wrote from
the Meridian jail: "I feel more rested and peaceful and cheerful than I have for months. Two days and I know for sure what
you can never know for sure until you have gone to jail—that
there is no shame in being in jail. Two days and I understand

so well the truth that Thoreau said that sitting in a jail cell you can feel—and you can be—completely free."

Gail Falk was serving out a twelve-dollar fine for allegedly making an improper traffic turn. Why? "I do not believe I owe the city of Meridian any money. We have precious little money in the movement and we certainly don't have any extra to hand over to the city treasury. However if the city undertakes to give me food, clean sheets, blankets, a shower, towels, bathroom facilities, heat and a room to myself where I can catch up on some reading, writing, thinking, and sleeping, I am not going to object. It will cost them more than $12.00 before the four days are up. It seems like a big fuss over a little $12.00 fine, but all fall there have been a constant succession of these fines which add up to a considerable drain on our funds. It seems the only way we can put pressure on the city to stop these harassment fines is to start going to jail for them. So that when a policeman decides to stop us, he will not be adding money to the city treasury but rather will be costing the city . . . money and effort."

A professor of philosophy from Yale, having witnessed the civil rights workers in action, has made a sane appraisal: "But what of the COFO workers themselves? Who were these people who came from all over the country to work with the Negro community? Again and again, one heard from white Mississippians (who had no contact with the workers) that they were 'beatniks, weirds and degenerates!' Even up in the North, I have heard similar appraisals. After all, weren't they in it for the kicks, for a little adventure? It is important to keep in mind that a substantial proportion of the summer volunteers were not college students, but teachers and other professionals committed to the civil rights struggle. And every COFO worker in Mississippi was risking his life. There were some 'fringe' people in the project, but I came to feel that the great majority of workers were perceptive and level-headed. They had an acute sense of the dangers of the situation and of what they could honestly achieve. They were neither rabble rousers nor starry-eyed idealists. They were idealists, but idealists without illusions. Many of them lived in primitive conditions and a good deal of their work was drudgery. In many places they lived under constant harassment, with no opportunity to let off steam or to escape the constant pressure. Yet, despite the discomfort and the tensions, they performed their tasks efficiently and intelligently, with even a healthy sense of humor."

Aside from the professional staff of COFO (numbering about a hundred, three-fourths from SNCC) and the summer volunteers, there were hundreds of others who came to Mississippi in the summer of 1964, either individually or under the auspices of specialized groups. (COFO's mailing list contained 1,500 names and addresses, though this was no indication of the efficiency of its office force, whose chief administrative task seemed to be "that of reducing chaos to disorder." In the Jackson headquarters a sign on the wall read, "NO ONE WOULD DARE BOMB THIS OFFICE AND END ALL THIS CONFUSION.")

Some individuals, like the Harvard honors graduate now a law student in the University of Chicago and the high official on the verge of retirement from the New York office of the National Council of Churches, quietly came to Tougaloo and Rust colleges as volunteer, unpaid teachers. The NCC sent ministers by the dozen to Mississippi for consultation with the summer workers, and committed itself to maintaining the community centers set up during the summer.

COFO saw in June the need for a "medical presence" in Mississippi, and the Medical Committee for Human Rights was organized under the sponsorship of such renowned physicians as Benjamin Spock, Paul Dudley White, Alan Guttmacher, and Albert Szent-Gyorgyl. Previously Dr. Robert Coles and Dr. Joseph Brenner, psychiatrists from the Boston area, had written all Mississippi doctors urging the best of care to the civil rights workers, a letter which caused understandable resentment in the Mississippi medical profession. Nevertheless, the Medical Committee, backed enthusiastically by the National Medical Association, quickly instituted a four-point program of recruiting outside professionals for short periods in Mississippi, of arranging and providing payment for medical care of the rights workers, of drafting health projects and requests of foundations and federal agencies, and of providing information to begin to remove discriminatory patterns in health services. By summer's end more than a hundred health volunteers had gone to Mississippi,[6] a state which in 1960 had 59 Negro physicians, 37 Negro dentists, and 376 Negro professional nurses (of 207,611 Negro housing units, 100,138 had no piped water, 137,881 no indoor toilet facilities, 160,413 neither tub nor shower). A planned health program, including a rest and recreation house, was set up at Tougaloo. There was satisfactory communication with the majority of white Mississippi doctors and "particularly cordial" relations with the University of Mississippi Medical Center.

Under the auspices of the Medical Committee, and representing the Schwerner and Chaney families, Dr. David M. Spain, pathologist from New York City, performed an autopsy on the body of James Chaney on August 7, 1964 (witnessed by University of Mississippi pathologists as well as by Dr. Aaron Wells and Dr. Charles H. Goodrich). Dr. Spain's report included the following: "In lay terminology—the jaw was shattered, the left shoulder and upper arm was reduced to a pulp; the right forearm was broken completely across at several points, and the skull bones were broken and pushed in toward the brain. Under

---

6. For example, Dr. Edward J. Sachar, research associate in psychiatry at Harvard, examined "battle fatigue" in civil rights workers. Interviews helped determine whether workers could withstand pressures. One of the summer volunteers wrote: "It wasn't until after the Sheriff threatened me that I really realized that I was in Mississippi, that I could be killed and nobody would protect me. That night in my room, I began to get more frightened than I had ever been in my life. I felt like I was drowning. I saw I could be shot through the windows, so I slept on the floor. During the day, it wasn't so bad when I was busy, but at night it really got to me. It lasted 6 or 7 nights, and then I got over it. I stayed with the Negro families, but I kept changing where I stayed, so as not to get them in trouble. I'd come in late and leave before dawn. You never knew for sure who you could trust. Once one of my own people told the police where I was for $2."

the circumstances, these injuries could only be the result of an extremely severe beating with either a blunt instrument or chain. The other fractures of the skull were the result of bullet wounds. . . . In my experience of 25 years as a Pathologist and as a Medical Examiner, I have never witnessed bones so severely shattered except in tremendously high speed accidents such as aeroplane crashes."

By 1965 there were fourteen chapters of the Medical Committee in the country, a medical director (Dr. Alvin Poussaint, a Cornell M.D. who had completed his residence in psychiatry at U.C.L.A.) and five public-health nurses in Mississippi, as well as a team of nine medical, nursing, and social-science students oriented for summer work in Mississippi at the University of Pittsburgh Graduate School of Public Health. In co-operation with the Tufts University Medical School and the Delta Ministry of the National Council of Churches, a Mississippi Community Health Service had come into being, as well as a Health Improvement Association in Holmes County. The Medical Committee had by 1965 adapted itself to the shift of emphasis to local definition of projects.

In the very nature of the Mississippi problem there was great need for professional legal assistance. No white Mississippi lawyer would take a civil rights case, and there were only three practicing Negro lawyers in the state. In response to the urgency there appeared on the Mississippi scene the Lawyers' Committee for Civil Rights under Law, the Lawyers' Constitutional Defense Committee, the Legal Defense and Educational Fund of the NAACP, and the National Lawyers' Guild. The last was suspect in Mississippi from the beginning because of an attempt by Senator Eastland and others to brand some of its members with the communist label.

The Lawyers' Committee for Civil Rights under Law was formed at the request of President Kennedy on June 21, 1963, and includes in its prestigious membership ten past presidents of the American Bar Association, four past presidents of the American College of Trial Lawyers, presidents of more than half the state bar associations, and the deans of fifteen leading law schools. In 1964 it sent eighteen volunteer attorneys into Mississippi to provide visiting clergymen with legal aid. Representatives of the committee met with members of the Mississippi State Bar Association, which, a couple of months later, adopted a resolution authorizing the creation of a committee of its own members to provide liaison among courts, persons unable to obtain counsel, and lawyers willing to accept court appointments. Since June 1, 1965, a legal assistance project has had an office in Jackson, Mississippi. All volunteer lawyers are carefully screened and have special training in "Mississippi law, procedure, and rules of ethics, as well as the substantive law in the civil rights field." The Mississippi Bar Association has extended at least its nominal cooperation.[7]

The more militant Lawyers' Constitutional Defense Committee, incorporated in New York in June 1964, expended $56,-000 before the summer was done. Backed by such law firms as Paul Weiss, Rifkind, Wharton and Garrison, in New York, and Arnold, Fortas and Porter, in Washington, as well as by counsel for Aetna Life Insurance Company and the Celanese Corporation, LCDC set up offices in Memphis, Jackson, and New Orleans. It proceeded to defend hundreds of civil rights workers against charges ranging from criminal anarchy to insurrection and speeding. The Committee represented workers in negotiations with voter registrars, sheriffs, county attorneys, state and local police officers, and boards of education. Volunteer lawyers were asked to spend two uncompensated weeks in Mississippi, where they traveled a total of 150,000 miles in 1964. After the passage of the Civil Rights Act, these attorneys submitted com-

---

7. In June 1965, the Mississippi State Bar Association pledged an increased effort toward "the creation of better understanding on the part of every citizen of his duty to obey the law." It took notice of individuals and groups who "out of fanaticism, hatred, frustration or ignorance" set themselves above the law. "In our own state, there have been and yet remain such individuals and groups who have sought to substitute for the processes of law either clandestine violence or threats of violence on the one hand, or open defiance of duly constituted authority on the other." As Hazel Brannon Smith noted, the various resolutions were a little late in coming, eleven years to be exact.

plaints regarding segregation and loss of civil rights to the Department of Justice and the Community Relations Service. They also filed an omnibus suit challenging the constitutionality of sixteen Mississippi statutes enacted to "intimidate and coerce" plaintiffs from "helping Negro citizens of Mississippi to secure their constitutional rights." The laws, according to the LCDC, violated freedoms of speech, press, and assembly, and, taken together, defined a high-level conspiracy to frustrate efforts of Negroes to secure their constitutional rights. To sum up, the purpose of LCDC has been "to protect the Mississippi Negro who is associated with no organization but who awakens one morning, puts on his shoes, and decides that deputies or no deputies, *today* he is going to try to register, or talk to a civil rights worker in broad daylight, or eat at a white restaurant." As of April 1965, LCDC had a full-time attorney, Alvin J. Bronstein, in charge of its Jackson office, with three lawyers assisting him. At that time it was representing about 300 civil rights defendants. The American Civil Liberties Union has now taken LCDC under its wing, and has agreed to raise $75,000 of its $130,000 budget.

The largest legal group involved in the civil rights movement is, of course, the Legal Defense and Educational Fund of the NAACP. A great part of its $1.5 million budget for 1964 was spent in Mississippi, which, according to Director-Counsel Jack Greenberg, is becoming more like North Carolina, which, in turn, is beginning to resemble New York. The Legal Defense Fund has operated in Mississippi for a long time; it successfully took appeals of some of the 1961 Freedom Riders to the United States Supreme Court and championed the admission of James Meredith to the University of Mississippi. In 1964 it maintained seasoned specialists in Memphis and Jackson around the clock and furnished training seminars, office space, and law books for volunteer attorneys. At the end of the summer the Fund assumed responsibility for more than a hundred cases initially handled by volunteers.

According to the Fund's annual report, "The list of these

cases reads like a catalogue of petty annoyances punctuated by outrageous instances of atrocity. Among pending charges were 'vagrancy' (for talking on the sidewalks), 'trespassing on school property' (conversing in a playground), 'resisting arrest' (being brutally beaten by two police officers), 'breach of the peace' (attending a voter registration meeting), and 'loitering' (reading a bulletin board in a court house). Many of these arrested were held incommunicado for several days; some were beaten. Officials frequently denied their right to telephone, set absurdly high bail, and sometimes withheld any opportunity for defendants to retain counsel."

In the summer of 1964, there were remarkable individuals who came to Mississippi unsponsored but with fresh ideas and much initiative. There is no more heartening story than that of the working mission of Abe Osheroff and Jim Boebel, California carpenters who not only raised the $10,000 required, but who planned and themselves constructed the community center at Mileston.

Sponsored by the National Council of Negro Women and including individuals from the Young Women's Christian Association, the National Council of Jewish Women, the National Council of Catholic Women, the League of Women Voters, the American Association of University Women, and the United Church Women, forty-eight women, calling their organization "Wednesdays in Mississippi," visited the state in 1964 in an attempt "to ease racial tensions" and "to build a bridge of communication with their southern counterparts, white and Negro." They came as observers, not demonstrators, and talked at length with some 300 Mississippi women, about half of them white. This small band of women was more significant than numbers would indicate because it was made up of educators, psychologists, lawyers, journalists, and social workers, and included wives of a former governor of New Jersey, of the director of Brandeis University's Communications Research Center, of the dean of science at Massachusetts Institute of Technology, of the director of the Twentieth Century Fund, and of a former board chairman of Inland Steel. For 1965, "Wednesdays in Mississippi" had set a budget of $37,665.

As Leslie Dunbar of the Southern Regional Council saw it, COFO and the summer workers "shook the structure" of a Mississippi now forced to confront itself. The movement was building into the deepest recesses of the state an awareness of wrong and the possibility of change. These constructive and missionary implications of the revolution were largely ignored by a nation fascinated by vivid accounts of what was going on. In COFO the dominant force from the beginning was SNCC, and it was SNCC's purpose to make life so miserable for the white supremacists that they would either accept change or retaliate with violence, which would bring in the federal government. After the Philadelphia murders, the United States did beef up its presence in Mississippi, but neither this nor the Civil Rights Act did much for the state's Negro families, two-thirds of which had annual incomes of less than $2,000.

On the basis that "only a renegade Democratic Party exists in Mississippi," the freshly conceived and organized Mississippi Freedom Democratic Party demanded the state's seats at the Democratic National Convention in 1964. The new party, with less than a shadowy legal claim to existence, completely out-pointed the bankrupt white political leadership of Mississippi in putting on a spectacular propaganda exhibition at Atlantic City.[8] Though its candidates for the federal House and Senate fared worse than poorly in the fall elections, the party's real promise was for the rapidly approaching future, when large numbers of Mississippi Negroes would secure the franchise. Most of the old-line Mississippi leadership in and out of politics was solidly arrayed against the platform of these neo-Populists, which included antipoverty programs, medicare, federal aid to education,

8. Although the Freedom Democratic Party, in characteristic SNCC fashion, refused the compromise offered by the Atlantic City convention, that compromise insures that Mississippi Negroes, and all other disenfranchised Negroes, will have fair representation in the 1968 and (unless the rules are changed, which is doubtful) all subsequent Democratic National Conventions.

urban renewal, rural development, and the guarantee of constitutional rights.[9]

The fate of all Mississippi Negroes would be determined by
events beyond the borders of the state, and the simple truth is
that the summer civil rights workers achieved their most remarkable success in convincing the nation as a whole that it
could no longer tolerate the deplorable living conditions of four
out of every ten Americans who happened to reside in Mississippi.

Political Bankruptcy

As long as Mississippi was determined to keep its medieval caste
system there was no place for it in either of the great national
parties. The state's electoral votes, in consequence, have often
been donated to bizarre and hopeless candidates—Strom Thur-
mond in 1948, Harry Byrd in 1960, and Barry Goldwater in
1964. A suggestion that such conduct indicates political bankruptcy (which implies a former solvency) is as meaningless as
a prognostication as to who will control Mississippi's electoral
votes in 1968.

As crisis deepened with the summer, Governor Paul Johnson
lived up to the promise of his inaugural address. Probably satisfying no one, Johnson kept his own counsel, and his mouth
closed to demagogic outbursts, while treading the uneasy path
between the demands of the Citizens Council (which had helped
elect him) and the imperatives of the situation. As one astute
observer saw it, the governor was "tempering political expedi-
ence with common sense, yet still attempting to ease down the
more radical, emotional, and ignorant groups without losing
these votes." And so "ambivalent Paul" could denounce in pic-
turesque and biting language the impending civil rights law and
could declare that "It is an odd thing that so much hell is being

---

9. Senator Eastland told Mississippians what they wanted to hear, that
the FDP was communist infiltrated. It had long been a communist tactic
to create new parties. "And now," he said, "they have created the Freedom Democratic Party in Mississippi."

raised over three people missing in Mississippi when 10,000 are missing in New York," while welcoming Allan Dulles and J. Edgar Hoover to Mississippi and firing a couple of Ku Kluxers from the Highway Patrol. While castigating the civil rights workers and refusing even to meet with responsible Negro leaders, he did come down hard for law enforcement and played a major role in ending the violence in Pike County. It is more than a reasonable guess that the two Johnsons, President and Governor, kept each other informed, though neither could have admitted that to his public. In fact, it is likely that PBJ would have come out for LBJ in the fall of 1964 had it not been for the Mississippi debacle in August at Atlantic City. As it was, both Mississippi senators and Governor Johnson were present when the "Ladybird Special" pulled into the station at Gulfport during the presidential campaign. In the meantime, the old "watchdog of segregation," the State Sovereignty Commission, lapsed into desuetude from deliberate withholding of gubernatorial appointments, and the Citizens Council prepared its own death watch.

By Mississippi standards, Erle Johnston, the director of the State Sovereignty Commission,[10] is a reasonable man. During Barnett's administration, however, the Commission had turned over $193,500 to the Citizens Council, and had contributed mightily to the cost of the Coordinating Committee for Fundamental American Freedoms (under the direction of John Satterfield), created for the purpose of defeating the 1964 Civil Rights Act. Yet Johnston went along with the new Mississippi image of compliance with that act, and his agency refused to counte-

10. From public relations director, Erle Johnston moved up to director of the Commission in March 1963, replacing Albert Jones, who resigned to run for sheriff of Hinds County. The inept and clumsy Jones, appointed by Barnett, had blundered badly in the Billy Barton case. An initial grant of $20,000 was made to the Citizens Council in June 1960, and $5,000 monthly was paid for about nine months. From April 1961 to October 1962, the give-away amounted to $4,500 per month. From the latter date it was reduced to $2,000 a month until Paul Johnson had all payment stopped late in 1964. So the bulk of Commission money was transferred to the Citizens Council under the direction of Albert Jones.

nance further resistance to court-ordered desegregation of Jackson schools in September. He declared that "extremism is on the wane in Mississippi as more of the leadership in business and in government recognize that the federal government is going to enforce its laws. . . . Things are being done now that many years ago people said would never happen here." Robert E. Lee and Jefferson Davis, he added, were not considered traitors because they "knew when to stop destroying and start rebuilding." Henceforth the Sovereignty Commission would concern itself with "subversive forces within the integration movement" rather than with opposition to integration itself.

Somewhat later Mr. Johnston began to burn some of the Commission's old files, stuff collected by spies and informers under the Barnett regime. For the record, it may be well to remember just one report circulated by the Sovereignty Commission in 1962. It said that Hazel Brannon Smith "came to Mississippi in 1936. Since that is the year the Sherwood Eddy group, with Cox and Minter, came to Mississippi, and since their mutual interest is promotion of racial integration, the question arises as to whether or not their arrival in Mississippi in the same year was coincidental. After the unusual happenings at Providence commanded the attention of the people of Holmes County, it became evident that other individuals were participating. . . . Will D. Campbell and Mrs. Smith . . . and two Negro integration leaders, Dr. Felix Dunn and Dr. Gilbert Mason, who have been trouble makers on the Mississippi Coast and were prominent in the Biloxi beach integration issues in the state."

It will probably do the Sovereignty Commission no great harm at this late date to record the facts: 1) Minter came to Mississippi in 1938. 2) Cox met Mrs. Smith for the first time in 1943. 3) Prior to late 1955, Mrs. Smith had never visited Providence Farm. 4) Neither Cox nor Minter had met Campbell before October, 1955. 5) While a medical student, Felix Dunn was employed by Minter for a summer in the 1940's. From that time until late 1955, Cox saw Dunn on one occasion, when he passed him in a car in Jackson. Since then Cox has visited Dr. Dunn in his Gulfport office once only. 6) Cox has never met Dr. Gilbert Mason. (It's really a shame for Mr. Johnston to burn those files. I would be grateful for a look at them, even though I am somewhat disconsolate that the Commission did not list me among those conspirators who entered the dream world of Mississippi in 1936.)

Perhaps because of its rural background and because its members took seriously the oratory they forced upon each other, the state legislature during 1964 worked night and day "outlawing the federal government and the Supreme Court." These stalwart champions of the status quo seem to have learned nothing from the experience of Little Rock, Oxford, and Birmingham. As already indicated, they prepared to meet the summer invasion with the mailed fist, and, when token integration appeared inevitable, passed private-school subsidy bills with just enough money appropriated to ensure the failure of such an enterprise.

In September, Governor Johnson announced that "Mississippi's debt to the national Democratic Party is now paid in full and we are absolutely free to act in the best interests of our people. . . ." Mississippians proceeded to take advantage of their new-found freedom by voting for Goldwater over Johnson 359,693 to 53,063—in spite of an LBJ consensus in all-Negro Mound Bayou, 257–0. A freakish result of the people's frustration was the election of Mississippi's first Republican Congressman since Reconstruction. Prentiss Walker, an intimate of Ross Barnett, had been chairman of the 1960 unpledged electors drive, and was heralded as an opponent of socialism and a proponent of state rights, as well as a prosperous chicken raiser and a fox hunter de luxe (Mississippi "watched his adept handling of dogs in the field trials and knew him for a sound man"). He was, furthermore, a patriot who could write, "I can sincerely state that I have no personal knowledge of the denial of the right to vote to any citizen in Mississippi who is legally qualified." Predictably, he would blame the Los Angeles riots in August 1965 on President Johnson and his "Great Society."

When the results of the election were in, one Mississippi

voter declared, "I can foresee two Federal projects remaining in Mississippi when the air bases and space projects are nailed up . . . the Federal Bureau of Investigation and the Internal Revenue Service." An imaginative woman thought work should be started immediately to dig deep ditches around Mississippi's borders in hopes that the state would drift silently and swiftly into the Gulf of Mexico. Some grim humor was evident in various predictions: a Berlin-type wall around the state, with rigid application of visiting regulations; secret importation of the boll weevil; enforcement of prohibition; abolition of football; division of all Mississippi into three parts, as gifts to Tennessee, Arkansas, and the Virgin Islands; elimination of mosquito control; and the forbidding of revivals. One young office worker said sadly, with more wisdom than he could possibly have known, "It's going to be a long four years."

No account of Mississippi political bankruptcy would be legitimate without passing reference to the symbol of intransigency, Ross Barnett. Unable to succeed himself, Old Ross began his 1967 gubernatorial campaign about the time of his repudiation in Paul Johnson's inaugural address. He continued to titillate the emotions of frenzied right-wing audiences throughout the country, including crowds drummed up by the Americans for the Preservation of the White Race, and to amuse college groups who came to hear him in order to prove that such a phenomenon really did exist in the twentieth century.[11] He sounded off against all laws and executive orders coming out of Washington and made it clear that he was unhappy with a good deal of Mississippi legislation, though he did not dare to attack his successor openly. In October 1964, after having plugged unpledged electors once again, he gave the country the benefit of his clairvoyance regarding the coming election: "It has become plain that there is now no need for Mississippians to sacrifice their public schools for considerations of national politics. In fact, intelligent resistance to Federal force could well turn the tide of

---

11. It has been my pleasure to recommend Barnett for several college speaking engagements, which he has filled. (He does not charge a fee.)

the 1964 election, and display to the entire nation the duplicity of the Counterfeit Confederate who seeks re-election."

Barnett, who loathed all "outside agitators," has been doing his share of agitating in other parts of the country. He told an April Fool's Day audience in Iowa City: "The record will show no proof that any qualified applicant in Mississippi has ever been denied registration because of his color." He informed Lawrence Spivak on national television that he did not know of a single Negro who had been discriminated against in Mississippi. When asked about murder and intimidation of Negroes who sought to register, Barnett said, "None ever complained to me." He urged the school boards in Mississippi not to sign the federal pledge prepared by the Department of Health, Education and Welfare. To a Citizens Council audience, he revealed that "The secret purpose of our enemies is to diffuse our blood, confuse our minds and degrade our character as a people, that we may not be able to stand against the wiles of the devil. . . . It is their purpose to liquidate us socially, religiously, politically, economically, or, as was done by the revolutionists in Russia and Red China, we are to be slaughtered." The ex-governor's reference to international affairs reminds one of his retort to a chief aide who once asked him what he thought should be done about Matsu and Quemoy. Barnett had a ready reply: "Put 'em on the Game and Fish Commission."

The terrifying prospect for Mississippi is that, though dispossessed at the moment, the die-hards are building up a legacy of hatred and suspicion which may explode politically once more in the state. Unless the feelings which prevailed in the fall of 1964 can be dissipated by moderate leadership, it is at least conceivable that Barnett could a second time "cry nigger" his way to the governor's mansion. I have listened to the Barnett buffoonery on a number of occasions, at least enough to know that he makes only one speech—racism overlaid with double talk is his specialty. The following is taken from an appearance at Western Michigan University in the fall of 1963 because the transcript of a tape recording is scrupulously accurate and completely fair, while showing (as any speech would do) what a clown Mississippi once elected to her chief office in time of crisis.

The governor felt it good to come to Michigan, which had given to the nation such men of genius as Henry Ford, Thomas Edison, and Edgar Guest. "More than at any time in this century men and women are rallying to the defense of constitutional government. . . ." The August march in Washington had been "mob action." Barnett exposed his curious fund of historical knowledge in speaking of "Thomas Jefferson and other founding fathers when they wrote the Constitution," and in the incredible statement: "Hitler offered the people of Germany a short cut to human progress. He gained power by advocating human rights for minority groups." But it was in the question and answer period that Mississippi's chief ambassador gave to the outside world reason enough for the state's sorry image:

QUESTION   Mississippi in 1962 paid $275 million in federal taxes and received federal money up to $650 million. Do you consider this an intrusion on state rights?

BARNETT   I think you're incorrect. You're wholly incorrect in the figures. Wholly incorrect.

QUESTION   Are you against integration in the armed forces where there is no fear of mongrelizing the races?

BARNETT   It's best for both races to be segregated in order to maintain the purity and integrity of both races.

QUESTION   If you are so insistent on state rights, why doesn't Mississippi have civil rights legislation?

BARNETT   Well, we don't need any civil rights legislation in Mississippi. Let me tell you this: The Negroes in Mississippi are a lot better off than in many of the other states. Ninety per cent of the Negroes finishing high school and college remain in Mississippi because they love our way of life. You take Jackson State College there in Jackson. I think it's better equipped than most any other school in Mississippi. They won the national championship in football. And it was my privilege to issue fifty-two certificates of appreciation to the Negroes of the football team. Last December, right in the governor's office—because we spent more money on their school facilities than on the whites', in many instances.

QUESTION   I'm wondering if you consider Negroes people in Mississippi.

BARNETT   I would say that the Negroes, the Indians, the Eskimos, and all the whites—ninety per cent of them are against Kennedy in Mississippi.

QUESTION   Who should interpret the Constitution if not the Supreme Court?

BARNETT   The Supreme Court reversed what it had been holding for nearly a hundred years, and said that they would follow the advice of Gunnar Myrdal, who admits he's a socialist, instead of following the law of the land.

QUESTION   Do you condone the use of violence?

BARNETT   I am unalterably opposed to turmoil, bloodshed—and we have practiced it—we've tried to.

QUESTION   How does a Negro get to be registered in Mississippi?

BARNETT   He has the same rights that a white man has to vote in Mississippi, and you'll see that if you go down and watch the registrars. They treat the Negroes just as fairly as they do the white people.

QUESTION   Would you be as willing to address an integrated audience in the South as you are here?

BARNETT   Well, I'd have to get the invitation first and study it a little while.

QUESTION   Why did you attempt to cancel Meredith's graduation?

BARNETT   Because two federal judges said he was not qualified. And the Army said he was a troublemaker. In fact no white man in the United States could have entered Ole Miss with his qualifications.

QUESTION   The Jews were a minority group in Germany. Do you call what they got human rights or an equal opportunity?

BARNETT   I don't know whether they had equal opportunities or not. I suppose they did [fading away to very faint] . . . probably did.

The Businessman and the Image

A nationally known economist returned to his alma mater (class of 1919) on April 30, 1964, to speak at the dedication of the Self Building on the Mississippi College campus. Murray W. Lattimer, whose father had been professor of Greek and Latin at the Clinton institution, had used the resources of his firm for four months to prepare his message, and now he told an astounded audience that Mississippians had been kidding themselves about their economic progress. His hearers probably knew that the state's per capita income in 1963 was the country's lowest and that Mississippi was second from the bottom on the index of indigency. The shocker came in his estimate that, at the rate of improvement since the beginning of World War II, Mississippi would catch up with the national income average in the year 2051 and, at the rate of increased income in the previous fifteen years, the state would achieve the national average in 360 years. "Mississippi's need for physicians," he said, "is being met only about half as well as the need of the average American." Its economy was particularly vulnerable to depression, and its ill-advised hostility to responsible trade unions was costly to the state, as was its insistence on a racial caste system. Mississippi needed capital, tools, a skilled labor force, and imaginative business leaders. Its "main safeguard against recession is the federal purse." The economic status of Mississippi Negroes "is not three-tenths of that of all of the American people." Virtually half the population "exists on income of not much over one-fourth the national average and has wholly inadequate access to education. The future economic progress of Mississippi depends largely on making color irrelevant in law, in economics, in housing, in education, and in public behavior." He told of the vice-president of a great corporation who had put a large plant in North Carolina instead of in Mississippi because "he concluded that North Carolinians were the more teachable."

Business leaders had known the truth of the Lattimer speech for some years, and a few politicians were beginning to react. Paul Johnson admitted that "the racial trouble has hurt us economically," as at least a dozen companies considering Mississippi for new locations decided to go elsewhere after the 1964 summer. The $37 million spent on new plants in the state in 1964 represented a drop of 28% from the previous year, while Arkansas and Louisiana were making big gains. At least fifteen industrial prospects made it clear they were afraid of the Mc-Comb atmosphere. An aluminum fabricator in that troubled city lost a quarter of a million dollars in sales "because of people refusing to buy Mississippi products." One manufacturer moved his shipping point to Louisiana. Some of the smaller motels on the Gulf Coast lost 50% of their business in 1964, and the state travel director admitted a drop of from $40 million to $60 million in tourist spending that year. State tax receipts were up 7% annually for five years; expenditures had risen 20%. A $38 million treasury surplus left by Governor Coleman in 1960 was gone.

A Jackson manufacturer in a position to know wrote that Sears, Roebuck was then shipping out the $175 million worth of Mississippi products it bought annually in boxes marked "Tennessee." A chamber of commerce representative from the coast area said, in December 1964, that hotel-motel occupancy in the Gulfport-Biloxi area was only 8%. At that time the Syracuse University football team, bound for the Sugar Bowl, chose Florida as a place to train rather than Mississippi, as had been customary. In January 1965, Lieutenant Governor Gartin spoke in Greenville of the Ohio industrialist who refused to consider expansion of two Mississippi plants until the state "decides to become a part of the Union again," of the Virginia contractor who canceled orders for the product of a southeast Mississippi plant, and of an industrialist who had complained of the difficulty of moving thirty key personnel to Mississippi. But the biggest scare of all must have come from Arthur Miller, vice-president of a Mississippi-based engineering firm doing 80% of its business out of the state, who told the Jackson Rotary

Club his firm would be forced to move unless the state dealt firmly with racial strife. Had the Mississippi image not deteriorated, "we could have approximately 50 additional employees resident in Jackson," he added. Other corporation executives let public officials know that they would not remain in Mississippi if violence continued, if law and order broke down, or if the public schools were closed. (On the other hand, a New England president of a large plant opened in Amory praised Mississippi for its Goldwater vote, saying "I'm glad to be back in the United States.")

A perpetual optimist about Mississippi's future wrote from the Gulf Coast a month before the fall elections: "Prejudice is a strong emotion but it can't hold a candle to self-interest. No busted millionaire ever jumped out of an office building window because of prejudice. A man who has built up a business and sees it threatened by racial turmoil doesn't react in the same way that he would if his wife and children were threatened. He reacts as if *he himself* was threatened. He loves his wife and children but his business, career or property are a *part* of him.

"In dealing with the racial problem, business men and politicians have to weigh one threat against another. Until Johnson became president, the weight of the Citizens Councils was the greater threat. Now they are beginning to see that the threat of federal power in the hands of Johnson is the greater threat. The passage of the Civil Rights Bill pulled the rug out from under the Citizens Councils by giving business a legitimate excuse to go along with radical changes."

After the disappearance of Schwerner, Chaney, and Goodman, civil rights leaders made a big plea for federal troops in Mississippi. Instead, President Johnson sent J. Edgar Hoover, who announced the establishment in the state of the largest branch of the FBI in the country, and Allan Dulles, who talked like a Dutch uncle to the governor, clergy, chamber of commerce, and civil rights leaders. According to one who listened attentively, Dulles "was most understanding of Mississippi's problems, but also most insistent that Mississippi was under a gun and if it didn't begin to act, outside action would be forced."

And so the business power structure of Mississippi, fearful of the disastrous economic impact of the state's image, spurred by the Philadelphia murders and the passage of the Civil Rights Act, as well as by the impending school desegregation, exerted its strength for law and order and compliance with the national will. Paul Johnson was in a tight spot with Citizens Council and redneck pressure heavy on him, but he finally went down the line. Mayor Allen Thompson, famous for his policy of "instant arrest" but now afraid of bloodshed and riots, called for a meeting with the executive committee of the Jackson Chamber of Commerce. Out of this came the chamber's ringing declaration for compliance, which lost it only four out of a membership of 1,500. Condemnatory statements by the Citizens Council and the House of Representatives made very little impression. It was generally known that eighty-two House members had signed a blank piece of paper while waiting two hours for the resolution. The Senate failed to concur. At the strategic time, the mayor backed the Chamber of Commerce and the fight was won. The impetus had come from men whose security and prestige were assured, whose motivation was neither spiritual nor intellectual but largely economic. It was mainly a matter of property rather than human rights, of profits rather than honor and justice. These leaders had at long last broken openly with the Citizens Council, whose period of glory and power was now to give way to a grim fight for survival.

A question that has long troubled many Americans is the practicability of reforming any close-knit society from the outside. In an absolutely closed society the chances for imposed change would be minimal, indeed, but Mississippi has always had many citizens anxious to break away from the old customs. Now at last these moderates began to lose their fear of speaking up. With the passage of the Civil Rights Act, the shopworn argument that integration was a usurpation by the Supreme Court and not the will of the people was no longer tenable. While there was no rush to be first in line, a powerful movement to obey rather than defy federal law had been inaugurated. It culminated in the statement of principles by the Mississippi Economic Council on February 3, 1965, which declared that "Mississippi is not an island unto itself, but an integral and responsible part of the United States. We recognize the Civil Rights act of 1964 . . . cannot be ignored and should not be unlawfully defied. Resistance to the law should be through established procedures . . . the ballot boxes and the courts. We should adjust ourselves to the impact of the legislation, regardless of personal feeling and convictions, and limit our resistance to the stated methods.

"For the purpose of furthering justice, harmony and continued development in Mississippi, we respectfully urge: 1) Order and respect for law must be maintained. Lawless activities in the state by individuals and organizations cannot be tolerated. The penalty for law violation should be fairly and equitably applied to all law violators. 2) Communications must be maintained between the races within the state. 3) Registration and voting laws should be fairly and impartially administered for all. 4) Support of public education must be maintained and strengthened. We call upon all Mississippians to take positive action toward these ends."

More than fifty chambers of commerce, business organizations, and law enforcement groups throughout the state endorsed the Economic Council's firm stand. Opposition from the unreconstructed was to be expected. Barnett talked about the new "fuzzy" thinking, Charlie Hills suggested that Mississippi's so-called troubles were "all MOUTH," and Joe Bullock, director of the Agricultural and Industrial Board, suggested that "the person who is worried about our image is one of three things: a fool, a politician seeking the Negro vote, or a person who has a yellow streak up his back." Notwithstanding these pinpricks, at least for the present (and, one hopes, for the future), according to Nat S. Rogers, president of Jackson's Deposit Guaranty Bank, "What we are trying to say is that the people of Mississippi want to adopt a more realistic relationship with the rest of the country."

The Church Takes a Stand

In the fall of 1964, a prominent Methodist layman wrote, "We are undergoing a revolution. I am more optimistic than a year ago. However, the changes that have taken place have not been in my own church, nor do I feel my denomination has contributed significantly to those changes. Since church work is my primary interest in life, this doesn't make me feel very good." Father Bernard Law, editor of the Catholic *Mississippi Register,* noted, "One of the distressing aspects of the Mississippi scene has been the almost total silence of organized religion, when one could have reasonably expected to hear the clear prophetic voice which is religion's traditional role in times of moral crisis." A Mississippi circuit judge agreed that "The churches are mostly in the middle of the road; now and then you find a Duncan Gray or a Selah, but as a whole the ministers are not leading but following the thinking of their congregations." A visiting clergyman from California was told that Bishop Gerow had been silent in public on racism for thirty-six years. He had insisted that Notre Dame seminarians not come to Mississippi in the summer of 1964 and had, in fact, sent six priests home to Oklahoma City after one week with students of the freedom project.[12] Rabbi Schultz continued to move about the state shouting that America was about to be taken over by Communists, the U.S. intelligentsia, and the Madison Avenue-Harvard-Hollywood axis, through control of communications. They "are diluting the will of our people to survive," he insisted. A virtual

12. The visitor from California, Father Tom Fry, wrote: "The priests are keenly aware of the emotional problems of their white parishioners. All Negro Catholics are served by order priests, so the diocesan clergy are protected from pastoral experience with Negro frustrations and emotions. It is almost impossible for the diocesan priests to say with Dr. King, 'Daily I meet young Negroes whose disappointment with the churches has grown to almost outright disgust.' In a white parish, they cannot even say, 'Daily I meet young Negroes.' But there is a growing awareness that the Body of Christ cannot remain as it is—the White Church and the Negro missions."

ultimatum was issued to Methodist Bishop Edward J. Pendergrass complaining about church literature and Methodist connection with the National Council of Churches. On the other
hand, a liberal Methodist deprecated the vague role of the NCC:
"They were very defensive in their effort to let people know
this summer project was not theirs and not in their regular
budget. They lost as much support acting in an advisory capacity as they would have had they jumped in with both feet.
But this defensive action is so typical of the church at this time.
Of course the local churches washed their hands of the whole
project. A few individual churchmen helped as advisors."

Therein lay the truth and the heart of the matter. Although
Mississippi denominations were slowly beginning to follow the
lead of their national churches, it was still a fact that almost
every congregation in the state was composed of individuals
who ranged from liberal to racist. Many moderates were biding
their time, desiring to act effectively, like Bishop Gerow whose
"silence yielded to eloquence." "We are all responsible," he
had written, "for the death of Medgar Evers. The only way to
prevent this from being repeated is to meet the just grievances of
the Negro community." Just before public-school desegregation was carried out, he announced that the parochial schools
would be open to all persons. At Galloway Memorial in Jackson, the church from which Dr. Selah had resigned because of
its racial policy, the Board was told quite frankly by Bishop
Arthur Moore that its no-admittance policy was wrong. According to one present, "This did not evoke the bitter denunciations
such words provoked on former occasions." [13] Bishop Pendergrass made it plain to the Methodist Conference that a vital
church could not bar Negroes from its service: "No congregation can deepen the spiritual eyes of its members and make an
effective witness to Jesus Christ by placing special ushers at the

---

13. At a meeting late in the fall of 1965, the official board of the church
voted 60–40 to table a motion calling for seating Negro visitors to the
church. Yet, a week later, an integrated party was seated—in a pew
just beyond that occupied at the time by Mayor Thompson and his
family.

doors to ·select who will and who will not be allowed to participate." In the fall of 1964, Father Law commended the Mississippi Baptist Convention for "recognizing that the racial problems which beset Mississippi can only be solved through the leadership of the church," an action antecedent to that of the Southern Baptist Convention, which, in June 1965, according to its president, "brought to an end five or six years of reactionary and negative thinking." Every month saw increasing numbers of Mississippi churches quietly opening their doors to all who would come to worship.[14]

In the early spring of 1965, the "Sunday Bulletin" of Catholic Saint Benedict the Moor Church of Indianola, in the heart of the Mississippi Delta, contained these pertinent messages: "There has been uncalled-for police brutality with regard to picketers and bystanders last weekend simply because the majority of our Indianola peace officers are poorly trained. Brice Alexander is basically a good man but he is not a free police chief. He is pressured by various members of the White Citizens Council. We hope that Mr. Alexander will emancipate himself from this undue pressure and show us real leadership in Indianola law enforcement." And, somewhat later, "How can Mississippi pretend that it fights Communism when it tolerates a 'closed society,' another characteristic of Communism. If Indianola is in good faith, its civic leaders will demonstrate their Americanism by raising funds to replace the burned FREEDOM SCHOOL. The challenge is theirs. All decent people everywhere are waiting." The "Beacon" of the First Baptist Church in Biloxi suggested to its readers that "Christians in Mississippi have not understood that to raise their voices against the evils of their state would be the finest thing they could do for her. Far from being disloyal, this would be loyalty of the highest sort." And the unsinkable Father Law declared in the *Missis-*

---

14. Reports are conflicting. An occasional Negro visitor does not mean that a church is integrated. A congregation may shift its policy from time to time. As far as I know, there is no record of a white church welcoming a Negro to membership.

sippi Register that "The time has come to emancipate our politicians. Mississippi has the leadership, if it can be freed, to push
the state forward on many fronts. For too long we have been
wasting time, talent, effort and money in a senseless doomed
struggle to maintain the corpse of enforced segregation." In
June 1965, Methodist Bishop Ellis Finger asked candidates to
the ministry, "Are you willing to relate yourself in ministry to
all persons without regard to race, color or national origin, including receiving them into membership and fellowship of the
Church?" All answered in the affirmative.

When Millsaps College opened its doors to Negroes, the
North Mississippi Conference "deplored" a program of vilifica-
tion of the church by the Mississippi Association of Methodist
Ministers and Laymen (MAMMAL), which "falsely implied
participation in a 'blue print for Communist control' on the part
of the interboard council." When Mississippi College refused to
open its doors to Negroes, the Griffith Memorial Baptist Church
in Jackson pledged itself to help replace lost federal funds. The
College was praised for not selling its honor and respect—"the
government would have paid for the school's heresy in destroying the purpose and the soul of the institution by integrating the
races therein."

Early in 1965, MAMMAL prepared a petition, signed by
7,000 Methodists, asking Bishop Pendergrass to help destroy
integration and socialism. "We have succeeded in exposing, but
have not succeeded in defeating their influence," the ultimatum
read. If the bishop did not maintain separation of white and
Negro churches, "there can be no alternative to the creation of
an independent Methodist Church in Mississippi." The North
Mississippi Conference responded by voting down (126–73) a
proposal calling for "an inclusive church in an inclusive society."
Subsequently, MAMMAL, having switched its name to Association of Independent Methodists, organized two new churches in
Jackson and appropriately called for the first service to be held
in the Robert E. Lee Club (formerly the Robert E. Lee Hotel).
Citizen Council members of the new Methodist ventures de-

nounced the social gospel ("an effort to debunk Christ, humanize God, and minimize sin"), those in control of the NCC ("the same bunch of rotten radicals"), and bishops in general ("We are tired of them"). Undertaker John Wright decried communist influence in the church as he professed his own belief "in the virgin birth and the infallibility of the Holy Scriptures. The no. 1 problem is sin. No series of fair deals, new deals, raw deals and great societies can solve the problem." He did not say who would interpret the Scriptures. Previously, the Holy Trinity Anglican Church, composed of former Methodists, Baptists, Episcopalians, Presbyterians, and Catholics, had in an open letter welcomed to membership "those who feel a Divine Discontent." The invitation noted that, while "Winston Churchill was an Anglican [and] Queen Elizabeth is an Anglican," this new church is founded not "on snob appeal" but in the knowledge that "not one penny we contribute goes to espouse causes alien and dangerous to our Christian way of life."

To many people, the most shocking reprisal of white malcontents against the freedom movement in Mississippi was the burning of forty-one Negro churches. The church, as a kind of command post in the struggle for equal rights, the only sanctuary and secure meeting place for black and white civil rights workers, thus became the focal point of attack and defense. Yet out of this wholesale arson came the most promising evidence of the compassion of thousands of Mississippians in the creation, in September 1964, of the interfaith Committee of Concern. In exactly twelve months the committee had collected $119,435.04 (with that much again in labor, furniture, fixtures, supplies, and discounts) from every state and eighteen foreign countries, had rebuilt twenty-nine churches, had dedicated twenty-two, and had five more under construction.

The inspiration for this ecumenical movement came from Dr. William P. Davis, secretary of the Department of Work with Negroes of the Mississippi Baptist Convention Board. On August 14, Davis had met with the pastor and members of the seventy-five-year-old St. Matthew Baptist Church to examine the ruins of their church, burned the night before. Their faith

prompted him to walk to a charred picnic table, where he laid
down his Bible and opened it to Isaiah 61:1-4.

The spirit of the Lord God is upon me; because the Lord hath
anointed me to preach good tidings unto the meek; he hath sent me
to bind up the brokenhearted, to proclaim liberty to the captives,
and the opening of the prison to them that are bound;
2 To proclaim the acceptable year of the Lord, and the day of vengeance of our God; to comfort all that mourn;
3 To appoint unto them that mourn in Zion, to give unto them
beauty for ashes, the oil of joy for mourning, the garment of praise
for the spirit of heaviness; that they might be called trees of
righteousness, the planting of the Lord, that he might be glorified.
4 And they shall build the old wastes, they shall raise up the former desolations, and they shall repair the waste cities, the desolations of many generations.

"From that picnic table," he later remembered, "I steadfastly
set my face to create beauty for ashes and to build bridges for
better human relations." Next came an editorial, "Smoke Over
Mississippi," in the *Baptist Record,* which insisted that "murder,
rioting, bombing, arson, threats, mob action, will not solve Mississippi's problem." The Committee of Concern, with enthusiastic support from Protestants, Catholics, and Jews, was created
to "make it possible for men, women and children of good will
to respond to violence, hatred, and destruction with concern,
compassion, and construction." The Mississippi Baptist Convention in November deplored all actions of violence and commended the committee for its work of restoration.

Help came from many sources. The Mennonite Disaster
Service pledged $15,000 worth of skilled labor.[15] Students from
Oberlin College, Queens College, the University of Mississippi,
Mississippi State University, the University of Notre Dame,
Mississippi College, Millsaps College, the University of Arkansas,
Jackson State College, Tougaloo College, and many others

15. The Society of Friends in Philadelphia, New York, and San Fran-
cisco also recruited skilled labor and raised money; $15,000 came from
Jewish organizations.

sacrificed vacation periods to offer their willing hands. The Council of Churches of Southern California raised $8,000 to help rebuild one church, and $5,000 to help rebuild others.[16] The American Bible Society donated a magnificent pulpit Bible to each church when it was rededicated. The building program must have had considerable effect on local public opinion, as evidenced in these words from the Memphis *Commercial Appeal*: "He who sets a match to a church or hurls a fire-bomb into it, desecrates more than a building. He profanes God. In a sense, he joins those Roman soldiers who drove spikes through the hands and feet of Christ and then pierced His side with a spear."

The new churches are beautiful fireproof (but not bomb-proof) structures designed by Mississippi architects. Each dedication service has been biracial. For example, the Zion Hill Baptist Church outside McComb was organized in 1868, its building was burned on July 17, 1964, and the new $15,450 edifice was dedicated on May 14, 1965. The church had raised $1,500 to add to $3,100 received in insurance, and the committee had done the rest. In his dedicatory remarks, Dr. Davis said that "no one should be denied a place in the church because of race, creed or nationality." To the Civil Rights Commission, meeting in Jackson, Davis added, ". . . anarchy, bigotry, demagoguery and violence shall not be allowed to prevail in Mississippi—we the people of Mississippi will not stand for it. A new sunrise of inter-faith and biracial good will stands at the gate of the morning in Mississippi 'to bind up the broken-hearted and give unto them beauty for ashes, and to build the old waste places, the desolations of many generations.' 'Let no man's heart fail.' Indignities and injustices shall not prevail. Tyranny must go. A power structure designed to deprive citizens of their voting rights and to discriminate in the administration of justice because of race or creed is tyranny. It is not treason to challenge tyranny. It is the highest act of patriotism

16. The Committee of Concern of Richmond, Virginia, contributed $12,000.

and obedience to the eternal command of Almighty God: 'LET
MY PEOPLE GO.' "

It would indeed be difficult to quarrel with such piety, yet
the fearless Tom Ethridge managed it: "Inside jobs of church
burning can be financially or psychologically profitable to
leaders and adherents of the Negro Revolution. There is nothing
to prevent outside agitators or inside opportunists from burning
colored churches and blaming it on white terrorists. The propaganda value of this is quite obvious—especially since the nation
is being conditioned to believe the worst about our state and
region."

The church organization whose civil rights work caused most
screams of rage in Mississippi was the militant Commission on
Religion and Race of the National Council of Churches. According to a lead editorial in the Jackson *Clarion-Ledger*, the
NCC sponsored unchristian teaching of hatred toward Mississippi in its school for summer workers in Oxford, Ohio. The
Clarion-Ledger quoted from the Lynchburg *News*: "What
would you think of a school which specializes in teaching
hatred of other human beings?—Which teaches one how to
act during street violence, how to protect oneself during riots,
which teaches one how to lie, cheat and break the law?—Which
teaches fear and distrust and creates the impression that there
is not a single decent white person in an entire state?—Which
teaches its girl students that if they are arrested, they have
a choice of being horsewhipped or submitting to the desires
of their jailer?—Which uses filthy words and actions to depict
the type of treatment to expect from people one has never seen
and who have not harmed them in any way?"

Another excerpt from a quoted editorial included the advice
given the workers by R. Jess Brown, a Jackson Negro lawyer
who had handled dozens of civil rights cases: "If you are
snatched out of a car some night by a policeman, 'Don't stand
out there at midnight and try to teach him constitutional law.
He's got a second grade education. A club and a pistol is all he
knows about rights.' "

The *Clarion-Ledger* did not attempt to show wherein this

advice fell short of reality. Hazel Brannon Smith was one of the few Mississippi editors who pointed out that 1) the NCC did not originate the Mississippi project or recruit students for it, 2) the NCC spent on the training only money specifically donated for that purpose, 3) the training was in the nature of orientation, 4) the young people in the COFO project did not go to Mississippi to demonstrate, but to conduct literacy and voter registration classes. As a matter of further fact, the NCC had since the early 1950's sponsored a rural development program to help wipe out pockets of persistent poverty complicated by racial injustice. Its Delta Ministry was later to be met with more sustained animosity from most of the whites in Mississippi.[17]

---

17. In the summer of 1964, Claude Ramsay reviewed "from stem to stern," with clergymen associated with the Delta Ministry, the question of agricultural labor in Mississippi. He concluded, as have most impartial observers, that the plight of the part-time farm worker could not be remedied from a trade-union point of view. Machines and chemistry have already done away with the need for most labor in the Mississippi Delta except for about 3,000 equipment operators and some 25,000 men, women, and children needed each year for no more than eighty days of cotton chopping. Tractor drivers usually live on the farms, where they work for $6.00 a day, while unskilled laborers normally reside in town and receive $3.00 for working from sunup to sundown. In such a situation, the only organizable people are the mechanics spread over an area 150 miles long and up to 75 miles wide.

Under the sponsorship of the Freedom Labor Union, an offshoot of the Freedom Democratic Party, and with the active help of the Delta Ministry, tractor drivers walked off the Andrews plantation and several others nearby in the summer of 1965. In spite of widespread publicity, as well as involved court action, this "strike" was notoriously unsuccessful because of the few people involved and the ease with which they were replaced. The moderate *Delta Democrat-Times* looked upon the ministerial leaders of the dispute as "inept, inefficient revolutionaries," while others remembered futile efforts to organize farm labor in the Depression days before automation came to Mississippi agriculture. Bishop Paul Moore made it clear, however, that the Delta Ministry, whose end is social action rather than religion, would push aggressively its fight to improve living conditions of tens of thousands of depressed and largely unemployed workers. The Ministry looked beyond its own resources to those

In his last sermon delivered in St. Peter's Church in Oxford, Episcopal priest Duncan Gray, perhaps the most dedicated and eloquent of all the ministers who carried the gospel of equal rights to Mississippians, told the parishioners he had shepherded for eight controversial years: "We are called not only to lead the way into the new age, but also . . . to minister constantly in loving care and concern to those who cannot yet accept it. . . . The new age must be for all men, and we should never allow one prejudice to be swapped for another."

The Press Takes Several Stands

One Mississippi businessman thought, "Even the *Clarion-Ledger* sees the handwriting on the wall," which may have been true, but veteran *Commercial Appeal* reporter Kenneth Toler was exceedingly accurate when he wrote, "Very little editorial support to acceptance of change is being given by Mississippi newspapers." [18] All through the summer of 1964 and, in fact, well

---

of the federal government for a massive infusion of economic assistance. The great need seemed to be, in the fall of 1965, for co-operation between the determined churchmen and the heretofore lethargic white community. The Delta Ministry would find it immeasurably difficult, if not impossible, to bypass established local political structures, while the old conservative leadership needed to show evidence of good faith in its willingness and desire to upgrade the Negro community. Need for biracial compromise and understanding was apparent and would probably be forthcoming, as usual, with the persuasive prodding of the federal government.

18. The Hederman press has often quoted out-of-state editors favorable to the conservative Mississippi position. One of those most frequently quoted has been James J. Kilpatrick, editor of the Richmond *News-Leader*. For some reason, Jimmy Ward missed the following statement from the pen of Mr. Kilpatrick: "Mississippi isn't perfect. Of course not. Not even the most sympathetic observers can excuse or condone some of the senseless segregation that persists. There is, in truth, a terrible sickness there, made all the more tragic by the unwillingness of so many Mississippians publicly to acknowledge the cancer that exists. They are paying a fearful price socially and economically and culturally."

into the spring of 1965, the press as a whole continued to mis-
inform its readers in an effort to stem the inevitable tide of
revolution.[19] When Mississippi editors finally came around to
recommending the scrapping of the state's laws and constitutional provisions framed to maintain white supremacy, it was
merely a staying action aimed at keeping out a horde of federal
registrars, with a view to recapturing much of the old way of
life as soon as the heat was off.

For unfathomable reasons, the Hederman press has for years
carried Drew Pearson and has printed letters to the editor of
all descriptions. Its press association stories are, of course, of
known accuracy, though the cautious reader must beware of
the headlines and the many news accounts that fail to list their
source. WAS DEAD RIGHTS WOMAN A COMMIE? for
instance, introduced a UPI dispatch carrying the testimony of an
Alabama investigator in the murder trial growing out of the
shooting of Mrs. Viola Liuzzo. " 'Did you see a communist party
card in her billfold?' Murphy demanded. 'No sir,' Dixon replied."

---

19. The following excerpts are from two personal letters written by a
prominent newspaper publisher in southwest Mississippi. July 24, 1964:
". . . the Negroes are not being taken advantage of in Mississippi . . .
they are proud of their schools . . . have their own football teams,
basketball teams, majorettes. Really, their situation is about as ideal as
one can imagine, considering their capabilities. Many people are wondering why it is that every time a bombing takes place, no one gets hurt and
little damage is done. It has long been a 'nigger trick' to set a man's house
on fire if he gets in trouble with him. Many responsible people believe that
a goodly proportion of these bombings are being done by militant agitators who are seeking publicity for their cause, with a purpose of pointing a finger at whites. Take the three missing beatniks who disappeared
at Philadelphia. Most people here believe that this was another publicity stunt. . . . It would be pretty hard to hide three bodies and not
have at least one show up." August 18: "As I told you previously,
many people here believed that these three men were a part of a publicity
stunt and that they probably had escaped to Cuba or Greenwich Village.
This belief was based on factual information that there are Communists
working in the state with the invading college students. We were wrong,
in this case. The murder of these men was a terrible thing regardless of
how one looks at it. While they doubtless had it coming, obviously there
is nothing right about murder."

(An Ethridge column was headed, HUSBAND SHOULD BLAME HIMSELF FOR PERMITTING WIFE TO LEAVE CHILDREN.) Another UPI story, listing the provisions of the voter registration bill before Congress, was introduced with the words "NEGRO CONTROL?" An Associated Press report of "dramatic signs of progress in racial harmony" was headlined NEGROES TAKING OVER TUSKEGEE. When, in August 1965, two young SNCC enthusiasts recommended that Mississippi Negroes resist the draft, the *Clarion-Ledger* carried a front-page story headed LEGION URGES U.S. PROBE FDP ACTION, while on page 24 there reposed another item, one-tenth as long, FREEDOM DEMOCRATS RAPPED BY NAACP. A caption accompanying a clear reproduction of an Associated Press photograph showing Dr. June Finer, "head of a medical group supporting the agitators," protecting a small Negro boy in the presence of eight state and local uniformed officers of the law, read as follows: "UNFORTUNATE INCIDENT in the arrest of FDP political demonstrators at the Governor's Mansion Friday included that of a Highway Patrolman taking a flag [American] away from a Negro boy, who accompanied his demonstrating mother. Waving of flags [Confederate?] and signs is considered picketing. The boy was said to be surrendering his flag to the patrolman on demand when his mother shouted at him not to give it up. The boy tugged and the officer, acting on reflex apparently, responded to the unexpected tug with a strong pull of his own, which lifted the child off the ground. At this instant, a press photographer for the New York Times snapped a shot that doubtless will arouse reaction."

In January 1965, a *Clarion-Ledger* news story of undetermined origin carried this information:

The White Christian Protective and Legal Defense Fund was formed by a group of patriots from all walks of life, and representative of no particular political viewpoint, in response to the immense and ever increasing political pressure that is being brought to bear on Mississippi, its institutions, and its citizenry.

It was formed to provide monies for adequate legal defense to any White Christian Patriot who has or may be indicted and forced to stand trial for some real or imagined infraction of the Communist inspired Civil Rights Act or other acts passed by Congress (Acts which the Communists themselves declare to be the greatest single advance they have made in the capture of the United States).

Agents of organized Communist revolution and savagery have come into our state with the deliberate intent of inciting race war: their aim is the destruction of our Christian civilization. The agents of the Federal Government have prevented our local officers from defending us from them. The National Government has provided the finest lawyers and unlimited financial resources to protect our enemies. Any society which cannot or will not protect and defend its domestic tranquility against atheistic revolution cannot expect to survive.

The Board of Directors call on all Patriotic Christians everywhere to join in this common endeavor; and wish to report that the response from the public has been very enthusiastic. (Checks from all parts of the country have begun to come in.) Already more than 925 collection jars have been placed throughout Mississippi. And, within the next month, the goal of 7,500 jars will have been achieved.

At least the *Clarion-Ledger* placed its report of Judge Russell Moore's charge to a grand jury at Raymond on the editorial page where it belonged. A contract to comply with federal insistence on school integration, according to Moore, "amounts to taking an oath to insure integration of the state school system." He pointed out that "just such compliance would not only result in integration of the children, integration of faculty, and eventually of textbooks, but with complete control of all facets of the children's education." He said, "the loss of the right of a state to operate its school system . . . can only result in eventual dictatorship. 'Our forefathers were not concerned with federal aid. Their concern was liberty and freedom.' The slow poison of Communism and its related isms might well find itself a major subject required of every student from the elementary grades through our colleges and universities. The acceptance of social reforms contrary to local custom or desire follow just as easily through such money-bait tactics."

The afternoon Jackson *Daily News* also ranted against the

"nefarious civil rights law, written by Fabian socialists and rammed through Congress by leftist liberals. . . . The government has seized control of the nation's schools, not only to force racial mixing, a proven evil, but worse, if possible, to condition school children to accept social doctrines and fit into a submissive and conforming way of life . . . to put Russia and other communist countries in a more favorable light." [20]

Much of the local press of the state carries on in the same vein as the Jackson papers. When Tunica County was designated by a federal agency as "the most poverty-stricken area of the nation," it was only natural for Editor Paul Phillips of the Tunica *Times-Democrat* to come back in a fighting mood. But he defended his county (median family income: $1,260) by saying that its Negroes "are getting along pretty well. They are getting free rent and a government check . . . have cars and television sets . . . aren't working and don't want to work." If the plantation owners "would turn these Negro families out . . . you would really see poverty." Harvard-educated Clayton Rand, the leading racist editor on the Gulf Coast, declared in the fall of 1964: ". . . how proud we are that Mississippi is coming through another crisis strong and triumphant. If she does not falter in her effort to preserve racial integrity, she will achieve her purpose. Hers is no lost cause." And zealous Mary Cain, head of the Women for Constitutional Government and editor of the Pike County *Summit Sun*, who scorned "gutless" capitulation to the federal government, was sick and tired of hearing about the McComb bombings when everyone with

---

20. The *Daily News* was understandably opposed to all three aims of the Head Start program (to attack poverty, to raise educational levels, and to narrow the chasm separating whites from Negroes). According to a lead editorial on May 21, 1965: "On the face of this undertaking, it appears to be the most wholesome and humane, appealing to the most tender senses in assisting infant youngsters who otherwise might be relegated to slum dwelling influence, undesirable home background, and lack of basic necessities. However, as all federal programs are now designed, here is one of the most subtle mediums for instilling the acceptance of racial integration and ultimate mongrelization ever perpetrated in this country."

a grain of sense knew COFO itself was guilty. After local whites signed confessions (the Americans for the Preservation of the White Race had guarded her house when she got a crackpot letter), Mrs. Cain couldn't believe that Mississippians could be so cruel and admonished her readers to withhold judgment until they were proven guilty.

There has always been a responsible Mississippi press, and in the last year or so it has become more outspoken. Billy Mc-Millan, editor of the Kosciusko *Star-Herald,* admitted that, until the passage of the Civil Rights Law, "Tempers ran short, leaders made intemperate remarks . . . that appeared to the illiterate, unlettered and naive segments of our population to be calls to arms . . . [they] sensed official approval of violence." Now "it's time we change, or be destroyed by change. This act was passed by the Congress of the United States, and quite overwhelmingly so. In essence it was apparently endorsed over-whelmingly by the majority of the people of the United States, who voted for President Johnson as opposed to Senator Gold-water in a clear-cut choice between one who supported the Act and one who opposed it. We must obey the law, and there is no other alternative." The Winona *Times* confessed that the state had "been sadly lacking in the leadership department." Those who had piously cried "Never" were seeking to promulgate their own interests; "they knew well that their promises were pie-in-the-sky and that they would be tromped into the mud when the day of confrontation came." The *Deer Creek Pilot* remarked "on the hopeful signs growing day by day that no longer will it be sufficient for seekers after public places of trust to 'cry nigger.' " In a front-page editorial the Laurel *Leader-Call* defended a COFO advertisement accepted by the paper. It would continue to print ads that "are legitimate, not libelous, blasphe-mous or obscene." (All of the windows had been blown out of the press room seven months before. No arrest was ever made.) The Hattiesburg *American* commended "the strong and coura-geous words" of Judge Darwin Maples' charge to a Jackson County grand jury. "These so-called leaders," said the Judge, "have contributed to these bombings and other acts of violence

in going up and down the length and breadth of the state preaching hatred, disrespect for law and order, and they have condemned the courts and the constituted authorities in this country
in an attempt to drape themselves in a cloak of patriotism."

There is no room here to list the courageous, intelligent, and
constructive programs sponsored by such papers as the Greenville *Delta Democrat-Times*, the Lexington *Advertiser*, the
Tylertown *Times,* the Clarksdale *Press-Register,* the Batesville
Panolian, or the Tupelo *Journal.*[21] The last named paper, a
genuine community leader for thirty years, had spearheaded a
biracial movement that was meeting the economic requirements
of all the people. Instead of crying state rights and deprecating
the federal government, the *Journal* joyously admitted that the
2,000,000 inhabitants of Mississippi had, since World War II,
received more "foreign aid" from Washington than had the
450,000,000 of India.

In somewhat arbitrary fashion, I have chosen to sketch the
failures and successes of a gallant and intelligent editor in
McComb, the church-burning capital of the world. By the middle
of 1964, a reign of terror prevailed in Pike County, evidenced
by widespread rumors, alarming suspicions, underground activities, and a frightened people. "Political leadership said little
about the need of exercising moderation at a time when the
community powder keg was readied for an explosion." This
intolerable situation developed despite the efforts of Oliver
Emmerich of the *Enterprise-Journal* to prepare his community
for proper action. In a series of front-page editorials in May, he
had conducted a campaign of information and had suggested a
course of action: 1) The coming civil rights workers, he contended, quoting the New York *Times,* "are seriously motivated,
emotionally stable individuals, intent on participating in social

---

21. Papers from Memphis, Birmingham, and New Orleans are widely
read in Mississippi. The Scripps-Howard papers contributed greatly to
peaceful desegregation in Memphis and undoubtedly had some influence
in Mississippi. It is not true that the Memphis *Commercial Appeal* went
for Johnson-Humphrey in its Tennessee edition and for Goldwater-Miller
in its Mississippi edition.

change." 2) "The people of Mississippi," here he was repeating the words of Governor Johnson, "are asked to avoid emotionalism; to go about their affairs dispassionately and to leave the problem of law enforcement to Mississippi's well-trained law enforcement officers." 3) On the county level, "We cannot tolerate anyone taking the law into his own hands. If this should happen mob law would prevail and under mob rule anything could happen." 4) The city's officials had promised that "So long as demonstrators are not violating the law nor interfering with the rights of other people, we will exercise restraint," and 5) thus the people of McComb and Pike County were asked to relax, while allowing law enforcement officers to handle the situation.

Nevertheless, the terrorists took over, as all the world knows.[22] In one weekend early in the fall, the *Enterprise-Journal* raised $5,000 as reward money to be used to purchase information regarding the violence. Somewhat later, eleven men confessed to crimes of bombing and arson, and though justice remained blinded, the community settled down in an uneasy tranquillity. Editor Emmerich (who has at various times had crosses burned in front of his home and his business, had his office plate-glass windows shattered by bullets, triumphed over a circulation boycott, and been slugged on the streets of McComb) continued his pursuit of peace with justice:

October 14: Negro churches have been burned. Negro houses have been bombed—and homes of some white people as well. A Negro store has been dynamited. And with a sense of irresponsibility we have blamed the Negroes. This is the ugly record of our community, the sordid story of McComb.

October 16: This sacred cow, like nullification and interposition, is unrealistic. It is the belief that the U.S. Constitution does not

---

22. One resident of McComb later wrote, "When the invasion [of civil rights workers] got under way the tempo of resistance stepped up to the point of fury. Houses were bombed. Churches were burned. Flogging of individuals occurred. Gun blasts were fired into residences and places of business. These things were accompanied by boycotts, forced firing of employed workers, expanded KKK activities, harassment arrests and general lawlessness."

uphold the right of franchise to Negro citizens . . . unreality because it is contrary to the facts of the Constitution.

October 19: It is easy to be irresponsible and effective. Governor Ross Barnett proved this to be true in the Ole Miss crisis.

October 20: Elected leadership has led us through the epochal trials of the Southern Manifesto, nullification, interposition, violence, mass resistance, the closing of schools, boycotts and economic pressure. But negation has served only to prove the fruitlessness of such efforts. Many legislators urged our people to ignore the law, refusing to comprehend that such action would arouse violence and create the potential climate for martial law.

October 22: . . . many people are afraid to venture an opinion, to speak out, or even to make a suggestion at a time when the good name of our community is in ill repute, or progress stalemated and community frustration . . . prevails.

October 23: At Tupelo, Miss., the economics of the racial problem is being met successfully. The project [based on Federal economic aid] in Tupelo was preceded by a meeting of responsible Negro ministers, Negro business leaders, Negro teachers who met with responsible white Tupelo leaders.

October 26: [Emmerich made an appeal for community action directly to bankers, merchants, lawyers, industrial workers, school teachers, insurance people, railroadmen, housewives, ministers, farmers and doctors.]

October 27: A team of researchers is now studying the means of applying economic pressure upon the City of McComb. . . .

October 28: Our people are a frightened people. Frightened people cannot achieve progress. Nor can a frightened people re-establish peace and tranquility. . . . [McComb is] a sick community with lack of faith in the future, undue sensibility, susceptible to wild rumors, with a low boiling point, tolerant of a dual system of justice, with undiversified conversation devoted almost exclusively to racial matters, and with a feeling of blamelessness.

October 29: With a positive program we can move in the direction of permanent progress with increased personal liberty and a higher standard of living for all our people.

October 30: A few weeks ago McComb was threatened with martial law. This is not hearsay. The threat was imminent. Roughly one thousand soldiers, 60 per cent Negro and 40 per cent white, were scheduled to patrol the streets and roads in this area. [Governor Johnson came to McComb to appeal for law and order.]

November 2: The city board of mayor and selectmen held a meeting this past week to check into what has been described as "harassment arrests." They usually are founded upon technical violations of law which are made not primarily because of the law violations but because of public antagonism to the individuals arrested.[23]

November 3: The first step toward community responsibility in McComb is the public will to restore law and order to the point where every citizen has the assurance of protection. The second step of responsible men and women must be to uphold the laws governing voter registration.

November 9: There is nothing more American than our Bill of Rights.

November 10: When we become involved in excessive community emotionalism our minds are often trapped. Our opinions set like cold concrete. Our judgment becomes inflexible. Our minds close like clams on a New England beach. We must not forget to be concerned.

November 11: [The Pike County Board of Supervisors resolved:] "All acts of violence, violation of law, intimidation, threats and coercion by and to any and all citizens of Pike County, are condemned."

November 16: McComb is getting nearer and nearer to the goal of responsible action with which to cope with our persisting and costly racial problems.

November 17: Tomorrow representatives of the NAACP are scheduled in McComb . . . to test some of the civil rights law. The city of McComb has two choices: 1) To meet the situation responsibly and attain a new sense of stability and serenity . . . or 2) to ignore the successful patterns of Southern cities and bog deeper in chaos and retrogression.

November 18: We Support McComb's Statement of Principles—

---

23. The case of Willie Dillon on August 27, 1964, may serve as an example of a harassment arrest. He was picked up at his home on the Holmesville Road near McComb shortly after he had refused to stop repairing a COFO car. Sheriff R. R. Warren came to investigate an alleged explosion in Dillon's front yard, but ended up by arresting him for operating a garage without a proper license and for stealing electricity from the Mississippi Power and Light Company. Altogether, he was fined $600 and costs and sentenced to nine months in jail. Judge Mize refused to accept the petition of removal to federal court.

signed by more than 650 McComb people. . . . [This statement condemned terrorism and called for equal treatment under the law for all citizens and for obedience to law. It decried harassment arrests and insisted that subversives (Ku Kluxers) should not be allowed to hold public office. Economic threats and sanctions must be stopped. Avenues of communication between the races must be re-established. Jury duty was not to be avoided.] We urge our fellow citizens to take a greater interest in public affairs . . . and to approach the future with a renewed dedication and . . . attitude of optimism about our country.

November 19: Things are looking upward in McComb. The new spirit manifested here will change the bad image of our community. Our people are determined that our problems must be solved within the framework of law.

Life in Mississippi in the past couple of years has not been completely frightening. Among six chosen as "Women of Influence" by the *Mississippi Magazine* and Theta Sigma Phi (their pictures were adjacent in the journal) were Mrs. Fannie Lou Hamer, ex-sharecropper of Ruleville, and Mrs. Florence Sillers Ogden, aristocrat par excellence from Rosedale. Mrs. Hamer was best known for her eloquence at the Democratic National Convention. Mrs. Ogden, who accepted her new honor graciously, is well known for "DIS AN' DAT," her Sunday column in the *Clarion-Ledger*. A healthy sign for Mississippi was Mrs. Ogden's shift from a plea for noncompliance in taking federal funds, in February 1965, to a call for changing the state constitution to conform with the new federal voting law, in August.

The Federal Presence

Without the drive, authority, and power of the federal government, the Negro in Mississippi would be doomed to live out at least this century bound in the shackles of the caste system. (The chief function of civil rights workers of whatever description has been to offer their bodies and their minds as catalysts in the creation of a nation-wide public opinion that, in turn, would demand action in Washington, a mission in which they have been eminently successful. Their efforts have been mightily aided, of course, by the colossal stupidity of their chief opponents: Ross Barnett, Bull Connor, George Wallace, Jim Clark, the die-hards in the Mississippi legislature, the Citizens Council, the Ku Klux Klan, and the right-wingers who captured the Republican Party in 1964.) Basing its decisions on the explosion of knowledge which had for at least fifty years been stripping away the intellectual basis for white supremacy, the U.S. Supreme Court had led the way. Congress followed with the civil rights acts of 1957, 1960, and 1964 and with the Voting Rights Act of 1965. Under a southern politician turned statesman, the executive branch of the federal government finally took the lead in the crusade to eliminate second-class citizenship in America. Lyndon Johnson had become, as Louis Lomax stated, the number one civil rights leader in America.

Rather than authority, it was more a matter of policy made in Washington (and policy that reflected the mood of the nation) that seemed to matter in Mississippi. For years civil rights workers had expressed anger and scorn over what they considered the apathy (and even collusion with local officials determined to frustrate federal law) of the Federal Bureau of Investigation, whose chief maintained that his agency was largely investigative and couldn't "wet-nurse everybody who . . . tries to reform or educate the Negroes in the South." It was, however, Assistant Attorney General Burke Marshall who explained most clearly the delicate state-federal system of law enforcement, which, until the civil rights movement, had served the country well since its founding. He was most reluctant to encourage a tendency that might have led to the establishment of a federal police force. Yet the Constitution left the control over normally routine decisions affecting the daily lives of all citizens to state institutions, which, in Mississippi, were not only unwilling to co-operate, but were in fact militantly organized to deny clearly established civil rights. Marshall illustrated the problem with the case of the 1961 Freedom Riders in Alabama, where state authorities failed to protect federal rights and failed to maintain order (thus bringing in U.S. marshals), and in Mississippi, where order was maintained but federal rights were not. Whenever local officials (as in the case of James Meredith's entry into the University of Mississippi) had tried to resolve the matter at hand by terror and violence, the federal government had had to step in with its own counterforce. In every such conflict, the federal courts have eventually enjoined state authority from illegal action and the local police have sooner or later met their responsibility for maintaining order on a proper basis. In Mississippi, the Freedom Riders did suffer from harassment arrests and were victimized by jail sentences and fines. In theory, at least, these grave indignities were not irreparable, but could be appealed from and invalidated, which is exactly what happened when Freedom Rider cases reached the U.S. Supreme Court.

The courts move slowly. It took five years of enormously patient and exhausting work on the part of the Justice Department to bring Forrest County Registrar Theron Lynd to terms. But it was done. In 1965, the Fifth Circuit Court of Appeals not only held him in contempt for disobeying orders of 1962 and 1963, but ordered him to pay court costs as well as to register 280 Negroes whom he had rejected. The Justice Department's John Doar had told the court, "For the first time, we have overwhelming proof that there is universal white suffrage in Forrest County," and had advocated that all Negroes be registered also. At one point a judge asked Lynd, "Do you think you can do better in the future than you have in the past?" His answer: "I think so, your Honor, I learn something every time I come into court." The painful education of a slow-learning registrar is of no great significance. Of enormous importance is the fact that the Justice Department had triumphed over a most obstreperous foe and that federal court orders similar to that given Lynd were the order of the day as early as 1964. In the excitement over the implementation of the Voting Rights Act, this climactic victory was largely forgotten.

As a matter of fact, it had been the willingness of states like Mississippi to use every means, legal and illegal, to block the course of justice that had been instrumental in bringing the voter registration law to passage. It may be argued that the executive and legislative branches of the federal government were willing by 1965 to risk a violation of that part of the Constitution granting states the power to determine voter qualifications in order to surmount state invalidation by subterfuge of the 15th Amendment. To many people, two wrongs did make a right.

The country was simply fed up with Mississippi. Until the summer of 1964, agents of the FBI had usually been on hand during or after racial disturbances, but their role seemed the casual one of investigating violations of toothless federal law. For Mississippi, they worked out of Memphis and New Orleans. But after the Philadelphia murders, the FBI took a five-year lease on the eighth floor of the First Federal Building in Jackson to set up the largest local bureau in the country. It began an intensive campaign of public education regarding respect for law, helped to purge terrorist elements from state and local law enforcement groups, heightened its infiltration of the Ku Klux Klan, and even made a few arrests. It was most effective in its identification of alleged criminals in Hattiesburg, McComb, Philadelphia, Itta Bena, Greenwood, and Meadville. Irrefutable evidence, however, sometimes including written confessions of bombers and arsonists, did not mean that Mississippi juries would indict or convict or that judges would measure sentences to the crimes. When J. Edgar Hoover visited Mississippi, he spoke highly of the co-operation of Governor Johnson but later castigated a state judge for suspending the sentences of nine men convicted of terrorism. He declared, furthermore, that "in the southern part of the state, in the swamp country, the only inhabitants seem to be rattlesnakes, water moccasins, and redneck sheriffs. . . ."

Incredible as it may seem, there are still Mississippians who profess to believe that Negroes in the state have been free to register and vote, that colored citizens have simply been apathetic about exercising their rights. The 284 pages, made up largely of Negro testimony, of the *Hearings before the United States Commission on Civil Rights* (the hearings were held in Jackson, February 16–20, 1965) should somehow be made required reading for those who are capable of facing truth. Apathy has indeed been a factor in the fact that less than 7% of Negroes of voting age were on the registration rolls at the time of the hearings, but it has been an apathy "born of decades of disenfranchisement and poor education rooted in poverty. Fear of the white man, both physical and economic," has also played a major role. In its seventy-four-page pamphlet, *Voting in Mississippi,* the Commission declared that "since 1875 Negroes in Mississippi have been systematically excluded from the franchise by legislative enactment, fraud and violence." County registrars have deprived Negroes of basic rights in the administration of voting tests, the poll tax was established as a discriminatory device, threats of violence and economic reprisal have prevented Negroes from voting, and the quality of public education for Negroes now of voting age has been so poor that any test of educational skills as a prerequisite for voting is inherently unfair. So said the Commission.

In the fall of 1964, all of the whites over twenty-one in Issaquena County were registered, and not one of the Negroes (who make up 68% of the population) was registered. Between July 1961 and February 1965, every one of the 150 white applicants had passed the voter registration tests and nine (some after repeated attempts) of the 128 Negro applicants had satisfied the registrar of their competence. Rural Issaquena was not an unusual Mississippi county. Evidence before the Commission established that many sheriffs refused to accept Negro poll taxes, and others took pictures of Negroes who tried to register. Low income meant economic dependence, so that "near destitution of many Negroes makes an economic reprisal a major disaster." Teachers were most susceptible to intimidation because of the autocratic power of all-white school boards. Despite official Mississippi propaganda, appropriations for white and colored education were grossly unequal (in 1961–62, Jefferson County spent $96.29 on the white child, $2.60 on the Negro).

Injunctive relief against county officials had been sought in twenty-six Justice Department cases, but the elapsed time from filing a complaint to the entry of judgment had averaged 17.8

months. An appeal from an unsatisfactory judgment took a year, and only three cases had been concluded. It was the Commission's opinion that "judicial remedies have not proven effective in eliminating discrimination in voting or the effects of intimidation and reprisals against Negroes attempting to exercise the right to register or vote." There had never been any affirmative state action to encourage all citizens to participate in the elective process.

In the testimony of Humphreys County Registrar G. H. Hood, the following colloquy took place:

COMMISSIONER GRISWOLD. I hand you a copy of section 182 of the Mississippi constitution. Would you please make a reasonable interpretation of section 182 for the Commission?

(Pause.)

MR. HOOD. You say 182?

COMMISSIONER GRISWOLD. Yes.

MR. HOOD. I'm sorry, sir. I've been reading 183.

(Pause.)

MR. HOOD. Well, it means that the power to tax corporations, their property, shall never be surrendered or abridged by any contract. And—

COMMISSIONER GRISWOLD. I didn't ask you to read it, Mr. Hood. I asked you to interpret it.

MR. BRIDGES. (Aside to Mr. Hood).

COMMISSIONER GRISWOLD. Mr. Chairman, I think it should be the witness' interpretation; not his counsel's.

MR. BRIDGES. If you please, gentlemen, the conference between the witness and his attorney had nothing to do with the question. It was a question whether he was to answer it or not.

MR. HOOD. Which I will not.

MR. BRIDGES. Which he will not.

COMMISSIONER GRISWOLD. You decline to interpret section 182?

MR. HOOD. On pressure being put on me before a Committee like this.

COMMISSIONER GRISWOLD. On the ground that it may incriminate you?

MR. HOOD. That's right.

COMMISSIONER GRISWOLD. I find it a little hard to see how citizens of Mississippi are expected to interpret the section if the registrar is unable to do so and he is the person who grades the interpretation which is made by a citizen of Mississippi.

On May 18, 1965, the Commission on Civil Rights transmitted its report to the executive and legislative branches of the federal government.[24] Its recommendations included:

24. The United States Civil Rights Commission, largely as a result of its investigations and hearings in Mississippi, also made an extensive report on the administration of justice in civil rights matters. This report (*Law Enforcement: A Report on Equal Protection in the South,* Government Printing Office, Washington, D.C., 1965) summarized exhaustive inquiries into 1) the legacy of violence, 2) failure to investigate and solve incidents of racial violence, 3) failure to protect or prosecute, 4) official interference with the exercise of federal rights, 5) state and local enforcement, 6) federal criminal legislation, 7) federal civil remedies, and 8) executive action to protect the exercise of federal rights.

The Commission, with its eye principally on Mississippi, on October 6, 1965, made specific recommendations which unquestionably will be thoroughly considered as the basis for further civil rights legislation and federal executive action. The recommendations follow.

"I. *Criminal Remedies*
"Failures of State and local law enforcement officials to prevent or punish crimes of racial violence and the inadequacy of the current Federal criminal statutes urgently require additional legislation to protect persons exercising rights guaranteed by the Constitution and by Federal statute. The Commission *recommends,* therefore, that Congress consider enacting a criminal statute based on its powers to regulate interstate commerce and to enforce the 14th amendment by appropriate legislation.

"Part 1, based on congressional power over interstate commerce, would make criminal any act of violence, threat, intimidation, or punishment against a person engaging in certain protected activities if the perpetrator used or was using the mails or any facility of interstate commerce or if the victim was using a facility of interstate commerce. The protected activities should include the exercise (or attempted exercise) of any right created or secured by a Federal statute relating to equal or civil rights, or any activity protected by the 1st amendment, when undertaken for the purpose of obtaining equality for individuals of a particular race or color.

"Violation of the statute should be a felony and the penalties for its violation should be graduated according to the seriousness of the unlawful act.

"Part II, based on the equal protection clause of the 14th amendment,

Recommendation No. 1

In past reports to the President and Congress, the Commission has recommended a variety of corrective measures to eliminate dis-

---

would permit the prosecution in Federal court of cases of racial violence that violate State law where the failure of local officials to act, or the nature of their action, constitutes a denial of equal protection in the administration of justice or where it is determined that justice is administered in the community involved in a manner so as to deny equal protection of the laws. Punishment should be the same as if the case had been prosecuted in State court. To minimize interference with State criminal procedure, the determination of whether a Federal prosecution is justified should be made by a three-judge Federal court. If the three-judge court determines that a Federal trial is appropriate, the trial should proceed before a single judge sitting with a jury.

"II. *Civil Remedies*

"1. *To Increase the Authority of the Attorney General to Initiate and Intervene in Civil Rights Cases*

"Title IX of the Civil Rights Act of 1964 provides that the Attorney General may intervene in any case of general public importance brought in Federal court where relief is sought 'from the denial of equal protection of the laws under the 14th amendment to the Constitution on account of race, color, religion, or national origin. . . .' The Commission *recommends* that Congress consider amending this statute to empower the Attorney General to initiate, as well as to intervene in, such proceedings and to intervene in or initiate proceedings to prevent denials to or interference with persons exercising 1st amendment rights directed at obtaining equal treatment for all citizens regardless of race, color, religion, or national origin.

"2. *To Provide Relief to Private Persons Against Unlawful State Court Proceedings*

"While private persons may seek relief against *prospective* prosecutions under State statutes unconstitutional on their face which abridge 1st amendment rights or where State statutes are applied for the purpose of discouraging protected activity, such relief is not available once a prosecution is instituted. The Commission *recommends* that Congress consider amending section 1983 of Title 42 to permit injunctive relief, notwithstanding the Anti-Injunctive Statute, where State prosecutions are brought against persons for exercising 1st amendment rights directed at obtaining equal treatment for all citizens regardless of race, color, religion, or national origin.

"3. *To Strengthen Civil Remedies Against Unlawful Official Conduct*

"In 1961 the Commission recommended that section 1983 of Title 42 criminatory denials of the right to vote. Prime among these recommendations have been proposals calling for the elimination, as a

of the United States Code be amended 'to make any county government, city government, or other local government entity that employs officers who deprive persons of rights protected by that section, jointly liable with the officers to victims of such officers' misconduct.' The Commission again *recommends* that Congress consider the need for this revision. The Commission also *recommends* that Congress consider amending section 1983 to provide that in all cases brought under this section—actions for injunctions, as well as for damages—the court, in its discretion may allow the prevailing party reasonable attorney's fees as part of the costs.

"4. *To Extend the Equal Employment Law to Public Employment*

"In order to help assure that justice is administered in a nondiscriminatory manner, employment in law enforcement agencies should be available to all persons, regardless of race, color, religion, or national origin. Title VII of the Civil Rights Act of 1964, providing for equal employment opportunities, does not cover public employment. While discrimination in public employment can be challenged in private law suits, administrative and judicial remedies should be provided to enforce this constitutional right. The Commission *recommends* that Congress consider amending Title VII to extend its coverage to public employment.

"III. *Executive Action*

"*Methods of Federal Law Enforcement*

"The employment of Federal force to curb racial violence should not depend upon the existence of a Federal court order. Federal protection should be accorded where local authorities fail to protect persons exercising constitutionally guaranteed rights or where general racial violence, unchecked by local law enforcement officials, deters individuals from exercising such rights. The Commission *recommends* that the President direct that Federal law enforcement officers be stationed at the scene of likely violence, that increased numbers of Federal officials be assigned to communities where violence has occurred, that more extensive investigation and surveillance activities be undertaken by these officials, and that Federal law enforcement officers be authorized to make on-the-scene arrests for violations of Federal law. In addition, the Commission *recommends* that Federal law enforcement agencies should be staffed with sufficient personnel to carry out these functions and, if necessary, the President should consider requesting Congress to strengthen and train a force of Federal marshals to be maintained on a contingency reserve basis.

"*Assistance to Local Law Enforcement Agencies*

"Congress has enacted the Law Enforcement Assistance Act of 1965 prerequisite for voting, of any test or requirement of literacy, and the establishment of a system of Federal registrars to provide an effective administrative procedure for securing the right to vote in areas where racial discrimination exists.

The Commission wholeheartedly supports the legislation now pending in Congress which would accomplish these objectives. For the legislation to be fully effective in securing the right of citizens to vote, we make the following recommendations:

(a) All literacy tests, including any requirement that the applicant complete any form, should be abolished in view of the fact that such tests and requirements have been established and used for discriminatory purposes.

(b) In areas where Federal examiners have been appointed, applicants should be free to seek registration with such examiners without prior recourse to the State registration process.

(c) The requirement of any poll tax payment as a prerequisite to voting in any election should be abolished, in view of the fact that poll taxes have been intended and utilized as a means of discrimination. In the opinion of the Commission, there can be no reasonable doubt of the power of Congress to enact such a provision as an exercise of the power expressly granted to Congress to enforce the 15th amendment.

(d) Provision should be made for the assignment of Federal poll watchers at election places (in districts where Federal examiners have been appointed) to determine whether persons entitled to vote are being permitted to vote and have their vote counted.

Recommendation No. 2

The Commission recommends to the President that the resources of the Executive branch be explored for the purpose of establishing

---

which provides Federal funds to assist in training State and local law enforcement officials and to improve techniques, capabilities, and practices in local law enforcement in order to prevent and control crime. The Attorney General administers this Act. The Commission *recommends* that in administering this Act particular attention should be paid to assisting communities with problems of law enforcement raised by crimes of racial violence. Effort should be made to develop techniques for recruitment, selection, screening, and training procedures which will improve the quality of local law enforcement."

an affirmative program to encourage persons to register and vote. Such a program should:

(a) Assure better dissemination of information concerning the right to vote and the requirements of registration. (In this connection consideration should be given to the use of branch facilities and personnel of such agencies as the Post Office and the Department of Agriculture.)

(b) Provide training and education to foster better understanding of the rights and duties of citizenship and the significance of voting, and to encourage persons to register and vote. (In this connection consideration should be given to the use of programs of adult education, literacy and community action which are administered by the Department of Health, Education and Welfare, the Department of Agriculture, or the Office of Economic Opportunity.)

The Voting Rights Act, signifying failure in this area of civil rights under the legislation of 1957, 1960, and 1964, received the enthusiastic assent of the President. The Attorney General of the United States immediately filed suit in federal court to have Mississippi's poll tax declared unconstitutional. Federal registrars moved into Leflore and Madison counties, where, respectively, 7,348 of 10,274 and (curiously) 6,256 of 5,622 whites of voting age were registered, compared to 281 of 12,567 and 218 of 10,366 adult Negroes. Lyndon Johnson was still visibly concerned about the future: "Presidents and Congresses, laws and lawsuits can open the doors to polling places and open the doors to the wondrous results which await the wise use of the ballot. But only the individual Negro . . . can really walk through those doors and can use that right and can transform the vote into an instrument of justice and fulfillment.

"So let me now say to every Negro in this country: you must register; you must vote; you must learn so your choice advances your interests and the interests of our beloved nation. . . . It means that dedicated leaders must work around the clock to teach people their rights and their responsibilities. . . . There is no room for injustice in the American mansion."

Then, as if to the vast majority of Mississippi whites, the

President had a word of compassion: " . . . there is always room for understanding toward those who see the old ways crumbling and to them I say simply this: It must come.

"It is right that it should come and when it has you will find a burden has been lifted from your shoulders, too. It is not just a question of guilt, although there is that. It is that men cannot live with a lie and not be stained by it."

Using the carrot as well as the stick, the federal government poured at least $20 million into Mississippi in 1965 under various aspects of the War on Poverty. Thirty-seven counties in the state with per capita incomes of less than $750 were declared eligible for 100% aid by the U.S. Office of Economic Opportunity. Community action programs from one end of Mississippi to the the other were approved by Governor Johnson and set to work on health, welfare, rehabilitation, and employment problems.[25] An example was Star Incorporated, a nonprofit organization initiated by the Catholic Diocese of Natchez-Jackson, which received a grant of $7 million for the education of 75,000 adult illiterates. Another, the Child Development Group of Mississippi, conducted 84 Head Start schools in 45 communities with some 6,400 pre-first-grade underprivileged

---

25. The white people in Coahoma County expressed no interest in a community action program until it looked as though the Southern Educational and Recreational Association (SERA) would get the money from the Office of Economic Opportunity. After months of negotiation, a biracial committee of twenty-eight men (sixteen whites, twelve Negroes) was formed and is now a going concern.

On the other hand, a blue-ribbon biracial committee of thirty members launched and efficiently carried out the Head Start program for Jackson. A Negro professional worker served as the executive director. Under her were 80 teachers, 130 instructional assistants, and 150 volunteer workers. The facilities of the Bethlehem Center, a Methodist social service agency for almost three decades, served as headquarters. The city school buildings being unavailable, some 1,200 children were taught during the six weeks, for the most part, in Negro churches. Medical and dental examinations were made at the University Hospital. Altogether, this was an impressive though far from perfect example of interracial co-operation.

children in what Director Dr. Tom Levin declared was an "aggressive compliance with the Civil Rights Law of 1964." [26] The $1.4 million from the Office of Economic Opportunity was only the largest of several such grants in the state. Altogether, 21,347 children in 284 centers were exposed to the Head Start program, at a total cost of $4,579,926. There was some financial mismanagement, and, in a few instances, perhaps too close a connection with activists in the civil rights movement (in the very nature of things a problem of considerable difficulty), but few people took seriously the old familiar charges of excessive sin and communism. In the meantime, all federal agencies were increasing the number of jobs, skilled and unskilled, open to Negroes, and this in itself was a destructive blow to the caste system. Federal money and federal insistence on integrated employment as well as services were influences beyond calculation and beyond counteraction.

Tokenism with a Vengeance

The court-ordered desegregation of the first grades of Jackson and Biloxi schools took place in September 1964 without an

---

26. Potential tragedy is just around the corner in Mississippi these days. In one instance in the summer of 1965, the Iuka city marshal got a telephoned warning that from fifty to sixty Negroes were on their way by train from Corinth. Whether the invaders were COFO oriented and how they planned to demonstrate were not clear. But, acting in military fashion, the marshal rounded up his auxiliary police. Dozens of white men, mostly armed, gathered at the station. In a council of war, they determined that the incoming Negroes would be treated politely, would be asked to stay on the train, and that only in case of a refusal would force be used. After all, Iuka was a peaceful place and wanted no trouble. As train time approached, the tension grew. There was a look of quiet determination in every eye. It was a dramatic scene right out of *High Noon*. At last the moan of the diesel engine's whistle was heard. The train itself was sighted. It roared into the station. And the rumor was true. Some fifty Negroes jumped off the train, all primed for action. And action there was, plenty of it. For these were underprivileged youngsters, five to six years of age, from the Corinth Head Start program, out to see the world on their first train ride.

unpleasant incident.[27] Ten years of massive resistance were over. The cry of Aleck Primos, speaking for the Citizens Council, that "No education is better than integrated education" fell on deaf ears as some thirty-nine Negro children trudged off to school with their white neighbors in the capital city of the state. Fear of bad publicity and federal intervention had resulted in careful planning "to make certain we did not have a lot of brawling in the streets." School officials came in from Louisville, Kentucky, to give the benefit of their experience, and local leadership (which even at this late date must remain anonymous) was, according to John Doar, "absolutely magnificent."

Judge Claude Clayton's order for desegregation of the first grade in Clarksdale was frustrated by a new zoning system based on "natural boundaries" formed by the Sunflower River and a railroad which divides the city. The town fathers also found it convenient to engage in "slum clearance" by purchasing Negro property in the "white" section of the newly zoned community. In his home county Ross Barnett and his allies succeeded by "persuasion" tactics in preventing all except the merest of tokenism. At the beginning of the term, lone little Debra Lewis was forced to sit in the back of the first-grade room and to stand at the end of the line for lunch in the Carthage elementary school. Her father lost his job, the landlord filed suit when the family refused to move, and their house was set on fire. But Debra stuck it out and six months later Mrs. Lewis said, "I think I would do it all over again if I had to."

With considerable fanfare, a Citizens Council school was opened in Jackson, backed in part by tuition grants of $185 per

---

27. This does not mean that the idea of token desegregation was generally accepted in the state. On November 3, 1964, to take one instance of contrary evidence, a school bond issue of over a million dollars was defeated in Rankin County. At least part of the reason for this decision may be found in a newspaper advertisement which stated that "in case of integration, our choice will be private schools which will leave many empty class rooms in our present schools . . . if we follow the plan laid out by the United States Court, all of our white schools will be vacated."

pupil set up by the legislature. According to Council literature, the two-story frame building at 555 Hartfield Street was "good-as-new," and accreditation ("it need not be despised, but it should not be revered") could hardly be a problem at the elementary level. The lack of free textbooks was deemed an asset, as this kind of state handout had become "an instrument of cultural retardation and socialistic regimentation." [28] By October the Council School Foundation sponsored two committees, one on library and the other on patriotism. At Christmas their educational venture, somewhat handicapped by a basic tuition of $375 per pupil, had become a going but not glowing concern with twenty-four students distributed among its six grades. A couple of dozen charters were issued by the state for private, white, segregated schools, but these were largely for stand-by use in future cases of compulsory desegregation.

Thirty-nine Negroes going to school with 2,380 whites in Jackson were almost forgotten by the turn of the year when rumors of the real meaning of the 1964 Civil Rights Law began to seep into the state. The accommodations provisions of the law had brought a summer and fall of discontent, but their real impact in Mississippi was more psychological than basic. Now it appeared that each and every one of the school districts in the state would have to sign desegregation compliance pledges for the 1965 fall term or have its federal school aid cut off. To make matters more difficult, the Department of Health, Education and Welfare soon defined compliance as desegregation of at least four grades in September 1965 and complete integra-

---

28. By 1965, the eccentric Medford Evans had somehow become adjusted to the subjection of children in Council School No. 1 to that obnoxious "instrument of cultural retardation and socialistic regimentation," the free textbook. He took all of the slim July-August issue of *The Citizen* to promote the virtues of "the school that can't be mixed . . . not only jewel-like in perfection, it was, like a jewel, small!" Just how small, he kept to himself, though the same three children appeared in five of seven classroom pictures in the magazine. Public education, Evans observed, had "served a noble purpose in its day," but having been captured by the revolution, a glorifier of "ignorance . . . filth, and disarray," had now become "venal, bureaucratized, and mindless."

tion by 1967. There is no question that the majority of white Mississippians would have voted against compliance if segregation could be maintained, but, as Governor Johnson made plain in February, the alternatives to the local school board were to have its desegregation plan drawn and implemented by a federal court or by HEW. Although at first Johnson said, "I would not sign," a week later he abandoned resistance with the pious proposal that "Each district should give prayerful consideration to this problem." The attorney general, secretary of state, and state superintendent of education went to Washington to explore the possibilities of minimizing requirements, but returned empty-handed.

Thus Mississippi was face to face with her most serious civil rights problem. Though classroom salaries were low (in 1963–64 the Mississippi average was $3,824 compared with $4,979 for the South and $5,963 for the country) and pupil expenditure was $233.28 against a national average of $455, the state was spending 5.3% of its (1962) income on schools. In this category, it ranked among the states putting forth the greatest financial effort compared to resources. Of the total public-school revenues for 1963–64 of something less than $150 million, 8.3% had come from the federal government, and Mississippi could least afford to relinquish these funds. And so the pressure was on.

There could have been no other outcome. The Mississippi Women for Constitutional Government watched with growing shock and disbelief the capitulation of the state's leadership "to the forces of communism exemplified in the Civil Rights Compliance Act, so called." By the middle of September, eighty public school district plans for desegregation had been accepted (sixty-one approved by HEW and nineteen under federal court order) and thirty-five plans were under consideration, with more to come. A dozen or so districts made it clear that no plan would be submitted. The School Board of Montgomery County (1,406 Negro students, 850 white) requested the Board of Supervisors to increase taxes to make up for the $14,000 it planned to forego in federal aid (along with $235,000 in grants under the

Aid to Education Act). In Amite County the supervisors agreed to an increase of up to 25% in school taxes to offset a loss of $57,000 in federal money.

In September 1965, almost a thousand Negroes were attending previously all-white schools. This was still tokenism, to be sure, but tokenism with a vengeance.[29] The 1954 Supreme Court decision was at last being implemented in Mississippi's most rural areas, in counties like Neshoba and Pike and Madison, long known to the outside world only for their racial violence. Economic, physical, and psychological harassment of Negroes continued, and local private schools sprang up here and there, but the real heart of the "Never Never" opposition was gone.[30]

---

29. Admittedly, tokenism with a vengeance has real meaning only in relation to the *number* of schools newly involved in enforced compliance. For the Southern Regional Council estimated that in September 1965 there were 928 Negro children (or .34% of those in school) attending previously white schools.

30. Several people who know Mississippi well have already challenged this statement. Each has evidence of Negro children being driven by harassment tactics from an integrated school in a specific situation. In many districts which have desegregated under pressure, Negro children are still confronted with illegal segregation practices. The so-called "freedom of choice" concept has been used with great hypocrisy to frustrate the intent of the law. Achievement tests and bus transportation have been turned into vehicles of harassment. All six Negro twelfth-grade transfers dropped out of the Madison-Ridgeland High School when it was suggested to them that they would not graduate with their class inasmuch as full academic credit would not be given for work done at colored schools. In addition, one student's father was severely beaten and his mother lost her job. At the time of this writing, it is too early to determine how widespread such undercover opposition to compliance will be and what counter measures will be taken by the federal government.

In October 1965, the NAACP and the Justice Department were challenging a state law prohibiting the enrollment in the public schools of any child whose parents were not residents of Mississippi, unless a tuition payment were made. The law, passed in July 1965, required payments up to $360.75 a year per student. The NAACP called it Mississippi's "War on Orphans." Of the 7,000 youngsters affected, 85% were Negroes. Representative Jimmie Walker of Quitman County, author of the law, had made it clear during the legislative session that

A few of the private schools, such as that of the First Presbyterian Church in Jackson, might survive, but most were destined for failure. For one thing, it was a simple matter to set up a new elementary school for a few of the lower grades, but many of the desegregation plans called for a lowering of racial barriers in some grades of both elementary and high schools. It was impossible to set up a chemistry laboratory in a ramshackle abandoned building made overnight into a schoolhouse. Even Dr. Medford Evans, the Citizens Council's leading theoretician in education and race, couldn't solve that problem.

Mississippi higher education is controlled by the Board of Trustees of the Institutions of Higher Learning, which, besides doing the minor bureaucratic damage normal in state schools, openly interfered with academic freedom in the summer and fall of 1964. In an August resolution it complained of the Mississippi Project in which COFO "have sought to activate and accelerate a trend opposed to states rights and local self-government and for extreme liberalism and a strong central national government." More disastrous, from the Board's point of view, was the "reputation for membership in the communist party" of some of the summer workers. Naturally, "a concerted effort should be made . . . to avoid these dangerous movements and to support conservative constitutional government and to preserve and protect" both the United States and Mississippi. Therefore, the heads of the state institutions were authorized "to protect student life from undue pressure by those engaged in activities contrary to the laws of the state of Mississippi and to the image of citizenship of the state," and to do all things proper "to eliminate the development of socialistic and communistic trends among the college or university youth where violence is done to constitutional government . . . and to prohibit as far as possible invasion of state institutions by out-

---

his measure was aimed at Negro children whose parents had left the state to find jobs outside of Mississippi. Toward the end of October, Judge Harold Cox granted a temporary injunction restraining the State Board of Education from implementing the law, whose constitutionality would later be decided by a panel of three federal circuit judges.

side influence contrary to the established and well-known policies of the State of Mississippi relating to good government. . . ." A few days later, all Negroes not enrolled as students or working as employees were denied access to public buildings on the campuses of the white institutions. On September 9, the parents of two Negro students at the University of Mississippi were not allowed to eat in the school cafeteria, and, later that fall, Chancellor Williams restricted attendance at college functions to students, faculty, staff, and alumni. (In one homemade crisis in the fall of 1964, when there was great fear of an invasion by Memphis State colored students, the chancellor suggested that Memphis Negroes be allowed to sit with other visitors on the east side of the stadium—looking into the sun—and that "our Negroes" be allowed to take their seats on the Ole Miss benches. A Johnson appointee to the Board, Senator George Yarbrough, insisted that all Memphis State Negroes be arrested at the city limits.[31] Luckily, the Negroes failed to put in an appearance.) In April 1965, the Board rescinded its order deputizing white employees of the cafeteria with the power of arresting colored intruders who might try to eat there.

In March 1965, the American Association of University Professors made available its confidential report on higher education in Mississippi, which criticized the Board for its pressure to make the academic faculties "conform to orthodox segregationist views." The report was critical of the failure of University officials to protect a liberal student from bodily harassment and of the screening of speakers by an administrator "who appeared to have no particular academic qualifications except that he had been in charge of FBI training." Freedom of public utterances by college faculty members in Mississippi was restricted pri-

---

31. In moments of stress, tempers come to the surface quite easily. And so it was with an alumnus of the University who, in one of the normal traffic jams at the time of a big game in Oxford, spied an out-of-state car with a Johnson-Humphrey sticker on it. He yelled at the attractive woman driving the car, "You'd better get that thing out of here before something happens to you." "Oh," she replied sweetly, "I thought you only burned station wagons down here."

marily by fear rather than official policy—"a man has about as much freedom as he has guts." The report conceded that "It is something of a compliment to the University of Mississippi that it is the place where important issues have most often been raised and fought about, even though the fighting has not been a pretty spectacle." Then it explained the tranquillity on the campus of the University of Southern Mississippi by quoting the president, William D. McCain, who had stated in a public address: "There has been a lot of trouble with college professors on the matters of integration and segregation. We don't have that trouble at Southern. Each year I tell our instructors they are employed to teach . . . and I will handle all other problems."

According to the AAUP study, all state Negro institutions were watched very carefully by the Sovereignty Commission for subversion; it might have added that they were more tightly controlled than the white schools. Students of private Tougaloo College had been aggressive in the civil rights movement, so much so that Lt. Governor Gartin had called for an investigation to determine whether Tougaloo's charter should be revoked. Gartin described Tougaloo as "a haven for quacks, quirks, and political agitators," and suggested the college must not be performing its educational function when its students spent a major part of their time demonstrating in the Jackson streets. Faculty members admitted it was hard to teach students in jail, especially when they were refused books in their cells. Nothing came of a Senate resolution seeking the repeal of the charter, perhaps because of the second thought that if Tougaloo were abandoned, its students might attempt to transfer to white state institutions.

Administrative officials at the University of Mississippi have been liberal enough in their personal views concerning race and have, in fact, at times encouraged inevitable racial change at Ole Miss. They have been badgered, though, by continuous and often conflicting pressures, and at times they have shown unpardonable weakness. Under the National Defense Education Act, summer language institutes were held at the University in 1961 and 1962. In the aftermath of the Meredith affair, no grant was made for the summer of 1963. The University withdrew its application for an NDEA language institute (federal appropriation approximately $90,000) for the summer of 1964 because of its unwillingness to comply with HEW nondiscrimination regulations. In October 1964, the administration insisted on changes in the wording of the contract, but this was unacceptable to HEW, and plans for the summer of 1965 fell through. Shortly thereafter came the breakthrough: Chancellor Williams signed the compliance pledge. Thus, in January 1965, the School of Education was awarded money for a summer institute to assist public-school teachers and administrators in facing problems in newly integrated school systems. Backed, of course, by the Board, the University of Mississippi had finally caught up with national policy.

From its beginning in 1955 as a four-year institution, the Medical Center has been the most liberal segment of the University. Dependent to a great extent on federal grants, it quickly accepted compliance orders from Washington and even went so far as to employ a Negro assistant professor of pharmacology. In the meantime, the Law School had taken a Ford Foundation grant to expand its course work on "civil rights, individual rights and criminal justice" and to seek out Negro students from low-income families. In the *Clarion-Ledger*, Tom Ethridge called it a "sell-out . . . to voluntarily negroize Ole Miss."

Yes, the University was making progress. In June 1965, the first Negro guest was put up at the Alumni House. Such hospitality was a far cry from the action two years before, when the Board of Directors of the Alumni Association had instructed its alumni secretary to welcome James Meredith if he dropped in for a cup of coffee at the Snack Bar, but to have it arranged that the employees would openly rebel against serving the University's only Negro student. Football-minded alumni have been most difficult to assuage on the racial question. How they must have suffered when, in December 1964, Ole Miss was soundly whipped by Tulsa University in the Bluebonnet Bowl, largely due to the terrific charging of a 240-pound Negro lineman from Mississippi! But surely their spirits were revived by announcements that the University of Mississippi would sponsor, as usual, the thirteenth annual Dixie National Baton Twirling Institute (beginning, intermediate, and advanced twirling, strutting, drum majoring, etc.) July 11–16, the fifth annual Young and Beautiful Charm Camp (figure improvement, make-up, business techniques, poise, inner beauty, beauty-contest competition, etc.) July 18–21, and the Mid South Cheerleaders Institute (crowd management, sportsmanship, chants, bonfires, novelty yells, etc.) August 1–6.

Almost three years after the admission of Meredith, Chancellor Williams issued a "statement of University policy concerning student assemblies," which spelled out the law about gentlemanly conduct. Like most such administration policy edicts, it was a kind of apology for lax control of students with a promise to do better. In this case the pronouncement came after the wrecking of a car in a student demonstration against a biracial group from Tougaloo College attending the Southern Literary Festival on the Ole Miss campus in April. An unimpeachable witness, the executive director of the Mississippi Council on Human Relations, thought that while student conduct was reprehensible, University officials, under heavy pressure from state politicians and Citizens Council adherents, had acted intelligently and were "making a conscientious effort to comply with the Civil Rights Act." He was complimentary of the leadership demonstrated by the vice-chancellor, the professor in charge of the festival, and the dean of women. What infuriated many loyal friends of the University was the quiet readmission, less than six weeks later, of a football player who had been expelled for his part in the demonstration.

An amusing repercussion from the campus exuberance was a blast from E. L. McDaniel, Grand Dragon of the White Knights of the Ku Klux Klan, who saw "a conspiracy going on to liberalize the University of Oxford." Critical of the holding of the "literate festival" in the first place, McDaniel charged that a group of "three nigger girls, two white nigger boys and a professor" was brought to the campus "without the students knowing of it." He insisted that the integrated delegation "started kissing and showing their affections in public," which resulted, strangely enough, in a car being "slightly damaged . . . by a bunch of COFO workers." A "fine Christian, conservative, segregationist student" was proven innocent and then expelled by "the students' council . . . which is controlled by the liberals." McDaniel also charged that Chancellor Williams had "called a meeting of all the nigger employees and told them to use the bathrooms and cafeteria . . . and other facilities at Ole Miss . . . and to urge their friends to do the same." Furthermore, the language department had "already hired three nigger teachers." The Grand Dragon understandably carried "a great burden" because of the goings-on at the University.

An exceedingly hopeful sign for the future was the apparent freedom of faculty and students to criticize at will official University action. The local chapter of the AAUP expressed its "complete disapproval" of the return of the expelled demonstrator, but it remained for students to excoriate "the spinelessness and cowardice," and even the integrity, of the administration. A disenchanted law student wrote withering editorials for the *Mississippian* declaring that University officials "had been too paralyzed by politics" to mold a fair but forceful discipline program. "The policy of don't-rock-the-boat or keep-the-University-open-at-any-cost is ridiculous in light of the past three years." The administration "has proven itself incompetent and inadequate to handle the problems. . . . There are too many Indians and not enough chiefs. One would think it a bank the way the bucks are passed inside. People are waiting for acts of wisdom and strength from Ole Miss policy-makers. . . ." The indignant writer was pleased with student protests in favor of law and order (and conformity with the national will) and thought the vision shown by student leaders "is superb evidence that the University as an institution has not passed the point of no return."

Though the University of Mississippi still has considerable time to run on its "ten years of entrenched mediocrity," it has not been destroyed and even now shows promise of living up to its potential of greatness. Ole Miss has suffered grievously in

loss of competent faculty,[32] in the retention of timeservers, and
in reputation, but the dedicated people who remain will see it
through the difficult days ahead.

The Forces of Reaction

From the moment of Paul Johnson's inaugural, the Citizens
Council was on the defensive. Soon it was evident that the governor had no intention of continuing the flow of state funds
into the Council treasury. But it was not until the summer of
1964 that Bill Simmons and company began to absorb the
really lethal blows. They fought compliance with the new Civil
Rights Law and lost. They ridiculed and tried to intimidate
Mississippians for Public Education and lost. Most significant
of all, they battled against the acceptance of token integration,
demanding that schools be closed, and again they lost. By September, the people of Mississippi knew that the Citizens Council
had failed in the one promise it must keep to stay alive; desegregation was a fact. The Council prediction of a decided Goldwater victory in November was more of a long-shot gamble for
the recovery of public esteem than the result of intelligent prognostication.

As the financial "take" from Mississippi decreased, Council
officials began to sense the possibilities of tapping the frustrations of many troubled people throughout the country. After all,
a five-dollar membership fee from California or Indiana was
just like money from home. It was, of course, more difficult to
keep up with outside agitators, and the Council was sharply

---

32. An evaluation of the losses suffered by the various departments
since the beginning of racial turmoil and political interference is too
subjective an undertaking for me. I would hesitate, for instance, to judge
the competence behind a letter written in 1964 to Robert Frost, requesting correspondence with Stark Young, but returned with a Vermont post-
mark and the simple notation, "Gone." Or the eagerness of a middle-
aged medievalist, vegetarian, and "sentimental segregationist" to come
down from his ivory tower to run for governor. As this grotesque political prospect had been the only professor publicly to endorse Barnett in
office, would his candidacy be attributed to race or reason?

embarrassed when one of its Maryland chapters became infiltrated with liberals who, in a frivolous mood, voted a merger with CORE. By the spring of 1965, Council professionals privately expressed disappointment that their national campaign had never really caught fire.

After the Goldwater debacle, the Jackson Citizens Council reiterated its belief in good government and harmonious race relations and deprecated violence, "including the reprehensible burnings and bombings of churches." When school compliance pledges were asked by HEW, Executive Secretary Robert Patterson announced that "Tyranny is no longer a threat—it is upon us." And Dr. Willie Caskey pathetically insisted that "We are determined to maintain our traditional Southern way of life . . . the problem is nothing more or nothing less than the survival of our Anglo-Saxon race." He added, ominously, "God forbid that we might be forced to resort to any extremities."

In the November 1964 issue of *American Opinion,* Medford Evans still pressed the absurdity that the "disappearance act" of Chaney, Goodman, and Schwerner was "the work of *agents provocateurs.*" Either they had been killed by "wet squads" on their own side or they had not been killed at all. "Identification was made by the Ole Miss Medical Center. Is that an infallible source?" he asked derisively. "Everyone was struck by the uncanny accuracy of the dragline that exhumed the bodies from the 600-foot-long dam. The first scoop got 'em. Even if an informer had at one time known the *precise* spot of burial, he would have had to be extraordinarily accurate to guide anyone, so unerringly, six weeks after the event. But, of course, if three stiffs from the morgue had been planted only a day or so before, the strain on the memory would be comparatively trivial."

In a speech to the New England Rally for God, Family and Country in July 1965, Professor Evans (who presently heads a committee of the Congress of Conservatives to explore the possibilities of a new party to the right of the GOP) expanded his Citizens Council case. Negro revolutionaries were seeking to destroy the United States, beginning with Mississippi. "The concept is one in which all the features of the USA are to be obliterated—its racial composition, its form of government, its economic system, its religion, its culture, even its ideals of romance. America's sweetheart is no longer to be a nonsexy pretty blonde like Mary Pickford, or a sexy pretty blonde like Marilyn Monroe, but a homosexual middle-aged man, preferably though not necessarily mulatto.

"A conspiratorial enemy such as the Communist Party, could find no surer way to erase America from history than to begin with an assault on any one state, and having liquidated its proper social and political institutions, to proceed with suitably-modified attacks on the others. As the states vanished to make way for administrative districts, the Union of the States would automatically vanish to become a region of the World Soviet Republic." Obviously, the first state to go would be Mississippi and the way to get Mississippi was to indict a local sheriff or to challenge the Mississippi Congressional delegation. Either Dr. Evans had not been to the movies in a long time or he followed the practice of writing his speeches after the late-late show, if he did not fall asleep to dream of South Africa, that promised land without television.

On the way out as it unquestionably had been for some time, the Citizens Council was still able to whip up an audience of 6,500 people at the state's new coliseum for a "White Monday in Mississippi" rally in the middle of May 1965. Delegates from Selma and Bogalusa trooped in to hear Governor George Wallace declare, "The South is winning its battle to preserve segregation." It was just a matter of time, "when the rest of the nation wakes up," until the people of the United States would get on "our side." Bill Simmons presided, Ross Barnett introduced the speaker, Mayor Thompson boomed Wallace for President, and Confederate flags and convention posters ("We're through with LBJ and PBJ") were all over the carnival scene. Governor Johnson was conspicuous by his absence. But the new hero of the hour, Sheriff Jim Clark, was introduced. As reported by Charlie Hills, "The crowd, as it realized who the husky sheriff was, leaped to its feet, cheering wildly. The uproar lasted several minutes as the appreciation of the audience was poured out to the Selma sheriff."

The business establishment may well have deserted the Citizens Council because of the larger pressure from Washington, but there were thousands of lesser whites who were determined to maintain the caste system without counting the cost. Though the history of Mississippi reveals that organization is not required for violence, it was only natural that the bitter-enders turn to the Americans for the Preservation of the White Race and the several varieties of the Ku Klux Klan available as early as the spring of 1964. The APWR may have been responsible for a portion of the terror which gripped southwest Mississippi and were respectable enough to provide forums for politicians, such as Fred Ross and Ross Barnett, still hopeful of riding racism into public office, but their total effect was puny compared to the Klan's. The participation of Klan members in bombings, arson, and murder during 1964 was well known. It was rather thoroughly infiltrated by the FBI, remained on the subversive list of the U.S. Attorney General, and was repudiated, at least in public, by Mississippi leaders generally. It could be and was constantly exposed for taking the law into its hands. With its new image as a law-abiding state, Mississippi could not afford long to tolerate the excesses of this hate group.

The threat was real enough. In the July 1964 issue of *The Klan Ledger,* official publication of the White Knights of Mississippi, Allan Dulles ("arch traitor and long-time betrayer of patriots the world over") was attacked for blaming the disappearance of the three civil rights workers on the Klan.

We were not involved, and there was NO DISAPPEARANCE. Anyone who is so simple that he cannot recognize a communist hoax which is as plain as the one they pulled on Kennedy in Dallas . . . had better do a little reading in J. Edgar Hoover's primer on communism, "MASTERS OF DECEIT."

There is no racial problem in this state. Our system of strict segregation permits the two races to live in close proximity and eliminates any racial problem. Bi-racial groups are the greatest danger . . . have brought violence and bloodshed. . . . We are

not going to recognize the authority of any bi-racial group, NOR THE
AUTHORITY OF ANY PUBLIC OFFICIAL WHO ENTERS INTO ANY AGREE-
MENT WITH ANY SUCH SOVIET ORGANIZATION. We knights are working day and night to preserve Law and Order . . . by the control
of the social structure in the hands of Christian, Anglo-Saxon White
men, the only race on earth that can build and maintain just and
stable governments. We are not going to sit back and permit our
rights to be negotiated away by a group composed of atheistic
priests, brain-washed black savages, and mongrelized money-wor-
shippers, meeting with some stupid and cowardly politician. Take
heed, atheists and mongrels, we will not travel your path to Leninist
Hall, but will buy YOU a ticket to the Eternal if you insist. Take
your choice, SEGREGATION, TRANQUILITY AND JUSTICE, OR BI-RACISM,
CHAOS AND DEATH.

According to the FBI, the Philadelphia triple lynching resulted from a Klan conspiracy and Klan members were responsible for the burning of churches as well as the bombing
of homes and places of business. Although the original KKK
spilled over from Louisiana in July 1963, it was not until the
formation of the White Knights in the Brookhaven area in
February 1964 that the Mississippi reign of terror began. Led
by Sam Bowers of Laurel, the night-riding White Knights
shunned the robes and paraphernalia generally associated with
Klan activity, were secretive and tough.[33] Their tools were the
shotgun, rifle, pistol, bull whip, gasoline-soaked rag, cluster
of dynamite sticks, and Molotov cocktail. It took only a handful
of determined men to bomb a church or flog a Negro or a
white in the dark of night. According to recruiting posters,
"The issue is clearly one of personal, physical SELF-DEFENSE or
DEATH for the American Anglo-Saxons." Besides Negroes, the
enemy included "Jews, Papists, Turks, Mongols, Tartars, Orien-

---

33. As a congressional investigation was getting under way in October
1965, Laurel and Jones County officials listed thirty-five acts against
life and property (houses hit with shot, houses burned, dynamite blasts)
in their county. Admitting that such efforts were "long since due," the
city and county officers of the law pledged themselves to stop further
lawlessness, no matter by whom.

tals." After the passage of the 1964 Civil Rights Act, the choice was all the more clear: "If we don't win in the next eight months, we're all destined for Communist slavery and our wives and daughters will be chattels in Mongolian and African brothels. . . ." But by the end of the year, state and federal pressure had brought Klan activity to a temporary standstill. J. Edgar Hoover claimed that there were only 480 Klansmen in Mississippi: "I had our agents in Mississippi interview every member of the Klan there just to let those individuals know the FBI knew who they were and had an eye on them."

The accelerating pace of erosion of the old way of life in 1965, marked by widespread compliance in token school desegregation, the effort of the legislature to convince the world that Mississippi had at last changed its spots, and the passage of the Voting Rights Act, brought a resurgence of the Klan and the invasion of White Knights territory by the United Klans of America. Led by Imperial Wizard Robert Shelton, the public-relations-conscious UKA held a half dozen rallies in Mississippi, featuring a revival atmosphere with cross burnings and sometimes Sheriff Rainey in uniform. At nine-thirty on the eve of July 2, the date for implementation of the employment provisions of the Civil Rights Act, between eighty and ninety crosses were burned simultaneously throughout the state. So the battle lines were drawn, and in September Governor Johnson sent the national guard into Natchez to prevent a possible race war between the Klan and Negroes enraged because the local president of the NAACP had been dynamited in his car.

Right-wing organizations continued to spring up, such as the Conservative Leadership Council (composed of representatives from the Citizens Council, APWR, the John Birch Society, and the Women for Constitutional Government) and the Association of Christian Conservatives, "a leadership group without rank-and-file members" formed for the purpose of opposing the constitutional amendments sponsored by the governor.

Two propaganda sheets were distributed widely. The first was a gimmick purporting to be a facsimile copy of *The Crusader,* "published in Cuba," recommending black nationalism and violence, with the following crudely hand-printed across the front page: THIS LEAFLET BEING DISTRIBUTED BY SNCC AND COFO WORKERS AMONG U.S. NEGROES. The other, resembling the *Rebel Underground* published at the University during James Meredith's short and turbulent undergraduate career, was a hate sheet called *A Delta Discussion*. The discussion was on a rather low level, attacking the "COON CODDLING" FBI, slandering former Congressman Frank Smith as "OUR MOST INFAMOUS SCALAWAG. THIS BIG BELLIED, HOG-JOWLED, LYING, DECEIVING [*sic*] RAT . . . THIS SMELLY VARMIT [*sic*] HE SHOULD BE TREATED LIKE THE YELLOW DOG, IMMORAL TRAITOR HE IS," and deciding the fate of local schools, "YES, WE HAD RATHER SEE THEM RAZED TO THE GROUND AND SALT SPREAD OVER THE SOIL THAN TO SEE THEM TURNED INTO 'MODEL' INTEGRATED INSTITUTIONS."

The perennial champion of lost reactionary causes, Elmore Greaves, was associated with *The Southern Review,* an eight-page, three-dollar-a-year literary effort which labeled Paul Johnson, Allen Thompson, and Jim Eastland as left-wingers. Appropriately, this literary treasure was published by a Jackson funeral-home operator. In its first issue, the intellectual tone was set by reprinting an article on race by James K. Vardaman from the *Saturday Evening Post* of April 27, 1907.

As Walker Percy has written, Mississippi is no longer mysterious. Reports of continued violence have a numbing effect on the recipient. In-fighting has supplanted talk. In spite of its new image, Mississippi continues to be the scene of bombings, arson, assassinations and attempted killings, economic reprisals, persecution of moderates of both races, police brutality, beatings, legal harassments, and collection of funds to protect "white, Christian" murderers. Magnolias and mayhem is still more than an alliterative phrase, with the near-successful homicidal attacks on a gentle white minister in Jackson and a moderate Negro leader in Natchez in the late summer of 1965.

Here, in brief compass, are a few cases which Mississippians should not allow themselves to forget:

1) Thirty-five-year-old Thatcher Walt, editor of the Green-

wood *Commonwealth,* had written a mild editorial against the Klan that resulted in threats and his sitting up with a loaded shotgun. His real crime came later when, on a Friday night in July 1964, he took his family to see *The Chalk Garden* at the newly integrated Leflore Theater. Local bullies, including DeLay Beckwith, paraded in and out of the building armed with baseball bats and flashlights. That night an explosion took place on the Walt lawn and a threatening note was thrown on his porch. Word came of specific plans to kill him; he requested, but did not get, police protection. On Saturday he moved his family to Clarksdale. The FBI was alerted through friends in Washington, and local officials were informed. On Monday morning Walt returned to Greenwood, found that his picture window had been smashed by gunfire and that his name had been removed from the masthead of the newspaper. He now resides in Florida.

2) Clyde Harvey, an illiterate Negro residing in Harmony, had permitted five COFO workers to live in his home. On July 10, 1964, he was arrested without a warrant for possession of two cans of beer. Justice of the Peace Jack Adams sentenced Harvey, *in absentia* on July 23, to pay a $500 fine and to serve ninety days in prison. Harvey was not arrested until September 4, too late to appeal the verdict, and was sent to jail. After he had served sixty-two days, the Fifth U.S. Circuit Court of Appeals set aside the verdict on the grounds that Harvey had been denied his constitutional right to a lawyer.

3) In August 1963, the deacons of the Belzoni Baptist Church adopted strict segregation resolutions including a prohibition on "teaching or preaching advocating integration of the races." On October 29, 1964, partly to avert a vote to oust him, Chester A. Molpus, pastor of the church for twenty-one years, resigned, saying, "I cannot imagine Jesus standing on the church steps and turning a man away because of the color of his skin." He hoped to remain in the pastoral ministry but doubted whether he could do it in Mississippi.

4) Ollie Shelby, an eighteen-year-old, fourth-grade drop-out Negro from Flora, moved to Jackson in January 1965 in search

of a job. He was picked up, tried without counsel, and sentenced
to six months in jail for making indecent gestures at a white
woman. A few hours later, unarmed, the slightly built youth was
being transferred by four officers from one section of the Hinds
County jail to another. According to the coroner's jury, Shelby
attacked two officers and began beating jailer Neal Hollings-
worth. The boy was shot in the head and killed by O. E. Sander-
ford, deputy sheriff. Charles Evers commented: "The Mississippi Negro is the only animal in the world that doesn't have
a closed season."

5) With two other Mississippians, Fred Berger, fifty-year-old
Natchez lawyer, signed the loyalty pledge at the Democratic
National Convention in August 1964. Upon his return home he
found himself denounced in newspapers as a traitor, received
threatening telephone calls, felt it necessary to hire guards to
protect his home and family.[34] Berger commented: "These
people were convinced that John Kennedy and Lyndon Johnson
were Communists. They really believed it. There was a frenzy.
Violence was going on. The Mayor's home was bombed and
I'm convinced that mine would have been bombed if it weren't
for the guards." Though he thought of himself as a liberal,
Berger had "never crusaded on racial matters." Today he lives
in Washington. (By innuendo, Tom Ethridge attacked Berger's
integrity, suggesting that he might have been unsuccessful as a
Natchez lawyer—his income was about $25,000 a year—and
hoped for material rewards for his conduct at Atlantic City.)

6) Here is an abbreviated chronology of one month in the
life of Albert Heffner, prosperous insurance agent in McComb:

July 2, 1964: Civil Rights law passed. Heffners in Delta for a
wedding.

July 5–12: Pressure builds up in McComb—bombings.

---

34. Berger played on the University of Mississippi tennis team about the
time that I arrived as an assistant professor. When asked on national
television at the Democratic Convention whether Mississippi was a
closed society, he answered in the negative. But after he had been back
home in Natchez for a spell, he told Frank Smith in a telephone conversation, "Hell, Mississippi ain't a closed society; it's padlocked!"

July 13: Meeting in Heffner home; Rev. Don McCord, National Council of Churches, present.

July 14: Requested men's clubs of Baptist and Presbyterian churches to allow McCord to speak. Turned down. Set up talk between McCord and sheriff.

July 15: Followed McCord back to home from Magnolia. McCord ate spaghetti supper with Heffners.

July 16: Malva [Mrs. Heffner] got anonymous call advising against association with civil rights workers.

July 17: Supper with McCord and two white civil rights workers. Daughter Carla called from New York City. Mentioned name of Dennis Sweeney, who was present. Shortly thereafter a woman called, asked to speak to Sweeney. Neighbors said they were upset about car in front of Heffner home. Cars circled house. The two boys left. Called FBI and local police.

July 18: Rumor mill. "That night I did load my pistol." Highway patrol "protected" house on tip it was to be bombed.

July 19: To church. Malva stayed at Holiday Inn. Harassment telephone calls.

July 20: Malva and Jan [daughter—reigning Miss Mississippi] stayed at motel.

July 21: Malva and Jan left for Miss Mississippi pageant at Vicksburg. Got office eviction notice.

July 22: Left for Vicksburg with dresses for Jan. Spent night in Jackson.

July 23: Talked with Erle Johnston in Jackson. Sympathy, but no help.

July 27: Returned to McComb. Sheriff put statement in paper saying not informed about actions around Heffner home.

July 28: Calls pick up.

July 29: Wild rumors: Carla said to be dating Negro in New York City and living with known Communists. ("Just pure crap.")

July 31: Talked with Bishop Paul Moore. Had to pick him up at a neutral place.

August 1: Moved out of office.

August 3: First adult McComb visitor since trouble started. Business completely gone. Clients afraid to talk. [Shortly afterward, the Heffners sold their home and moved to Washington.]

A complete account of the Heffners' experience may be found in Hodding Carter's *So the Heffners Left McComb.*

7) At two o'clock one April morning in 1964, Lafayette County Sheriff Boyce Bratton and his deputies stopped a car and trailer on the Oxford square. Three colored and three white men were searched and locked up in the county jail for about ten hours. Their trailer was filled with books from the Greenwood COFO library, destined for the Holly Springs Freedom House. The driver of the car was fined about twenty dollars because the taillight on the trailer was not burning. One of the Oxford policemen present, a retired U.S. Navy chief petty officer and an Ole Miss graduate student, had noticed that when the car and trailer were stopped the rear light *was* burning, and surmised that the wires had been jerked loose by one of the sheriff's aides. In disgust, this man resigned from the police force. The next day the front page of the Oxford *Eagle* was filled with pictures of the six men, captioned with such titles as "The Line Up," and with a hysterical account of the so-called leftist convictions of those arrested, derived in part from an examination of their billfolds and mostly from imagination. The editor of the paper congratulated the sheriff and his boys on knowing how to handle outside agitators. Her last word was to the effect that the culprits had been picked up in Holly Springs for "wreckless [*sic*] driving." No one in the complacent home town of William Faulkner and the chief center of learning in the state of Mississippi protested against this high-handed miscarriage of justice.

8) The following excerpts are taken from three signed confessions of McComb terrorists whose sentences (maximum possible penalty: death) were suspended by Judge W. H. Watkins, partly on the basis that they had been unduly provoked by outsiders of "low morality, some of them unhygienic," and because they came from good families "who were shocked at their involvement." [35]

---

35. It was generally believed that Judge Watkins (who had presided in the Clyde Kennard case but later had a cross burned in *his* yard) hit upon the suspended sentences in the belief that the confessed bombers, if tried one by one, would not be convicted by a local jury. On the same day the Ku Kluxers went free, twelve civil rights workers were

Ernest Frederick Zeeck, Jr.

I am 25 years of age and reside at 302 South Fifth Street, McComb, Mississippi where I am employed at the Western Auto Associate Store.

I wish to state that on the night of 20 September 1964, I rode in a car to the residence of a Negro woman in McComb, subsequently identified as Alyene Quin. This was a black car and was driven by Jimmy Wilson, operator of a Pure Oil service station in McComb, Mississippi. Sitting opposite Jimmy was an unknown man. I was sitting on the back seat on the right hand side as you look toward the front of the car and to my left was Paul Wilson, an employee of the Illinois Central Railroad in McComb.

The time was before midnight of the night of September 20, 1964 and pursuant to a prearranged agreement. Paul Wilson lit a bomb and handed it to me. I got out of the car and threw this bomb in the direction of the Quin house, after which we sped away. This bomb was a round object approximately 5 or 6 inches in diameter and about 18 inches long. It was wrapped in some kind of brown wrapping paper.

We bombed this house because it was the residence of a Negro woman whom I had been told was feeding COFO workers in the McComb area. I do not know what kind of explosives were used in the bomb or where it came from.

Jimmy Prinston Wilson

I reside at 136 North Cherry Street, McComb, Mississippi, and I operate the Edgewood Pure Oil service station, Georgia Avenue, McComb, Mississippi.

I joined the United Klans of America sometime after the first of 1964 and sometime in August, 1964, several of us split off from Ray Smith's Klan and organized a Klan of our own with Paul Wilson being appointed as E. C. and Allen Lee being appointed as Treasurer.

After forming this Klan, we made two or three meetings at Bubba Gillis' Upholstery Shop on Park Drive, then on September

---

arrested (and later sentenced) for cooking their own meals in a Freedom House without a health permit. Also, there was some distress in the community when a colored residential section called Beartown, added to McComb in 1961, was "de-annexed" in 1965, probably to keep down the potential Negro city vote.

20, 1964 I was contacted by Paul Wilson to help to do this job. I was contacted on Sunday, September 20, 1964, by Paul Wilson, and he told me he had a mission that he wanted me to go on.

We were supposed to go fishing about 6:00 P.M. which we had planned. I was at home that evening, and I decided to go on to the river myself earlier, and I went on out to the river fishing, and Paul Wilson, Billy Wilson and Ernest Zeeck came out roughly about 6:00 or 6:30 P.M., and we went out and set out hooks and fished about 10:00 and all four of us drove into town in Paul Wilson's car. I drove, Billy Wilson was in front with me and Paul Wilson and Ernest Zeeck was in the back. The bomb was in the back seat between Paul Wilson and Ernest Zeeck.

We drove around the block where Ailene Quin lives several times, which is on the old Summit Road, and the lights were on, and we could see that there wasn't anybody in the house around and on about the fourth round, I stopped the car in front of Ailene Quin's house. Paul Wilson lit the fuses and handed it to Ernest Zeeck who opened the car door, got out and threw the bomb toward the house. He got back in the car, and we drove back to the river. We drove north to Summit and back to the Bogue Chitto River Hoover Bridge. We fished awhile and took up the hooks and Billy Wilson and me came back in my station wagon which is a 1955 Mercury, black and white, to my home. Paul Wilson and Ernest Zeeck were behind us and Billy Wilson got out of my car and helped me unload some fishing gear, and I went in the house. He got in the car with them and went on with them. It was midnight or after when I got home. I went home; got undressed for bed, got in bed and went to sleep.

I was not present when this bombing was planned and had no knowledge of it until I was contacted by Paul Wilson to go along.

Billy Earl Wilson

I am 22 years old, was born April 22, 1942 at McComb, Mississippi and am employed by the I.C. Railroad at McComb.

I joined the Ku Klux Klan in McComb, Mississippi about May or June 1964. In about August, 1964 several members of the Klan to which I belonged decided to leave this Klan and organize a Klavern of our own to be known as the South Pike Marksmanship Association. This new Klan met mostly on Tuesday nights in an upholstery shop operated by "Bubba" Gillis. This upholstery shop was located behind Gillis' residence, in McComb, Mississippi.

At a meeting of this Klavern on Tuesday or Wednesday night, September 15 or 16, 1964 which was attended by Paul Wilson, Jimmy Wilson, Bubba Gillis, Al Lee, Charles Womack, John Paul Westbrook, Hilton Dunaway and I, a drawing was held for jobs to be pulled. I drew a piece of paper from a hat which bore the name of Alyene Quinn, 304 Old Summit Road, South of the Border night club.

After this drawing I got Paul Wilson, Jimmy Wilson and Earnest Zeeck to help me in bombing the Alyene Quinn residence.

On Sunday morning, September 20, 1964 I got a dynamite bomb consisting of about 12 or 15 sticks of dynamite from Al Lee.

On the night of Sunday, September 20, 1964 Paul Wilson, Jimmy Wilson, Earnest Zeeck and I went to the Alyene Quinn residence at which time we were riding in a 1961 black Ford owned by Paul Wilson and being driven by Jimmy Wilson. We stopped in front of the Alyene Quinn residence at which time Jimmy Wilson turned off the headlights of this automobile and Paul Wilson, who was seated in the back seat of this automobile and Paul Wilson lit the fuse to the dynamite bomb which Zeeck stepped out of the car and threw toward the Quinn home. We then drove at a high rate of speed away from the Quinn home.

These eight cases involving the dark forces of reaction were selected at random and could be duplicated a dozen times over.[36]

---

36. Another well-known case in which justice miscarried many times is taken from the report of the United States Commission on Civil Rights, *Law Enforcement: A Report on Equal Protection in the South.*

"In Greenwood, the county seat of Leflore County, two Negro brothers, Silas and Jake McGhee, tried repeatedly in July 1964 to attend the previously segregated Leflore Theater. The manager admitted them, as required by the Civil Rights Act of 1964, but angry crowds of whites gathered frequently at the theater, attempted to keep white patrons away by picketing with signs saying, 'This is a nigger theater,' and beat and harassed Negroes when they attended the theater. The building was also stoned by the crowds.

"Silas McGhee first attempted to attend the theater on July 5. He was attacked by a group of men. Although he reported the incident immediately to the city police, no arrests were made. His brother Jake McGhee was attacked at the theater on July 8. Following this assault, the police attempted to persuade the manager of the theater to sign a warrant for his arrest. On July 16 Silas McGhee was abducted by a

They are not just something frightening out of a dismal past, but represent a state of mind accurately descriptive of a large proportion of Mississippi whites today. There is no way to eliminate the propensity to inhumanity, legal trickery, and outright

---

gang of men who referred to his having attended the theater and who then beat him with pipes and boards. Although McGhee swore out a warrant before the justice of the peace, no arrests were made by local officials.

"During this period the manager of the theater and the McGhees made repeated requests to city officials for protection but received none. The police made no attempt to stop the violence or to disperse the crowds which, for three weeks, gathered in front of the theater. The only action taken by city officials was to close the theater temporarily, pursuant to a special ordinance enacted for that purpose. According to the manager of the theater, on one occasion the city officials told him that they were occupied protecting the city's other theater, which continued to refuse to admit Negroes.

"On July 26 the McGhees attended the theater and when they attempted to leave, they found a large, noisy, hostile crowd blocking their way. They called the police from inside the theater and requested protection. The police came but refused to escort the McGhees from the theater or disperse the crowd. The McGhees were told: 'You got yourselves in this damn mess, so get yourselves out.' As they left the theater, Silas McGhee was struck in the face by a white man. Other whites in the crowd pummeled, kicked, and spat at them. When the McGhees drove away, a bottle was thrown through the car window, spraying glass in their faces. Followed by the hostile crowd, they were taken by a friend to a local hospital to be treated for injuries. The police chief refused to escort them home and, after several hours, the sheriff escorted them through the crowd. No arrests were made although numerous police officers were present at both the theater and the hospital.

"A few weeks later Silas McGhee was shot and received a near fatal wound as he sat in a car in the Negro neighborhood. The police investigated but, again, no arrests were made.

"Following these events, the Department of Justice brought suit against the police and city administration contending that the failure to provide protection constituted a denial of the right to public accommodations in violation of the Civil Rights Act of 1964. An order was sought compelling the authorities to provide protection. Trial before a three-judge court was held in January, 1965, but the case has not yet been decided."

violence except through a long evolutionary educational process. The best that can be hoped for in the short run is that pressures for the maintenance of law and order based on justice will be accelerated by those state and federal powers in a position to enforce their will.

The Emerging Negro

One of the great shockers of the revolution that must sink into the mind of every white Mississippian sooner or later is the destruction of fictions long accepted regarding the personality of the Negro. The black man cannot be stereotyped, fitted into any well defined pattern, any more than the white man. As a debased sharecropper, he may be satisfied with steerage citizenship; as one who somehow has made it into the middle class, he may be overly cautious or indifferent toward change; as an emancipated partisan, he may be a revolutionist on the verge of violence. Furthermore, any one individual may be possessed by mixed feelings and motivations that lead him to react differently as the scene changes from day to day. It cannot be said that there exists a new Negro except as the white man takes another look at the colored brother he thought was there. This is true regardless of the unwillingness of Governor Johnson and Mayor Thompson to deal with any except those "responsible" from the white view, or of the tendency of leaders in small towns, where Negroes still give the appearance of docility, to believe that "our nigras" are untouched by universal human desires for betterment. The facts of life are not changed when an intemperate federal judge refers to Negro voter applicants as "a bunch of niggers who are acting like a bunch of chimpanzees."

Robert Parris Moses, an intellectual from the outside, and Fannie Lou Hamer, a nonintellectual from the inside, represent the explosive force of the black revolution in Mississippi. The legendary Moses came to Mississippi in 1961 by way of New York City, Hamilton College, and Harvard to push rural voter registration in the strongest bastion of segregation. For almost four years he lived on borrowed time, surviving jailings, beat-

ings, and attempts at assassination. Described by *Newsweek*'s
Karl Fleming in 1963 as "the most effective worker in the most
helpless areas," Moses inspired a few Negroes to shake off their
fear of attempting registration and giving testimony in federal
court for the Justice Department. Quiet, reflective, philosophical, not as religiously bent as Martin Luther King, Moses ate,
slept, and worked with local Negroes. Still, he wasn't really
getting anywhere in his try at tearing down the monolithic white
supremacy society until, in co-operation with William Higgs and
others, he brought in a hundred or so eager college students to
help with the mock election campaign of Aaron Henry and
Ed King in the fall of 1963. This experiment led to the 1964
summer invasion by civil rights workers, who "through con-
nections back home will give the project more projection, and
bring the Justice Department into Mississippi in a bigger
way." Regardless of whether COFO (with Moses as project
director) won or lost the immediate summer battle, it turned
the tide of the war as the nation itself became committed to
civil rights for all.

A lengthy conversation with Bob Moses in February 1965
convinced me that he was unconcerned with integration as such,
that his real mission was to uplift a whole people in the shortest
possible time. His prophet's role, unembarrassed by personal
ambition, took him into visionary paths such as the proposition
for setting up Negro courts in Mississippi.[37] "It's important to
recognize in the struggle certain humanitarian values," he told
Robert Penn Warren, "that you have to struggle for people,
and . . . you try to eke out some corner of love or some
glimpse of happiness within. . . . The dichotomy is whether
you can learn to be a victim any more and also not be what
Camus calls an executioner. For when people rise up and
change their status, usually somewhere along the line they
become executioners, and they get involved in subjugating other

---

37. A friend of his suggests that Moses really had in mind the establishment of special federal courts, in the tradition of the customs or
patent tribunals, to handle civil rights matters. It now seems likely that
some such legislation will be considered by the Congress.

people. The problem is whether you can move Negro people from the place where they are now the victims of this kind of hatred to a place where they don't in turn perpetuate this hatred. In the end the Negroes and the whites are going to have to share the land, and the less overlay of bitterness, the more possible it will be to work out a reconciliation."

It is possible that such reflection directed the humble Moses, once he had become the "executioner" in blocking compromise at Atlantic City, to change his name and leave the Mississippi scene (where he worried about his own predominating role). At least it helps explain his movement into larger areas of conflict such as the controversy over American participation in Vietnam and his willingness to challenge even the President of the United States.

Fannie Lou Hamer, indomitable, untutored philosopher from Jim Eastland's county and darling of SNCC, dominated the training period at Oxford, Ohio, contested the spotlight at the Democratic National Convention with LBJ, and challenged Congressman Jamie Whitten for his House seat in the fall of 1964. The whole country watched and listened to her eloquence at Atlantic City: "They carried me into a room and there were two Negro boys in this room. The state highway patrolman gave them a long, wide blackjack and he told one of the boys, 'Take this . . . and if you don't use it on her, you know what I'll use on you.' I had to get over a bed flat on my stomach and that man beat me . . . that man beat me till he give out. And by me screamin' it made a plainclothes man—he didn't have on nothin' like a uniform—he got so hot and worked up he just run there and started hittin' me on the back of my head. And I was trying to guard some of the licks with my hands and they just beat my hands till they turned blue."

Mrs. Hamer assured the students at Oxford, Ohio, that they were the answer to the faith of her people in Sunflower County. "Faith is the substance of things hoped for, the evidence of things not seen," she said as she warned the prospective rights workers, "our religion is very important to us—you'll have to understand that." Hatred of the white man was no part of the problem's solution: ". . . the white man is the scaredest person on earth. Out in daylight he don't do nothin'. But at night he'll toss a bomb or pay someone to kill. The white man's afraid he'll be treated like he's been treating the Negroes, but I couldn't carry that much hate. It wouldn't solve any problems for me to hate whites because they hate me. Oh, there's so much hate! Only God has kept the Negro sane."

So the existentialist and the fundamentalist came together to move the Mississippi Negro. Most of the civil rights workers, like Schwerner and Goodman, were skeptics when it came to organized religion, but they took to heart the warning: "Don't talk about atheism. If God wants to start a movement then hooray for God." Sometimes Fannie Lou Hamer forgot her feeling of love for all mankind. At one of the rallies of the Mississippi Freedom Labor Union pressing the first Delta farm labor strike in a generation, she lashed out against the faint-hearted: "We got to stop the nervous Nellies and the Toms from going to the Man's place. I don't believe in killing, but a good whipping behind the bushes wouldn't hurt them."

Participation in the movement for any length of time has a tendency to "radicalize" the rank and file in SNCC, which makes a profession of having no authoritarian leadership.[38] SNCC, therefore, is seldom amenable to compromise—as shown at Atlantic City—and thus the breakup of the SNCC-dominated COFO was to be expected before the summer of 1964 was over. Radicals in control of the movement were trying to achieve what NAACP liberals thought was unattainable. These activists were unimpressed with legalism and constitutionalism; they were the "new abolitionists," not sure they wanted to integrate the Negro into a society they saw as sick. They decried bourgeois values in their desire to remake not only Mississippi and the South but all of America along egalitarian, proletarian lines. In

---

38. The clearest insight into the Student Nonviolent Coordinating Committee, the most militant phase of the Negro movement, is a thirty-four-page pamphlet, *Encounter with the Future* (Atlanta, 1965), by Pat Watters, senior staff member of the Southern Regional Council.

Mississippi their demand was for a second Reconstruction, with a redistribution of political power, or perhaps it is more accurate to say that their hope was for an alliance of poverty-stricken whites with poor Negroes, a new Populism. To say that SNCC leadership was communistic, as many did, was to miss the obvious, for SNCC wanted nothing less than a revolution to be carried out with the power of the federal government, hardly a Marxist conception. Help from any source was gratefully received by SNCC; communism was irrelevant. It may have been disillusionment with conditions in the ghettos of the big cities that had sent fiercely aggressive Negroes into Mississippi in the first place, but they were gradually being replaced by equally aggressive native young rebels, as exemplified by Lawrence Guyot, able chairman of the Mississippi Freedom Democratic Party.

A contempt for bureaucratic control made SNCC vulnerable to slashing attacks from the enemy. The challenge of the Mississippi Congressional delegation in 1965, for instance, was discredited in part when two workers in McComb suggested in a newsletter that Mississippi Negroes should not honor the draft, which might send them to Vietnam to fight "for the white man's freedom." Though quickly disclaimed by Guyot and disavowed in content by the NAACP, this blunder allowed the American Legion and the *Commercial Appeal* to cry "Treason." Likewise, the promotion of a short film strip called *The Peoples Wants Freedom,* a rather crude assembly of old-style Marxist propaganda, was of questionable value to the cause.

In Mississippi for more than a year the liberals and the radicals have been slugging it out over spoils which are not only ephemeral but whose slight value is further endangered by the feud. Jack Newfield pointed out the basic problem: "The liberals are practical, and SNCC is utopian; the liberals are sophisticated, and SNCC is primitive; the liberals want reform, and SNCC wants what is tantamount to a revolution; the liberals are bureaucratic, and SNCC is spontaneous; the liberals are middle-aged and middle-class, and SNCC is young and classless; the liberals are relativist, and SNCC is absolutist; the liberals

are adjusted, and SNCC is alienated." When the Democratic
Convention was over, Bob Moses explained his refusal to compromise: "The FDP delegates were the only people at that
whole convention who were free in any meaningful use of the
term. The President told everyone else . . . what to do. All I
cared about was the insides of those 68 delegates and the future
of the FDP in Mississippi. It wasn't my responsibility to care
about Humphrey or the backlash. We couldn't let others single
out two people and appoint them our spokesmen. The whole
point of the FDP is to teach the lowest sharecropper that he
knows better than the biggest leader what is required to make
a decent life for himself." Mr. Moses had got to the heart of
what some of the radicals meant by "participatory democracy." [39]

If all Negroes of voting age in Mississippi were registered, if
they block-voted (as whites have done historically to preserve
the caste system), and if their votes were cast for the Freedom
Democratic Party, they could not carry now, or at any foreseeable time in the future, a single office in a statewide election.
That is, if the Voting Rights Act were totally implemented,
Negroes would control slightly more than one-third of the Mississippi vote. This Utopian possibility, moreover, ignores the
plain fact that almost all Mississippi Negroes will for a long time
be almost completely at the mercy of whites who employ them.
"There are plenty of folks around here who will fire their
Negroes for registering," said Rice Pritchard, who for thirty
years has run a cotton gin and lumber yard employing twenty-
five Negroes in Tallahatchie County. "My people," he added,
"aren't registered—I don't fool with those smart niggers. But
if any of them did, I'd sure call them in and ask them what they
mean." According to A. D. Beittel, former president of Tougaloo College, "Economic intimidation is far more powerful and
common in the race issue than violence . . . economic in-

---

39. For a sympathetic advocacy of this point of view by an activist who
participated in the Mississippi Summer Project in 1964, see Staughton
Lynd, "The New Radicals and 'Participatory Democracy,'" *Dissent*,
Summer 1965, pp. 324–333.

timidation is the thing these people live with every day." [40]

Except as they may help choose a moderate over a racist white in a local election, then, Mississippi Negroes have no prospect of major political influence, whatever the course of the Freedom Democratic Party. Their capacity to swing elections where rival candidates divide the white vote will soon achieve some basic Negro demands, such as the elimination of police brutality, more and better community services, and recognition on school boards. Such a prospect presupposes wheeling and dealing with white politicians, an impossibility (at least in the open) at the moment in Mississippi, however far along such a course may already be in other southern states.

In the last year or so, a predominantly Negro group led by SNCC has failed twice to obtain a state charter from the Young Democratic Clubs of America. It was blocked by Mississippi liberals (Charles Evers' NAACP and Claude Ramsay's AFL-CIO) who fear an all-Negro party and "episodes to kick off more hatred in Mississippi." R. Hunter Morey, white secretary of the radicals, claimed in a burst of anger that the liberals were out to control the Negro vote "to accommodate the civil rights movement to the status quo," their conduct being "not only shocking but revolting." For good measure, Morey included in his denunciation the Mississippi Council on Human Relations, most biracial committees, and "white segregationists whose opportunism is even stronger than their racism." In August 1965, when the Young Democratic liberals walked out of a radical-controlled meeting in Jackson, Charles Evers returned the compliment: "They are anti anybody that wears a suit of clothes . . . that comes in clean . . . that combs his hair." The Mississippi liberal establishment, whose strength at the moment is nominal, hopes to build for the future with control of the colored vote plus whatever whites can be induced to

---

40. Separate but equal was hardly the case in a rural Madison County Negro school whose children had no toilet facilities. Judge Cox ordered the school board to install flush toilets, but when this project proved expensive, the judge approved *the removal of the school itself to existing flush toilets.*

forget their supposed superiority, together with the manifold blessings expected to flow from Washington. Their blueprint calls, not for another party to be carved out of the Mississippi Democratic Conference, but for use of the conference to infiltrate and capture at least a considerable part of the regular Democratic following in the state. As of September 1965, the disputing groups in the Young Democrats had reconciled their differences in a merger whose strength was unlikely to disturb the professional politicians of Mississippi.[41]

Claude Ramsay, president of Mississippi's AFL-CIO, has fought the good but unrewarding fight to put Mississippi labor on the side of the angels in matters of race and civil rights. His views coincide with the thinking of the more enlightened business community, which, however, is more than content with the "right-to-work" proposition firmly embedded in the state constitution. Antiunionism so dominates Mississippi that, on the verge of an election in the Superior Coach Corporation's Kosciusko plant, the somewhat enlightened *Star Herald* could argue that if the workers declared for the union "they will be guilty of destroying our local industrial development effort." Ramsay complains of Klan, Birch, and APWR infiltration of the unions, although, as a matter of fact, his wage earners, with a long tradition of Negrophobia, are the natural allies of the status quo in racial matters. Hence, a vicious circle results: labor leaders go along with business officials on race, but disagree on union policy; in the short run, at least, industrial workers are unsympathetic with their officers on civil rights, but

---

41. Early in October 1965, the executive committee of the liberals almost unanimously rejected the "uneasy compromise" between the two factions. Thereupon the radicals withdrew from the fight, probably fearful of their national image once it was widely known that the Freedom Democratic Party was opposed in the state by a labor-white liberal-Negro coalition. Two weeks later the integrated liberal Mississippi delegation was welcomed and granted a charter by the Young Democratic Clubs of America, who pledged "every form of assistance necessary for the Mississippi Young Democratic organization to grow and flourish." At least a beginning had been made in the direction of eliminating racism and white supremacy from Mississippi politics.

agree on the need for unions. The industrialist, of course, could help insure Mississippi's future prosperity by his endorsement of the inevitable organization of Mississippi factory labor, a course not appreciably opposed by the great corporations with plants in the state.

When the income of the ex-redneck as an industrial worker approaches the national average, the problem may very well be on the way to solution. In the meantime, an occasional beating by Klansmen of union officials who go along with the economic dictates of the Civil Rights Law of 1964 and with national union policy may help the workers to see that future solidarity of white and black labor transcends the perpetuation of racial prejudice. The good society will be on its way when Negroes are accepted in unions as well as in factories. Claude Ramsay not only understands this, but goes a step further: "It is a foregone conclusion," he says, "that labor will not attain its political goals as long as the Negro is systematically denied the right to vote. . . . If and when large numbers of Negroes are allowed to vote, organized labor will probably find the political strength to become an effective force in Mississippi." For the first time in history, Mississippi has more industrial than agricultural workers. The educational problem requires great finesse: to prevent racism and prejudice, historically employed by white supremacy politicians and fly-by-night industrialists, from exploiting the masses, black and white, as has been the case for almost a hundred years.[42]

---

42. In the *New Republic* for December 26, 1964, Gerald Johnson wrote with emotion about the age-old problem: "What force could conceivably propel any man into commission of a crime more hideous than plain murder? The answer is not far to seek. It is the policy, pursued by the proper gentlemen of Mississippi, of controlling and manipulating the wool-hat boys, the rednecks, the lint-heads, by stuffing them with lies that blind their eyes to the real world. The policy of white supremacy could be justified, of course, only on the theory of white superiority. In the realm of physical force white superiority did and does exist; the lie was in extending this superiority into the realm of moral and intellectual force, and attributing it to a biological factor, which is to say, the propagation of racism."

"Most Mississippi Negroes are silent in the current struggle," wrote John Herbers of the New York *Times*. "But they are not strangers to violence, and when it comes they speak of it as something they have long had to bear." A colored minister who had lost two churches to fire bombs said philosophically, "I guess they were trying to scare somebody." The radicals, according to Bob Moses, were putting themselves "in the place of Negroes who have been subjected to violence without anyone on the outside knowing it or doing anything about it." The apathy among Negroes in regard to their rights was portrayed by a young farm worker: "I'm not sure Mrs. T. would fire me for registering, but I suspect she would. At any rate I'm certainly not going to register unless she encourages me."

Middle-class Negro schoolteachers have been more than hesitant to risk economic security and status by antagonizing whites who have absolute control over their jobs. The principal of the Oxford Training School has for twenty years been registered in Hinds County, 165 miles away. This convenient resolution (one couldn't be expected to travel over 300 miles just to vote) of a real dilemma is eminently satisfactory to the local school board. In the summer of 1965, I got acquainted with an aspiring young teacher who had gone to Rutgers University to pursue his graduate French degree, assisted by financial help from the state of Mississippi. He had, he said, been too busy to try to register in Jackson, where he taught, and he was doing exceedingly well on his $5,000-a-year salary. It was obvious that he had no feeling of obligation to his race if it necessitated risking the wrath of the white man. Besides, he remembered with some satisfaction a pleasant conversation he had had with Dr. Jobe of the Board of Trustees of the Institutions of Higher Learning when he picked up his expense check. In a similar case, an elder brother, himself an aggressive civil rights worker in Jackson, expressed to me great dismay when he learned that his sister would attend Howard University instead of the University of Mississippi. "She's plumb scared to go to Ole Miss," he declared with some disgust. James Meredith felt the same discouragement with those middle-class Negroes who sent their children out of state, even to prestige Eastern schools, rather than follow in the path he had opened up.

About a year ago, I talked with some 300 Negro high-school social-science teachers. I came away convinced that these educators knew what they wanted but were hesitant about expressing themselves in or out of class for fear of economic reprisal. In private conversation, one Negro college president usually designated as an Uncle Tom made it clear that he would rather act the role of a DuBois than a Washington but that he had been ridden hard by the state Board of Trustees. Another state college president has, on occasions when the Board met at his institution, doffed his suit coat for a white jacket in order to *serve* his white guests properly. In 1965 the Mississippi Teachers Association (Negro) held its meetings in the state coliseum. President C. J. Duckworth was at least outwardly happy. "This is a giant step forward," he purred; "it lends dignity to our educational and cultural pursuits." Speakers included Mayor Thompson, the superintendent of the Jackson schools, the state superintendent of education, the executive secretary of the college board, and the president of Bishop College, an exceedingly conservative Texas college. Duckworth pleaded with Governor Johnson to encourage teachers to vote: "I'll be darned if I can see how a teacher with enthusiasm and conviction can teach the 13th, 14th and 15th amendments . . . and cannot exercise that right themselves." Paul Johnson, he added, should "find an avenue to bridge the gap that severs the communication line between the educated Negro citizenry" and the governor's office. There was no report of serious objection to this impertinence.

Who will cast the first stone at the thousands of Mississippi Negroes who have achieved middle-class status and perhaps some peace of mind by adjusting to the caste system? In the case of Percy Greene, whose Jackson *Advocate* was sent out to Negro high schools by the Sovereignty Commission, the decision is relatively easy. Nobody raised an eyebrow when Greene challenged the Freedom Democratic Party's "comic vote mockery" in the fall of 1964 as a "colossal joke . . . a mock-

ery of the elective system, invented by the communists who
. . . exercise their greatest influence with COFO in order to
undermine Negro confidence in the Democratic elective process." Another Negro publisher complained that his people had
"not taken advantage of the opportunities that have been opened
to us." He wrote the *Clarion-Ledger* that Mississippi Negroes
should "tell their agitators and extremists to pack their carpet-
bags and . . . return the leadership of the Negro community
back to the local people. . . ." In his column, Charlie Hills
printed a letter ostensibly sent by a penitentiary inmate, au-
thenticated by the Parchman chaplain, to his daughter graduat-
ing from a Los Angeles high school. An excerpt: "I hope you
had a wonderful Christmas. . . . By the way did you like the
Band from Mississippi Vocational College? Or did you see them
on television at the Rose Bowl parade? To me they were wonderful, because they represent the mind and spirit of the decent
Negroes in Mississippi who do not bow to the people who come
to stir up trouble. This is my home and I should know. And I
am not a cotton-patch raised Negro. I know that the educational facilities in this state for Negroes is second to none anywhere, but will they go? No, they would rather lay around town
and indecent places, and then blame the white people because
they make constructive elements for the future and the present.
This is the truth, so help me." Evidently Parchman is a superior
educational facility.

Mississippi Negro publisher Jessie Gillespie, of the *Mid-South
Informer,* took up the refrain of separatism: "There seem to
be a never-ending stream of so called Freedom Workers invading The South. The White and Negro workers I have seen are
unkept [*sic*], unsanitary and uncouth. Actually they are an
insult to our dignity, for the immoral example they are showing
is not conducive to the progress of Negroes. Dr. Booker T.
Washington worked on the theory that the Negro would have
to prepare himself to meet the challenge of the day in the fields
of industry and agriculture. . . . W. E. B. DuBois, a known
Communist agitator said the only hope for the Negro was for
him to completely integrate into the White man's society. Dr.

Washington's theory . . . would encourage him to build things for himself, it would make him proud to be a Negro. So let us try to build . . . a great heritage for our posterity as Negroes that our children will be proud of us and will not try to lose the identity of our great race."

There are in Mississippi, it would seem, about as many kinds of Negroes as there are kinds of white people. But day by day, as they discover that they do have a chance to go beyond the confines of the old society, more and more Negroes lose their reluctance to speak their minds. Dozens of them risked violence to spread their grievances before the United States Commission on Civil Rights. In December 1964, thousands of Negro farmers participated for the first time in county elections of Agricultural Stabilization Committees. (They carried positions in Holmes and Madison counties and swept the top three places on a five-man committee in Benton County. In the last case the victors failed to get an advertisement into the Ashland *Southern Advocate* which would have informed all farmers that: "We do not intend to serve our race exclusively. We do not intend to cast stone for stone. We intend to carry out our function with justice and equity . . . regardless of race, as good, true, and honest committeemen.") Three Coahoma County Negro women filed suit in federal court contesting the constitutionality of a 1964 Mississippi law making repeated conception of illegitimate children a misdemeanor. A Citizens Coordinating Committee in Jackson, "representing the combined Negro leadership," issued a proclamation in the form of an open letter to Mayor Thompson, declaring its support of all who challenged "the validity of elections which were held under unfair and discriminatory laws." The same group sponsored a march of local Negroes protesting lack of justice in Mississippi courts and with some asperity announced: "We're going to get equal rights through the federal government and the churches." Mrs. Henry Lorenzo, who lives in the new Negro community house in Mileston, commented on the new courage born of purpose: "Every night Negro volunteers come and guard the building. They are armed with shotguns and one carries a tommygun. All the Negroes are armed. They have to be. People outside cannot imagine how it is here." [43]

There is little reason to question the judgment of a visiting northern professor who was surprised to find the "so-called un-educated Negroes articulate, self-respecting and courageous." While he admitted he had met only a small proportion of Mis-sissippi Negroes, he was sure that the "Mississippi project would never have gotten off the ground if the Negroes themselves had not been willing to risk their jobs, property and lives. It was they who found the churches and other buildings for the Free-dom Schools and community centers, who attended the schools in the oppressive summer heat, who took the COFO workers into their homes. The courage that this required can scarcely be estimated; every Negro who became identified with the free-dom movement was risking economic and physical reprisal. In Mississippi there is no sanctuary for the Negro; the 'law' is not a source of protection but the chief instrument of intimidation and persecution." To which one who has lived in Mississippi for thirty years can say, "Amen."

The Future Is Clear

About two years ago, I saw "little evidence that the closed so-ciety will ever possess the moral resources to reform itself. . . . [The nation] will not much longer indulge the frustration of its will. . . . It cannot be long before the country, seeing that per-suasion alone must fail, and perhaps acting through the power and authority of the federal government, will, with whatever reluctance and sadness, put an end to the closed society in

---

43. James Chaney was buried on August 8, 1964. At the funeral serv-ice, his mother said: "This has been an awful thing. It is even more important now that the guilty ones be brought to trial and justice, and be punished. If not, other mothers of Negro sons may be caused to grieve as I have grieved. God must forgive them; it is very difficult for me to . . . if we don't stand up for our rights now [my son's] death will have been in vain, and the death of the other two boys."

Mississippi." Inspired by radicals in the civil rights movement, all branches of the federal government, since the above was written, have pursued the relentless course which has brought about more change in Mississippi than in any other part of the Union. The courts, the Congress, and the Chief Executive of the United States have not faltered and their actions have been overwhelmingly endorsed by the people of the whole country.

On the surface at least, Mississippians have grudgingly accepted their inevitable destiny. In fact, the civil rights legislation of 1964 and 1965 has allowed those who contended all along that they were not opposed to constitutional measures to save face. The big question, posed by the historically-minded who look back to the country's experience with federal fugitive-slave legislation and to the dreary record of national prohibition, has been whether social change can be permanently imposed from the outside against the will of a solidly defensive community. In the present case of the country's mandate to end Mississippi's caste system by bringing first-class citizenship to her Negro population, that question can be answered tentatively in the affirmative. The answer must remain tentative for some years because the evidence seems to indicate that if, for any reason, the nation relaxes its insistence on justice, the cause of the Mississippi Negro will still be lost.[44]

Former Governor James P. Coleman, in his testimony before the Senate Judiciary Committee, which recommended his appointment to the Fifth Circuit Court of Appeals, spoke for Mississippi when he said the civil rights war was over, that integration was the law of the land and no longer debatable. Fundamental resistance is dead, though a few are still arguing

---

44. Though he has done his share of whistling while passing graveyards, it is well to remember that as late as December 1964 Robert Patterson, Citizens Council executive secretary, could write: "Frankly, I believe the current era may be Mississippi's finest hour. We know we are right and all we have to do is to hold what we have got. The rest of this nation will eventually come to its senses especially as a result of the extreme negro attitudes in the North and throughout the world."

points long ago settled. Ross Barnett has become an anachronism, yet there is reason to believe that he and his Klan-minded friends are unaware of their real status. Civil rights has moved on from a protest to a political action movement.

Mississippi whites have matured a good deal since 1954. Mississippi Negroes will suffer further indignities and disappointments before they mature. Modern communities are dominated by economic power structures which cannot tolerate chaos. Able Mississippians are still moving out of the state for economic advantage, but capable outsiders are at the same time coming in to run the new industry. The Negro exodus continues, lessening pressures. Middle-class Negroes have shown no great understanding of the revolution which engulfs them, but will become more involved in the changes taking place. Every civil rights crisis since 1954 has had its instructive value for Mississippians of both races. The country is determined to move disadvantaged Negroes and whites out of their hopeless cycle of poverty and ignorance, and in the process thousands of Mississippians will be exposed to constructive, integrated experiences.

The roll of moderates in responsible situations in Mississippi who have been speaking out since the passage of the 1964 Civil Rights Act has been lengthening month by month. State Treasurer William Winter, a prime gubernatorial prospect for 1967, was the first politician to call for new leaders "willing to say frankly that we do our state no service when we counsel defiance of the laws of this nation. We must," he said, "not only condemn acts of violence after they've taken place, but we must create a climate in which they will not be attempted in the first place." A past president of the Mississippi Bar Association admitted sadly that Mississippians had lost faith in the courts "in the backwash from irrational and emotional criticism" of the Supreme Court. Lieutenant Governor Gartin, worried about industries lost to the state because of its racial climate, declared, "We cannot build fences around our state . . . we have to adjust to change . . . or be destroyed by change." With a similar apprehension, the president of the state

Manufacturers Association declared, "Nothing can be gained by a continuation of the past." One of Mississippi's most prominent Baptist laymen, the president of the Mississippi Economic Council, recognized that in the passage of the Civil Rights Act of 1964 the state had "lost the battle" and must henceforth obey "the law of the land." He added, "It's no longer taboo to talk about these things." Bishop Joseph Brunini thought "the time to talk is past. We must move into actual integration. There should be no trouble." The head of the Bankers Association suggested: "We must sweep aside the misconceptions people have about us, obey the law, and rise above criticisms of the past." And Paul Johnson said it best of all: "The day for a lot of bull-shooting is over."

There has been, indeed, a new mood abroad in the state. In asking support for legislation and constitutional amendments to remove restrictions on Negro suffrage, many highly placed politicians freely admitted their hypocritical political chicanery of the past. A prominent North Mississippi banker concluded that "we've had the most trouble" when the Citizens Council was in the ascendency. "I'm sorry now I had anything to do with the council. I used to think it was the answer to our problems. Now I see it has only contributed to them." A Mississippi-born novelist concluded that the ordinary citizen, "sick and tired of the climate of violence and of the odor of disgrace," would help to bring about the new dispensation. "Most Mississippians were and are still good people. The weakness was a failure of the leaders, a failure of the press, a failure of the professions especially the bar, and saddest of all, a failure of the churches." An editor of the Ole Miss *Mississippian* wrote that those doing the state the most harm were not out-of-state agitators, biased journalists, or left-wing television commentators: "The people who are doing the most to drag Mississippi down are Mississippians who attempt to live in a dream world of moonlight, moonshine and magnolia blossoms, Mississippians who burn churches, Mississippians who refuse to recognize that two-fifths of the population of this state is non-white."

As must be true in all societies in a state of flux, there is conflicting evidence as to what is going on.[45] A look at only the

---

45. The United States Commission on Civil Rights liked what it found in its investigation of Greenville. Its report:

"The contribution that community support for impartial law enforcement, a professional police force, and firmly expressed intentions to enforce the law can make towards preventing racial violence was revealed in the Commission's study of Greenville. Greenville is the county seat of Washington County and the fourth largest city in Mississippi. When Negro leaders from Greenville appeared before the Commission, they were unanimous in expressing confidence in their law enforcement officials. James Edwards, chairman of the local NAACP, testified that the attitude of the Negro community towards law enforcement was 'good' and that Negroes believed 'we have one of the best police forces in the State, one of the best police forces that you will find. . . .'

"The confidence of the Negro community in Greenville police can be attributed to the determination of city officials to have impartial and professional law enforcement.

"The chief of police, William C. Burnley, Jr., had served as a law enforcement officer in Greenville for 25 years and is a graduate of the FBI National Academy. Members of extremist groups were not permitted to join the police departments, and this policy was enforced by means of FBI checks of recruits and lie detector tests. Burnley's entire immediate staff (seven officers) have attended the FBI National Academy. Other officers have received training as detectives. Unlike other police forces in Mississippi, since 1950 the Greenville police force has included Negro officers. At the time of the Commission's hearing there were seven Negro police officers and several Negro crossing guards.

"In the spring of 1964, when many Mississippi communities feared violence because of the announced arrival of civil rights workers, officials in Greenville took steps to prevent trouble. The mayor and the city council issued statements which underlined the city's determination that law and order would prevail. Mayor Dunne told the Commission: 'This we meant and the people knew that we meant it.' The city's position was supported by public statements from citizens' groups in Greenville and by the local newspaper.

"The police displayed a similar attitude. Police Chief William C. Burnley, Jr., began a program of orientation and training for his officers in which he stressed their duty to enforce the law fairly and to prevent incidents of violence. The chief told his men that the policy constructive side of the picture makes for distortion, but the fact of widespread desegregation of schools and compliance with court-ordered integration of accommodations cannot be gainsaid. Negroes and whites use the municipal golf course in Jackson; civil rights marchers moving into Brandon were treated

---

would be, 'Arrest no person regardless of who they are or what group they belong to unless they have violated the law.' Those who felt they could not accept this policy were invited to leave the department. The police chief and other officials also took steps to advise themselves fully of the membership and activities of the Klan and similar organizations.

"The community was apprised in April 1964 of police determination to prevent violence. When the Ku Klux Klan, in a show of strength, burned crosses in communities throughout Mississippi, Greenville was the only place where the persons responsible for cross-burnings were arrested and prosecuted. Later, when civil rights workers arrived in the community, there were no incidents of violence against them, nor was a single worker arrested by the Greenville police on any charge.

"On August 10, 1964 a white attacked a Negro, and, in a separate incident, a Negro attacked a white. Arrests were made almost immediately in both cases and identical fines imposed. Following these incidents, Police Chief Burnley issued a statement:

" 'The issue with us is not which race assaults the other, but rather the idea of professional law enforcement. We intend to enforce the laws of the state and city as written without regard to one's station in life. This is the only way that peace and order can be obtained and continued.'

"Chief Burnley testified at the hearing that his policy received 'tremendous support from the community,' and that without such support he believed his effectiveness would have been greatly diminished. Two leading members of the white community, Albert Lake and Leroy Percy, testified that they thought that the business and professional community contributed to the quality of law enforcement in the city of Greenville. As Mr. Lake commented, 'Voluntary groups . . . have basically operated to give support to the governing body of the city and to the police force and to see that law and order was maintained.' Mr. Percy expressed a similar view:

" 'I think that the basic reason for Greenville being the community it is, is this: there has been a long history of responsible citizens willing to participate in local government, not only to involve themselves in voting and getting the vote out, but to serve as city councilmen, as members of the school board and so forth. I think that is basic.' "

with respect; a biracial committee is functioning in Clarksdale; the 1964 state fair, with 150,000 attending, was integrated, as was an arts festival in Jackson. For the first time since Reconstruction, a Negro is serving on a high-level municipal commission unaffiliated with administration of federal funds. The Mississippi Council on Human Relations is not only a healthy reality, with a paid executive director and a paid assistant, but it has several branches meeting regularly in several parts of the state. Three white state universities have been desegregated, with about a dozen Negroes attending Ole Miss in the summer and fall of 1965. The chairman of the U.S. Commission on Civil Rights called the testimony regarding Greenville "a breath of fresh air." Cities like Corinth have made great progress under a variety of federal aid programs and have no Citizens Council or Ku Klux Klan. A Baptist preacher is moderately hopeful about the future, saying wistfully, "The children of Israel left a big graveyard in the wilderness before they made it to the Promised Land." Students at the University of Mississippi have been quite outspoken in their denunciation of weak leadership from their school's administration. At least one of the men put on probation for bombings in McComb has been sentenced to six months in jail for breaking his pledge of good behavior, and McComb itself has become a relatively peaceful place. Racial demagoguery may become a profitless venture even by the next gubernatorial campaign in 1967. Barriers to Negro participation in heretofore white religious services have quietly been taken down in all parts of the state.

Two little-known legal cases arising in Greenville in the summer of 1964 are cause for hope that the old customs are no longer inviolate. Two white lawyers defended seventeen-year-old Negro Oliver Lee, accused of raping a white girl. The only real question involved was one of consent. The young woman had engaged in sexual relations with many whites and blacks and was married, the mother of two small children. Little short of a prostitute, she had taken up with Negroes partly because the whites were fearful of venereal disease. Yet the prosecution, in normal Mississippi fashion, spoke of her as "this young housewife and mother." Three whites testified as to her reputation. A lawyer involved in the case remarked, "It turned out that most of her former bedmates are presently either in the army or in Parchman." The trial resulted in a hung jury. Later, the district attorney dropped all charges, telling the court that "a statement by the victim made further prosecution of the case impossible." He did not elaborate.

In another case, a Negro hospital orderly was clubbed by a deputy sheriff and then charged with disturbing the peace. Lawyers' Constitutional Defense Committee attorneys appeared to defend the accused, but six local lawyers offered their services free of charge. On the day of trial, civil rights lawyers observed as the defendant was acquitted. Both of these cases are minor straws in the wind, and yet they indicate a degree of change from the past when a Negro had little or no chance for justice if involved in court against a white person.[46]

Opposed to these miscellaneous evidences of change in the direction of a new, healthier society in Mississippi must be placed facts on the other side. The state's official stance of compliance with the demands of the country is superficial and minimal and could easily be reversed. (For a time, George Guy was both chief of police of McComb and president of the local chapter of Americans for the Preservation of the White Race.) Police brutality, legal harassment, economic intimidation, beatings, bombings, arson, and murder are still commonplace. In June 1965, I listened to and largely believed the stories of five women who complained at a freedom rally of brutalized treatment they claimed to have received in the Jackson stockade that very day. I thought they were, in the main, telling the truth despite blanket denials of police brutality by Mayor Thompson.[47] Children who come from environments which caused them

---

46. In November 1965, a Mississippi white man was sentenced to life imprisonment for the rape of a Negro girl.

47. Ed King commented bitterly on the conduct of Jackson police: "They've learned to take brutality off the streets." Some Negroes among the 800 sent to the "Fairgrounds Motel" for illegal demonstrations had, according to Chief of Detectives Pierce, bruised themselves while

to applaud in school the assassination of President Kennedy are not likely to have turned into little saints in the meantime. There was a minor riot on the Ole Miss campus one night during the Southern Literary Festival because of Negro members in attendance. The old Alcazar Hotel in Clarksdale, now the Regency Club, is for whites only. The home of Aaron Henry is protected every night by an armed guard. In the wake of widespread token desegregation of schools, at least fifty new private institutions are contemplated, and many are already in operation. The world knows about the 650 McComb citizens who signed the declaration for law and order, but few seem to have heard of the satisfaction-with-the-status-quo statement from the same city, with twice as many signatories.

No white office-holder in Mississippi has yet encouraged Negroes to vote. There has been no effort to increase the number of Negroes on juries beyond the legal minimum.[48] It is still true that only the very boldest people dare speak out in criticism of the old order. A liberal rabbi was driven out by his congregation, and moderates continue to leave the state, one remarking sadly that his departure was "for the sake of my children." In September 1964, the *Center Light* declared, "If there is one person in Greenwood truly free, he ought to come forward and identify himself so that we can offer him as proof positive that there is such a thing as a free man in our community. We are . . . scared of our shadows because in the shadow may be someone listening to our words, reading our thoughts, ready to pounce on any action which does not comply with local stand-

---

playing tackle football on the concrete floor with an old shoe for the ball. At the time, Mayor Thompson was under pressure from the governor to "lay off" the troublemakers, at least until the challenge of the Mississippi delegation in Congress had been decided.

48. There has been some talk in Mississippi of a movement to reform the jury system, now in the hands of the boards of supervisors. Whether "blue-ribbon" juries, composed of the most respectable and supposedly least biased and least corruptible people, would improve the present intolerable situation is debatable. If this change were possible, at least the "best" people, the so-called "good" citizens, would then be responsible for the state's image.

ards and traditions." I have received dozens of letters filled with valuable information from people of various political views living in all parts of Mississippi who have asked that their names not appear in print. One factory owner dared not dictate a letter to his confidential secretary, but wrote twenty pages longhand in the privacy of his home.

The course the Mississippi Negro will take in politics is reasonably clear. As was demonstrated at the Democratic National Convention, the Freedom Democratic Party is of doubtful legality, is controlled by those who want to revolutionize American society, and is almost all Negro. By the time this book is published, 100,000 Mississippi Negroes may be eligible to vote. In the years to come, the number may expand to 400,000, but even then they will be in the minority in Mississippi. The future of the Mississippi Negro is assured. Time will bring him not only political emancipation, but economic and social freedom as well. This fine promise could, however, be endangered if it were tied up with causes which do not arise in his situation. For the Negro to identify his future with draft-dodging or any side in a dispute, say, about the nature of the American commitment in Vietnam is simply beside the main point.[49] An all-Negro party is, on the face of it, statistically absurd, as well as a kind of reverse racism. The Negro leadership that counts most in Mississippi and in the nation knows this.

Mississippi Negroes have time and again shown their conservatism; as they acquire more wealth they will tend to line up with whites of property. The average Negro is no more concerned with the destruction of bourgeois society than the average white man. He wants a greater share of high-school diplomas and college degrees, of inside plumbing, of cars and television sets. If he did want to abolish middle-class America, he couldn't do it. It would be criminal folly for him to place his destiny in the hands of those who call for revolution, simply because revolu-

---

49. It is hardly necessary to add that such a view does not suggest that whatever views any Negro or any organization, black or biracial, may hold on any question of public policy should be withheld, suppressed, or swallowed. The issue is an obvious one of priorities and tactics.

tion—whatever that term means—is nowhere in sight.[50] There is nothing in any impoverished Mississippian's situation that could not be sufficiently improved by winning the war on poverty. Such a victory would be revolution enough.

The Freedom Democratic Party will in all probability die if it follows SNCC leadership as presently constituted.[51] It may be that SNCC has already served its historic purpose in Mississippi. Its heroic accomplishments, let there be no mistake, are beyond praise.

SNCC has not penetrated in many areas of the state, but its existence and potential have frightened white leadership into making concessions and into acceding to federal pressures. These leaders, however, will deal as far as possible with the most conservative local Negroes. Some such biracial committees are already functioning. Most Negroes are going to follow liberal rather than radical leadership, liberal in the sense of the Democratic Party and the Great Society. For Negroes will benefit, above all others, from such a program. They will work with liberal whites, and together the two, with help from Washington, will try to control, and may in time control, the state Democratic Party. The more conservative whites will go over to the Republican Party, as will the more affluent Negroes, and Mississippi will

---

50. Aaron Henry believes the Freedom Democratic Party "should be a reform, a protest movement within the National Democratic Party within the state of Mississippi." The head of Mississippi's NAACP has said a number of times that all of the state's problems can be solved when the Negro gets the vote.

51. Discussions I've had with SNCC workers on the kind of change they would bring about in American society have been remarkably unprogrammatic. The essential push of a SNCC worker's position is usually that the last thing he wants to encourage is the absorption of the Negro into American middle-class society. He believes such a result is no more than the exchange of one form of slavery for another. He is sure capitalism is wrong and that it must exploit, that it requires poverty at home and war abroad. All of which is familiar leftist rhetoric at least as old as Populism. It is not convincing in an affluent society waging (slowly and tentatively in 1964 and 1965) a voluntary war on poverty. To Mississippi Negroes it is Greek. The siren song of FDR is now being sung by LBJ—and that is the music that will command.

have its first two-party system since the 1840's. Once this happy state has been achieved, the further likelihood is that, because of its economic backwardness, Mississippi more often than not will give its support to the Democratic Party.

A psychiatrist now practicing in the state, a man of high intelligence and impeccable scientific training who obviously loves the land of his birth, not long ago took a hard look at the white people of Mississippi.

In order to avoid examining their own feelings as to why they fear giving equal rights to Negroes, and wrestling with their guilt if they accepted the responsibility for crushing fellow humans over the years, they must not make a moral issue but a legal one out of the conflict. To say that the 14th Amendment is invalid because it was not properly ratified removes the responsibility for and the anxiety of facing the realization that laws should not be necessary to assure that people are treated like human beings, that we should want to treat people decently because we are civilized, loving humans.

People only see and hear and read what they want to (need to). This is discouraging but we must accept it as a necessary defense, though a rather desperate one, of the mind against a fantasied assault on the very life and security of the individual in Mississippi. Denial of reality is a last-ditch defense to ward off fear of dissolution, disorganization, and death of a way of life. We must expect and respect this defense, giving it due consideration, and not expect too much lest we then be disappointed, disheartened and dejected in our fight against prejudice and for a greater Mississippi.

I am afraid that Mississippi is a paranoid society. You can't tamper with its defenses until you can substitute something better —something that will make it no longer necessary for Mississippians to defend so desperately against their fears and to continue to deny reality. *And the only way is for them to try "the new way" which apparently is coming about by the external force of the federal government.*

When present-day German children ask their parents about the Jews, concentration camps, and the most awful atrocities of this or any century, the answer is always the same: "We didn't know these things were going on." As a matter of fact, they should have known and did know, as Hitler was anti-Semitic from the start and never tried to hide his feelings or what he was having done. In sad comparison, many Mississippians have seen and heard and read only what they wanted to (needed to).[52] Now, when fact has been placed upon fact in a crushing refutation of what they have said and have perhaps believed about their society, when it has been demonstrated beyond the least doubt that the civilized world demands that they transform that society, and that the demand will be enforced, they are indeed in great need of compassion and understanding.

This is not said to suggest that the enforcement of the new order be slacked or slowed; rather, the situation demands that all Mississippians have it made irrefutably clear to them that there will be no turning back, that the law of the land will be fully implemented, that there is no alternative. The job, in short, is to turn "Never" into "Now."

On the other hand, it should be recognized that the white hoodlum in Mississippi who engages in violence and terrorism is as much the product of his environment as the black hoodlum who operates in Harlem. The Mississippi outlaw is almost always a man not long off a submarginal farm, a truck driver, an un-

---

52. I have long wondered whether a great many Mississippians have been aware of the cruel treatment used to keep the Negro in his place. Some have developed moral calluses to the point that they are indifferent to injustice. A few years ago a student told me that he had never seen any case of brutality to Negroes. Later, after we became more closely acquainted, he admitted to me that once his father, who owned a large mercantile establishment in one of the state's smaller county seats, sent him over to the jail to get out a Negro held on some minor charge. On entering the jail, the boy heard piercing cries from one of the cells. In it he found the drunken jailer, an enormous man, cracking a bull whip at the heels of (but not touching) a teen-aged naked Negro girl, who was thus forced into a wild dance until she fell exhausted.

A sensitive Mississippi girl wrote her parents in the summer of 1964: "I have not been totally blind for seventeen years. I have seen much to remember as beautiful, and I have seen much to cringe at in horror. Yet, there is so very much that I have never seen. I have never seen these things because they did not affect me in my sheltered, pretty way of life. Nothing has been hidden, and yet, it has not been in clear view."

skilled worker, a gas-station attendant, who hates the Negro out of his own frustrations. He needs a doctor and rehabilitation more than a policeman and a stretch at Parchman. The criminal, in Harlem or Mississippi, should pay the proper penalty called for by the law. But the nation's supreme objective should be the elimination of discrimination and lack of opportunity, the *causes* of crime and poverty.

It may be necessary from time to time to send federal troops to Mississippi, though the occasion for such action should not arise again. But it is more essential to send hundreds of millions of dollars to help whites and blacks in Mississippi achieve full participation in the "Great Society," and the sooner this is done the better. In the meantime, continued and improved legal protection must be afforded by the various lawyers' organizations and the Justice Department. The police power must no longer be used on the side of the mob. Federal registrars may be needed to see not only that Negroes are properly registered, but that they be allowed to vote freely. Education of the poor of both races must be accelerated. The many federal poverty programs must be extended. Mississippi's labor force must be not only upgraded but made color blind. Enforcement of the Mississippi Supreme Court's decree against systematic exclusion of Negroes from the jury system must be implemented. Meaningful communication between the races on a basis of equality must be encouraged and achieved, for political racism will not be destroyed until such communication has become habitual and routine at every level of society. Not just the federal government, but all of the country will have to keep a watchful eye on developments in Mississippi for years to come. It is not the Mississippi image, after all, that requires changing, but Mississippi reality.

In a closed and sick society the crisis has been met and passed. What Mississippians now face is a long period of controlled convalescence. The possibility of relapse cannot be denied. The effort at understanding and change that thousands upon thousands of conventional white segregationists will have to make will be enormous. The effort Negroes shall have to continue and enlarge passeth understanding. What is required of all Mississippians is nothing short of the transformation of the traditions and social structure of a settled and outmoded society. The stakes are high and the margin for error thin. No honest student of Mississippi's long past and recent history could fail to agree, however, that its prospects for genuine democracy have never been better. The day will yet come when Mississippi not only accepts the end of segregation but welcomes and embraces integration simply because it is right.

Index

DATE DUE